ADDRESSING CHILDHOOD ADVERSITY

edited by
David Donald, Andrew Dawes & Johann Louw

DAVID PHILIP
Cape Town & Johannesburg

*All royalties from the sale of the book will be donated to
the Child Welfare Society, Cape Town*

First published 2000 by David Philip Publishers (Pty) Ltd, 208 Werdmuller Centre,
Claremont 7708, Cape Town, South Africa

ISBN 0-86486-449-3

Printed and bound by
Creda Press, Eliot Avenue, Epping, Cape Town.

Contents

PREFACE

In 1994 two of the current editors were involved in the publication of *Childhood and adversity: Psychological perspectives from South African research.*[1] This volume focused on research that had a bearing on the nature and consequences of psychosocial adversities facing South African children in their development. Subsequently, the need has been expressed for a sequel which would focus more on ways in which these adversities may be addressed. One of the initial motivations for the production of this volume, therefore, was to present a selection of community-based programmes[2] which have, in one way or another, attempted to intervene in the broad areas of childhood adversity addressed in the original volume. In this way it was felt that the earlier focus on 'problems' could be appropriately shifted to a focus on 'solutions', particularly at a time when South Africa is attempting to address the challenges of social reconstruction.

As the project has developed, this purpose has also evolved. What has become apparent is that, probably because of its years of isolation, South Africa has in some ways not kept pace with international developments in programme planning, implementation and evaluation. In other ways, unique features and demands of working in southern Africa have dictated an evolution of child-oriented, community-based intervention programmes which have different, and perhaps very important, things to say in other developing contexts.

What is also true is that financial and human resources for such interventions in this region are limited. Governments are under pressure to make provision for very basic needs. Although there have recently been a number of important policy developments relating to the lives of children in South Africa, there has been little in the way of really concrete and effective action in reducing the adversities which beset them. On the other hand, non-governmental organisations (NGOs) which have, for a long time in South Africa at least, carried the burden of interventions for the children in the most adverse of circumstances, have been progressively restricted in their funding as international donors have tended to shift their support to government. All this has created a situation in which it has become increasingly important for those programmes that do aim to benefit children suffering various forms of psychosocial adversity to be effective – and to demonstrate that they are effective. The resources are simply too limited for ineffective interventions to continue to be justified.

While incorporating the original motivation, therefore, the purpose of producing this volume has shifted to a position which not only is illustrative but which also actively attempts to stimulate the development of effective community-based interventions in the region. Thus, through adopting a proactive theoretical position, through presenting a range of examples of the ways in which childhood adversity is currently being addressed, and through drawing out the issues and insights which these programmes illustrate, we hope to contribute to a growing theory of practice in this area.

One way in which we have tried to achieve this goal has been through selecting only projects which met certain minimal criteria of design and evaluation for inclusion in the book. It is important to state that we do not claim that these projects are 'the best' in the region. There are undoubtedly others which may not have come to our attention, and which may be equally good or better examples. What we do claim, however, is that those that have been included all contribute, in one way or another, to our understanding of good practice, and illustrate at least the following minimal principles of design and evaluation:

• The project should demonstrate sensitivity to local context and the community in which it is situated
• The project should be informed by appropriate theoretical principles and relevant research
• The project should have explicit aims
• The project should show evidence of evaluation in terms of these aims

Within these broad principles, a great deal of variation is possible. Thus, the projects selected address a range of childhood adversities, from the effects of violence on children to the quality of schooling in underdeveloped contexts, and from the effects of under-nutrition on cognitive performance to the consequences of stress in organisations dealing with children in need. Variation is apparent not only in the issues that are addressed, but also in the scale of different interventions. This varies from large-scale programmes which have spanned several years and have extended into different communities across whole regions, to smaller-scale projects which usually have had more limited goals and focus. Most notably, the authors of the projects described here range from academics to practitioners in state departments, NGOs and schools, and their academic backgrounds include psychology, psychiatry, education, economics, sociology, social work and child health. In itself this is an indication of the value of cross-disciplinary co-operation and collaborative engagement in intervention projects of this nature.

Briefly, as regards structure, the volume is divided into three sections. Section 1 contains three chapters that we regard as central to the aim of contributing towards a theory of practice in this area. Chapter 1 develops some key connections between factors that influence the psychosocial development of children, the processes through which adversities may compromise development, and the reasons why interventions need to draw explicitly on these understandings. These links are too often neglected, the consequence being interventions which are less than optimally effective.

Chapter 2 provides current information and a very important overview of the situation of children in the wider South African context. In particular it draws attention to the gap between well-intentioned policy making and effective practice, which is so starkly apparent in South Africa at the moment. Developing an effective theory of practice has particular significance in this context. Not only can it inform the larger-scale programmes which government must in due course attempt if policy is to be enacted, but it can guide the continuing development and refinement of the sorts of NGO-run, community-based projects which will always have a place in the larger scheme of things.

Chapter 3 addresses the critical issue of programme evaluation. That some form of evaluation had been undertaken was a requirement of projects selected for this book. However, it is a topic which is extremely complex and has many dimensions to it, not all of which are readily illustrated or exemplified in the project descriptions. This chapter, therefore, provides a framework for readers to understand how the process of evaluation needs to enter into every phase and dimension of the life of a programme. This framework acts as both a specific guide to reading the chapters that follow and a broad background to the important topic and theory of programme evaluation.

Section 2 is devoted to the different project descriptions and analyses. To assist readers to draw the threads across these quite widely different endeavours, authors were asked to construct their chapters using five major headings: Background and Aims; Theoretical and Research Base; Project Description, Outcomes and Evaluation; and Issues and Insights. Where authors have not used these specific headings, they have generally covered the equivalent areas so that the overall pattern should still be apparent.

The projects selected for inclusion are all, with one exception, South African. This was not a conscious intention to exclude other worthy projects that may exist in the wider southern African region. It was simply that the project conducted in Angola was known to the editors, and since it exemplified important principles of intervention, it was included.

Section 3 of the book consists of a single chapter. It is the logical conclusion and attempt on the part of the editors to extract the lessons that can be learned from the foregoing two sections. Although readers will have drawn many of their own conclusions, and will hopefully have begun to construct their own theory of practice in relation to what has been presented, this final chapter is our attempt to crystallise out central elements of a theory of practice which we believe have emerged through this volume.

[1] Dawes, A. & Donald, D. (1994) *Childhood and adversity: Psychological perspectives from South African research* Cape Town: David Philip.

[2] Although the term 'programme' may sometimes be interpreted as referring to large-scale initiatives and 'project' to smaller-scale initiatives, this usage is not consistent. In this book the terms are used interchangeably, according to the preference of the authors of different chapters. The term 'intervention', although closely synonymous with the former two terms, tends to connote the actual activity of a programme rather than its whole organisational structure.

ACKNOWLEDGEMENTS

The editors wish to acknowledge the support from colleagues as well as from the administration of the University of Cape Town in the course of producing this book. To all those involved in different ways in the projects described here, but who in many cases remain unnamed, we would also like to extend our thanks.

IMPROVING CHILDREN'S CHANCES 1

Developmental theory and effective interventions in community contexts

Andrew Dawes & David Donald

The central argument of this chapter is that the design, delivery and effectiveness of psychosocial interventions with children and adolescents will be enhanced if they are underpinned by theory and research. This may seem an obvious point. However, it is often the case that practitioners and researchers work in different worlds. The former frequently face enormous demands on their time, and the pressing needs of those they serve call for a quick response. On the other hand, researchers commonly do not make their findings accessible to their applied colleagues (Donald & Dawes, 1994).

A lack of dialogue between practitioners and researchers can lead to expensive and inappropriate investment in programmes that are not effective, and that could have been improved had they had a more adequate research base (Sinha & Mishra, 1993). This is a situation that developing countries with few resources can ill afford. It is therefore a central purpose of this chapter to show how links between developmental knowledge, research and intervention may be constructed, thereby strengthening programme design.

It goes without saying that the growth of psychological capacities is a highly complex process, and there are many ways of understanding it. Nevertheless there is sufficient agreement for us to make certain claims that can assist the design of interventions. In this chapter, we adopt a definition of development provided by Aber, Gephart, Brooks-Gunn and Connell (1997, p. 47) who see it as 'the acquisition and growth of the physical, cognitive, social and emotional competencies required to engage fully in family and society'. While the definition has been formulated by researchers in the United States, it is applicable to children[1] worldwide. Its value lies in its neutrality. The type of society and family is left open, and development is seen as the acquisition of competencies that are appropriate for their societies. A definition of this nature is valuable for a region such as southern Africa where the importance of particular developmental competencies may be seen differently in different cultures and contexts (Nsamenang & Dawes, 1998).

Indeed, professional psychological knowledge about children, ideas concerning their rights and their welfare, and provisions for the advancement of their development have largely been developed in Europe and North America (Kessen, 1979). This modern ideology of child development is being increasingly spread around the world as it is exported to developing regions. These regions often have rather different understandings of childhood human nature and natural rights from those of the West (Boyden, 1990; Stephens, 1995). A particular force for this pattern of globalisation has been the adoption by the United Nations of the Convention on the Rights of the Child in 1989. The Convention is informed by Western concepts of rights and psychological knowledge. It seeks to extend certain protections and conditions of development to children throughout the world. It also informs the practices of many aid programmes to families and children in developing regions. These commonly carry with them Northern assumptions about what is best for children (Boyden, 1990). South Africa has signed and ratified the Convention, and is required to ensure that its Articles are given expression in all policies and programmes for children. This commitment constitutes both an opportunity and a challenge in the developing context of southern Africa.

The interlocking set of ideologies and practices referred to above is increasingly being brought together in the search for effective intervention programmes for children in difficult circumstances (Dawes & Cairns, 1998). Undoubtedly, there is much in these developments that has universal applicability, and it would be foolish not to attempt to incorporate what has been learned in other contexts into our own. However, it is equally important to be wary of what might not apply, and to search for models and solutions that are most relevant in the social, cultural and material contexts that characterise the southern African region. An understanding of children's lived contexts is thus central to the design of effective interventions, as is an appreciation of the manner in which children's contexts influence their physical and mental development.

In this chapter we explore some key linkages between developmental research and theory and interventions with children growing up under adverse conditions. We begin by considering a model of the relationship between the contexts of children's development and their emerging psychological capacities. These contexts include the family and wider sources of influence such as the school and the neighbourhood. A particular focus of our discussion is research on psychological development in poverty environments. We then consider the role of cultural practices in child development and interventions with children. The chapter concludes with some key principles for the design of interventions for children living in difficult circumstances in developing regions such as southern Africa.

THEORISING DEVELOPMENT IN DIFFICULT CIRCUMSTANCES

Huston (1994) points out that most research in developmental psychology does not consider the role of the larger social context in shaping developmental processes. It therefore tends to have little impact on public policy and community-based interventions for children. He suggests that 'If child development research is to have an impact on public policy for children, it needs to be conceptualized and framed in terms that can be communicated to policy makers and translated into policies and programs' (Huston, 1994, p. 5). In short, programmes designed to improve children's developmental outcomes require an understanding of the way the contexts of development influence emerging psychological processes.

In recent years there has been an increase in efforts to understand and ameliorate the impact of contexts of poverty on children's physical and psychological development (Brooks-Gunn, Duncan & Aber, 1997a, 1997b; Chase-Lansdale & Brooks-Gunn, 1995; Dawes & Donald, 1994; Fitzgerald, Lester & Zuckerman, 1995; Rogers & Ginsberg, 1990). Significantly, these initiatives, which in their focus on poverty and its effects have much relevance to the southern African region, have all benefited from the study of child-context relationships.

In the next section, therefore, we have chosen to highlight work that has proved particularly useful in understanding how children's development is shaped by their material, social and cultural contexts. Probably the most influential contribution has been the ecological framework formulated by Bronfenbrenner (1979, 1986). A closely related and complementary perspective is transactional developmental theory (Sameroff, 1975, 1991). Research within the latter tradition maps the impact of children's developmental contexts onto their emerging psychological capacities at different points in the life cycle. Once one knows how these pathways operate, this knowledge can be used to design more effective interventions.

An Ecological–Transactional orientation

Psychologists such as Bronfenbrenner and those who have followed his lead (e.g. Garbarino, 1992) see context as a 'socially constructed system of external influences that is mediated by individuals' minds … whatever influences local environments have on children must be seen as a product of how these environments are perceived and interpreted by parents and children' (Furstenberg & Hughes, 1997, p. 27). Bronfenbrenner (1979, 1986) introduced four interacting dimensions that need to be considered when attempting to understand child development in context. They include *person* factors (e.g. the temperament of the child or parent); *process* factors (e.g. the forms of interaction process that occur in a family); *contexts* (e.g. families or neighbourhoods); and *time* (e.g. changes over time in the characteristics of the individual or the environment).

Bronfenbrenner has demonstrated that it is enduring proximal interaction processes that are commonly the most important in shaping stable aspects of development. Proximal processes refer to face-to-face interactions between children and other people. Examples might include a boy's relationship with his father, as well as his relationship with his teacher. Proximal interactions are affected by the characteristics of the child and the other people involved in the interaction, as well as by the nature of the contexts within which they occur (e.g. the home or school). These context, person and process elements change over time due to children's maturation, as well as changes in the environments themselves.

Children's learning, across all areas of development (e.g. early relationship formation and cognition), is seen as occurring in four nested systems, the microsystem, the mesosystem, the exosystem and the macrosystem. The systems may be seen as surrounding one another, and influencing one another to varying degrees. Children's perceptions of their contexts are central to an understanding of how they engage with their developmental settings. The environment therefore does not simply impact on the child. Rather children are active participants in their own development. The way they perceive their circumstances will influence the way they respond to their human and physical contexts. For example, if a young child has a secure sense of the social world, exposure to new people will not evoke as much anxiety as it would for a child who has an insecure orientation. Central components of this ecological model are illustrated in Figure 1.

Microsystems are interactive situations in which the child is in face-to-face contact with another person. As illustrated in the figure, these would include a parent's relationship with her child (Richter, 1994), and the teacher–child learning context of the school (Liddell, Lycett & Rae, 1997). Another example of a microsystem is the child's enduring relationship with close friends in the neighbourhood (Berndt & Ladd, 1989). A key feature of the microsystem is its bi-directional nature. All parties to the interaction influence its outcome. Thus a child with an easy temperament is likely to evoke a more positive response from its caregiver than a child of irritable disposition, even when the caregiver is under emotional strain (Scarr, 1992).

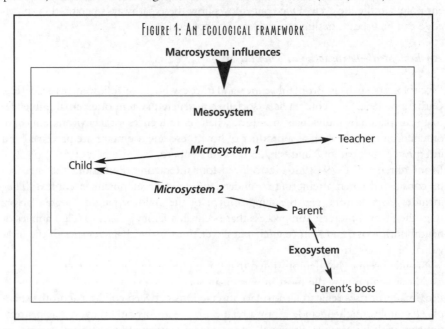

FIGURE 1: AN ECOLOGICAL FRAMEWORK

The mesosystem is a set of associated microsystems. For example, the economic strain on a single mother may reduce her ability to respond to her young child's emotional needs, thus placing the child at risk for an insecure orientation to other people (McLoyd & Wilson, 1990; Richter, 1994). However the child may also have an attentive and caring teacher who is able to provide a positive environment which boosts the child's self-esteem. Thus, the experience in the microsystem of the school provides a protective influence (Rutter, 1985) which reduces the impact of the stress within the microsystem of the family. In another situation, a distressed family may have a supportive neighbour who has a warm relationship with a vulnerable child, protecting him to an extent from psychological effects of emotional neglect in his own home (McLoyd & Wilson, 1990). The mesosystem therefore links the different microsystems in which the child is involved, two of which are illustrated in Figure 1.

Exosystems are settings that do not involve the child directly, but include the interactions of those who have a relationship with the child. These are contexts that directly affect people who have proximal relationships with the child. Thus the parent's relationship with an employer, as depicted in Figure 1, does not involve the child, but its stresses or benefits will influence the quality of that parent's relationship with the child. As another example, parental social isolation is known to increase the risk of child neglect (Garbarino & Sherman, 1980). Single parents who live in neighbourhoods that are characterised by low social cohesion are particularly at risk for isolation. In such a situation, a depressed single parent may be fortunate to have a neighbour upon whom she can call for emotional support. This is likely to reduce her isolation, have a positive effect on her mental state, and increase her capacity to deliver sensitive child care.

The macrosystem refers to the political and cultural level of influence on the other levels of the system within which the child is a participant. For example cultural values and ideas about childhood give rise to scripts for child-care. These values are also associated with the human and material resource constraints of the community (Scheper-Hughes, 1989). Cultural scripts, for example, may include developing obedience to authority and respect for senior members of the community as goals of child-care. In many African communities the means to the attainment of this goal is strict discipline (LeVine *et al.*, 1994). Obedience to authority as a desired outcome of socialisation may reflect long-established cultural values. Alternatively, the need for obedience may arise in contexts that are perceived as dangerous for children (such as are described in several chapters in this volume). Strict discipline that promotes obedience is a source of protection to these children. Compliant children who listen to their caregivers, regardless of who they are, will be safer than those who are freer to exercise their will. While obedience scripts are often negatively associated with authoritarian and punitive approaches to child-care (Dodge, Pettit & Bates, 1994), they clearly have survival value in dangerous contexts. However, these practices can also outlive their functional value. When social conditions have changed, they can live on as modes of discipline, and may continue to be seen as the 'right way' to bring up children although the original dangers no longer apply.

Chronosystem constructs reflect changes in the developing child, and simultaneous changes in his or her developmental context. One aspect of the chronosystem is the envelope of historical and cultural time that surrounds the other systems. The idea here is that development is influenced by the historical features of the period during which it is occurring. These may contain stable elements, as well as disruptions. Disruptions, for example, might include the influence of events such as economic depressions (Elder, 1974), political changes (Finchilescu & Dawes, 1998), or the information technology revolution. These phenomena mark the children who are growing up at that time in a way that is different for other generations. However, their particular impact will always depend on how they are perceived by the child and mediated by the child's caregivers in the microsystem.

The ecological framework has helped to foreground children's developmental contexts as central influences in the formation of their psychological capacities. In addition, it has allowed for the emergence of a more culturally sensitive approach to developmental psychology, and to interventions in this field (Ogbu, 1981).

Developmental transactions

Closely associated with Bronfenbrenner's framework, and central to understanding the effects of time on development, are what are known as transactional approaches (Sameroff, 1975, 1991). A transactional model provides an understanding of how individual–environment exchanges contribute to development differentially at various points in the life cycle. A key feature of Sameroff's model is his analysis of how the changing developmental status of the child contributes to these processes. That is, at any one point in time, the child brings existing psychological capacities, which are themselves a product of earlier interactions, to new microsystem interactions. The form of these capacities is also related to the child's developmental phase. Transactions of this nature are illustrated in Figure 2.

Here we depict two developmental pathways. In the first, we have a child who begins life with a positive temperament and warm and sensitive parenting. Having established a secure working model of relationships, the child approaches the challenge of moving from home to school in a positive manner. The school experience is positive, and the child's confidence and security are further enhanced. In the second path, we have a child whose earlier relationships are characterised by inconsistent parenting. In this case the orientation to school is anxious and fearful. However, this child is fortunate to encounter a supportive and understanding teacher, who through the nature of her approach is able to counter some of the negative aspects of the child's personality. In this case the early negative trajectory is interrupted by the later positive encounter with a caring teacher.

Figure 2 therefore illustrates how the socio-emotional capacities that the child brings to the first school day *transact* with the situation provided by teacher. Depending on how they turn out, these transactions may serve to consolidate or shift the script for relationships that the child has developed up to that point. This view challenges propositions that what is established early in development always has lasting or permanent effects. This is not to say that there is no enduring substance to psychological characteristics, or that there are no periods in the life cycle that are particularly sensitive to certain forms of stimulation or deprivation. Clearly this is not the case (Clarke & Clarke, 1986). There is evidence for several sensitive periods during which the stimulation that the child receives has a lasting influence on specific cognitive, social or other domains. Language acquisition is one example, and orientations to relationship formation in early childhood seem to be another.

Stability and change in personality, and other psychological characteristics, are a function of children's activities in shaping their development, as well as the complex interactions between their genetic endowment and contextual influences across the life cycle. Current research is attempting to tease out the relative influence of different contexts such as the family, the neighbourhood community, the school and the

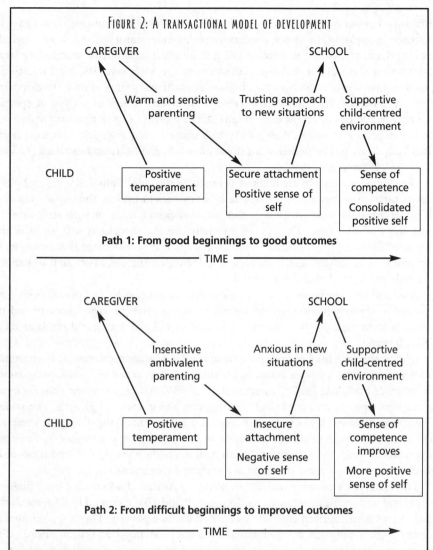

FIGURE 2: A TRANSACTIONAL MODEL OF DEVELOPMENT

Path 1: From good beginnings to good outcomes

Path 2: From difficult beginnings to improved outcomes

peer group on children's psychological development (e.g. Brooks-Gunn *et al.*, 1997a, 1997b). A transactional approach would suggest that these sources exert their influence in different ways during various developmental periods.

The role of developmental epochs

Aber *et al.* (1997) have defined a set of developmental periods which they have termed epochs. Broader than developmental stages or sensitive periods, they have been formulated to take account of the transitions that occur at significant points where new demands are placed on the young by their society. While they are particularly applicable to North American society, these epochs are also relevant to most established urban communities in South Africa. However, adjustments would have to be made in applying the epoch concept to some communities. These would include newly urbanised children of families living in informal settlements surrounding large cities and traditional rural, African communities. In such contexts, local traditional practices may create challenges for children at particular points in their development that are different from those characteristic of North American society. A specific example would be children's early involvement in forms of work that may replace, or be in parallel to, schooling. Also girls in such contexts may leave school before, or in, their early teens and be prepared for domestic work, child-care and marriage (LeVine *et al.*, 1994; Reynolds, 1997).

Developmental epochs are marked as much by the child's physical and psychological maturation as they are by the new tasks set by societies. Thus, the physical changes of puberty may be linked with increased social responsibilities, or with attending the next stage of schooling. The epochs are therefore also associated with shifts in the power of different environmental sources to influence development. For example, in the initial move to school, the sources of influence on the child now shift to include not only the home but also the school.

Aber and his colleagues (1997) consider four broad epochs: the period from conception to the commencement of formal schooling; the primary school period up until about the age of 10 years; early adolescence (11–16 years); and the later teens (17–20 years).

During the preschool period, the primary influences are home-based. Community influences are principally mediated in proximal developmental relationships by family members (Aber *et al.*, 1997; Bronfenbrenner, 1986). This is a sensitive time for emotional development and trust, and for cognitive and intellectual growth. The young child needs a reasonably consistent, predictable environment, together with a responsiveness on the part of caregivers which fosters self-regulation. Arguably, the environments in which the majority of South African children live do not lend themselves to the promotion of these positive developmental characteristics.

The family lives of many millions of southern African children have been disrupted by war and political violence (see Chapters 9 and 10). As noted in Chapter 2, the majority of South African children also live in chronic poverty. This is well known to compromise a range of developmental outcomes (McLoyd & Wilson, 1990). For many, relationships with caregivers are disrupted by factors associated with migration from rural areas to cities. Jones (1993) has reported that it is not uncommon for the children of migrant workers living in informal settlements and the former 'male hostels' to shuttle between grandparents in rural areas and mothers or fathers in town. Who their primary caregivers actually are, is often difficult to determine. Ramphele (1993) reports on the living conditions in overcrowded hostels where home is effectively the family bed, shared by both adults and children. Under such circumstances, proximal relationships are likely to be unstable and children are frequently exposed to alcohol abuse, domestic violence and other adverse condition associated with chronic poverty. These children certainly do not have consistent families – either nuclear or extended.

Self-regulation is a key attribute that begins to develop during this early period of life. It enables the child to delay gratification and improves impulse control – characteristics that help the child on entry to school. As Liddell *et al.* (1997) have found in their study of children in rural KwaZulu-Natal schools, attentive quiet children were highly rated by their teachers. Thus it can be seen that, during this epoch, children growing up in relatively inconsistent and chaotic situations are less likely than those brought up in stable environments to develop the qualities of self-regulation which predispose the child to successful schooling and peer relationships.

The epoch from 7 to 11 years is associated with a wider set of influences as the child increasingly encounters other adults and widens contact with peers (Berndt & Ladd, 1989). The social challenge of this time is to begin to learn skills that will be useful in the adult world – frequently, although not always, through schooling. New and powerful influences on cognitive and social development appear in the form of influential adults and peers. How children think about themselves as learners and as social beings becomes important. Schools are primary sites for the development of the self-concept. Peers have a significant impact on this aspect of development. Children who have not developed adequate self-regulation are aggressive, have poor attention and concentration, and are likely to invoke negative feedback from peers (Moffitt, 1993). This lack of social competence is likely to lead to social isolation, poor self-concept, and also may lead the child to be attracted to deviant peers. In contrast, pro-social children tend to choose pro-social peers (Masten & Coatsworth, 1998).

While the majority of South African children begin by attending school, it is evident that many of their schools are not well designed to retain them, to deal with their learning or other difficulties, or to prepare them for life ahead (Donald, Lazarus & Lolwana, 1997). Schools themselves are often unsafe environments in violent communities (Chapter 8). In the poverty contexts of the region in both urban and rural areas, many children during this age period have already left school after a brief period of attendance in order to earn money for their families (Gordon, 1987). Thousands have left schools that have failed to meet their needs, and their own dysfunctional homes, to make a living on the streets (Swart-Kruger & Donald, 1994). The strategies that such children are forced to adopt to survive on the street are often adaptive in the short term, but may also be seen as compromising their development in later phases of development (Donald, Wallis & Cockburn, 1997). Thus, for many children in South Africa, other sources of influences – such as peers on the street – may be more influential during this epoch than school. Of course some schools may themselves be a negative influence on development.

During the early adolescent epoch (11–16 years), changes in biology are usually linked to many changes in the child's social contexts and relationships. Influences outside the family become more significant. In the urban context in particular, there is normally a move to high school and a reduction in parental supervision. Increased risk-taking is common and in poor communities there is increased exposure to negative social influences such as gangs and risks such as drug-taking (Moffitt, 1993). Flisher and his colleagues (1993) have documented risk-taking among South African adolescents. Once more, there are a number of differences in life circumstances, and therefore developmental outcomes, for southern African children during this period. As may be deduced from the previous epoch, the continued influence of schooling cannot be taken for granted. Another example lies in the many thousands of Angolan and Mozambican children in this age group who have been shifted prematurely into adult roles through being forced to take up arms in civil wars (Honwana, 1997; Chapter 9). In South Africa, for many boys in urban slums, gangs begin to assume a similar role. In both cases, patterns of socialisation established in the home are likely to be disrupted as these children are inducted into violent life-styles.

During the final epoch (late adolescence), there is increasing preparation for adulthood and work, and further exposure to risks in the community. Millions of South African children have left school for one or other reason by this time (Chapter 2). Some have taken up forms of work, while the majority remain unemployed. As adolescents move into their late teens, they spend an increasing amount of independent time in neighbourhood and other community settings with peers. As Brooks-Gunn *et al.* (1997a, 1997b) report in their collection of studies, the direct effects on development of the child's exposure to neighbourhood influences increase significantly during this period.

Child–context relationships in poverty environments and developmental outcomes

Resilience, risk and protective factors

Studies developed within an ecological framework point to a complex set of interactions between developing children and the family, school and neighbourhood contexts that surround them (i.e. Bronfenbrenner's mesosystem interactions). This research has many implications for interventions in poverty environments, particularly in urban contexts. While there is still much to do to refine the models and the interventions they suggest, they draw our attention to significant sources of influence for the development of different psychological capacities at key points in the lives of children and adolescents. While the majority of studies have examined the risks posed by growing up in dysfunctional families and communities, more recent research is turning to an examination of how families cope successfully with neighbourhood poverty, and attempt to shield their children from its effects (Masten & Coatsworth, 1998; Rutter, Quinton & Yule, 1977). This work is particularly important for the planning of interventions because knowledge of coping strategies allows us to draw on existing practices that have been found to work for the very people who are the target of the intervention.

Factors that promote children's resilience under conditions of stress have been identified in a number of studies (Garmezy, 1993; Garmezy, Masten & Tellegen, 1984; Rutter, 1985; Werner & Smith, 1982). The quality of resilience 'generally refers to those factors and processes that interrupt the trajectory from risk to problem behaviours or psychopathology and thereby result in adaptive outcomes even in the presence of adversity' (Zimmerman & Arunkumar, 1994, p. 4). Factors that promote resilience and protect children from negative outcomes include capacities that are part of the child's physical and psychological makeup, as well as features of the social ecology in which the child is involved.

Garmezy *et al.* (1984) outlined three models of the way in which resilience operates. These are usefully summarised by Zimmerman and Arunkumar (1994). First they describe a compensatory model. In this case, a particular positive influence neutralises the impact of other stresses on a specific outcome such as educational achievement. For example, in a high-conflict marriage, the parents may nonetheless be very supportive of their children's academic work. Their attention and support for the child's study programme 'compensates' for the stresses that would otherwise be expected to affect school performance.

The second is the challenge model. Here the child's exposure to a moderate amount of stress acts to strengthen its ability to cope with difficulties at later points in life. This model explains the finding that children who have been exposed to adversity, and have learned to cope well, are likely to feel more competent in coping with future difficulties.

Third is the protective factor model. 'A protective factor is a process that interacts with a risk factor in reducing the probability of a negative outcome. It works by moderating the effect of exposure to risk [and modifies] the response to a risk factor' (Zimmerman & Arunkumar 1994, p. 6). For example, in many studies of the impact of political violence and war on children, it has been found that the presence of a supportive caregiver seems to 'protect' the child – and reduce the risk of the child developing serious psychopathology (Cairns, 1996).

Each of these models is useful in understanding how children may respond to the stresses associated with adversity. Equally, they are useful for the design of interventions. To return to the example of the high-conflict marriage, an intervention that draws on the compensatory model may encourage at least one of the parents to support the child's learning – despite the conflict. This could entail homework supervision and monitoring, as well as being generally supportive of the child's scholastic efforts. When children are exposed to continuous stresses, as is common in poverty environments, it makes sense to draw on the challenge model to design interventions that will enhance a sense of coping in the child, despite the continuing difficulties. This strategy could have long-term protective consequences if it equips the child to face further challenges in this environment from a position of strength. Strategies that strengthen caregivers are generally drawing on the protective model. Strengthening the capacity of parents and others to be effective caregivers in adverse environments acts to 'protect' children through moderating the risks they have to face in such environments.

Personal and structural features of the environment

All children's environments may be seen as having certain personal and structural features that influence development. Personal aspects include the attributes of teachers, peers and mothers which influence children's behaviour in proximal developmental settings. Structural characteristics, on the other hand, include the demographics of the area in which the child lives, as well as its physical features. The human structure of the environment (its demography) includes such characteristics as the ethnic mix of a defined community, the number of female-headed households and the proportion of people living below the Minimum Living Level (Barbarin, Richter, De Wet & Wachtel, 1998). Other important aspects include the quality and number of social networks in the area, the household density, age distribution and teacher–learner ratios in the schools. Structural physical qualities of the child's context would include the type of housing (shacks or brick houses), the quality of the recreation facilities, and the number and quality of the schools (Brooks-Gunn *et al.*, 1997a).

Research indicates that during the pre-school and primary school years, the impact of a range of neighbourhood characteristics is mediated primarily by family members, particularly primary caregivers and older siblings (Aber *et al.*, 1997). Because of this finding, it is important to understand how community characteristics influence the mental health of those who care for children. Research on this question has been reviewed by Wandersman and Nation (1998). They observe that stressful conditions in the community can undermine the coping capacities of adults. Negative structural characteristics of the neighbourhood produce stress in caregivers who, in turn, cannot cope or create the conditions needed for positive emotional outcomes for their children. Nevertheless, even in very poor communities, exposure to at least some well-functioning families can protect children against the deprivations of their situation. For example, such families may have somewhat better resources that can stimulate the cognitive capacities needed for school. They may also include positive role models. Local teenagers who are successful at sports or school would be examples. As we have noted earlier, adults in the community who are less stressed than their neighbours can also offer support to nearby parents who are living in difficult circumstances, thereby reducing the risks of abuse to the children of the stressed adults.

Other structural features that contribute to negative developmental outcomes due to parental strain include poor social cohesion which leads to the social isolation of families. This is common in areas of southern Africa that are characterised by high population mobility, such as the peripheries of cities that have large populations of recent migrants from the countryside. While country villages have been severely disrupted by migrant labour practices for many years, there is nevertheless likely to be a greater sense of history, stability and cohesion in these areas than in new urban settlements. In either context, however, the civil violence that is characteristic of so many communities in South Africa has been shown to fracture and disrupt social cohesion and mutual family support (Chapter 10).

The degree of disorder in the child's community, including signs of physical deterioration, garbage in the streets and dilapidated buildings, as well as social incivilities such as drinking, drug-dealing and violence on the street, increases the perceived danger and stress for both children and their caregivers. Garbarino (1995) describes such dangerous and decayed neighbourhoods as 'socially toxic'. In addition to the threats they pose to adult and child safety, they also provide opportunities for youth to be socialised into violent and deviant subcultures, particularly as they move into adolescence. As we have noted above, dangerous neighbourhoods encourage stricter parenting as adults strive to protect their children (see also below). A general model of the links between social conditions, child-care contexts and child development outcomes is depicted in Figure 3.

Most of the research we have cited has relied on large urban samples, surveys and psychometric measures. All are appropriate methods of describing and modelling effects of developmental contexts on children. By mapping the direct and indirect effects of sources of influence on particular areas of development at particular points in the life cycle, they provide guides for intervention. Qualitative methods also play an essential role in giving texture to these models, and suggest ways in which interventions can build on the strategies that community members have themselves devised. This approach is evident in Jarrett's (1997) study of the methods used by families to shield their children from the negative aspects of high-risk communities.

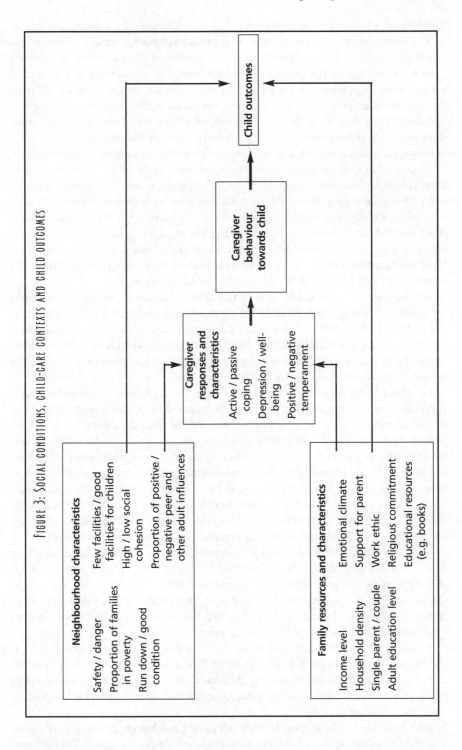

FIGURE 3: SOCIAL CONDITIONS, CHILD-CARE CONTEXTS AND CHILD OUTCOMES

Neighbourhood characteristics

Safety / danger
Proportion of families in poverty
Run down / good condition

Few facilities / good facilities for children
High / low social cohesion
Proportion of positive / negative peer and other adult influences

Caregiver responses and characteristics

Active / passive coping
Depression / well-being
Positive / negative temperament

Caregiver behaviour towards child

Child outcomes

Family resources and characteristics

Income level
Household density
Single parent / couple
Adult education level

Emotional climate
Support for parent
Work ethic
Religious commitment
Educational resources (e.g. books)

On the basis of interviews and observations Jarrett identified four strategies.

The first is the protection strategy. This included the selective use of the neighbourhood at safe times (e.g. before dark) and placement of restrictions on relationships with neighbours. For example, Jarrett observed that contact was only permitted with other families regarded as having a positive influence on the child. In addition, families that used protection strategies also tended to support mainstream value orientations. Thus they stressed the importance of advancement through school, they were anti-drug in orientation, and placed a lot of stress on self-improvement through employment. They also took steps to keep their children away from dangerous areas.

Child-monitoring strategies were identified by Jarrett as a second approach. Parents limited their child's exposure to larger influences using chaperoning (often by older siblings or supportive neighbours) and isolation (prohibiting contact with negative influences through keeping the child inside the house). These strategies become much more difficult as the child grows older. But the data suggest that chaperoning works best when started early and carried through into adolescence. This strategy can, however, cause resentment in the adolescent years, and possibly provoke the child's engagement with groups the family would consider undesirable.

A third approach was used by what Jarrett called 'competent parents'. They sought out capacity-building experiences for their children, such as involving them in educational or sporting activities. These parents also sought other personal resources such as alternative caregivers in the family and the community, when they were unable to see to the child's needs. Clearly this strategy relies for its success on the existence of a reasonably cohesive family or neighbourhood.

Finally, in-home learning strategies were used. These are both formal and informal approaches to learning, such as stressing the importance of homework or reading, which can enhance a culture of learning and reinforce what the child gains at school. This strategy has been found among Vietnamese-American immigrant families, who wish to promote the success of their children in their new country (Caplan, Whitmore & Choy, 1989). These refugee parents stressed the importance of education, read to their children in their home language, took part in their children's homework assignments and required twice as much daily homework as parents of other American children. Their children performed consistently well in school, often outperforming white Americans. Successful parenting practices such as these can, however, break down in communities that have high proportions of youth whose values are different from those of the child's family. This is a particular problem when the child forms an affiliation with deviant peers who reject the value of schooling (Maston & Coatsworth, 1998). In general, the evidence suggests that while the influence of the family remains powerful during the early years, factors external to the home become increasingly influential toward the teenage years.

An ecological–transactional model has considerable value in its ability to inform community-based interventions with children. It draws our attention to the way different sources of influence impact on children's development at different points in time. This provides guidance about what contexts to focus on, for what purpose, at what stage in development.

We turn now to a brief consideration of cultural psychology and its contribution. Key features of this approach include its implications for the design of culturally sensitive interventions. When using the term 'culture', we need to note that all children inhabit cultures, and our discussion is as relevant to children of modern middle-class communities as it is to children growing up in traditional or modernising settings.

Cultural practices and development

The key concept upon which we shall draw is the concept of a cultural practice (Miller & Goodnow, 1995). This approach to the role of culture in child development has an affinity with the Vygotskian tradition in developmental psychology (e.g. the cultural psychology of Cole, 1997). In this view, the developmental context is not treated as a variable (as in ecological approaches), or as a neutral phenomenon. Rather it is seen as invested with local cultural meanings. These are conveyed to children through the manner in which caregivers structure their everyday activities in the home and the community.

The study of cultural practices is important because it gives insight into the way adult behaviour towards children is embedded in local beliefs about what is good and what is bad for them. These beliefs and values are often quite resistant to change. Interventions need to take account of how such orientations may serve to block change. In addition, an understanding of local practices points the way to indigenous solutions to the challenge of bringing up children under difficult circumstances. These can be used to build appropriate interventions that do not alienate the client population (Gilbert, 1997).

According to Miller and Goodnow (1995, p. 7), cultural practices are 'actions that are repeated, shared with others in a social group, and invested with normative expectations and with meanings or significances which go beyond the immediate goals of the action'. They include ideas about what is natural and moral, and include activities that 'may easily become part of a group's identity' (Miller & Goodnow, 1995, p. 6).

The concept of a practice allows researchers and practitioners to describe development in context in a more holistic, dynamic manner. Practices provide the route through which children come to participate in culture, and practices allow the culture to be continued. In this regard, the everyday quality of cultural practices is important. Cultural practices embody activities that people do not even think about. They are the taken-for-granted activities of everyday life that we do not question.

Through participation in the practices that accompany the process of growing into society, we develop mental scripts for action in the world. Cole (1997) speaks of these scripts as 'cultural tool kits'. They contain representations of the social and material world. Representations, together with the practices in which the child is a participant, convey the taken-for-granted social assumptions of the family, local community and wider culture. They would include scripts for 'being a good child', dealing with father when he is in a bad mood, or 'being cool' as an adolescent. They would also include scripts laid down early in life, such as inner models of the degree to which others are to be trusted.

What is important for present purposes is that a cultural practice orientation helps us to appreciate that 'the way things are ordinarily done' in a particular community is quite deeply embedded. The adults who take them for granted will not easily give them up, and their children come to see them as part and parcel of life.

The acceptance of a set of disciplinary procedures in a school is an example of agreement around a cultural practice. Corporal punishment as a specific form of discipline symbolises a set of relationships between adults and children, as well as being the means to achieving certain cultural goals. Beatings were outlawed in South African schools due to the introduction of a new set of cultural practices that flowed from the adoption of the United Nations Convention on the Rights of the Child. The degree to which corporal punishment was a taken-for-granted component of the cultural practices of schools was evident in resistance to its abolition. For example, in a letter to *The Teacher* (April 1999, p. 19) the following comment regretting the loss of this form of discipline appeared: 'In the past, when you had the option of giving a hiding, the children were far more likely to behave and listen. I really dread to think of the calibre of adults we are going to be producing in the next ten years. I fear New Age philosophy is slowly eating away at the core of our moral fibre and destroying our children's lives.'

The adoption of the Convention and changes in education policy meant that the relationship between adult (teacher) and pupil was radically re-framed. The manner in which adult–child relationships were previously understood made it legitimate for an adult to physically assault a child. Beyond the physical act was the cultural goal of producing good citizens through teaching obedience to authority. Coupled to this was the cultural belief that beatings served this purpose well, as is illustrated in the above quote. While adults confirmed their power relationship with children, the young learnt a range of scripts about their place in society, as well as notions of power, justice and the use of violence to solve problems.

Clearly, from a developmental perspective, the reaction of children to a phenomenon such as corporal punishment is a function of their level of cognitive and emotional maturation. However, from a cultural psychology point of view, all psychological capacities are first cultural and then psychological (Cole, 1997). The child's inner psychological capacities reflect the available cultural resources of the surrounding community. A primary feature of these resources is that they carry the collective meanings that the community uses to make sense of social events. In this way, cultural templates for labelling events as violent or abusive are conveyed to children as part of their everyday induction into the cultural practices and conventions of their communities (Levett, 1994). The ability of the child to cope with difficult circumstances is therefore not simply a function of a psychological capacity that grows up 'independently' of the cultural learning context. They are both deeply intertwined.

The cultural practices approach alerts us to the fact that all communities have understandings of childhood and what is 'good' for children. These may or may not reflect 'mainstream' approaches to child development that are common to the Western mental health professional model. While the globalisation of many aspects of Western ideas about children and their welfare is occurring, there is more variation than commonality on these matters around the world (Boyden, 1990). What is regarded as optimal child development, a child's rights, a normal family, or an appropriate psychological intervention is not uniform. These differences are often most evident in the everyday practices within which children participate (LeVine *et al.*, 1994; Rogoff, Baker-Sennett, Lacasa & Goldsmith, 1995). They need to be clearly understood – and incorporated centrally in any psychosocial intervention.

The southern African region embraces a variety of cultural communities. These may be defined, and define themselves, in a number of frequently overlapping ways. They include religious, class, ethnic (and, for some, racial) identities, among others. While a number of common beliefs and practices bridge these divides, a range of different perspectives on childhood and cultural practices toward children is likely.

Such variations should prompt designers of interventions to take account of local knowledge and practices. As we noted earlier, taken-for-granted cultural practices are not easily changed. Indeed their disruption can cause distress and resistance. This is because the new practices brought by the intervention (e.g. new forms of discipline) may imply too radical a change to deeply embedded, existing ways of behaving and understanding the world (cultural scripts and forms of cognition). These have long been adaptive ways of understanding and addressing local problems (Gilbert, 1997). As Gilbert notes, the introduction of unfamiliar practices is most likely to be successful if they are shaped in a partnership between the bearers of the new ideas and the recipients of the intervention. When the intervention is designed to be in tune with local knowledge and practice, it is not an alien imposition, and this sensitivity is likely to increase programme effectiveness (see also Chapter 9).

LINKING DEVELOPMENTAL KNOWLEDGE AND INTERVENTION PROGRAMMES

In South Africa, millions of children live in urban poverty environments that are powerful predictors of negative psychological outcomes. These environments have both direct and indirect effects on the child's development, and families and schools play a major role in their mediation. The body of ecological–transactional research that has been considered points to the necessity of interventions being sensitive to both developmental domains and phases.

This introduction has stressed the role of cultural practices and local knowledge in shaping the developmental settings in which cognitive, social and emotional capacities emerge. This knowledge includes local understandings of children's needs and what constitutes appropriate care. Interventions that employ concepts and embody values that are not too distant from local frameworks of understanding are more likely to be supported by the target community (Chapters 9 and 10).

Interventions need to be clear about the particular area of development that they are designed to change, and at which level in the child's ecosystem it is probably best to intervene. Given a particular target problem, is it advisable, for example, to intervene directly at the level of the child, the mother, the family, the immediate neighbourhood, or the local community? As is evident from studies reported in this volume, the focus of the appropriate intervention is often on whole systems (e.g. the school as an organisation) or on adults as the caregivers. Particularly in poorly resourced environments, improvements in the child's condition may often be most economically and effectively achieved by improving the situation of those who mediate the child's experience. Improving the quality of the neighbourhood facilities to which the family has access may also be an appropriate intervention that promotes development. For example, the establishment of institutions that support child development and reduce parental child-care burdens, such as crèches or early child development centres, may be appropriate. Provision of sports facilities may draw children off the streets and into more constructive activities. Policing neighbourhood incivilities in a way that protects families from exposure to violence and criminal subcultures would be an intervention at yet another level.

However, Sameroff (1991) points out that the list of structural environmental risk factors that can easily be altered to improve developmental outcomes is short. Many of the variables that determine risk are stable, resist change, or are expensive to change. The evidence suggests that interventions in microsystems like family contexts, peer contexts, and schools – by altering the proximal relationship of the child and other actors – are frequently most likely to succeed. It is also possible to intervene directly to change the behaviour of the child, or of those with whom he or she may be involved. Changes in individual characteristics will alter the proximal situation. For example, reduction of hyperactive behaviour in a child is likely to reduce the stress on the child's mother, and thus improve the quality of her relationship with her child.

Programme designs also need to consider, on the basis of developmental theory and research, whether the problem is best addressed by a short-term or a long-term intervention, and whether single or multiple aspects of the child's situation need to be tackled. For example, psychosocial interventions have frequently targeted preschool or junior school children, or their caregivers, on the grounds that early intervention can prevent the manifestation of problems at later phases of development. However, transactional models persuade us that preventative programmes during early childhood are likely to hold their effects better if there are follow-up initiatives at later stages, when children face new vulnerabilities (e.g. in early and mid-adolescence). This is because new sources of influence such as peers start to have a significant influence at this time. This view is corroborated by Sameroff (1991, p. 169), who comments that characteristics of the child are 'frequently overpowered by factors in the environmental context of development ... while a continuous view of developmental functioning makes intuitive sense, it has not been borne out by empirical investigations'.

Unfortunately more complex long-term and multifaceted interventions are expensive, particularly for a developing country such as South Africa. Such projects are therefore not attractive to funders and policy makers, unless they can be persuaded of the significant benefits of the project for large numbers of children. However, smaller-scale projects can at least signal the potential effectiveness of larger and more expensive programmes.

CONCLUSION: SOME KEY PRINCIPLES OF INTERVENTION

In southern Africa, a major challenge to improving children's lives is poverty. The chronic and long-term poverty that prevails in South Africa and elsewhere in the region exerts powerful effects that no psychological interventions can seek to overcome. This is why in the North American case, McLoyd (1998) points to the importance of policies that will raise income levels and so enhance children's development, especially their educational attainment. She calls for welfare policies that seek to redress deep and persistent poverty particularly during the child's early years. Many poor children in dysfunctional families do, however, need continued educational support beyond this phase, if the gains are to hold. This was demonstrated by the failure of early Headstart initiatives, where under-resourced families, schools and neighbourhoods caused children who had been in the programme to lose the cognitive gains they had made (Sameroff, 1991).

In South and southern Africa, economic policies and financial resources are such that wide-scale poverty alleviation is simply not going to be achieved. Urban migration in the hope of escaping rural poverty is likely to continue, and this will contribute to burgeoning informal settlements with their associated risks. Despite these constraints, specific, effectively implemented and broadly applied interventions for the most vulnerable groups, during sensitive periods, may reduce the developmental threats of chronic poverty (Dawes *et al.*, 1997). Examples in the South African case include the government's provision of basic welfare support to indigent families with children under the age of 6 years, free medical care to the same population, and school-feeding schemes for disadvantaged junior-primary school children.

It is particularly important to acknowledge that South Africa has a low personnel and financial resource base from which to operate effective intervention programmes for children living in high-risk environments. The child research and intervention capacity is very low compared with developed societies. This is unlikely to change significantly. Indeed, while accurate figures are not available, the number of scholars in the country who are researching the issues we have been dealing with in this chapter could probably be counted on two hands. The number of mental health personnel who specialise in the treatment of child and adolescent disorders is also very limited (Dawes *et al.*, 1997), and those who, additionally, engage in community-based intervention programmes, even more so. This makes it critical for programmes to be clear about what they can achieve with the resources at their disposal.

However, if there is one general rule that can be used to guide intervention designs, it is ecological sensitivity. An analysis and understanding of the both human and physical aspects of the context of intervention is an absolute prerequisite. Such an analysis will reveal the potential supports and threats to the proposed intervention, and will help define its limits. It also allows the intervention to be presented in an ethical manner, making clear to both the target community and to funders what is likely to be achieved and what is not.

In conclusion, as an elaboration of the theoretical and research perspectives that have been discussed, and drawing also on criteria developed by Black and Krishnakumar (1998), Zimmerman & Arunkumar (1994), Huston (1994) and McLoyd (1998), we present some principles for community-based interventions with children in high-risk southern African environments. This is not a definitive list. It represents, rather, some key applications that flow out of our attempt to link developmental knowledge with practice.

Some principles for intervention

1. Interventions should be informed by a knowledge of developmental pathways and epochs. As children grow older, different areas of risk emerge, and different risk-reduction strategies become appropriate. For example, adolescence in urban settings is associated with active risk-taking (Flisher *et al.*, 1993). This group, therefore, becomes vulnerable in particular ways that require age-appropriate interventions.

A related observation is that early interventions do not necessarily hold unless they are supported at later stages of development. This point takes account of child–environment transactions. McLoyd (1998, p. 199) quotes Zigler and Styfco (1994) as follows on this point: 'Early intervention simply cannot overpower the effects of poor living conditions, inadequate nutrition and health care, negative role models, and substandard schools.' Short-term focused interventions that are designed to influence particular developmental domains may well be effective at particular phases in the child's life. However, as we have pointed out, child-context relations are very complex, and we cannot necessarily expect their effects to hold once the child enters a new context at a later point in life. Interventions which aim to produce long-term effects normally need to provide further support at these later points. This increases the expense and long-term commitment of the project, which is often very difficult to achieve. It is a point that is nevertheless important to bring to the attention of donors and target communities.

2. Where possible, interventions should be undertaken at multiple levels. As is emphasised in ecological–transactional approaches, children's development is a product of multiple individual–context relationships that change over time. Thus, problematic behaviours usually co-occur among children in disadvantaged communities, and they are associated with common risk factors. For example, families, schools and neighbourhoods can all be sources of risk for the development of violent behaviour. Optimally, interventions need to consider the relative influence of each source of risk (at different developmental periods), and shape the intervention to take these different sources into account. Multiple-level interventions are therefore more likely to be successful. For example, a violence prevention programme with young adolescents that focuses on the school, and pays no attention to sources of violence in the family and the neighbourhood, is unlikely to be as effective as one that attempts to address the problem at the other sources as well.

However, in most southern African intervention contexts resources are very limited. Multiple-level interventions and changes to the structural features of the context will be very difficult to achieve. The two sites of intervention that have frequently presented the best opportunities for intervention under such conditions are the family and the school (McLoyd, 1998). These are two key sites where adults are close to children for extended periods and can therefore have a relatively enduring and repeated influence on children's development at different phases in the child's life. This is particularly so during the pre-teen years. As we noted earlier, parental involvement in schooling helps to provide support for children, and the link between home and school provides continuity for the stimulation of cognitive development.

3. Interventions should combine cultural and developmental sensitivity. Culture, as we have observed, provides an envelope for all contexts within which development occurs. In this sense, all developmental settings in which other persons play a mediating role are infused with elements of the participants' culture. In addition, young people grow up in areas where subcultures operate (e.g. gangs). Cultures structure the settings within which the child's activities take place, they determine how children's needs are seen, they suggest what is or is not acceptable behaviour at different ages and for different genders. Cultures also indicate the signs of children's well-being and distress (Dawes *et al.*, 1997; Reynolds, 1997).

Failure to consider these aspects of the local situation is likely to hinder access to communities (who may resist unfamiliar practices) and reduce programme efficacy. Adult cultural practices toward children are also informed by what they believe to be best. Even when apparently dysfunctional, they may not be seen as such by adults in the target community. Adults need to be convinced that changing their behaviour will be of benefit to the children. This will be easier if interventions recognise (though not necessarily accept) local knowledge, values and practice, and attempt to develop co-operative interventions with those they intend to help. Ultimately, it is easier to intro-duce new behaviour in culturally supportive contexts.

4. *Interventions should promote community participation.* This proposition improves the local relevance and sustainability of the programme because it recognis-es the need for target communities to identify with the project and support it. It also suggests that sustainability will be promoted by local capacity-building, so that com-munity members can run key aspects of the project in the longer term. Involvement of the community also assists in the development of a partnership between the imple-mentation team and key members of the community. An important consideration is their understanding of local children's worlds as well as what is likely to succeed or fail. Involving local people also contributes to the building of relationships between community members. These are commonly fragmented in depressed areas, and rela-tionships can help improve conditions for children through reducing family isolation and increasing support for caregivers. This guideline also recognises the usefulness of integrating new programmes with existing services where appropriate.

5. *Interventions should build on, and promote, protective factors.* Here the impera-tive is to build intervention strategies that draw on protective factors at a number of levels, including the individual, the family and the community (Garmezy, Masten & Tellegen, 1984; Werner & Smith, 1982; Zimmerman & Arunkumar, 1994). As noted earlier, programmes may be strengthened if they have an understanding of whether protective, compensatory or challenge models of resilience (or all three) are most appropriate to the design of a particular intervention.

In general, a number of strategies have been found to be effective in promoting resilience. For example, early intervention with children whose characteristics are associated with developmental risks can reduce the probability of their developing dis-orders later in life (Desjarlais, Eisenberg, Good & Kleinman, 1995). Thus, early attention and conduct problems have been linked to delinquency in adolescence (Loeber & Stouthamer-Loeber, 1998). Strengthening the supportive capacities of adults can reduce the risk of emotional neglect of children (McLoyd, 1998). The child's connection to an adult (perhaps a teacher) who provides a supportive and safe developmental setting has been found to be of assistance in the development of resilience (Werner & Smith, 1982). Reducing the exposure of family members to negative components of the community is likely to reduce family stress and adult con-cern for the safety of the young (Wandersman & Nation, 1998). Encouragement of close monitoring of children in high-risk neighbourhoods is another protective inter-vention (Jarrett, 1997), as is the facilitation of family links to positive sources of devel-opment in the community such as schools. Following the challenge model of resilience formulated by Garmezy *et al.* (1984), the development of individual com-petence in the young can assist them to resist pressures to become involved in activities that are self-destructive such as delinquent activity and drug abuse. However, the nature of these strategies must take account of the child's developmental level and local resource constraints. At the community level, resilience can be promoted by the presence of cohesive, well-functioning schools and other social institutions. Social networks that intervene for the common good are important, as are families and networks that work to reassert control of their neighbourhoods. Social cohesion and local collective action are empowering to adults, who can then make their areas safer. A consequence of this is that adult well-being is improved, and this in turn has benefits for children.

NOTES

[1]   Throughout the chapter we will use the terms 'child' or 'children' to refer to both adolescents and young children, unless more specific terms are required.

REFERENCES

Aber, J.L., Gephart, M.A., Brooks-Gunn, J. & Connell, J.P. (1997). Development in context: Implications for studying neighborhood effects. In J. Brooks-Gunn, G.J. Duncan & J.L. Aber (Eds.), *Neighborhood Policy. Volume 1 Context and consequences for children* (pp. 44–61). New York: Russell Sage Foundation

Barbarin, O. A., Richter, L.M., de Wet, T. & Wachtel, A. (1998). Ironic trends in the transition to peace: Criminal violence supplants political violence in terrorising South African blacks. *Peace and Conflict: Journal of Peace Psychology, 4*, 285–305.

Berndt, T. J. & Ladd, G.W. (Eds.). (1989). *Peer relationships in child development.* New York: Wiley.

Black, M. M. & Krishnakumar, A. (1998). Children in low-income, urban settings. Interventions to promote mental health and well-being. *American Psychologist, 53*, 635–646.

Boyden, J. (1990). Childhood and policy makers: a comparative perspective on the globalisation of childhood. In A. James & A. Prout (Eds.), *Constructing and reconstructing childhood* (pp. 184–215). London: The Falmer Press.

Bronfenbrenner, U. (1979). *The ecology of human development. Experiments by nature and design.* Cambridge MA: Harvard University Press.

Bronfenbrenner, U. (1986). Ecology of the family as a context for human development: Research perspectives. *Developmental Psychology, 22*, 723–742.

Brooks-Gunn, J., Duncan, G.J. & Aber, J.L. (Eds.). (1997a). *Neighborhood Policy. Volume 1 Context and consequences for children.* New York: Russell Sage Foundation

Brooks-Gunn, J., Duncan, G.J. & Aber, J.L. (Eds.). (1997b). *Neighborhood Policy. Volume 2 Policy implications in studying neighborhoods.* New York: Russell Sage Foundation.

Cairns, E. (1996). *Children and political violence.* Oxford: Blackwell.

Caplan, N., Whitmore, J.K. & Choy, M.H. (1989). *The Boat People and achievement in America: A study of family life, hard work and cultural values.* Ann Arbor: University of Michigan Press.

Chase-Lansdale, P.L. & Brooks-Gunn, J. (1995). *Escape from poverty. What makes a difference for children?* New York: Cambridge University Press.

Clarke, A.M. & Clarke, A.D.B. (1986). Thirty years of child psychology: A selective review.

Journal of Child Psychology and Psychiatry, 27, 719–759.

Cole, M. (1997). *Cultural Psychology. A once and future discipline.* Cambridge, MA: The Belknap Press of Harvard University Press.

Dawes, A. & Cairns, E. (1998). The Machel Study: Dilemmas of cultural sensitivity and universal rights of children. *Peace and Conflict: Journal of Peace Psychology, 4*(4), 335–348.

Dawes, A. & Donald, D. (Eds.). (1994). *Childhood and adversity: Psychological perspectives from South African research.* Cape Town: David Philip.

Dawes, A., Robertson, B., Duncan, N., Ensink, K., Jackson, A., Reynolds, P., Pillay, A. & Richter, L. (1997). Child mental health policy. In D. Foster, M. Freeman & Y. Pillay (Eds), *Mental health policy issues for South Africa* (pp. 216–235). Cape Town: M.A.S.A.

Dodge, K.A., Pettit, G.S. & Bates, J.E. (1994). Socialisation mediators of the relationship between socio-economic status and child conduct problems. *Child Development, 65,* 649–665.

Donald, D. & Dawes, A. (1994). The way forward: Challenges to child development research and intervention in contexts of adversity. In A. Dawes & D. Donald (Eds.), *Childhood and adversity: Psychological perspectives from South African research* (pp. 261–271). Cape Town: David Philip.

Donald, D., Lazarus, S. & Lolwana, P. (1997). *Educational psychology in social context: Challenges of development, social issues and special need in southern Africa.* Cape Town: Oxford University Press.

Donald, D., Wallis, J. & Cockburn, A. (1997). An exploration of meanings: Tendencies towards developmental risk and resilience in a group of South African ex-street children. *School Psychology International, 18,* 137–154.

Elder, G.H., Jr. (1974). *Children of the Great Depression: social change in life experience.* Chicago: University of Chicago Press.

Finchilescu, G. & Dawes, A. (1998). Catapulted into democracy. South African adolescents' socio-political orientations following rapid political change. *Journal of Social Issues, 54*(3), 563-584.

Flisher, A. J., Ziervogel, C., Chalton, D., Leger, P. & Robertson, B. A. (1993). Risk-taking behaviour of Cape Peninsula high school students. Part ii. Suicidal behaviour. *South African Medical Journal, 83,* 474-476.

Fitzgerald, H.E., Lester, B.M. & Zuckerman, B. (Eds.). (1995). *Children of poverty: Research, health care and policy issues.* New York: Garland Press.

Furstenberg, F.F. & Hughes, M.E. (1997). The influence of neighborhoods on children's development: A theoretical perspective and a research agenda. In J. Brooks-Gunn, G.J. Duncan & J.L. Aber (Eds.), *Neighborhood Policy Volume 2 Policy implications in studying neighborhoods* (pp. 23-47). New York: Russell Sage Foundation.

Garbarino, J. (1992). The meaning of poverty in the world of children. *American Behavioral Scientist, 35,* 220–237.

Garbarino, J. (1995). *Raising children in a socially toxic environment.* San Francisco: Josey-Bass.

Garbarino, J. & Sherman, D. (1980). High-risk neighborhoods and high-risk families: The human ecology of child maltreatment. *Child Development, 51,* 188–198.

Garmezy, N. (1993). Children in poverty: Resilience despite risk. *Psychiatry, 56,* 127-136.

Garmezy, N, Maston, A. & Tellegen, A. (1984). The study of stress and competence in children: A building block of developmental psychopathology. *Child Development, 55,* 97–111.

Gilbert, A. (1997). Small voices in the wind: Local knowledge and social transformation. *Peace and Conflict: The Journal of Peace Psychology, 3*(3), 275–292.

Gordon, A. (1987). *Another mielie in the bag.* Pretoria: Human Sciences Research Council.

Honwana, A. (1997). Healing for peace: Traditional healers and post-war reconstruction in southern Mozambique. *Peace and Conflict: Journal of Peace Psychology, 3*(3), 293–305.

Huston, A.C. (1994). Children of poverty: designing research to affect policy. Social Policy Report. *Society for Research in Child Development, Volume VIII* (2), 1–12.

Jarrett, R.L. (1997). Bringing families back in: neighbourhood effects on child development. In J. Brooks-Gunn, G.J. Duncan & J.L. Aber (Eds.), *Neighbourhood Policy. Volume 2 Policy implications in studying neighbourhoods* (pp. 48–64). New York: Russell Sage Foundation.

Jones, S. (1993). *Assaulting childhood. Children's experiences of migrancy and hostel life in South Africa.* Johannesburg: Witwatersrand University Press.

Kessen, W. (1979). The American child and other cultural inventions. *American Psychologist, 34,* 815–820.

Levett, A. (1994). Problems of cultural imperialism in the study of child sexual abuse. In A. Dawes & D. Donald, (Eds.), *Childhood and adversity: Psychological perspectives from South African research* (pp. 240–260). Cape Town: David Philip.

LeVine, R. A., Dixon, S., LeVine, S., Richman, A., Liederman, H. P., Keefer, C. H. & Brazelton, T. B. (1994). *Child care and culture. Lessons from Africa.* Cambridge: Cambridge University Press.

Liddell, C., Lycett, J. & Rae, G. (1997). Getting through grade 2: predicting children's early school achievement in rural South Africa. *International Journal of Behavioral Development, 21*(2), 331–348.

Loeber, R. & Stouthamer-Loeber, M. (1998). Development of juvenile aggression and violence. Some misconceptions and controversies. *American Psychologist, 53,* 242–259.

Masten, A.S. & Coatsworth, J.D. (1998). The development of competence in favorable and unfavorable environments. Lessons from research on successful children. *American Psychologist, 53,* 205–220.

McLoyd, V. (1998). Socio-economic disadvantage and child development. *American Psychologist, 53,* 185–204.

McLoyd V. & Wilson, L. (1990). Maternal behaviour, social support, and economic conditions as predictors of distress in children. In V. McLoyd & C. Flanagan (Eds.), *Economic stress: Effects on family life and child development* (pp. 49–69). San Francisco: Josey Bass.

Miller P.J. & Goodnow, J.J. (1995). Cultural practices: Toward an integration of culture and development. In J.J. Goodnow, P.J. Miller & F.S. Kessel (Eds.), *Cultural practices as contexts for development* (pp. 5–16). San Francisco: Josey-Bass.

Moffitt, T. (1993). Adolescence limited and life course-persistent antisocial behavior: A developmental taxonomy. *Psychological Review, 100*(4), 674–701.

Nsamenang, A. B. & Dawes, A. (1998). Developmental psychology as political psychology in sub-Saharan Africa: The challenge of Africanisation. *Applied Psychology: An International Review, 46*(4), 73–87.

Ogbu, J. (1981). Origins of human competence: A cultural-ecological perspective. *Child Development, 52,* 413–429.

Ramphele, M. (1993). *A bed called home. Life in the migrant hostels of Cape Town.* Cape Town: David Phillip.

Reynolds, P. (1997). *Children and traditional healing in Zimbabwe.* Athens: Ohio University Press.

Richter, L. (1994). Socio-economic stress and its effect on the family and caretaking patterns. In A. Dawes & D. Donald (Eds.), *Childhood and adversity: Psychological perspectives from South African research* (pp. 28–50). Cape Town: David Philip.

Rogers, D. E. & Ginsberg, E. (Eds.). (1990). *Improving life chances for children at risk.* Boulder Colorado: Westview Press.

Rogoff, B., Baker-Sennett, J., Lacasa, P. & Goldsmith, D. (1995). Development through participation in socio-cultural activity. In J.J. Goodnow, P.J. Miller & F.S. Kessel (Eds.), *Cultural practices as contexts for development* (pp. 5–15). San Francisco: Josey Bass.

Rutter, M. (1985). Resilience in the face of adversity. Protective factors and resistance to psychological disorder. *British Journal of Psychiatry, 147,* 598–611.

Rutter, M., Quinton, D. & Yule, B. (1977). *Family pathology and child psychiatric disorder.* London: John Wiley.

Sameroff, A.J. (1975). Transactional models in early social relations. *Human Development, 18,* 65–79.

Sameroff, A. J. (1991). The social context of development. In M. Woodhead, P. Light & R. Carr (Eds.), *Becoming a person* (pp. 167–189). London: Routledge and The Open University.

Scarr, S. (1992). Developmental theories for the 1990s: Development and individual differences. *Child Development, 63,* 1–19.

Scheper-Hughes, N. (1989). *Child-survival: Anthropological perspectives on the treatment and maltreatment of children.* Dordrecht: Riedel.

Sinha, D. & Mishra, R. C. (1993). Some methodological issues related to research in developmental psychology in the context of policy and intervention programs. In T.S. Saraswathi & B. Kaur (Eds.), *Human development and family studies in India: An agenda for research and policy* (pp. 139–150). New Delhi: Sage.

Stephens, S. (1995). Introduction. Children and the politics of culture in 'late capitalism'. In S. Stephens (Ed.), *Children and the politics of culture* (pp. 3–48). Princeton New Jersey: Princeton University Press.

Swart-Kruger, J. & Donald, D. (1994). Children of the South African streets. In A. Dawes & D. Donald (Eds.), *Childhood and adversity: Psychological perspectives from South African research* (pp. 107–121). Cape Town: David Philip.

Wandersman, A. & Nation, M. (1998). Urban neighborhoods and mental health. Psychological contributions to understanding toxicity, resilience and interventions. *American Psychologist, 53,* 647–656.

Werner, E. & Smith, R. S. (1982). *Vulnerable but invincible: A longitudinal study of resilient children and youth.* New York: McGraw Hill.

Zimmerman, M. A. & Arunkumar, R. (1994). Resiliency research: Implications for schools and policy. *Social Policy Report. Society for Research in Child Development, Volume VIII* (4), 1–17.

SOCIO-ECONOMIC POLICIES

2

Their impact on children in South Africa

LINDA BIERSTEKER & SHIRLEY ROBINSON

The children of South Africa find themselves in a society where apartheid policy has left a legacy of severe disparities. The circumstances in which the majority of families have lived have impacted negatively on their capacity to meet the most fundamental needs of children. Deprivation, violence, malnutrition, poor health, inferior education and discriminatory social security systems have created profound inequalities between children in different racial groups and geographical areas and between genders. Rural as well as regional migration to urban centres in search of employment has led to the breakup of families as well as the exacerbation of poverty in high-density urban squatter settlements (Robinson & Tilley, 1998).

This chapter focuses on the implications of nationally planned policies for the delivery of socio-economic services to children by a range of different actors, including national, provincial and local government as well as non-governmental organisations (NGOs). National policies set the parameters within which services to children are to be delivered. Translating these policies into action may take place through different agencies. National government may take the lead such as in the implementation of the Primary School Nutrition Programme in the health sector; whereas in the delivery of primary and secondary schooling, it is the provinces that take responsibility. The delivery of many welfare services depends to a large extent on interaction with community-based NGOs.

The chapter begins by drawing a demographic picture of children in South Africa. This helps to situate the challenges facing children within the context of current political and socio-economic change, and outlines the policy framework for addressing childhood adversity. The focus falls particularly on the social sector. The second and main section takes an in-depth look at service delivery to children in key sectors – health, education, welfare and criminal justice. These sectoral reviews draw out the implications of policies for children, and evaluate how successful the implementation of these policies has been for uplifting their lives. We conclude with the identification of a common vision and strategic approach in the government's policies, and a discussion of factors constraining the implementation of these policies in practice.

Where are the children in South Africa?

A demographic picture, drawn from the 1996 census data, indicates that children, aged 0 to 19 years, form 44.22% of South Africa's population. Census results indicate that South Africa's population stood at 40.58 million in 1996. While the largest age cohorts are 5–9 years (11.5%) and 10–14 years (11.5%), the census results confirm that South Africa's population is not growing as fast as prior estimates suggested (Statistics South Africa, 1998). This means that South Africa's age profile is older than previously estimated. Nevertheless, children 18 years and under will dominate the age distribution of the population of South Africa in the short to medium term, and more so in some provinces than in others (see Figure 1).

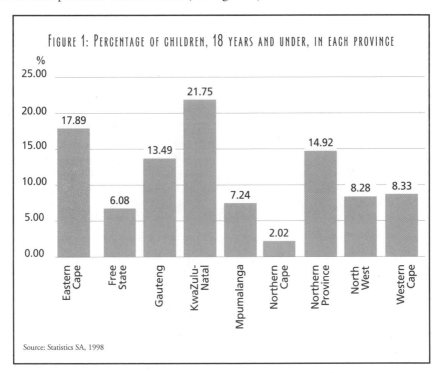

FIGURE 1: PERCENTAGE OF CHILDREN, 18 YEARS AND UNDER, IN EACH PROVINCE

Source: Statistics SA, 1998

Children living in poverty

Six out of every ten children in South Africa live in poverty, when 'poor' is defined as the poorest 40% of households (Office of the Deputy President, 1998). Children living in rural areas are more likely to be poor than those in urban centres. The poverty share of rural compared to urban areas is 70% – that is, seven out of every ten poor people in South Africa live in rural areas (Statistics South Africa, 1997). The broad picture hides stark provincial differences (see Figure 2) – in the Eastern Cape, for example, 78% of children live in poor households, compared to 35% in the Western Cape and 20% in Gauteng (Office of the Deputy President, 1998).

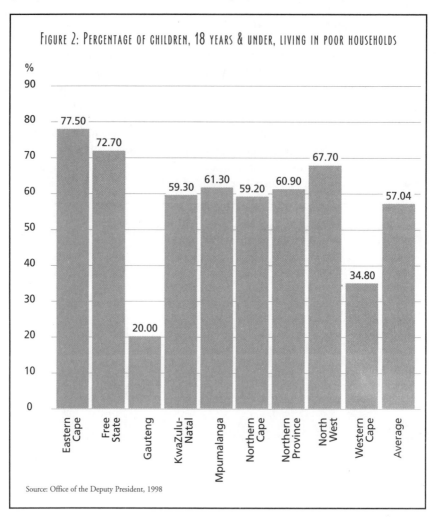

FIGURE 2: PERCENTAGE OF CHILDREN, 18 YEARS & UNDER, LIVING IN POOR HOUSEHOLDS

Source: Office of the Deputy President, 1998

Apart from a rural and regional dimension, poverty in South Africa is characterised by:
- gender (female-headed households are more likely to be poor than those headed by a resident male)
- increased numbers of very young or school-going children
- race (all black groups have higher probability of being poor than whites)
- unemployment
- education (less than secondary and post-secondary education increases the probability of being poor)
  (Office of the Deputy President, 1998)

At a macro level, the particular vulnerability of children to poverty is reflected in two quality of life measures: infant mortality rates (IMRs) and human development indices (HDIs). While the IMR is an indicator directly related to the vulnerability of very young children, the HDI provides an indication of the socio-economic environment and life opportunities facing children more generally. Human development indices, measured at the provincial level, present a clear view of provincial disparities in socio-economic development for children, highlighting the particular vulnerability of rural children to poverty in South Africa (see Table 1).

Infant mortality rates

The infant mortality rate (IMR) is a common measure of quality of life and socio-economic development. It is defined as 'the number of live-born children who die before the age of 1 year per 1000 live births' (South African Institute of Race Relations, 1997, p. 450). Estimates by the Health Systems Trust (1998) suggest that in 1994, 48.9 infants out of every 1000 live births died before age 1 year in South Africa. This is markedly higher than the IMR average of 17.3 for 15 similar upper-middle-income developing countries. This average hides large differences between population groups. The IMR for coloureds was 36.3, while it was 54.3 for Africans in the same period. The infant mortality rates for Africans and coloureds are substantially higher than those for Indians (9.9) and whites (7.3) (see also Box 1).

Predictions indicate a decline in South Africa's IMR by about 20% between 1996 and 2000. This forecast reflects a positive outlook for the quality of life and socio-economic development of South Africans (South African Institute of Race Relations, 1997).

Human development index

The human development index (HDI) is a composite indicator of socio-economic development. It comprises three factors: life expectancy, per capita income and level of education, and is measured on a scale from 0 to 1. An HDI below 0.5 indicates a low level of development, whereas an HDI above 0.5 indicates a higher level of development. The United Nations Development Programme (South African Institute of Race Relations, 1997) reports that in 1993 South Africa had an HDI of 0.649, and ranked 100th out of 174 countries. The South African government's Central Statistical Services reported a comparable value of 0.677 for South Africa in 1991, compared to an HDI of 0.557 in 1980.

Table 1 provides HDIs for the provinces in 1991, as reported by Central Statistical Services (South African Institute of Race Relations, 1997). The Western Cape and Gauteng have high HDIs, whereas the Northern Cape, Mpumalanga, Free State, KwaZulu-Natal, the North West Province and the Eastern Cape show a 'medium' level of human development. The Northern Province is the only one that has a relatively low level of human development as measured by the HDI. These quality of life measures reveal that poverty is still very much an issue of inequality of resources and appropriate service delivery in South Africa, in which extreme racial inequalities and provincial disparities play a major part. Poverty is concentrated in the rural areas, and therefore in those provinces which have a higher proportion of their population living in such areas. As the majority of employment opportunities are available in urban

TABLE 1: HUMAN DEVELOPMENT INDEX (HDI) BY PROVINCE, 1991

Province	HDI
Eastern Cape	0.507
Free State	0.657
Gauteng	0.818
KwaZulu-Natal	0.602
Mpumalanga	0.694
North West	0.694
Northern Cape	0.543
Northern Province	0.470
Western Cape	0.826
Average	0.677

Source: SA Institute of Race Relations, 1997

areas, migration to the urban centres depletes the income-generation potential and exacerbates poverty in the rural areas.

Children, especially those living in rural areas, are particularly vulnerable to poverty. Since its election in 1994 the South African government has put in place overarching policies which provide a framework for addressing the situation of children. Provisions specifically related to children, for example, were included in the Bill of Rights in the Constitution. In 1995 the government also ratified the Convention on the Rights of the Child.

The Convention on the Rights of the Child (CRC) is a legally binding international treaty which rests on four pillars, or groups of rights. These are survival rights (or the right to an adequate living standard), development rights, protection rights and participation rights. The state is obliged to undertake appropriate legislative, administrative and other measures for the implementation of the rights recognised in the Convention. For virtually all of the articles, this entails economic responsibilities for the public sector (De Vylder, 1996). Such responsibilities include financing services that are necessary to provide for some of the rights, as well as providing adequate resources for the enforcement of others, such as protection rights. While the Convention recognises that poorer countries may not have sufficient resources to implement it, there is the expectation that states will ensure the survival and development of the child to the maximum extent of their available resources (in Article 6).

Many of the CRC's provisions find expression in the Bill of Rights in the Constitution of the Republic of South Africa of 1996. Article 28, Chapter 2, relates specifically to children's rights, providing for basic socio-economic rights to nutrition, shelter, health care and social services without any limitation, as well as protection from neglect, abuse and exploitation, including particular provisions for children in detention. Article 29 provides for the right to basic education and the progressive availability of further education. Within this overarching policy framework, different departmental policies and programmes specifically address the provisions in relation to their own sectoral responsibilities. The National Programme of Action for Children (NPA) is the vehicle for integration of all policies and plans by government departments and NGOs to promote the well-being of children. It is overseen by an

Inter-Ministerial Steering Committee and housed in the Office of the Deputy President. As the government structure responsible for implementing CRC commitments, it reports on the NPA to the United Nations CRC Committee. The first report was submitted in 1997 and the next report is due in 2002.

The NPA has identified seven priority areas with a particular focus within each one on children living in difficult circumstances or with special needs (National Programme of Action Steering Committee, 1996). The areas are:
• nutrition
• child and maternal health
• water and sanitation
• early childhood development and basic education
• social welfare developmental services
• child protection measures
• leisure and cultural activities

The NPA is a key instrument for addressing childhood adversity, and will be used to monitor government progress in relation to the implementation of the CRC. Consideration of these priority areas will therefore provide the framework of discussion through the rest of the chapter.

PRIORITY AREAS IN THE NATIONAL PROGRAMME OF ACTION FOR CHILDREN

Child and maternal health, and nutrition

After education, health receives the highest level of government expenditure: R26.8 billion or 13.65% of the 1998/9 consolidated government budget. The new government has seen improved health care for children in South Africa as a priority in socio-economic delivery, and has enacted a number of significant policies to improve maternal and child health. These include the Primary School Nutrition Programme (PSNP), more recently the national Integrated Nutrition Programme (INP), health care for pregnant women and children under 6 years, and interventions against the HIV/AIDS epidemic. The move to greater decentralisation in health service delivery under the district health system approach will also serve to increase women's and children's access to primary health care services across the country.

A snapshot of child health and nutrition in South Africa (see Box 1) reveals a startling picture of extreme disparities in access to health services and consequent indicators of child health. Although South Africa has world-renowned specialist health facilities, many children, particularly those living in rural areas, do not have access to basic health care and other services, such as water and sanitation. These child health indicators point to the lingering effects of apartheid's racial, geographic and socio-economic policies. Poor children suffer and die from diseases, such as tuberculosis, measles, typhoid and diarrhoea, which could easily be prevented by improving basic health conditions and access to services.

A key challenge in the public health system is the need to address historical disparities in the distribution of health resources. One way in which this has been interpreted is to shift health resources from well-resourced provinces and regions to those that are most in need of health services. However, increasing the general amount spent on health care will not improve the basic health status for children, unless expenditure on health care is reprioritised specifically towards improving equity and access to primary health care facilities for women and children.

Box 1. child health and nutrition status

1. In 1994, the infant mortality rate (IMR) for Africans was 54.3 per 1000 live births, whereas the IMR for whites was only 7.3 per 1000.
2. There are wide provincial disparities in reported IMR figures – the Western Cape reported an average across all racial groups of 27 per 1000 in 1994, whereas the average IMR in the Eastern Cape was 72 per 1000 in the same year.
3. While the average immunisation coverage at 74.7 % (in 1994) is high in South Africa, there are significant differences between provinces, and children in rural areas had a far lower rate of immunisation than children in urban areas.
4. South Africa has a high incidence of low birth weight babies – approximately 16% of all births.
5. Chronic undernutrition is still a major problem among preschool children in South Africa – one in every four children is stunted and one in ten under-weight for age. The highest rates of malnourished children were reported in the Eastern Cape, Northern Province and KwaZulu-Natal.
6. In 1997, of every 100 women attending antenatal clinics, 16 were infected with HIV.
7. Of the total number of AIDS cases in South Africa reported up to December 1994, 10.7 % were children.
8. 2.3 % of all babies in South Africa were HIV-infected in 1994 – again there are wide provincial disparities, with KwaZulu-Natal reporting the highest rate of infection at 4.3% and the Western Cape the lowest at 0.35%.
9. In the next few years expectations are that there will be close to a million AIDS orphans.

Sources: (1, 3, 5) Health Systems Trust, 1998; (2) Department of Health, 1997a; (4) Department of Health, 1997b; (6, 9) United Nations Development Programme, 1998; (7, 8) Child Health Unit, 1998.

The Primary School Nutrition Programme

Malnutrition can severely impede the physical and psychological development of children (see Box 2). One specific intervention that prioritises poor children's nutritional needs is the Primary School Nutrition Programme (PSNP). This was initiated in 1994 as a Presidential Lead Project. Its stated goal is to contribute to the improvement of education quality by enhancing primary school pupils' learning capacity (by alleviating hunger), improving school attendance and punctuality, and enhancing general health development (Health Systems Trust, 1997). A recent evaluation of the PSNP highlighted the fact that although the overall objective of hunger alleviation has been met, the PSNP had not made significant inroads into addressing nutrition education, parasite eradication, or micronutrient supplementation. These problems were compounded by numerous allegations of mismanagement and corruption in the administration of the PSNP (Health Systems Trust, 1997).

The PSNP evaluation resulted in a number of key recommendations, noting the need to

- develop more stringent targeting criteria for schools
- improve the management system for school feeding
- optimise the quality and quantity of school meals
- transform the PSNP from a vertical feeding programme to a comprehensive school nutrition programme
- ensure the integration of the PSNP into the Community Based Nutrition Programme of the national Integrated Nutrition Programme
- ensure adequate funding for the PSNP
- control parasitic infection
- incorporate micronutrient supplementation
- incorporate nutrition education

(Health Systems Trust, 1997).

Implementation of the programme has been most successful in Gauteng and the Western Cape, whereas poor provinces such as Mpumalanga and the Eastern Cape have struggled. In Gauteng, 49% of schools were targeted, and children in schools in rural areas and informal settlements were given priority. In the Western Cape, the PSNP is integrated into established school-feeding programmes within the National Nutrition and Social Development Programme, reaching 100% of predominantly black and 76% of predominantly coloured primary school children. In the poorer provinces, where child poverty and malnutrition are more prevalent, logistical and administrative problems have meant that coverage by the PSNP has been poor and unreliable. However, these provinces have taken corrective steps and are overcoming administrative and institutional hurdles in implementing the programme.

While many of the problems in the implementation of the PSNP have arisen from inadequate management systems, and infrastructural and institutional constraints, particularly in the poorer provinces, anecdotal evidence does suggest that school feeding has led to improved school attendance and classroom performance. These results, if reliable, would confirm the appropriateness of a primary school nutrition programme. Provided it is effectively implemented, it has the potential to improve the general health and learning capacity of primary school children, particularly in the poorer provinces where child malnutrition is more prevalent (Health Systems Trust, 1997; Robinson & Sadan, 1999).

The Integrated Nutrition Programme for South Africa

The Poverty and Inequality Report (Office of the Deputy President, 1998) estimates that about 39% of people in South Africa face a daily reality of not having enough food to eat. Food insecurity and insufficient nutrient intake are closely associated with poverty and inadequate living conditions. Recent surveys indicate widespread malnutrition – again, particularly among those living in rural areas. A national nutrition programme therefore forms an essential element of a poverty alleviation strategy in South Africa. The primary objective of the national Integrated Nutrition Programme (INP) is to employ a series of activities to improve the nutritional status of all South Africans (Department of Health, 1998).

The INP recognises that malnutrition is caused by a multiplicity of factors, and is not only the result of inadequate food intake. The immediate causes of malnutrition include inadequate dietary intake, disease, and psychosocial stress and trauma. The underlying determinants, however, include food security, access to basic health services and a healthy environment (i.e. access to water and sanitation), care of women and children, and education and information (Department of Health, 1998).

The INP is an ambitious programme and will be phased in gradually, replacing the current Protein Energy Malnutrition scheme, the National Nutrition and Social Development Programme and the PSNP. The success of the programme is particularly dependent on effective intersectoral collaboration. This approach has been evident in a number of recent government policies and strategies. However, it presents extreme practical difficulties in planning, budgeting and implementation (Robinson & Biersteker, 1997). These difficulties may be partly alleviated by the implementation of management protocols, clearly identifying sector roles, responsibilities and procedures for interaction.

Box 2. NUTRITION AND CHILD DEVELOPMENT

The Carnegie Task Force on Meeting the Needs of Young Children (1994) notes evidence that brain development before 1 year is more rapid and extensive and vulnerable to environmental influence than previously realised. Inadequate nutrition before birth and in the first years of life can seriously interfere with brain development and lead to neurological and behavioural disorders.

Duncan (1997) acknowledges the argument that resilience can mitigate damaging effects of malnutrition, but notes that potentially damaging effects include permanent stunting if malnutrition occurs in the first five years of a child's life. Further, malnutrition leads to other physical problems such as bad teeth and bowed legs, and may have implications for the development of self-esteem when growth is stunted. There is also a high incidence of EEG abnormalities in malnourished children, which suggests that malnutrition could lead to organic damage as well as to vulnerability to infections and poor health. Poor health in turn may have adverse effects on a child's acquisition of various essential skills which normally develop very rapidly in the first few years of life. In particular, when brain growth and development are impaired, children cannot fulfil their intellectual potential.

Malnutrition can also affect the social and emotional development of children because it affects their caregivers. It seems to have a negative impact on caregivers' behaviour towards these children, who are difficult to care for and therefore makes caregiving less rewarding (Richter & Griesel, 1994). Others note that long-term childhood malnutrition may have effects such as aggression, release of latent behavioural abnormalities, and a general orientation to mistrust the world.

Free health care for pregnant women and children under 6 years

The Free Health Care (FHC) policy for pregnant women and children under 6 years was a bold move by the South African government to remove barriers (i.e. user fees) to health care and improve health conditions for women and young children. User fees for basic services impede access to these services for the poor and most vulnerable groups of the population. A recent evaluation of the FHC policy (McCoy, 1996) found that there was a significant rise in the utilisation of antenatal and maternal health services at public health facilities following the introduction of the policy. While there is as yet no conclusive evidence that this initiative has improved women's and children's health status, it is reasonable to assume that the FHC policy will contribute to achieving greater equity in access to basic health services for the most disadvantaged of the population.

The HIV/AIDS epidemic

The HIV/AIDS epidemic is fast becoming South Africa's priority health problem. The rate of HIV infections has soared, with the Department of Health estimating that at the beginning of 1996, 1.8 million South Africans were infected, and the epidemic has yet to peak. Children infected with HIV/AIDS form approximately 10.7% of all cases and there is an increasing prevalence of HIV-infected babies being born in South Africa – 2.3% of all babies in 1994 were born with HIV (Child Health Unit, 1998).

The Department of Health has placed interventions against AIDS at the top of its agenda, but bureaucratic delays have impeded the implementation of planned policies and programmes. The crisis clearly requires a response that is broader than the health sector, and presents a stark challenge to government, NGOs and communities to collaborate in developing and implementing effective strategies and programmes. The National AIDS Co-ordinating Committee of South Africa plays a critical role in co-ordinating the actions of key stakeholders and in monitoring programmes and activities. The epidemic presents a real crisis to the social and economic development of South Africa. The need for appropriate planning and prevention is critical, and will demand the effective collaboration of all key players – a challenge in itself.

The District Health System

The development of the District Health System (DHS) is seen as an important step in prioritising primary health care in South Africa's health system. The DHS is intended to lead to greater decentralisation in health service delivery, to improve efficacy in planning for community basic health needs, and to facilitate community participation in health service management (Financial and Fiscal Commission, 1997). The planning stage of the DHS has been completed and the process is moving towards implementation. However, key problems in implementation have emerged. These include the slow and uneven development of local government structures across the country, and differences amongst provinces as to whether districts should be accountable to local government structures or to provincial administrations (Office of the Deputy President, 1998). The need for additional personnel and essential drugs to cope with increased clinic attendance has also put the district health system under extreme budgetary pressures, and has made implementation difficult.

Summary: Child and maternal health, and nutrition
- The government has implemented a number of policies that prioritise primary health care services for women and children. These include the Primary School Nutrition Programme, the Integrated Nutrition Programmme, free health care at the primary level, and the decentralisation of primary health care at district level.
- The major obstacle to the successful implementation of these policies, particularly in the poor provinces, is lack of infrastructure and institutional (administrative) capacity.
- Free primary health care at the district level is a clear move towards improving access to health care in poor environments.

Water and sanitation

Access to basic water and sanitation facilities impacts directly on child health and complements the provision of basic health services. Availability of clean water and sanitation facilities reduces the susceptibility of children to killer diseases such as diarrhoea, and relieves women and children of the burden of time spent fetching water.

Water

About 12 to 14 million South Africans, especially those in the rural areas, do not have access to safe water (Financial and Fiscal Commission, 1997). In the Reconstruction and Development Programme (RDP), the government has committed itself to increasing access to water and sanitation services and to being responsible for providing access to safe water. In 1998/9 the government spent R2.3 billion on programmes for water provision under the Department of Water Affairs and Forestry (DWAF). These funds are also supplemented from the RDP fund.

The Community Water Supply and Sanitation Programme (CWSS) aims to provide water supplies to 90% of the currently non-serviced population, particularly those in the rural areas. Originally financed from the RDP Fund, the CWSS is now integrated into the programme activities of the DWAF. The Department has implemented the Water Services Bill – the first key piece of legislation that aims to bring 'some water for all, forever' – and has made great strides in attempting to realise the RDP promises of water provision to marginalised communities (Office of the Deputy President, 1998; Tilley, 1998).

The Consolidated Municipal Infrastructural Investment Programme (CMIP) is the main government programme that targets infrastructural provision towards poor households in urban areas. The majority of CMIP projects are targeted towards the provision of water and sanitation in urban areas (see below). In 1998/9 the government budgeted R585.6 million for CMIP programmes to provide basic infrastructure for poor households (Department of Finance, 1998b).

Sanitation

An estimated 21 million South Africans do not have access to adequate sanitation facilities. The main aim of national sanitation policy is to facilitate improvements in basic health care by providing guidelines for the provision of basic and adequate sanitation facilities (Financial and Fiscal Commission, 1997). However, improvements in sanitation are broader than simply providing toilets, and include health and hygiene education as well.

Summary: Water and sanitation

While these programmes are showing progress, the government faces a considerable challenge in addressing the backlog of infrastructural provision – essential complementary investments to expenditure on primary health care services. Nevertheless, with regard to water and sanitation, important initiatives have been launched to redress backlogs in the provision of basic infrastructure (safe water supply and sanitation services) to rural areas in particular.

Early childhood development and basic education

South African school enrolment rates compare favourably with other countries in the region and with other upper-middle-income countries. A high proportion of public expenditure is allocated to education. In 1998/9 the consolidated national and provincial education budget of R43.64 billion made up 22.2 % of the government budget. Despite this, there are high repetition rates at all levels, poor learning outcomes and unacceptably high adult illiteracy rates (Financial and Fiscal Commission, 1997). Matriculation results show poor performance overall and marked gender and geographic differences. The legacy of apartheid is vast, and achieving equity and redress is a major challenge (see Box 3).

The goals of the NPA in the education sector are of particular importance in addressing childhood adversity, namely:
- to expand activities that promote early childhood development, including appropriate low-cost family and community-based interventions
- to provide universal access to basic education, and the achievement of primary education by at least 80% of primary school-age children through formal school or non-formal education of comparable learning standards.

Policies aimed at transformation of the education system are designed to address issues of access, equity and quality. These include, for example, the new curriculum, language of instruction, a programme aimed at establishing a culture of learning and teaching, and recommendations in support of learners with special education needs.

Funding policies

Given the high budget allocation education already receives and the climate of fiscal constraint, the challenge has been how to redirect public education expenditure to the poor. This is of significance because there is a strong association between household income and educational enrolment. While at primary level 90% of children from rich households attend school and 85% from poor households, by the secondary level 90% of children from rich households attend school but only 46% from poor households still do. The disparity widens at the tertiary level, where 38% from rich households and 4% from poor ones go on to tertiary education (Office of the Deputy President, 1998).

Two important recent events have contributed to the project of redistributing resources amongst public schools in South Africa. First, in October 1998 the Minister

BOX 3. A SNAPSHOT OF EDUCATION IN SOUTH AFRICA

1. There are 12 million school children, 29 000 schools and 364 000 teachers in South Africa.
2. An estimated 5% of poor children between the ages of 10 and 16 are not in school.
3. Between 1.3 and 4% of children aged 4–14 years have a disability such as a serious eye defect, hearing/speech problem, and a physical or mental disability.
4. Studies suggest that only between 11 and 18% of children have access to organised preschool programmes of any kind.
5. In 1997, matriculation examination results were the worst recorded since 1979: the pass rate was 47%, and 12% matriculated with exemption. The number of failures increased by 23% and the number of students obtaining a matriculation exemption decreased by 13%.
6. In 1993, 60% of the school-age population from the poorest 40% of households received only 40% of public education spending, while 8% of the school age population from the wealthiest 20% of households received 23% of public education spending.
7. In 1994, 36% of teachers and 40% of women teachers did not have the officially required M+3 (Matriculation + 3years of teacher training).
8. The school register of needs revealed an average pupil–classroom ratio of 51:1 in the Eastern Cape whereas the official norm is 37:1.
9. In schools across the country there is a shortage of more than 57 000 classrooms, 10 000 boreholes, 15 000 electrical connections, 17 000 telephones, and 270 000 toilets.
10. Per capita spending on school education varied from R1650 to R3000 in the 1997/8 financial year.

Sources: (1) Financial and Fiscal Commission, 1997; (2, 6) Office of the Deputy President, 1998; (3) Central Statistical Services, 1997; (4) Biersteker, 1997; (5) Schindler, 1998; (7) Hartshorne, 1996; (8, 9) School Register of Needs, 1996; (10) Research Institute for Educational Planning, 1998.

of Education published the National Norms and Standards for School Funding (see Table 2). Second, in November 1998 the major educator unions reached agreement with the Education Department on norms and standards for the provisioning of teacher posts. This provides for members of executive councils in the provinces to set learner–educator ratios based on what budgets allow and specifies arrangements for surplus and temporary teachers. These two developments will allow provincial education departments to redistribute public funds from advantaged to disadvantaged schools. Advantaged schools still have two additional sources of funding – private sector contributions and school fees. The South African Schools Act grants school governing bodies the right to determine school fee levels and to appoint and pay

TABLE 2: NATIONAL NORMS AND STANDARDS FOR SCHOOL FUNDING

School quintiles	Expenditure allocation
Poorest 20%	35% of the resources
Next 20%	25% of the resources
Next 20%	20% of the resources
Next 20%	15% of the resources
Least poor 20%	5% of the resources

Source: Van Zyl, 1998

teachers from funds collected by the school itself. The Act thus partially 'privatises' education, while the two developments discussed above try to redress inequality. Nevertheless, a disadvantaged school may still have a considerably smaller budget than an advantaged school, even after the planned redistribution of public funds to schools has been completed (Van Zyl, 1998).

Access to early childhood development (ECD) programmes and basic education
    The South African Schools Act, together with provincial education laws, provides the legal framework for the provision of education to all learners and the protection of their rights in public and independent schools. The Act makes basic education compulsory for all learners from the age of 7 (or Grade 1) to 15 (or Grade 9). It furthermore focuses heavily on issues of school governance and funding. Unfair admission policies and discriminatory educational practices are banned, although school governing bodies decide on admission policies. While governing bodies may charge school fees there must be criteria and procedures for the partial or conditional exemption of parents who are unable to pay them. Corporal punishment is prohibited. Other provisions of the Act include norms and standards for language policy, and freedom of religion. Learners from Grade 8 have the right to representation on governing bodies of schools and to participate in matters which affect them.
    While the Schools Act guarantees the right to education, in practice approximately 337 000 children (see Box 3) between the ages of 10 and 16 are out of school. In addition, some children under 10 years of age are going to school later than the admission age of 7. Learners outside the system include children on farms, children who do not attend school on a regular basis, street children, and drop-outs from the early years of schooling. Policy commitments support a focus on out-of-school children, by providing flexible learning strategies and entry and exit points, for example. A recent study in Gauteng (Porteus *et al.*, 1998) investigated why children in Katlehong, Thokoza and Vosloorus are out of school. The most common factors were physical poverty (lack of material resources), social poverty (lack of social support networks), and power poverty (the inability to make bureaucracy work in one's favour). Other common reasons were the lack of supportive or stable families, and moving from place to place (see Box 4).
    With regard to disability, the White Paper on an Integrated Disability Strategy (Office of the Deputy President, 1997) estimates that as many as 70% of children with disabilities of school-going age are out of school. This is despite the provision of the Schools Act that learners with disabilities must, where reasonably practicable, be

---

BOX 4: STATEMENTS FROM OUT-OF-SCHOOL CHILDREN

'Both my parents are not working. They don't have money to pay for me at school and buy me a school uniform. My father use to do piece jobs but these days he is unable to get one.'

'I was staying at the farm with my aunt while my mother was staying at Thembisa. My aunt was my uncle's wife. But most unfortunately, my uncle died. And he was the only one who used to take care of me. After his death, my aunt started to treat me bad. I used to stay home so that I can clean the house and cook while her children are at school. I used to spend a half-day at school. I could not even spend a whole week or the whole month because she used to beat me when the house is not clean, or if there is no food at home. I used to wake up early in the morning, round about 4 am, start preparations for her own children, so that when they wake up, everything must be ready for them. At some stage I left school because I had to run away from the farm to Johannesburg, looking for my mother. But unfortunately, I did not find her.'

'The problem started when our parents separated. We were doing up and down. We had no one to take care of us. When my father wanted to stay with us we had to move with him and our mother also wanted to stay with us, and then we had to move with her again. And all these up and downs were happening during the year so we were in and out of school. Most of the time we were out of school. I started school very late at the age of 10 years.'

Sources: Porteus *et al.*, 1998.

---

admitted to ordinary schools. Those who cannot have to be educated at separate special schools, taking the wishes of parents into account. There is a lack of access both to special schools for children with severe disabilities, especially in rural areas, and to the general schooling system. Education support services, which should be an integral part of supporting children with special education needs, are lacking.

The Report of the National Commission on Special Needs in Education/National Committee on Education Support Services (Department of Education, 1997a) makes comprehensive recommendations on all aspects of special needs and support services in education and training in South Africa. It recommends an integrated and inclusive system for all learners. There is a strong focus on early identification of barriers to learning as well as early intervention, and therefore on programmes for children in the pre-formal schooling phase. However, without strengthened education support services, relevant teacher training and the development of barrier-free access to all centres of learning for learners with disabilities, the constitutional right to education for these learners cannot be implemented. It is of great concern that many special schools have been closed, while the ordinary schooling system is unprepared for the effective inclusion of children with disabilities.

Quality of basic education

As noted above, enrolment in South African schools is high, especially at primary level, but the benefit children derive from enrolment both in scholastic and broader terms is dependent on a number of other factors. Motala (1997) observes that these relate to socio-economic factors such as children's nutritional status, as well as to poor teacher–pupil ratios, textbook shortages, inadequate teaching practices, and limited provision for preschool and special education.

Several programmes and policies have been developed to address issues of quality. Curriculum 2005, the new national education curriculum for general education and training, was phased in from January 1998. It is an outcomes-based approach with a focus on skills, values and attitudes. The curriculum allows for considerable local-level input, which should assist in making the content more relevant to children. The system is also designed to be flexible, with learners moving through the different levels at their own pace and in their own time. Similarly, the intention is that learners will not be compared with other learners, but against their own past achievements. In terms of the new Assessment Policy for General Education and Training (Department of Education, 1998), any one school year should be repeated once only, so that multiple repetition in one grade is not permissible.

Prevailing difficulties in schools (including high learner–educator ratios, and lack of resources and facilities) do not create a welcoming environment for the new curriculum. One learning area in particular, namely 'life orientation', with its focus on a healthy life-style, life skills, problem solving, self-acceptance, respect for others, human rights, and interpersonal attitudes and skills, will require specific teacher training and support materials. If it is adequately delivered, it has great potential as a vehicle for addressing many mental health issues during the school years.

Language of instruction is another important variable affecting education. Donald, Lazarus and Lolwana (1997) note evidence that if the process of formal learning is abruptly cut off from a child's first language, this can negatively affect cognitive development in general and scholastic performance in particular. The Language in Education Policy (Department of Education, 1997b) promotes the principle of maintaining home language, while providing access to and the effective provision of additional languages. Recognition of all official languages as mediums of instruction helps address problems associated with having to learn in a second language. The policy requires only the chosen language up to Grade 3, but from there an additional approved language is required. Implementation of this policy is subject to considerations of practicability (as when the numbers of learners requesting a particular language are lower than prescribed learner–educator ratios for a class) and to the advice of the governing body and principals. In practice parents often demand English as the preferred medium of instruction as it is seen to be the key to better educational and employment opportunities.

Poor quality of schooling is also related to the deeply conflictual relationships among principals, teachers and students, and between schools and communities (Motala, 1997). Meyer, Loxton and Boulter (1997) note that the quality of relationships with peers and authority figures is an important factor in school adjustment. The national Ministry of Education has launched the Culture of Learning, Teaching and Service (COLTS) campaign to address this. It has two types of programmes: those aimed at building a positive perception of education by finding, recognising and publicising examples of best practice, and those which improve conditions in schools. The latter focuses on having all teachers teaching and all learners in schools, eliminating crime in schools, resourcing of schools, and involving communities in schools and schools in communities.

Transition to schooling

Appropriate early stimulation can assist children in their transition to schooling and their progress both in the schooling system and in later life (Chokski, 1996; Myers, 1992; Short & Biersteker, 1984; Vinjevold, 1996). Many children, especially in poor communities, are unprepared for the transition to formal schooling. Increased early childhood development (ECD) services are a goal of the National Programme of Action for Children and have been prioritised in the Poverty and Inequality Study (Office of the Deputy President, 1998). However, ECD has been and remains under-funded. In 1996/7 less than 1% of the education budget was spent on pre-primary education (Robinson & Biersteker, 1997). Estimates suggest that only between 11 and 18% of children have access to any sort of organised programme that either targets them directly or supports their caregivers (Biersteker, 1997). At present, large numbers of under-age children are enrolled in Grade 1 classes not designed to meet their needs. This is undesirable, but if the new admissions policy is enforced, it will leave potentially thousands of children without any form of care, as many parents use schools as a free child-care option.

The interim policy for early childhood development (Department of Education, 1996) introduced a reception year for 5-year-olds to facilitate the transition to formal schooling. The first step towards implementing it as a compulsory year throughout South Africa is the national ECD pilot project. This three-year pilot project, for which the national Department of Education allocated R50 million, is geared towards developing ECD policy, creating a subsidy system, developing standards and an accreditation system for practitioners, developing provincial capacity, and collecting and analysing data. A feature of the pilot project is that it utilises existing community based preschool projects to offer the reception programme and NGOs to train the teachers.

One concern is that a focus on the reception year or preschool facilities does not meet the need to support families in their child-care functions (Centre for Education Policy Development, 1994; National Education Policy Investigation, 1992; Richter, 1996). Even within the context of the pilot project there are concerns that the nutritional needs of the children are not being met (Khulisa Management Services, 1998), and its baseline study recommends that the PSNP be extended to children in the pilot project. The Gauteng Department of Education is exploring a family-based education approach to meet the needs of young children, linking families to a broad range of resources.

Summary: Early childhood development and basic education
• The government has put in place national policies to improve access to and quality in education. Legislation has made basic schooling compulsory for all children, and quality improvement is to be achieved through the redirection of funding to poorer provinces and schools, a new curriculum, supportive language policies, and recommendations for assisting learners with special education needs.

- Implementation of policies has been hampered by the need to reprioritise within a budget that has not grown in real terms. As more than 80% of education spending goes on personnel costs, mostly in the public schooling sector, all changes have been subject to lengthy negotiations with the Education Labour Relations Council. Where staff rationalisations took place, these have led to losses of experienced teaching and support staff, and have contributed to low morale in the teaching profession.
- Teachers need retraining and support to implement the new outcomes-based curriculum; and the lack of support staff, textbooks and equipment is a problem.
- Access to appropriate educational opportunities remains limited and elusive for marginal groups such as learners with disabilities, out-of-school children and children under 6 years of age.
- Socio-economic factors such as poor and dangerous living conditions, poor nutrition and health care, and unstable family lives make it difficult for children to benefit from schooling.

Social welfare developmental services

Many aspects of the responsibility for children under 18 years of age fall to the Department of Welfare and Population Development. The Welfare vote is the fourth largest in the budget, and in 1998/9 accounted for 9.48%, or R18.66 billion of the consolidated government budget. In the same year, 90.3% of the welfare budget was spent on social security, and 7.7% on social welfare and social assistance programmes (Department of Finance, 1998a). Budget cuts here too affected a number of activities.

In its social welfare component, the NPA focuses on facilitating the provision of appropriate developmental services, especially to those children living in poverty, those who are vulnerable, and those who have special needs. These services aim to include preventive and protective services, facilities, social relief and social security programmes. Particularly vulnerable groups of children targeted in the White Paper for Social Welfare include:

- preschool children from birth to 6 years
- children in out-of-home care
- disabled children
- children with chronic diseases
- street children
- commercially exploited children
- child survivors of abuse, neglect and violence
- substance dependants
- children of dysfunctional families
- under-nourished children (see Box 5)

Transformation of the child- and youth-care system

In 1995, an Inter-Ministerial Committee on Young People at Risk (IMC) was set up to manage the transformation of the entire child and youth care system. Chaired by the Department of Welfare and Population Development, the committee included representatives of the Ministries of Justice, Safety and Security, Correctional

---

BOX 5. A SNAPSHOT OF CHILDREN IDENTIFIED AS VULNERABLE IN THE WHITE PAPER
FOR SOCIAL WELFARE

1. 15.7 % of the population are children 0–6 years.
2. Between 1.3 and 4% of children aged 4–14 years have a disability such as serious eye defects, hearing/speech problems, physical disabilities or mental disabilities.
3. In the next few years there will be close to a million AIDS orphans.
4. In 1998, 8000 children were permanently living on the streets and a further 10 000 in children's homes and shelters.
5. In 1998, it was estimated that more than 200 000 children between 10 and 14 years were working as child labourers.
6. In 1997, there were 996 children in prisons awaiting trial and 1000 serving sentences.
7. In 1996, the Child Protection Unit dealt with 35 838 reported cases of crimes against children; 45% of these involved sexual abuse.
8. An estimated 60 000–160 000 children are arrested each year.

Sources: (1) Statistics South Africa, 1998; (2) Central Statistical Services, 1997; (3) United Nations Development Programme, 1998; (4) *Cape Times,* 2 April 1998; (5) Network Against Child Labour, *Molo Songololo,* March, 1998; (6, 8) National Programme of Action Steering Committee, 1997; (7) SA Law Commission, *Molo Songololo,* September, 1997.

Services, Education, Health, and the RDP – as well as some national NGOs. The focus was on children at risk of removal from their homes, and on those already in various facilities offering care and protection, education and treatment, or secure accommodation and detention. The investigation highlighted the fact that in a number of facilities children were receiving very poor services, and in some cases were even at serious risk of abuse.

The IMC defines 'at risk' as referring to 'young people who have their normal healthy development placed at risk because their circumstances and/or behaviour make them vulnerable to having to live away from their community and/or family on the streets or under statutory care, or they may be living in statutory care' (IMC, 1998, p. 10). While most of the provisions relate to behaviourally troubled young people or those in conflict with the law, the integrated framework stresses prevention and early intervention as first choices where possible. The policy identifies four intervention levels (see Box 6). There is a strong focus on the child within the context of family, extended family and community. The state's responsibility is to assist the family in providing an environment for the appropriate socialisation of the child. This focus on the family and community accords with findings on the International Resilience Project about factors which promote resilience in children (Grotberg, 1995).

Some prevention strategies identified by the IMC include:
• formal education which is accessible to all, is appropriate to the needs of the child, and is rooted in learning environments, rather than achievement or control-

---

BOX 6. IMC-RECOMMENDED LEVELS OF INTERVENTION FOR AT-RISK YOUTH

Level 1: Prevention
Young people and their families receive services or have access to resources which maximise existing strengths and develop new capacities that will promote resilience and increase their ability to benefit from developmental opportunities.

Level 2: Early Intervention
Children and young people receive support which maximises their potential to remain within their family or community.

Level 3: Statutory Process
In the event of statutory intervention, young people receive effective developmental assessment or referral, which leads to an appropriate placement, sentence or programme.

Level 4: Continuum of Care
Minimum standards are given for foster and residential care.

---

orientated environments
- school-based development programmes which include social skills training, emotional and self-development programmes, life-skills training, parenting awareness, etc.
- a range of early childhood care and development programmes in each community
- parent education and support
- sufficient day care, after-school care, recreation centres, weekend support programmes for parents, child-care services for working parents (especially single parents), overnight support and shelter programmes for families and youth
- adoption programmes (IMC, 1996).

This policy approach relies on multi-disciplinary teamwork for effective implementation. One example of intersectoral planning is the Multi-Disciplinary Protocol on Child Abuse and Neglect, which was jointly planned by the Departments of Welfare and Population Development, Justice, and Safety and Security (its Child Protection Services), and was piloted in the Western Cape.

One difficulty for an intersectoral approach is the lack of a single co-ordinated statute, or body of law, that deals with issues affecting children. The Minister of Welfare and Population Development has given the South African Law Commission Project 110 (South African Law Commission, 1998) the task to develop proposals for broad and appropriate child legislation for South Africa. The SALC has highlighted children in particularly difficult circumstances, such as those with disabilities, chronic diseases and HIV/AIDS, as well as abused and neglected children, street children, and refugees.

A second difficulty in intersectoral programme implementation is that there is a lack of effective joint planning and budgeting for programmes shared between departments. Departments generally plan and budget on a sectoral basis, which impedes intersectoral interventions. Without such joint planning and budgeting, however, intersectoral programme implementation is likely to be ineffective.

Moreover, the low budget available for social welfare services is a major constraint on prevention programmes. As already indicated, in 1998/9 only 7.7% of the welfare budget was spent on social welfare services and social assistance programmes. As the overall percentage allocated to welfare in the government budget is unlikely to increase in the medium term, social welfare services are likely to remain under pressure. One example of the budget constraints is that while early childhood services are a welfare priority area, less than 1% of the welfare budget in 1996/7 was allocated to subsidies for early childhood care and education facilities.

Social security

There is no universal social security system in South Africa, and old-age pensions account for approximately 58% of existing social security spending (Department of Finance, 1998a). As many poor children live in multi-generational households, pensions received by grandparents and great-grandparents are often the household's only source of survival. Grants that affect children directly are foster, disability and maintenance grants. At present a foster grant is cancelled when a child is adopted, and this discourages adoption and therefore permanency of care. The Law Commission is investigating this aspect as part of its review of legislation affecting children.

The grant which potentially will reach the largest number of children is the Child Support Benefit (CSB). This provides R100 per child a month for caregivers over 18 years who care for children under 7 years of age, and who qualify in terms of a means test weighted in favour of rural areas and informal settlements. It is intended to reach 390 000 children in 1998/9, and to extend to 3 million children once the programme is at full maturity (Department of Welfare, 1998). Unfortunately application procedures are cumbersome, and the take-up rate has been far lower than expected. It was announced in the 1999 welfare budget vote that 31 127 children were gaining the benefit of the grant (*Cape Argus*, 19 March 1999). This falls a long way short of the expected number. Take-up rates also were lower in the poorer provinces such as the North West Province and Eastern Cape, where administrative capacity to implement the CSB effectively is lacking (Robinson & Sadan, 1999). Although the group of children it targets is indeed a very vulnerable age-group, the lack of provision for children older than 7 is a great concern.

The Poverty and Inequality Report (Office of the Deputy President, 1998) recommends that the social welfare system should be a key component of government strategy for reducing poverty and inequality, and that current real levels of social welfare expenditure should at least be maintained as a central element of this strategy.

Social developmental welfare services

Overall welfare policy is intended to assume a developmental social welfare approach, in which people would be assisted to help themselves – through providing a socio-economic environment which assists those receiving social assistance to become self-reliant rather than dependent on handouts. This would require a change away from traditional social work services that focus largely on statutory obligations and individual counselling.

An initiative illustrating the new direction is the Flagship Programme – a three year pilot programme to assist single women with children under 5 years to develop income-generation skills, while at the same time providing developmental stimulation for their children. Fifteen projects across the nine provinces are being implemented, and include income-generating activities such as poultry-farming, communal gardening, a bakery, and leather works. There are 1043 women and 1535 children participating in the programme (Department of Welfare, 1998). An amount of R4.3 million was earmarked for the first year of implementation.

The Flagship programme has also provided access to early childhood development (ECD) programmes. Children are either placed in an existing ECD centre, or some of the women have been trained and provide care for the children at the project site. Robinson and Sadan (1999) indicate that the ECD component is being implemented quite slowly, and suggest that it highlights the danger that services for children may be marginalised when women and children are lumped together in programme activities. Children are too easily seen to benefit simply through the participation of their mothers.

The main constraint in the implementation of the Flagship Programme has been the lack of trained staff to facilitate the programmes at provincial level. Training programmes have been instituted, but staff turnover has hampered progress. Again it is clear that the level of local infrastructure plays a role in the success of a project, and in the places where a good infrastructure exists implementation has been easier. Indeed, the Flagship Programme has highlighted the complexities of implementing community-development programmes that depend on a variety of actors across different sectors. Limited human resource capacity has been a major constraint, but a lack of knowledge and skills that enable successful collaboration across sectors also limits delivery of services. At the same time, however, the programme has identified opportunities, such as working in partnership with communities, utilising the expertise of NGOs, and working across sectors (Robinson & Sadan, 1999).

Summary: Social welfare development services

Policy and service delivery for children in the welfare sector are characterised by a focus on poverty alleviation and on women and children as those most affected by poverty. They also emphasise policies and formulae for redistributing resources to the poorest 40% of the population, as well as a shift to a developmental social welfare approach, which emphasises prevention, community development and self-reliance.

Implementation of adequate services and safety nets faces many challenges:

- Poor people, especially children, find it difficult or impossible to access social welfare services. This is especially true in rural areas. Lack of administrative capacity especially in the poorer provinces has severely limited the implementation of the Child Support Benefit, which has the potential to benefit large numbers of poor children under 7 years.
- Nearly 90% of the welfare budget is committed to social security and this limits the resources available for social welfare services, which mainly provide for children.
- Social workers face a dual task, in that they are required to implement new devel-

opmental social welfare programmes as well as the many statutory services under the Child Care Act of 1983 (such as child protection, foster care and children's homes) which they have always delivered.

Child protection measures

The Country Report on the NPA comments on the mounting public concern over the extent and severity of violence against children, and their abuse and neglect in South Africa (National Programme of Action Steering Committee, 1997). This takes place at home, at school and in the neighbourhood. Children are abandoned, child labour continues and commercial sexual exploitation of children is apparently on the increase (although little is known about the scale of this problem).

The child protection goals of the NPA include ensuring that the criminal and civil justice system protect the best interests of the child, and that each child has the right to security, relevant social services and protection against abuse, neglect and exploitation. The task of protecting children cuts across different departments, such as the Departments of Welfare and Population Development, Justice, Safety and Security, and Correctional Services. This introduces, again, the problem of intersectoral collaboration.

BOX 7. FAMILY VIOLENCE

It is estimated that one in three women is being abused in relationships with male partners (Padayachee, 1994, quoted in Angless & Shefer, 1997). Similarly, Richter (1996) found in her Soweto–Johannesburg study that there was physical violence in the homes of one-third of 1615 families sampled. Angless and Shefer note that the impact on children witnessing violence varies with age and gender. However, the range of behavioural and emotional problems reported by researchers and practitioners is similar – emotional, cognitive and behavioural disturbances, including school adjustment.

A recent study of poor families in the Katlehong, Thokoza and Vosloorus areas notes another disturbing form of family dys   .tion. 'A theme which emerged in focus groups was the fear of older children (usually teenagers) both boys and girls. Caregivers are frightened to correct or scold their children, as they are threatened, often with guns. They feel that they cannot pass on what they learned as children.' (Kathorus Consortium/Third Wave Human Development Enterprises, 1998, p. 27).

Abuse of children

The South African Participatory Poverty Appraisal (1997) identified abuses to which poor children are subjected. These included sexual abuse (including rape and forced prostitution), fractured and unstable families, and alcohol abuse by parents (which leads to child abuse). In January 1997 alone, 1800 sex crimes against children were reported to the Child Protection Unit. At the end of March there were more than 1300 criminal dockets (*Molo Songololo*, September, 1997). Step-parents are often mentioned by children as a source or threat of abuse, and step-fathers in particular, for sexually abusing girls. Children frequently witness physical violence in their homes (see Box 7). Children are thus very vulnerable to violence of many kinds, public as well as domestic.

The Prevention of Family Violence Act of 1993 makes provision for reporting suspected child abuse. The Act provides for notification if ill-treatment or abuse is suspected by a dentist, medical practitioner, nurse, teacher, social worker, or children's home worker. It is a criminal offence for any parent, guardian or person having custody to ill-treat a child or allow a child to be ill-treated or abandoned.

Children in need of care and protection

Children in need of special protection and assistance can be brought before the children's court, and it they are found to be in need of care, they may be placed in alternative care. In a crisis a child may be removed without a court order and placed in a place of safety pending investigation. Children's court orders – usually two years in duration – can be extended if they serve the best interests of the child.

In 1997 there were 182 registered children's homes in South Africa with 13 565 beds and 32 places of safety with 3019 beds. There were 73 354 children in 43 998 foster homes (National Programme of Action Steering Committee, 1997). The IMC has identified inappropriate institutionalisation, human rights abuses in children's homes, and inappropriately trained staff as some of the defects in the care system. Children were often placed in state institutions outside their home provinces, which made it difficult for their families to visit them. Revised residential care policy proposals include a focus on family preservation and planning for permanency of care. Provincial welfare departments provide reconstruction services to parents whose children are in alternative care and training for foster parents to skill them in the care of children from troubled backgrounds.

The NCRC Supplementary Draft Report has raised a number of concerns about out-of-home care for children, similar to those raised by the IMC (National Children's Rights Committee, 1998). These again illustrate the slow process of policy implementation. In particular, they recommend that residential placement be used as a last resort once other alternatives have been explored, and that staff training be improved, individualised intervention programmes be utilised, and children in residential care be monitored.

Child labour

The Network against Child Labour estimates that in South Africa more than 200 000 children between 10 and 14 years are engaged in paid work (see Box 5). Most work is done within and alongside their families as domestic work. Many children living on farms are forced to work (at least one in three child workers lives in a commercial farming area). There have been reports of children on farms working before and after school for 4 hours a day for R40 per month. Work on farms may be hazardous as children are exposed to toxic substances such as pesticides. Studies, referred to in *Molo Songololo* (March 1998), reveal a negative impact on the education of children who work and attend school. Child workers who attend school are often less alert, less industrious and less regular. Children on farms also tend to start school later than other children.

The Basic Conditions of Employment Act of 1997 provides that no person may employ a child under 15 years of age (or under the minimum school-leaving age if this is 15 or older). No child may be in employment inappropriate for a person of that age, or that places the child's well-being, education, physical or mental health or spiritual, moral or social development at risk. Nevertheless, prohibition of child labour is a delicate issue. As a result of poverty, children's labour may be essential to the provision of family income.

Street children

Children working and living on the street are particularly vulnerable, and form a priority group for rehabilitation programmes. The Poverty and Inequality Report (Office of the Deputy President, 1998) draws attention to the extreme stress under which street children live. It cites Bedford's analysis of their self-portraits which indicated stress, anxiety, emotional regression and the lack of connectedness with the world. Violence and sexual abuse are also part of the lives of these children.

The NPA aims to develop systems for the early identification of children at risk of living as street children and for referral for assessment and intervention. While the Child Care Amendment Act of 1996 requires the official registration of street shelters, inadequate funding of these shelters is a concern, as is the closure of a number of existing facilities in some provinces for not meeting standards. Services are also uncoordinated, and the NPA notes the need to improve systems for assessing children who are in shelters and develop plans for their future so that they are not in shelters for more than six months. Younger children need to be prepared for formal schooling and older children skilled for employment. In line with the welfare policy of prevention, it recommends that community-based programmes for children and families be developed to prevent homelessness and living on the street.

Juvenile offenders

Until 1995 children involved in the juvenile justice system had limited protection. Even now the provisions that do exist are inadequate or difficult to implement. Children from 7 to 14 years are presumed not to have criminal capacity, but this is easily rebutted and children under 12 have been arrested and tried. Less than 10% of child offenders have legal representation. An NPA goal for child protection is that children in conflict with the law should be treated in a manner that takes account of the age of the child. A separate juvenile justice system is recommended as well as training for all personnel. The South African Law Commission is preparing recommendations and draft legislation.

No national juvenile arrest figures are available but an estimated 60 000–160 000 children are arrested each year (National Programme of Action Steering Committee, 1997). These children must appear in court within 48 hours, or within 24 hours if the child is 14 years or younger. In April 1998 there were 4000 children awaiting trial in prisons. At least half of these were not charged with serious offences, but could not be detained in the usual places of safety because they are understaffed or in crisis (*Cape Times*, 2 April 1998). Many child offenders are still victims of a system which is detrimental to their chances of rehabilitation (see Box 8).

BOX 8. PETTY THEFT AND THE HARSH REALITY OF JAIL LIFE

Max – 14 years old – was arrested on the charge of stealing a bicycle. The court referred him to Umtata prison for juveniles. Gang members in the cell beat him up, stole his clothes and sodomised him. Coerced, Max 'joined' the cell gang. Petty theft and the harsh realities of jail life may make Max a criminal for life. No rehabilitation, no future! (Testimony by 'Max' at the Children's Truth Commission, November 1996: Frank & Artz, 1997.)

Several pilot programmes have been established to test IMC recommendations. One such project is an arrest, reception and referral centre in Durban. There is a one-stop centre for youth justice services in Port Elizabeth, and a Family Group Conferencing Pilot Project in Pretoria. The Department of Welfare and Population Development led an initiative to build and upgrade a number of secure care facilities, particularly in the poorer rural provinces, which had few if any facilities for children. Two key projects were the building of the Hendrina Secure Care and Youth Development Centre (Mpumalanga) and the Enkuselweni Secure Care facility (Eastern Cape).

The policy focus of the Department of Correctional Services is on family reconstruction, and a parental guidance programme will be distributed to social workers in prisons. Establishing and developing services to convicted and unconvicted children is hampered by lack of a budget, severe overcrowding in prisons and human resource problems. For example, while the Criminal Procedures Act obliges police to notify parents or guardians of the arrest of a child under 18 if they live in the same magisterial district and can be traced, this does not work well in practice. Children awaiting trial thus receive few visits from their families.

For children who have been convicted of offences, juvenile justice advocates agree that non-custodial sentencing options are more desirable and should be used in as many cases as possible (Frank & Artz, 1997). The NGO sector has played a key role in such diversion programmes and, in 1995 alone, 4000 children were diverted from the criminal justice system.

On any one day, just over 1000 children are serving prison terms (National Programme of Action Steering Committee, 1997). The Department of Correctional Services has established a Sub-Directorate on Youth Offenders Services to determine national policy on the detention and treatment of juveniles. While the Department's policy is to provide separate detention facilities for young persons up to 21 years of age, in practice children under 18 are not always detained separately. Youth development centres for the treatment and rehabilitation of young people serving prison terms are being established, as many child prisoners have no access to education or vocational training. In 1997 eight of these centres were operational.

Summary: Child protection measures
• Violence against children, and their abuse and neglect are matters of mounting public concern. Child labour continues especially on farms, commercial sexual exploitation of children is on the increase, and many children live permanently on the streets.

- Legislation provides for notification of the ill-treatment and neglect of children, and children in need of care may be placed in alternative care. However, inappropriate institutionalisation, human rights abuses in children's homes and inadequate staff training have been problems.
- For the many children involved in the juvenile justice system, provisions to protect their best interests are inadequate and difficult to implement. Facilities are inadequate, prisons overcrowded and many staff are not appropriately trained. There is a shortage of non-custodial sentencing options.
- In order to address the problems the Inter-Ministerial Committee has developed policy and new minimum standards for a Child and Youth Care System. The South African Law Commission is investigating a single children's statute to co-ordinate all issues affecting children.
- Implementation of the Child and Youth Care policy is dependent on an intersectoral approach involving different government departments and NGOs, training and budget allocations for prevention, early intervention and rehabilitation programmes. The lack of adequate budgetary resources, staff cutbacks and inappropriately trained staff will be constraints on implementation.
- Progress has been made so far with pilot projects to test IMC recommendations, the construction of youth development centres for treatment, and rehabilitation of youth serving prison terms.

Leisure and cultural activities

Opportunities to engage in leisure, recreation and cultural activities form part of a child's development rights, according to the Convention on the Rights of the Child. The Inter-Ministerial Committee on Young People at Risk (1996) noted these as opportunities for protecting children and youth from problems which might place them at risk.

The White Paper on Sport and Recreation (Department of Sport and Recreation, 1998) promotes the health and educational value of sport, and mentions that 'success in sport and recreation may improve self-esteem' (Department of Sport and Recreation, 1998, p. 4). Similarly, the White Paper on Arts, Culture and Heritage (Department of Arts, Culture, Science and Technology, 1996) observes that participation in, and enjoyment of, the arts and culture are basic human rights and also have potential for healing and recreation. One programme, the Khulisa Pilot Programme, takes this as its premise, and tries to put African children who break the law in touch with traditional culture, arts and story-telling to help restore self-respect and a sense of responsibility. The programme is being piloted at Leeuwkop Prison, which has 700 juvenile inmates, and the Walter Sisulu Place of Safety and Secure Care Centre in Soweto (*Voice of Masibambane*, 1997).

The NPA's goal for leisure and culture is to provide all children with the opportunity to engage in leisure, recreation and cultural activities. These would include their heritage, visual arts, libraries and information services, language and literature, arts education, performing arts, sports, and recreational activities. Unfortunately there is a general paucity of such facilities, and of trained teachers, and a low level of funding for arts and culture. Such facilities and programmes that exist are mainly in urban areas. Nevertheless, government departments are involved in this aspect of children's lives. The Department of Arts, Culture, Science and Technology is in the process of building 43 community arts centres which will have a strong child and youth focus. The Department of Education has included arts and culture as a learning area in Curriculum 2005, and the Independent Broadcasting Authority has stipulated a quota for children's television and radio programmes.

Problems in regard to sport are the lack of recognition of physical education in the school curriculum, and the lack of provision for out-of-school children. A priority for the Department of Sport and Recreation is to motivate community members to develop active life-styles and channel those with talent into competitive sport. This will involve recruiting and encouraging youth and adults to participate. The South African National Games and Leisure Activities (SANGALA) in the Department of Sport and Recreation focuses on children and youth. One part of this is an investigation into the impact of recreation in rural and informal settlements. The project Movers in Action is aimed at developing the motor skills of 3–6-year-olds in child-care facilities, and involves training for teachers and distributing simple printed guidelines and some materials. Recrehab is a programme for the rehabilitation of youth in prisons. 'Training SANGALA' builds the capacity of recreation leaders (80% of whom are in rural areas) who render a set number of hours of volunteer services. 'Street SANGALA' is piloting a recreation and lifeskills project for street children; and by 1997, 1600 children had attended activities in various cities (National Programme of Action Steering Committee, 1997).

Summary : Leisure and cultural activities

The policies and pilot projects of the Departments of Art and Culture and of Sport and Recreation indicate that they recognise the benefits of leisure and cultural activities in bolstering child resilience and promoting full human development. Unfortunately, lack of resources makes it very difficult to meet the most basic needs. Even within education, which has a curriculum focus on arts and culture and physical education, very few resources are prioritised in this direction.

CONCLUSION

This chapter has explored current socio-economic policies and programmes affecting children across the six areas prioritised in the National Programme of Action for Children, as well as the implementation of some key policies and programmes. What emerges is a common vision and strategic approach in the way policy has been formulated across different sectors. Equally, what has become evident is a range of constraining factors, which limit the extent to which these policies can be implemented.

Vision and strategic approach

The principles of the Convention on the Rights of the Child, as expressed in the South African Constitution, provide a common vision which informs policies related to children. Similarly, the Reconstruction and Development White Paper has provided a framework for the targeting of the poorest communities and a prioritisation of children. Particular target groups for service delivery are rural children and others living in difficult circumstances. To ensure that the provinces with the largest and poorest populations, which are most dependent on public social services, receive proportionally more revenue from national funds for basic service delivery, the amount of funds each province receives is calculated according to its social and economic profiles. Socio-economic policies affecting children have prioritised investment in primary preventive services. In addition, policies across all sectors show a general recognition of the need for intersectoral collaboration if more effective and efficient service delivery is to be achieved.

At the conceptual and strategic level, therefore, there is an enabling environment for the delivery of socio-economic services to children. Policies are coherent. All departments are prioritising service delivery to the poor, and are moving to the delivery of primary preventive services which are more cost-effective. The question then is why the follow-through from policy to planning and implementation in the form of service delivery has been so slow and of such limited impact.

Constraints

What is evident is that the successful implementation of policies has been constrained by a range of very basic factors. These include:
• severe backlogs in services of all kinds
• lack of financial resources
• infrastructural problems (including transport, communication, electricity supply, etc.)
• lack of institutional capacity (both in administrative systems and in suitably trained staff)
• inadequate information systems (making it difficult to gauge the precise nature and extent of problems, and to monitor progress)

Since many of these factors co-occur, particularly in poorer regions, there tends to be a multiplier effect. Policies which are primarily directed at alleviating the adversities faced by poorer children are frequently *least* effectively implemented in those very contexts. Thus, developing the relevant infrastructure and capacity to support programme implementation becomes a primary challenge if government policies are to be successfully applied where they are most needed.

The South African government's macroeconomic policies have placed severe budgetary constraints on all kinds of spending. Redirecting social service provision to poorer provinces and regions has meant that services in previously well-resourced provinces have, in turn, been cut back. However, simply increasing the amount spent in the poorer provinces does not necessarily improve access to services for children. Apart from targeting the relevant infrastructure mentioned above, provinces also need to reprioritise expenditure towards building capacity and developing services which specifically benefit children. Thus, the Department of Health reprioritised its budget in very clear terms. Resources are now focused on primary health care – with free services for pregnant women and young children being an important element. However, programme priorities identified in other departmental policies – such as those affecting early childhood development, out-of-school youth, inclusion of children with special needs, and juvenile justice – have, for a variety of reasons, not seen the budgetary redirection necessary to affect them. In the case of the Department of

Welfare and Population Development, the statutory social security obligations swallow 90 per cent of the budget. In the poorer, more populous provinces social security obligations are even greater than in the other provinces, leaving even less of the budget available for desperately needed social welfare developmental services.

Social service delivery to children in most sectors is personnel-intensive. This means that efficient delivery of quality service depends on the adequate training of staff, as well as having the optimum number of staff in the right place to do the work. If service delivery depends on trained people being available in sufficient numbers, service providers, being few in number, will become overburdened and unproductive. It is difficult to over-emphasise the need for appropriate training of, and support for, staff. Generally, it is a relatively low-cost item in overall departmental budgets, and untrained staff are significantly more expensive in the longer term. Educators, for example, need training and support in order to manage the changes in school governance, the new curriculum, and the inclusion of learners with special needs. Child protection and juvenile justice experts have also identified the need for special training of staff.

Many departmental budgets have high fixed personnel costs (Education and Health are good examples), which has made development of an efficient public sector very difficult. The wage bill squeezes any possible expenditure on other items – including training and support – that might affect the quality of provision. Budgetary reform at a macro level is particularly dependent on reform of the public sector, given that the public service wage bill is the largest item of current government expenditure. On the other hand, while 'right-sizing' of the public sector is necessary, the extensive loss of more experienced personnel – such as those who have taken voluntary severance packages – may, as indicated, severely affect the implementation of social services. Achieving the right balance in such matters is a critical process.

While innovative programmes are being introduced, such as the various IMC pilot projects, the Flagship Programme, and the national ECD pilot project, they do remain pilot programmes. As such they can have only limited impact on children's access to services across the country. There is no indication whether resources are available, or will be allocated, for nation-wide implementation, should they prove to be effective. In the current financial climate, this is a very real constraint.

There are other constraints which are not primarily budgetary. As mentioned above, these include insufficient administrative and financial management capacity, lack of information systems, and inadequate infrastructure. Intersectoral collaboration has been emphasised in virtually all policy documents but this has not been easy to achieve in practice. While such collaboration is problematic, there have been certain promising interventions. The IMC pilot projects have shown that a number of factors are essential to the effective implementation of large intersectoral initiatives. These include:

- efficient management and co-ordination
- use of a range of intervention strategies in addressing service delivery concerns
- the importance of continued research and evaluation to ensure the effectiveness of interventions
- the importance of involving families and communities in the planning, development and implementation of each project

The lack of regularly updated child-related data is a significant obstacle to monitoring progress towards NPA goals. An information tool needs to be developed that will provide regular data on the impact of socio-economic policies on children in South Africa. Indicators should include:

- progress towards meeting stated NPA goals
- provincial and regional disparities in children's access to social services
- actual outcomes for children, particularly socio-economic indicators reflecting changes in the lives of children as a result of policy interventions

Finally, despite the constraints in operationalising policies for addressing childhood adversity in South Africa, the importance of having an enabling and coherent national policy framework in place should not be underestimated. This policy framework will determine national, provincial and, ultimately, local standards of provision for children. It provides for partnerships between different departments, communities, parents, NGOs and the private sector. In short there is, for the first time, a clear constitutional and policy commitment to the well-being of children in South Africa. The challenge is now to translate those policies into effective interventions which can address the huge unmet needs and disparities in service delivery to children across South Africa.

REFERENCES

Angless, T. & Shefer, T. (1997). Children living with violence in the family. In C. de la Rey, N. Duncan, T. Shefer & A. van Niekerk (Eds.), *Contemporary issues in human development – a South African focus* (pp. 170–186). Johannesburg: International Thomson Publishing.

Biersteker, L. (1997). *An assessment of programmes and strategies for 0–4 year olds: South African case study report of the Africa Integrated Early Childhood Development Services Initiative.* Cape Town: Early Learning Resource Unit.

Carnegie Task Force on Meeting the Needs of Young Children. (1994). *Starting points: meeting the needs of our youngest children.* New York: Carnegie Corporation.

Central Statistical Services. (1997). *The October household survey 1995.* Pretoria: Central Statistical Services.

Centre for Education Policy Development. (1994). *South African study on early childhood development – recommendations for action in support of children.* Washington D.C.: The World Bank.

Child Health Unit. (1998). Child health fact sheet. Cape Town: University of Cape Town.

Chokski, A. (1996). Early child development: never too early but often too late. Opening speech of Early Child Development: Investing in the Future Conference, Carter Center, Atlanta, Georgia, April 8–9.

De Vylder, S. (1996). *Developmental strategies, macroeconomic policies and the rights of the child. Discussion Paper.* Stockholm: Rädda Barnen.

Department of Arts, Culture, Science and Technology, Republic of South Africa (1996). *White paper on arts, culture and heritage.* Pretoria: Government Gazette.

Department of Education, Republic of South Africa (1996). *Interim policy for early childhood development.* Pretoria: Department of Education.

Department of Education, Republic of South Africa (1997a). *Quality education for all: overcoming barriers to learning and development.* Report of the National Commission on Special

Needs in Education/National Committee on Education Support Services. Pretoria: Department of Education.

Department of Education, Republic of South Africa (1997b). *Language in education policy.* Pretoria: Department of Education.

Department of Education, Republic of South Africa (1998). *Assessment policy in the General Education and Training Band, Grade R to 9 and ABET.* Pretoria: Department of Education.

Department of Finance, Republic of South Africa (1998a). *Medium term expenditure review, welfare.* Pretoria: Department of Finance.

Department of Finance, Republic of South Africa (1998b). *Estimates of expenditure to be defrayed from the National Revenue Fund during the financial year ending 31 March 1999.* Pretoria: Department of Finance.

Department of Health, Republic of South Africa. (1997a). Health trends 1995/6. Pretoria: Department of Health.

Department of Health, Republic of South Africa (1997b). *White paper for the transformation of the health system in South Africa.* Pretoria: Department of Health.

Department of Health, Republic of South Africa (1998). *Integrated Nutrition Programme for South Africa* (fifth draft). Pretoria: Department of Health.

Department of Sport and Recreation, Republic of South Africa (1998). *White paper on sport.* Pretoria: Department of Sport and Recreation.

Department of Welfare, Republic of South Africa (1998). Flagships: breaking the cycle of poverty. *Welfare Update, 4*(3), 4–5.

Donald, D., Lazarus, S. & Lolwana, P. (1997). *Educational psychology in social context.* Cape Town: Oxford University Press.

Duncan, N. (1997). Malnutrition and childhood development. In C. de la Rey, N. Duncan, T. Shefer & A. van Niekerk (Eds.), *Contemporary issues in human development – a South African focus* (pp. 190–206). Johannesburg: International Thomson Publishing.

Financial and Fiscal Commission (1997). *Public expenditure on basic social services in South Africa. A Financial and Fiscal Commission Report for UNICEF.* Johannesburg: Financial and Fiscal Commission.

Frank, C. & Artz, L. (1997). Justice. In S. Robinson & L. Biersteker (Eds.), *First call: the South African children's budget* (pp. 153–198). Cape Town: IDASA.

Grotberg, E. (1995). *A guide to promoting resilience in children. Early Childhood Development Practice and Reflections, 8.* The Hague: Bernard van Leer Foundation.

Hartshorne, K. (1996). The national teacher education audit, a review of the synthesis report. *Edusource Data News, 13,* 19–22.

Health Systems Trust (1997). *Evaluation of the Primary School Nutrition Programme (PSNP).* Durban: Health Systems Trust.

Health Systems Trust (1998). *South African health review 1998.* Durban: Health Systems Trust.

Inter-Ministerial Committee on Young People at Risk (1996). *Discussion document for the transformation of the South African child and youth care system, Second Draft.* Pretoria: Department of Welfare.

Inter-Ministerial Committee on Young People at Risk (1998). *Draft minimum standards: South African child and youth care system.* Pretoria: Department of Welfare.

Kathorus Consortium/Third Wave Human Development Enterprises (1998). *Kathorus ECD Project: Combined Research Report of the Action Research Project and the Family Based*

Project for the Gauteng Department of Education. Johannesburg: Gauteng Department of Education.

Khulisa Management Services (1998). *Baseline study on the National Pilot Project.* Pretoria: Department of Education.

McCoy, D. (1996). *Free health care for pregnant women and children under six in South Africa: an impact assessment.* Durban: Child Health Unit for Health Systems Trust.

Meyer, J., Loxton, H. & Boulter, S. (1997). A systems approach to the enhancement of self-concept. In C. de la Rey, N. Duncan, T. Shefer & A. van Niekerk (Eds.), *Contemporary issues in human development – a South African focus* (pp. 110–127). Johannesburg: International Thomson Publishing.

Motala, S. (1997). Education. In S. Robinson & L. Biersteker (Eds.), *First call: the South African children's budget* (pp. 115–152). Cape Town: IDASA.

Myers, R. (1992). *The twelve who survive.* London: Routledge and Kegan Paul.

National Children's Rights Committee (1998). *Draft supplementary report: convention on the rights of the child.* Unpublished document, Johannesburg: NCRC.

National Education Policy Investigation (1992). *Early childhood educare research report.* Cape Town: Oxford University Press/National Education Coordinating Committee.

National Programme of Action Steering Committee (1996). *National Programme of Action in South Africa: working document.* Pretoria: NPA Steering Committee.

National Programme of Action Steering Committee (1997). *Country report – South Africa: convention on the rights of the child.* Pretoria: NPA Steering Committee.

Office of the Deputy President (1997). *White paper on an integrated national disability strategy.* Pretoria: Office of the Deputy President.

Office of the Deputy President (1998). *Poverty and inequality in South Africa. Report prepared for the Office of the Executive Deputy President and IMC for Poverty and Inequality.* Pretoria: Office of the Deputy President.

Porteus, K., Clacherty, G., Mdiya, L., Pelo, J., Matsai, K., Qwabe, M., Momfungana, M., Raisa, M. & Zondo, V. (1998). *Vuk'uyithathe: out of school children and out of age learners' circumstances and needs: preliminary report.* Johannesburg: Vuk'uyithathe Research Consortium: Centre for Health Policy, Clacherty and Associates and the Kathorus Enhanced Learning Institute.

Research Institute for Educational Planning (1998). *Education and Manpower Development No 18, 1997.* Bloemfontein: University of the Free State.

Richter, L. (1996). *Characteristics of the care of children under four years of age in Soweto-Johannesburg.* Pretoria: Medical Research Council and Institute for Behavioural Sciences.

Richter, L. & Griesel, R. (1994). Malnutrition, low birth weight and related influences on psychological development. In A. Dawes & D. Donald (Eds.), *Childhood and adversity: Psychological perspectives from South African research.* Cape Town and Johannesburg: David Philip.

Robinson, S. & Biersteker, L. (1997). *First call: The South African children's budget.* Cape Town: IDASA.

Robinson, S. & Sadan, M. (1999). *Where poverty hits hardest. Children and the budget in South Africa.* Cape Town: IDASA.

Robinson, S. & Tilley, A. (1998). The impact of socio-political and economic transformation on children's rights in South Africa. Paper presented at the International Child Research 2000 Seminar, October 1998, University of the Western Cape, Cape Town.

Schindler, J. (1998). Analysis of the 1997 standard 10 examination results. *Edusource Data News, 20.*

School Register of Needs (1996). Quoted in Office of the Deputy President (1998).

Short, A. & Biersteker, L. (1984). *Evaluation of the effects of the Early Learning Centre centre-based programmes with follow-up through to adolescence. ELC Research Report No 5.* Cape Town: Early Learning Resource Unit.

South African Institute of Race Relations (1997). *South Africa survey 1996/1997.* Johannesburg: SAIRR.

South African Law Commission (1998). *The SA Law Commission: Project 110 Media Statement on Launch of First Issue Paper on Review of the Child Care Act.* Pretoria: Government Printer.

South African Participatory Poverty Appraisal (1997). *The experience and perceptions of poverty: the South African Participatory Poverty Assessment.* Durban: Data Research Africa.

Statistics South Africa (1997). *Earning and spending in South Africa. Selected findings of the 1995 Income and Expenditure Survey.* Pretoria: Statistics South Africa.

Statistics South Africa (1998). *Census in brief. Pretoria: Statistics South Africa* Pretoria: Statistics South Africa

Tilley, A. (1998). Social security – a necessary cost. *Budget Watch, 4,* 3.

United Nations Development Programme (1998). *HIV/AIDS and Human Development in South Africa.* Pretoria: UNDP.

Van Zyl, A. (1998). Education finance brief. Unpublished document. Cape Town: IDASA.

Vinjevold, P. (1996). Evaluation of the impact of ECD programmes. *Joint Education Trust Bulletin, 3,* 5–7.

Voice of Masibambane. (1997). Community Publication, Issue 1, December 1997.

IMPROVING PRACTICE THROUGH EVALUATION

3

JOHANN LOUW

The notion of evaluation is often not appealing to programmes, their management staff and service deliverers. In the face of sometimes overwhelming need, programme staff want to get on with alleviating that need. They do not want to spend time and money on an evaluation exercise which may place the programme at risk, or which may reflect negatively on programme staff. Yet the practice of evaluating one's own efforts is part of everyday life, of trying to do things better, and of improving the performance of even the most routine aspects of our activities.

This chapter is not an overview of evaluation methodologies, or a summary of 'How to conduct an evaluation'. Rather, it is an attempt to answer the question 'How can evaluation be used to strengthen or improve interventions?' In the light of the tremendous demands made on human services in South Africa, especially in relation to children, evaluation will not serve a useful function if it is seen as something threatening and punitive, or as a trial to be endured and then forgotten. However, programme staff are generally interested in improving their performance and would like to establish whether their activities are making a difference. If they are convinced that evaluation can help in this, they may begin to incorporate an evaluative way of thinking into their everyday activities. Even better, they can be encouraged to integrate evaluation into programme processes, to strengthen the intervention and to make the evaluation a built-in part of it.

Programme staff are themselves frequently certain that their interventions are effective. They know how relevant their work is, and they see evidence of this in feedback from the people with whom they work. Despite this sense of making a difference, programme activities and results have to be accounted for to a wider audience. Staff need to be able to provide documented evidence supporting their claim that the programme is effective. Obviously, this evidence must be convincing, otherwise funding agencies, policy makers, and the general public will simply not believe it. The programme staff's sense of 'certainty' referred to above and anecdotal evidence of effectiveness are, on their own, certainly not going to be enough.

Also common is a converse 'impression', or unsupported belief, that nothing is working and that a programme's interventions are futile within the wider problems of society. This perception is equally unreliable – and undesirable in terms of staff motivation. Systematic evaluation can be just as helpful in showing that certain outcomes are being achieved, and in counteracting a sense of futility in staff.

Thus, as opposed to a process of forming chance or subjective impressions, programme evaluation is ultimately a conscious and systematic process. This is evident in the following definition: 'Program evaluation is the systematic collection of information about the activities, characteristics, and outcomes of programs to make judgements about the program, improve program effectiveness, and/or inform decisions about future programming' (Patton, 1997, p. 23). In drawing the distinction between unsystematic judgements and opinions about programme performance and programme evaluation, Newcomer, Hatry and Wholey (1994, p. 3) say: 'In the public arena and in the private nonprofit sector, there is always a cacophony of unsystematic feedback on program performance. *Program evaluation* is the systematic assessment of program results and, to the extent feasible, systematic assessment of the extent to which the program caused those results.'

THE LOGIC OF PROGRAMMES

There is a certain logic to programmes and to programme evaluation, awareness of which may be of assistance to programme managers and staff. Making this logic explicit, and examining the sequence of events of which it is comprised, may serve to clarify many difficulties that are commonly experienced with programme evaluation. Put in the simplest terms possible, the logic consists of the sequence of components represented in Figure 1.

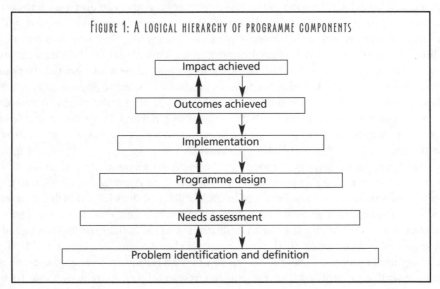

FIGURE 1: A LOGICAL HIERARCHY OF PROGRAMME COMPONENTS

Impact achieved

Outcomes achieved

Implementation

Programme design

Needs assessment

Problem identification and definition

This sequence of components is represented in a hierarchy of steps, one building on the other, as indicated by the bold ascending arrows in Figure 1. Continuous cycles of feedback should also be understood as occurring between the various levels, as indicated by the thin descending arrows in Figure 1.

One way of understanding this logic is to say:
- The more clearly the problem is identified and *defined*
- The more clearly the needs are *assessed*
- The more appropriately the programme is *designed* to address the needs
- The more effectively the programme is delivered and *implemented*
- The more the short- or medium-term outcomes are *achieved*
- *The greater the long-term impact will be.*

Too often, evaluation is seen as coming only at the end of the process. The argument here is that programmes can be strengthened at every step of the way, and that the successful completion of each step strengthens the programme's ultimate impact. In a school-feeding scheme, for example, we may find (by monitoring the activities of the programme) that there is such large-scale theft that very little food actually reaches the children for whom it was intended. If we find this at the implementation level, it does not make sense to do an outcome evaluation, because the programme has not really been delivered.

As emphasised, feedback loops are also important in the process. Feedback is created when information gathered at one level of the programme process is used to inform goals or activities at a preceding level. Often this acts so that the next cycle of activity is modified appropriately. Chapter 9 illustrates well this cyclical process of feedback and modification in the evolution of a programme. Or, using the school-feeding example again, let us say that, as the result of a needs assessment, a specific target group has been defined as being in need of extra nutrition, say children under the age of 7 years. A set of activities is then planned to provide each child directly with a food parcel. However, in the design phase, it may be decided that it would be more practicable to deliver the food to the child's primary caregiver. In doing so, however, the target group is modified. In effect, the intervention will now work directly with primary caregivers, and only indirectly with the 7-year-olds. Note how this creates a different set of problems for monitoring the implementation of the intervention. Who actually receives the food in the household would need to be checked. In poor households, it is very likely that the food would be distributed to augment the whole family's food supply (see Chapter 4). This then might negate the specific outcomes expected from the intervention with the original target group. Programmes that have been careful with the processes of problem definition and needs assessment are, however, likely to be alert to this kind of problem.

Thus programme logic is a property of the whole programme rather than the evaluation. It is something that programme planners and managers need to build into the entire process. Usually it can be traced in the documents, theories and beliefs of planners and managers about what they believe to be the links between inputs and expected outcomes. One of the tasks in an evaluation is to make these assumptions about linkages clear and explicit so that reflection on their validity becomes possible. By making the assumptions explicit, we are in a better position to discuss whether they are reasonable in terms of what the available research literature tells us about these kinds of strategies, or the findings from case studies, or from the insights and perceptions of people involved in similar programmes.

Most programmes assume that their input will lead to some immediate outcome. Frequently it is assumed that this, in turn, will lead to one or more intermediate outcomes and ultimately to a longer-term outcome. This longer-term outcome is usually described in terms of the need the programme is addressing. A typical, simplified example could be a community education programme (say, in child health promotion) where one part of the intervention is to broadcast a message targeting mothers. The exposure is intended to provide them with new knowledge or skills (an immediate outcome), which is then assumed to change their behaviour (an intermediate outcome), which in turn is assumed to impact on the original problem of improving child health (the ultimate outcome).

However, insufficient attention is paid to the distinction between 'outcomes' and 'impacts', or, to put it differently, between immediate, intermediate and longer-term outcomes. As a result, almost everybody involved in the programme may have unrealistic expectations of when the programme can reasonably produce what effect. This is often to the detriment of the programme. Conversely, a clear understanding of programme logic can lead all stakeholders to have clearer expectations of what the programme can deliver at what time, and for what it can be held accountable. In designing an evaluation, clarity about these different levels of outcome can provide a useful framework for negotiating with stakeholders about which outcomes to focus on. It can also serve to reduce unrealistic expectations of politicians and senior managers.

This view of the logic of programmes is obviously not the only one and there are other ways to understand complex adaptive systems. Nevertheless, all models attempt to provide simplified, comprehensible ways to understand complicated things. This way of looking at programmes attempts to do just that. Hopefully it does not lose sight of the interdependencies that exist within a programme, and between the programme and its environment. The rest of the chapter addresses the different steps in the programme logic.

Problem identification and definition

All interventions start with the realisation by someone, an individual or a group, that a problem of some kind or another exists within a community. Examples are numerous: battering of pregnant women; high unemployment rates in certain neighbourhoods; the incidence of sexually transmitted diseases among teenagers; criminal behaviour; and road deaths as a result of high-speed head-on collisions. These problems are not objectively given in society. They have to be 'made into' social problems by one or more interest groups, who identify them and lobby for them to be taken seriously.

Evaluators very seldom enter the picture at the stage of 'diagnosing and defining the problem'. But they often ask the relevant stakeholders to think back to this stage, and to how the problem came to be defined in a certain way. Time spent in the initial stages of the process, by either group, would be time extremely well spent. Indeed, one of the greatest sources of failure to conduct evaluations that prove useful in informing programme decisions – by any stakeholders, from clients to funders – is lack of adequate consideration of what happens (or happened) at the beginning of the process. Taking the field of child health and nutrition as an example, Chapter 2 identifies a set of immediate causes of malnutrition. These include inadequate dietary intake, disease and psychosocial stress and trauma. In addition, underlying determinants of malnutrition are identified as food security, access to health services, care of women and children, and education and information.

In relation to such an analysis of causes, two considerations are important – to understand, theoretically, the practical problem that is faced, and how the intervention might act as a change mechanism. Evaluators will ask programme planners and managers to think about the question 'Is the programme intent appropriate to the problem it wishes to address?' This requires an understanding of the nature of the social problem that is being addressed and the processes that produce it (Chen & Rossi, 1989). Social science knowledge provides numerous pointers to the social causes of problems. Evaluators familiar with this literature (e.g. on the psychological effects of malnutrition) can provide important support to planners in understanding the problem, and in designing a programme which has a reasonable chance of success.

This is sometimes referred to as problem theory. The problem is defined in as exact terms as possible, possible causes are specified, and the persons or groups who are typically affected are identified. This is not really an area for programme evaluators as such, but more for specialists in the relevant content areas. Nevertheless, evaluators can play an important part in identifying problems and describing them empirically. They can also help by directing attention to the relevant literature on the nature and causes of social problems.

When evaluators talk of research and theory, it is not unusual for programme staff to say that they are not in the theory business or that they are practical people interested in making a difference, and not interested in theoretical or research issues. But this is a false dichotomy. Take for example the importance of knowing the literature on a particular problem area. Literature searches and reviews are playing an increasingly important role in the accumulation of knowledge, not only in the social sciences, but also in the world of practice. The importance for social scientists as well as practitioners of knowing the literature in a specific problem area cannot be overemphasised. For a start, it makes it less likely that what others have tried already will be duplicated. This is the well-known 'reinventing the wheel' accusation. In addition, it integrates and summarises the state of knowledge in a given domain, allowing overall conclusions to be drawn from many separate studies. Finally, knowing the literature often allows implications for policy and practice – such as establishing the conditions under which an intervention is likely to be more or less successful – to be clearly stated and understood.

'Research' at the early stages of programme development need not include only literature searches. It can also be as practical and down-to-earth as searching for programmes and initiatives in the same problem domain, with objectives similar to one's own. This draws attention to the importance of networking and of sharing information between different agencies and service deliverers, so that all can benefit from learning through the experience of others.

Needs assessment

In more specific terms, part of the process of problem identification is to ask questions about the assessment of need, to assist in the selection of problems on which to focus resources. Needs can be defined as those things without which, or without a sufficient amount of which, a negative or undesirable state occurs (Lipsey, Wilson, Shayne, Derzon & Newbrough, 1996). A negative state may be defined objectively, such as poor health, or subjectively through social construal. Negative states of a social variety are the sorts of problem commonly addressed by social services. Part of a needs assessment therefore is to identify and rank the gaps between problem areas and the social services available to address them ('gaps analysis'). For Lipsey *et al.* (1996) this definition helps to avoid the confusion of solutions with needs. We do not need psychotherapy; we need psychological well-being. It is the absence of the latter which is an undesirable state. Psychotherapy may well be a means of achieving psychological well-being, but it is not the need.

If the evaluator takes part in the planning of a new programme (and it is clear that evaluations are most useful if they are built into the planning process), he or she will ask about the unmet needs to be addressed by the programme. Needs assessment is a sub-discipline of evaluation in its own right, and has developed a methodology of its own. It relies on many sources of information to describe as accurately and reliably as possible the 'things without which a negative or undesirable state occurs'. The sources may include social indicators, community surveys, site visits and situation analyses, key informant interviews, and rapid appraisal techniques – several of which are illustrated in the chapters which follow.

Needs assessment, done before the programme starts, also provides a baseline measure against which the situation, after completion of the programme, can be compared. If parasitic infection among 4–6-year-old children in a particular region was defined as a problem, and the need to address it was identified, it would help to be able to say that prior to the programme 80% of the children were affected, but after the programme only 60% of the children were still infected.

Needs assessments are also important in planning the delivery of services. If the assessment has been thorough, it enhances the chances of reaching and serving the population of interest. Thus the evaluation described in Chapter 7 identified the lack of a 'systematic and rigorous needs assessment survey before embarking on actual implementation' as one of the major oversights in the planning of the intervention.

Assessing the programme design

Generally, more attention needs to be paid to the question 'Why should this intervention work?' With new programmes in particular, special attention ought to be paid to understanding how the intervention is supposed to bring about the desired changes. In Chapter 4 for instance, the authors base their intervention of a school-feeding scheme on 'sound conceptual and empirical evidence linking nutrition and school performance'. In this case, therefore, there is a clear theoretical basis for expecting the intervention to have its desired effects.

However, practitioners are not always aware of their programme theory, and evaluators may serve to help them articulate it. Argyris (1982, p. 83) introduced the notion of a theory of action: 'We begin with the proposition that people hold theories of action about how to produce consequences they intend. Such theories are theories about human effectiveness. By *effectiveness* we mean the degree to which people produce their intended consequences in ways that make it likely that they will continue to produce intended consequences.' Argyris and Schon (1978) earlier distinguished between espoused theories of action (what people say or believe is the theory undergirding their actions) and theories-in-use (the bases on which they act). Patton (1997) suggests that the evaluator assist practitioners to articulate their espoused theories of action while, at the same time, continuing to test these against their actual theories-in-use, so that differences may be identified and dealt with.

According to Lipsey, treatment or intervention theory is 'a set of propositions regarding what goes on in the black box during the transformation of input to output, that is, how a bad situation is transformed into a better one through treatment inputs' (1993, p. 11). Such a treatment theory would specify at least the following elements: a problem definition that articulates what condition is treatable, for which populations, and under what conditions; the necessary inputs and the interrelationship between them; the important links in the transformation process, and the mediating variables in the process; the expected output; and other elements, such as contextual or environmental factors which may affect the treatment process.

The important point here is that programme design is more effective if assumptions about the best way to bring about changes (and assumptions about the causes of the problems) are made explicit. Many educational programmes, for example, assume a particular model of change – that if you give people knowledge about the condition and about what they have to do, their attitudes will change, and the attitude change will lead to a change in behaviour. Thus, if faced with the problem of malnutrition, an educational campaign may be launched to inform mothers in poverty-stricken areas on how to prepare nutritious meals from very basic ingredients. In this case the implicit treatment theory may be that the increase in nutritional knowledge brought about through the educational campaign will lead to a change in attitude regarding 'basic ingredients'. In turn, the theory might hold that the change in attitude would lead to the mothers cooking differently and more nutritiously. Such a theory of change could be challenged along a number of dimensions. For a start, it is very hard to change human behaviour by information input alone. Media campaigns to inform people about practising safer sex to reduce the risk of exposure to HIV/AIDS may very well increase knowledge and awareness (see Coyle, Boruch & Turner, 1991), but whether such campaigns lead to change in sexual behaviour is very much in question. Certainly, theorists like Fishbein and Ajzen (1975) and Bandura (1977) have demonstrated quite forcefully that the knowledge–attitude–behaviour sequence of supposed change does not necessarily hold true. Despite this, programmes are frequently designed in which it is assumed that information or knowledge will lead to a change in people's behaviour. Thus, not being clear about one's programme theory, or following an implausible theory, has the very practical consequence of decreasing the chances of the programme making a difference to the condition of its recipients.

Monitoring implementation

If we return to the example of a school-feeding scheme provided earlier, we can see why a focus on implementing the programme is important. Many things can go wrong with the treatment plan of delivering food parcels to children under the age of 7. People may defraud the scheme of either its funding or the actual food; children or parents may not accept the type of food provided; and the schools, as delivery points, may not have the administrative capacity to carry the intervention through effectively. But anticipating what might happen enables us to track the contextual factors operating on the programme, and may eventually lead us to take other steps in order for the children to benefit.

Just as programme personnel may have espoused theories of action and theories-in-use, so we can expect discrepancies between the programme-as-designed and the programme-as-delivered. Not only that, but there may very well be variations in delivery between the different sites at which the programme is delivered. Thus the programme cannot be regarded as a single entity delivered in a uniform way in all settings. Posavac and Carey (1997, p. 121) describe monitoring the operation of programmes as 'the most fundamental form of program evaluation', and refer to it as 'an examination of the program itself – its activities, the population it serves, how it functions, and the condition of its participants'. Indeed, de Wilde's (1967) collected studies showed that programme implementation and administration were of critical importance in developing countries. If service delivery in developing countries is very poor, as these studies suggest, it makes it impossible to say anything about impact, since poor delivery or implementation virtually guarantees that the programme will fail. It would be unfair in such a situation to conclude that the intervention is ineffective, since it has not been given a proper opportunity to bring about the desired change. This lack of valid evaluation data is one reason why it is difficult to design more effective projects in developing countries.

Why should this be the case? Several reasons can be given for the importance of monitoring implementation or of 'process evaluation' (as it is sometimes called) in the overall logic of the programme and its evaluation. In the most extreme case, this part of the evaluation enterprise provides evidence that planned activities have actually taken place. This information is important for purposes of accountability to funders and others. In less extreme terms, it is important to know not only that the programme has been implemented, but that it has been implemented at a strength that will make it likely to have an effect. Weak implementation is often identified as a major cause of failure of the programme to bring about change. A potentially strong treatment may be built into the design phase, but if it is weakly implemented, it has little chance of being effective.

As indicated already, we also need to know whether the programme was delivered uniformly to the appropriate recipients at the right time, or whether delivery was degraded in some way. Yeaton and Sechrest (1981) have referred to this as the 'integrity of treatment'. The best safeguard to ensure that strength and integrity of service delivery are adequately monitored is to actually measure or determine the level of treatment received by participants. We need to have a description of what happened in the delivery of the actual intervention and its activities. For example, in the delivery of sexuality information workshops to teenagers, we would need to know how many workshops each teenager actually attended (strength of treatment), and whether the trainers were all following the same curriculum (integrity of treatment). Chapter 7 illustrates a number of instances of how the integrity of treatment was degraded in terms of inconsistency of delivery. Drawing attention to the importance of monitoring the integrity of treatment does not imply that the programme should be fixed and unchanging. Programmes need to adapt to specific local conditions. The point is that these must be documented. If one adaptation is more successful than another, we need to understand exactly how and why this occurred.

These measures of programme implementation also provide feedback on the quality of service delivery. If an assessment can be made quite early in the life of the programme on how well services are being delivered, and problems and difficulties can be identified, such information can be fed back on a very short feedback cycle to improve the programme. This kind of evaluation-of-progress is best used to make adjustments to the delivery of the programme in its early stages.

Whether people are participating in sufficient numbers, and whether the intended recipients are being reached, is another aspect of implementation which needs to be monitored – i.e. the actual population being served (see Posavac & Carey, 1997 above). For example, community workers may be employed to deliver an intervention intended for 15–18-year-old teenagers. When an assessment is done of who actually comes to the events, however, it may turn out that it is mainly 10–12-year-olds (the reason being that community workers found it easier to work with younger children, and were unwittingly arranging activities which appealed more to the younger children). Furthermore, one needs to know, as soon as possible, whether those who participate in the programme are doing well or better.

Finally, simply documenting the progress of the programme, describing its identifiable components (activities, behaviours, products, strategies, materials, etc.), and its planning and delivery, is very useful to others who might want to engage in similar work. It is probably fair to say that in South Africa a vast amount of knowledge about psychosocial interventions goes unused because not enough attention is paid to a careful and detailed description of programmes, their components and processes.

Outcomes and impacts

Questions such as 'Did the programme work?', 'Did it achieve its objectives?', 'What were its effects?' are clear indications that there is an interest in the overall outcomes of the intervention. The programme logic outlined above draws our attention to the important distinction between immediate and longer-term effects. Some of the effects achieved by the programme may happen quite soon after the programme has been delivered. Let us call these 'outcomes', after Linney and Wandersman (1991). These are observed or measured changes in the behaviour of target populations. For example, an intervention may change people's knowledge of what causes parasitic infections, or enhance their skills to negotiate with health officials for assistance, or raise awareness in the community of the detrimental effects of parasitic infestation on children's lives.

Other effects are further removed in time from the programme, being long-term or ultimate effects. Let us call these 'impacts', also after Linney and Wandersman. These are changes observable only at the community level, such as changes in social indicators (like the infant mortality rate and the human development index quoted in Chapter 2). These are clearly effects to be achieved only after a number of intermediary outcomes have been achieved, such as reducing parasitic infection, increasing caloric intake, and increasing school attendance. If the outcomes have been achieved, one may expect the infant mortality rates to decrease and the human development index to rise.

Why is this distinction important, and how can it help programme staff? For a start, the distinction clarifies our expectations of what should happen as a result of the intervention and when. It might also guide us as to what to try to measure, and at what phase of the whole programme. Returning to the example of a school-feeding scheme, if the implementation has been closely monitored and has been delivered at full strength, we may expect improvements in the children's health (measured, for example, as an increase in body weight) fairly soon. The improved nutrition should then increase their ability to pay attention in school (which could be measured through systematic observation of their classroom behaviour). Finally, this should lead to more effective learning (which could be gauged through general measures of school achievement). This could then be seen as an ultimate outcome or impact of the programme. Chapter 4 contains a description of such a causal chain.

Another example could be found in a job skills training programme delivered to groups of unemployed youth. We may ask whether the intended skills were actually acquired as an immediate outcome. But the question of whether those skills enabled the young people to find employment is an impact question. This would have to be asked further down the line. If the outcomes (job skills) have not been achieved, however, there is less chance that the impacts (employment) will be achieved (assuming, of course, that the treatment theory is valid!). The outcome question is therefore an important one to ask.

Furthermore, clarifying the distinction helps to protect the programme against unrealistic expectations. When dealing with intractable social problems (e.g. high infant mortality rates), it is unreasonable to expect the intervention of one programme, by itself, to have demonstrable impact. But the programme may well demonstrate significant outcomes. On the basis of these, a programme can legitimately defend itself, as these outcomes may ultimately make a contribution towards achieving an impact at community level. Social problems are recognised as very difficult to change. Evaluations of specific outcomes can therefore help in preventing discouragement if impact is not clearly evident.

Although outcomes and impacts are normally considered as a final stage of the programme and its evaluation, one can monitor outcomes from earlier on in the life of the programme. As pointed out, monitoring service delivery forms the basis of the implementation phase of the programme, but if the programme staff know what outcomes they wish to achieve, they can keep track of them from the beginning. Thus they can develop indicators of change (in knowledge, in behaviour, in functioning) which ought to occur as a result of their intervention. For example, although a score on a standardised reading test may be an imperfect approximation of reading ability, it can serve its purpose as an 'indicator' of that ability. Recording changes in the indicator over time acts as warning system if things are not changing as they should be for the programme recipients. The consequences for the programme, when this kind of outcome monitoring is absent, can be severe.

In the evaluation of the Thousand Schools Project described in Chapter 7, a failure to define and monitor measurable and observable indicators of progress was seen as a major difficulty in the programme not being able to diagnose early problems of implementation. The World Bank has reported that very few impact studies have been done in developing countries, especially of the randomised control nature (Newman, Rawlings & Gertler, 1994). The authors argue that such a neglect 'handicaps the development community's ability to demonstrate what has been achieved and so to win political support, design more effective projects, and set priorities for resource allocation' (p. 181). The evaluation reported in Chapter 7 is a large-scale impact study that utilised a non-equivalent comparison group design and is therefore a welcome addition to this literature.

Programmes cost money

Is an intervention worth its cost? This is a tough question to ask, and is not often asked of local interventions (Louw, 1998). However, now more than ever before, questions are being asked about the efficiency of psychosocial interventions, and very few interventions would even be considered for funding if not accompanied by cost estimates. Funds are limited, and choices have to be made either to support a particular programme, or to choose between alternatives.

Broadly speaking, one can address the question of programme cost in two ways: one can ask at what cost does the programme achieve what strength of effects (cost-effectiveness); or at what cost does the programme achieve certain savings, expressed in monetary terms (cost-benefit). The difference between the two ways of thinking lies in the way the outcomes are expressed. In the latter, the relationship between costs and outcomes is expressed in monetary terms. In the former, programme outcomes are expressed in terms of substantive improvement or change. The following example illustrates how choices might be made as to which approach to take. When a crèche is established in the workplace for the children of parents who cannot afford to get child-minders, the employer would be interested in what it costs – salaries, supplies, space, electricity, telephones, etc. – as against what it achieves for the children, the staff and the company (cost-effectiveness). These would be difficult to assess. In cost-benefit terms, however, the benefits of the crèche might be more directly expressed in money terms – reductions in staff turnover, less absenteeism, staff loyalty, and length of maternity leave taken.

These are technically difficult questions to answer. They also provide decision-makers with difficult dilemmas to resolve. Decisions have to be made on how to allocate scarce social resources in such a way that communities obtain maximum benefit from them. Some programmes may be more effective than others, in that they achieve more for less money. Chapter 4 refers directly to the costs of the nutrition programme in relation to its effectiveness compared to other programmes aimed at educational improvement. For our society, this is important to know. Indeed, cost-effectiveness and cost-benefit questions may take us right back to the question of priorities. Scarce resources cannot be spent on problems with low priorities.

CONCLUSION

In an attempt to answer the question 'How can evaluation be used to strengthen or improve interventions?', this chapter has presented a way of thinking about programmes and their evaluation. Central to this way of thinking is the notion of a feedback system. In the early stages of the programme, information needs to be fed back to programme staff on how the components of the programme are being delivered: in the intended format, at what strength, and to whom. This relatively short feedback loop is intended to make service delivery more effective. Thus individual psychosocial interventions can be strengthened by receiving practical and timely information about their functioning, and perhaps by meeting the need for a credible judgement of the programme's value.

There are also longer feedback loops involved in interventions and their evaluation, which can also be used to improve them. Programmes can be improved in the long term, through attempts to accumulate knowledge from the many evaluations of individual interventions (see Lipsey, 1997, for a discussion of this). For present purposes, it is sufficient to point out that we can improve our interventions in the long term if we apply, accumulate or synthesise knowledge at every step of the model. At a basic level, for instance, understanding the dynamics involved in the relationships between malnutrition and school achievement, and parasite infection and school achievement, may very well determine initial priorities and choices.

At the level of programme theory, research that goes beyond the immediacy of individual programmes can develop valid, generalisable knowledge about how interventions ought to be implemented, and how the programme processes are supposed to bring about change. Attention has been drawn to programme theory as specifying how the programme is supposed to work. It specifies the change processes that must have taken place in order to link the treatment with the desired outcomes. Thus a causal theory of how the programme works is useful in terms of improving interventions. Understanding and specifying how a particular intervention works gives guidance to the evaluator in a number of ways. It contributes to specifying relevant populations for the treatment; it assists in identifying contextual variables likely to be important; it distinguishes between intermediate and ultimate effects; it focuses attention on treatment strength and integrity; it allows stakeholders to understand why and how a treatment will or will not work; and it provides insight into the appropriateness of the programme for the particular social problem.

It ought to be possible to transfer lessons learned from one programme to another. Thus, Schorr (1988) gave a set of lessons derived from successful programmes in poverty relief:

- They offer a broad spectrum of services
- They have organisational flexibility, in that professional and bureaucratic boundaries are crossed regularly
- They are holistic in their approach, in that they see the child in the context of the family and the family in the context of its surroundings
- They contain coherent and easy-to-use services
- They employ committed and results-orientated staff
- They find ways to circumvent professional and bureaucratic limitations to meeting

the needs of clients
• They have comprehensive, responsive and flexible programming
   Such a belief (or hope) that lessons can be transferred between programmes under-
lies this whole book. In Lipsey's (1997, p. 9) words: 'Feedback from cumulated
knowledge gained through evaluating thousands of past and present programs should
be available in efficient form to help successive generations of programs become progressively better.'

REFERENCES

Argyris, C. (1982). *Reasoning, learning, and action.* San Francisco: Jossey-Bass.

Argyris, C. & Schon, D. (1978). *Organizational learning.* Reading, MA: Addison-Wesley.

Bandura, A. (1977). Self-efficacy: Toward a unified theory of behavioral change. *Psychological Review, 84*, 1185–1193.

Chen, H-T. & Rossi, P. (1989). Issues in the theory-driven perspective. *Evaluation and Program Planning, 12*, 299-306.

Coyle, S.L., Boruch, R.F. & Turner, C.F. (1991). *Evaluating AIDS prevention programs.* Washington, D.C.: National Academy Press.

de Wilde, J.C. (1967). *Experiences with agricultural development in tropical Africa.* Baltimore, MD: Johns Hopkins University Press.

Fishbein, M. & Ajzen, I. (1975). *Belief, attitude, intention and behavior: An introduction to theory and research.* Reading, Mass.: Addison-Wesley.

Linney, J.A. & Wandersman, A. (1991). *Prevention Plus III. Assessing alcohol and other drug prevention programs at the school and community level.* Rockville, MD: US Department of Health and Human Services.

Lipsey, M. (1993). Theory as method: Small theories of treatments. *New Directions for Program Evaluation, 57*, 5–38.

Lipsey, M.W. (1997). What can you build with thousands of bricks? Musings on the cumula-tion of knowledge in program evaluation. *New Directions for Evaluation, 76*, 7–23.

Lipsey, M., Wilson, D.B., Shayne, M., Derzon, J. & Newbrough, J. (1996). *Community needs assessment: The challenges of classification and comparison across diverse needs.* Research Report, Vanderbilt Institute of Public Policy Studies, Nashville, TN.

Louw, J. (1998). Programme evaluation: A structured assessment. In J. Mouton, J. Muller, P. Franks & T. Sono (Eds.), *Theory and method in South African human sciences research: Advances and innovations* (pp. 255–268). Pretoria: HSRC Publishers.

Newcomer, K.E., Hatry, H.P. & Wholey, J.S. (1994). Introduction. In J.S. Wholey, H.P. Hatry & K.E. Newcomer (Eds.), *Handbook of program evaluation* (pp. 1–10). San Francisco: Jossey-Bass.

Newman, J., Rawlings, L. & Gertler, P. (1994). Using randomized control designs in evaluat-ing social sector programs in developing countries. *The World Bank Research Observer, 9*, 181–201.

Patton, M. Q. (1997). *Utilization-focused evaluation. The new century text* (3rd ed.). Thousand Oaks: Sage.

Posavac, E.J. & Carey, R.G. (1997). *Program evaluation. Methods and case studies* (5th ed.). Upper Saddle River, NJ: Prentice Hall.

Schorr, L. (1988). *Within our reach: Breaking the cycle of disadvantage.* New York: Doubleday.

Yeaton, W.H. & Sechrest, L. (1981). Critical dimensions in the choice and maintenance of successful treatments: Strength, integrity, and effectiveness. *Journal of Consulting and Clinical Psychology, 49*, 156–167.

THE PSYCHOLOGICAL IMPACT OF A SCHOOL-FEEDING PROJECT

4

Linda Richter, Dev Griesel & Cynthia Rose

Hunger and poor growth are widespread among poor South African children. In 1995 it was estimated that nearly a quarter of South African children under 6 years of age were stunted, or shorter than expected, as a result of long-term nutritional deficiencies (Wigton, Makan & McCoy, 1997). For much of the apartheid era, issues of hunger, poor growth and malnutrition were obscured by technical debates about how malnutrition and growth should be assessed, and whether the measurements of local children should be compared to international grades (which would make local children appear thinner and shorter, and more children would be classified as malnourished) or to South African norms (which would make fewer children appear malnourished) (Griesel, Richter, Windell & Oberholzer, 1986). This particular debate was only resolved in the 1990s in favour of using universal growth grades against which to evaluate measures of South African children.

The history of nutrition policy in South Africa reflects apartheid priorities and divisions. In the 1940s a National Nutrition Council was established to implement a wide range of efforts to promote nutrition. This included practical support for farmers, improved marketing of basic foodstuffs, nutritional surveillance, direct food aid and school feeding. A free-milk-in-schools scheme was introduced in 1938 for children in white and coloured schools, and this was extended to African schools in 1943. A programme to provide one meal a day for all primary school children was introduced in 1944 and, although it was later discontinued, it was justified by the assertion that 'school feeding is recognised in all civilised countries as a useful and economic method of combating malnutrition' (Harrison, 1995, p. 156).

A separate government department for nutrition was established in 1951 but, with improved living standards among whites by the 1970s, nutrition took a back seat to other health issues and was addressed mainly through programmes of nutrition education to avert emerging diseases of life-style. In 1975 a protein–vitamin–mineral supplement was introduced into clinics for malnourished children and an Emergency Food Scheme was initiated in 1985 to provide relief in very vulnerable parts of the country. The appointment of a Committee for the Development of a Food and Nutrition Strategy for Southern Africa in 1989 was the first attempt by the Nationalist government to begin to address the impact of poverty and social development on nutrition. The National Nutrition and Social Development Programme (NNSDP) was established in 1991 to serve women and young children at risk, mainly in rural areas. Reviews of these efforts suggest that they were dogged by administrative problems, poor targeting, inadequate control and a lack of evaluation (Harrison, 1995).

In September 1994 the Primary School Nutrition Programme (PSNP) was launched as a Presidential Lead Project of the Reconstruction and Development Programme. The purpose of the PSNP was to contribute to the improvement of education quality by enhancing primary school pupils' learning capacity, school attendance and punctuality, and to contribute to general health development. There is both sound conceptual and empirical evidence linking nutrition and school performance. Pollitt (1994), for example, argues that poor nutrition and concurrent illnesses interfere with the schooling of children in low-income countries, and that educational interventions have to include children's health issues, including chronic protein-energy malnutrition, iron-deficiency anaemia, iodine deficiency and intestinal helminth infections. In parallel with poor growth, there is widespread academic failure among young South African children in the earliest years of formal schooling. It has been estimated that, for more than three decades, at least 24% of Grade 1 children have failed or been held back for an additional year (Gordon, 1986; Liddell & Kemp, 1993). Although this high failure rate is more than twice that at any other grade in primary school, it does set the pattern for faltering school achievement for many children (Taylor, 1989). A causal link between undernutrition and cognitive performance among South African samples is suggested by several reviews (Griesel & Richter, 1987; Griesel, Richter & Belciug, 1990; Richter & Griesel, 1994).

Although children's achievement at school is dependent on many factors, the PSNP aimed to address education in a number of ways: the alleviation of hunger by providing 30% of Recommended Daily Allowance; micronutrient supplementation where indicated (iron and Vitamins A and C); parasite control where needed; nutrition education; and community participation in nutrition. The PSNP began with a goal of reaching 3.8 million children. By 1998 it was estimated to be reaching nearly 6 million children at an average annual cost of around R500 million per annum. Two major reviews of the PSNP have been conducted, indicating a number of weaknesses and shortcomings of the programme (Health Systems Trust, 1997; National Progressive Primary Health Care Network, 1995). Both reviews highlighted lack of controls over expenditure, insufficient targeting of children, inadequate community participation, and the lack of administrative and other infrastructure to achieve the goals of the programme.

In addition, this major financial outlay on feeding school children was not seen by many stakeholders in nutrition to be the optimal investment. Their opposition stemmed from the recognition that the PSNP would not address, and indeed would probably divert money and energy away from, preschool children who are the most vulnerable group nutritionally. In reality, none of the goals of the programme, apart from the direct supply of food, have been systematically implemented. Despite glaring deficiencies and repeated reports of fraud and corruption in the delivery of the service, 'anecdotal' reports of increased attendance and punctuality at school, and a rapid sampling of pupil and teacher responses to the scheme showing general appreciation for the food received, have been taken as evidence of success.

Apart from the study described below (originally published as Richter, Rose & Griesel, 1997), no other South African evaluation of the impact of school feeding on children's learning capacity has been published, nor have any comparative analyses been undertaken to examine whether the intervention has produced benefits in school performance, achievement and progression in the early school grades.

CONCEPTUAL FRAMEWORK

School feeding was introduced in the United States and the United Kingdom in the 1930s, in various forms, with the intention of increasing the growth of children (Baker, Elwood, Hughes, Jones & Sweetnam, 1978). While a general claim is made that supplementary nutrition and school feeding can improve the nutritional status of school children, as well as improve performance and reduce absenteeism (Makorapong, 1987; Myeni & McGrath, 1990), not many controlled studies have been reported which can demonstrate these effects unambiguously (Levinger, 1984). It is important to note, though, that there is a great deal of variation in what is meant by school feeding. This can range from free or subsidised milk distribution, to specific nutrient supplementation, to serving part or full meals at full price, reduced price or free. In developing countries, evaluations also have to take account of the fact that food distribution programmes, including school feeding, are not always adequately implemented. Owing to problems of supply, storage and administration, there is little chance of demonstrating beneficial effects.

School-feeding programmes, as was the case with the PSNP, are also motivated by wider concerns than the provision of direct food aid. For example, it is hoped that providing a meal at school will increase attendance, particularly among children from poor families in marginal communities, and that this too will contribute to improvement in school performance (Babu & Hallam, 1989). It is also hoped that school feeding will increase knowledge about nutrition at the community level, stimulate local industry and create employment (Beaton & Ghassemi, 1982). The focus of this evaluation, however, was on the expressed purpose of the PSNP as an RDP project; namely, to increase the learning capacity of young children and increase educational achievement.

Even in developed countries, nearly one-third of children are found not to have breakfast regularly (Chao & Vanderkooy, 1989). The figure is likely to be substantially higher among poor children in developing countries. These children may also not have had a substantial or nourishing supper the night before. As a result, children may be hungry during the school morning and even hypoglycaemic (Jooste, Wolmarans & Oelofse, 1993). This hungry state reduces children's ability to pay attention, concentrate, learn and remember, and therefore diminishes the benefit of their school attendance. Poor children may also have specific micronutrient deficiencies, particularly iron deficiency anaemia, which is known to affect cognitive functioning (Pollitt, Gorman, Engle, Martorell & Riviera, 1993).

Three pathways, not necessarily independent of one another, have commonly been suggested to explain the link between nutritional deficiencies and cognitive functioning:

- by directly causing structural and biochemical changes in the brain which reduce cognitive capacity
- by reducing arousal and activity levels, resulting in a withdrawal from, and lack of responsiveness to, environmental stimuli
- by causing changes in emotionality, particularly in attentional processes, which interfere with cognitive functioning

Recent reviews and theoretical analyses support the view that prolonged nutritional deficiencies produce lasting changes in emotional control and motivation, with wide-ranging effects on all aspects of personal functioning, including cognition (Barret & Frank, 1987; Pollitt *et al.*, 1996; Strupp & Levitsky, 1995).

Unfortunately, the effects of undernutrition are much easier to study in the laboratory than in real-life situations (Pollitt, Cueto & Jacoby, 1998). This is because many other co-occurring influences, especially poor living and schooling conditions, produce effects on children's cognitive performance that are not easy to separate from the effects of poor nutrition. For example, one of the obvious and immediate consequences of not eating is a drop in plasma glucose levels. Under laboratory conditions, administration of glucose can be shown to have an immediate and noticeable effect on improving attention (Benton, Owens & Parker, 1994). Although not impossible, it is much more difficult in real-life situations to show effects on cognition of hunger, undernutrition or specific micronutrient deficiencies – or to show educational benefits that can be directly attributed to school feeding.

The major theoretical model guiding research on nutrition and cognitive performance assumes that deficits in emotional, attentional and arousal regulation disrupt information processing at several stages and affect cognitive performance (Kopp, 1987). For this reason, measures are usually made of activity levels, impulse control, frustration tolerance, attention, concentration, persistence and distraction, and short-term memory.

PROJECT DESCRIPTION

In 1992 the authors were asked to evaluate a school-breakfast programme funded by a local food company at a farm school near Muldersdrift outside Johannesburg. In response to observations that children were arriving hungry, weak and inattentive at school, the introduction of a breakfast was the combined idea of the school staff and their major sponsor, a local food-manufacturing firm.

From the outset, it was accepted that the measurement of school achievement is a complex process, and that several methods would have to be used to investigate it. A pilot study was undertaken to test the feasibility of a broadly outlined evaluation plan. It was also specifically intended to:

- establish good working relationships with the staff and to hold discussions with them about relevant classroom behaviours which they considered to be related to school achievement
- ascertain the routines of the school and the first-grade classrooms so that the con-

straints associated with these activities could be accommodated in the process of data collection

- test the ceiling and floor levels, as well as the means and ranges, of several psychometric measures of cognitive performance
- examine the practicalities of videotaped behavioural measures of task-related classroom behaviour
- estimate the costs of a pre- and post-test study

The piloted measures included psychometric measures of attention, concentration and short-term memory; videotaped observation of classroom behaviour; and rating by the teacher of a child's customary behaviour in the classroom. On the basis of the pilot study, a formal evaluation was designed with the following characteristics. The design adopted was a pre- and post-test, non-equivalent group comparison: that is, the performance of two groups of children was measured and compared both before and after the school breakfast had been introduced to the one group (the intervention or experimental group). While the two groups were comparable in terms of school grade and the time between pre- and post-testing, they differed from one another in a number of important respects. Thus, children in the intervention group were compared with children at an inner-city school in Johannesburg where the staff and parents were prepared to co-operate with the investigation. Although the children at the inner-city school were considerably better off than the intervention group, the ethical impossibility of establishing two randomised samples in one school, and the bureaucratic difficulty of getting permission to do the study at schools other than these two, led to the chosen design. Also, history, maturation and testing experience are known to be the main threats to the internal validity of before–after designs (Reichardt & Mark, 1998). One way of addressing these, when randomisation is not practicable, is through non-equivalent group comparisons such as these.

First and second graders were targeted for the evaluation on the basis of evidence that younger children are more likely to benefit from school feeding because their faster rate of growth creates increased nutritional demands (McKay, Sinisterra, McKay, Gomez & Lloreda, 1978). The evaluation was conducted before and then after six weeks of the school breakfast intervention, a continuous period without any vacation break.

The farm school served the children of extremely poor farm workers in the Muldersdrift district. Not all children in the district attended school because some farmers insisted that whole families work their lands. Most children were obliged to work on the farm after school and during holidays. Very few caregivers among the farm workers were available in homesteads to care for young children and prepare their meals. In contrast, the school itself was generously funded by the farmer and his personal network of benevolent contacts, and was well provisioned and staffed by good and dedicated teachers. The buildings, classroom facilities and educational materials were equivalent to those provided in many private schools in South Africa.

The comparison school was a well-run government school in the centre of Johannesburg which catered for local children as well as immigrants, many of whom were Portuguese-speaking refugees from Mozambique. The principal had managed to persuade the Portuguese government to supply the school with additional teaching staff, as well as staff to assist children to learn English, the medium of instruction in the school. Although many were latchkey children, who went home to empty high-rise apartments while their single mothers were working long hours, the staff at the school had instituted several voluntary programmes to assist the children and their families. For example, the school ran a free after-care facility together with sandwiches for children who were collected very late in the afternoon by their caregivers. The evident teamwork, energy and innovation of the staff produced a school which, although comparatively poor in facilities, provided a strong educational experience for children and was responsive to the needs of inner-city families. On the surface, the two schools thus showed similar strengths and weaknesses. Both served vulnerable children and families, both had a group of dedicated teachers, and both sought additional help from external sponsors to assist them to provide for their pupils. There were, however, also clear differences as shown in the baseline descriptive results which will be discussed below.

The food company supplied money to the experimental school for the purchase of a nutritionally balanced breakfast, consisting of cereal, milk and a banana for each child in the school each day of the school year. The principal, in collaboration with the parent–teacher association, administered the funds. The housekeeping staff at the school, teachers and volunteer parents all assisted in collecting and preparing the food. An early break was scheduled before 09h00 to allow children to have their breakfast. The programme was introduced simultaneously throughout all grades in the school and has remained in place ever since. Although the sponsors, we and the staff tried, sufficient funds could not be raised to subsidise the afternoon sandwiches given to children in the comparison school. However, we undertook and met the commitment to give talks to parents and teachers at the comparison school on matters of child development of interest to them, in exchange for their participation in the evaluation.

Evaluation methods

The methods used to conduct the evaluation were triangulated to assess school performance from three perspectives of children's functioning.

1. Individual cognitive functioning

This was assessed by performance on the following psychometric tasks:

- *WISC Coding A and B and WISC Digit Span.* These are supplementary tests to the basic Wechsler Intelligence Scale for Children (Wechsler, 1949). The Coding subtest is believed to measure, among other things, attention, freedom from distractibility, psychomotor speed, short-term memory and visual–motor co-ordination. The abilities associated with the Digit Span test are attention, auditory memory, concentration, freedom from distractibility, sequencing and short-term memory (Sattler, 1986).
- *Vigilance.* A set of seven items was designed for the study to measure attention, based on the vigilance-scanning task used by Soemantri, Pollitt and Kim (1986). In the information-processing model of cognition, vigilance is conceptualised as one aspect of arousal or attentional intensity and is studied by requiring individuals to be alert to the occurrence of a target in the context of distracting information (Haber & Hershenson, 1973). In these items, children were asked to mark a single

letter (an X) in increasingly complex arrays of similar letters within a time limit. The total score of correct target detections, as well as errors of omission and commission, was recorded.

2. Teacher assessment of child behaviour

Class teachers were asked to complete the ADD-H Comprehensive Teacher's Rating Scale (ACTeRS) (Ullmann, Sleator & Sprague, 1988). This 24-item scale was designed to systematise teachers' observations of children in primary school by way of scores on four scales: attention, hyperactivity, social skills and oppositional behaviour. Test–retest reliability is reported to be good (0.78 to 0.82) and the internal consistency very high (above 0.95) (Bacon, 1992; D'Costa, 1992).

3. Observed classroom behaviour

Children's behaviour in the classroom was videotaped by means of a camera with a wide-angled lens mounted on a panning motor to afford continuous coverage of the classroom. The videotape was installed two weeks before the start of the study to allow children to become used to it. With the panning movement of the camera every child was visible for a duration of 2–4 seconds every 10 seconds. This allowed almost continuous observation of each child's behaviour and coding, during each observation interval, along a number of dimensions of behaviour. Only observations made during structured learning activities when children were required to sit at their desks, pay attention to the teacher or perform some oral or pencil task, were coded for analysis. The pre- and post-intervention observations used in the analysis were selected to ensure that they were made on the same day of the week, and included approximately the same kind of teaching and classroom activities. Using these criteria, it was possible to select 100 comparable pre- and post-intervention observations for each child.

For a variety of reasons, much of the videotaped data could not be used in the final analysis. For example, a particular child was recorded on a Thursday during the pre-testing period but was absent from school on the Thursday during the post-test period. In addition, children in Grades 1 and 2 spent a good deal of time out of their seats, usually gathered in a circle on the floor in front of the teacher's desk, during which time they moved inconsistently in and out of the view of the camera. Also, it was not clear during these activities what exactly constituted appropriate on-task behaviour.

The analysis of the videotaped data was based on codes assigned after complete agreement was reached about the allocation of a particular behaviour to a category. The coding was done using an editor, which allowed the tape to be slowed down to a still picture and then 'jogged' forward frame by frame. Analysis involved calculating the total number of behaviours observed in each category for each child in both the intervention and comparison groups, and by computing a duration score which reflected the mean number of observation periods during which any particular code was assigned.

Baseline descriptive measures

Baseline descriptive measures were taken of each child during the pre-test. They were not repeated at the post-test because they were collected to describe and classify the children in both the intervention and the comparison group. One of the measures was Raven's Coloured Progressive Matrices (Raven, Court & Raven, 1990), which was used as a non-verbal measure of intellectual ability. According to the authors, the Raven's is believed to be one of the best single measures of 'g' or general ability. Several cross-cultural validity studies indicate that the test is a valid measure of non-verbal intelligence among children from culturally, economically and linguistically diverse backgrounds (Carlson & Jensen, 1981).

The other measure was a home interview with the child's primary caregiver administered by the child's class teacher or one of the research assistants specially employed and trained for the project. The interviews were done after hours and over weekends to ensure that contact was made with the child's primary caregiver. Caregivers were asked to provide basic social, health and historical data on the child and the family, including caregiver educational levels, occupation and income. They were also asked their opinion on the school-breakfast programme.

Post-test evaluation of school performance

School attendance of each child for the period of the intervention was taken from the class records maintained at both schools. School results, in the form of a pass or a fail of the school grade at the end of the year during which the intervention took place, were taken from the schools' files.

The intervention, a school breakfast, consisted of 30 g corn flakes, 100 ml skimmed milk and a banana. The nutritional components of this breakfast were 919 kj of energy, 6.6 g protein, 0.5 g fat, 50 g carbohydrate, 1.4 g dietary fibre, together with sodium, potassium, folic acid, iron, niacin and vitamins B1, B2, B6, 1B2 and vitamin E. A schematic representation of the design is given in Figure 1.

FIGURE 1: INTERVENTION AND EVALUATION DESIGN

INTERVENTION GROUP   **COMPARISON GROUP**

Baseline descriptive measures
Raven's Coloured Progressive Matrices
Caregiver interview

Pre-test assessment
Psychometric tests
• *Digit Span*
• *Coding*
• *Vigilance task*

Teacher rating of child behaviour in class

Videotaped observation of class behaviour

SCHOOL BREAKFAST   **NO INTERVENTION**
Continuously in place for 6 weeks

Post-test assessment
Pre-test assessment repeated for both groups
Post-test evaluation of school performance

OUTCOMES AND EVALUATION

Baseline differences between the intervention and comparison group children

Previously published research on the nutritional status of children at the experimental and comparison schools indicated significant differences between them (Reitsma *et al.*, 1994; Vorster *et al.*, 1994). Of the children in the experimental school 12% were found to be below the 5th percentile of height-for-age, and 18% below the 5th percentile of weight-for-age. The energy intake of the children was below the recommended daily allowance, as was their intake of calcium, iron, zinc and the major vitamins. Clinical examinations indicated that approximately 20–25% of the children showed signs of malnutrition, including spongy and bleeding gums and muscle wasting. Information from dietary histories suggested that few children received nutritious meals at home. In contrast, no signs or symptoms of malnutrition were found among the children attending the comparison school.

The same patterns were found in respect of statistically significant differences between the two groups on the demographic and social parameters assessed (Richter, Rose & Griesel, 1997). The experimental group were patently disadvantaged in relation to the comparison group on a number of social indicators. These included a higher household density, a higher number of children in the household, lower maternal and paternal educational and occupational levels, and lower household income. For example, the majority of mothers of the experimental children (72%) had received only primary education in contrast with only 4% of the mothers of comparison children. Similarly, 90% of the experimental households reported a monthly income of less than R1000, whereas the majority of the comparison households (66%) reported incomes above R1500 per month.

The 1986 American norms for the Raven's Coloured Progressive Matrices were used to convert raw scores into age-equivalent percentile points, and then categorised into five grades (Raven *et al.*, 1990). Of the experimental children, 62% scored below the 5th percentile, while 50% of the comparison children scored above the 50th percentile.

The nutritional, social and intellectual baseline measures indicated that the two groups of children were not equivalent and that nutritionally based educational intervention among children in the experimental group was strongly justified. These results also indicated that differences in post-intervention measurements between the two groups could not be used as indicators of intervention effects because the groups were substantially different to begin with. In such cases, two analytical procedures are recommended. The first is the use of change scores: both mean change scores for the groups, and individual change scores from pre- to post-intervention measures (Rogosa, Brandt & Zimowski, 1982). A second is the use of covariance analysis to remove the effect of baseline differences between groups. Since this procedure is appropriate only to randomised designs (Lipsey, 1998), it was not used here.

In all, 108 children participated in the study: 55 children in the experimental group and 53 children in the comparison group. The numbers of children in each group were evenly distributed between Grades 1 and 2, and between males and females. While the two groups were reasonably well balanced in terms of school grade and gender, the children in the experimental group were significantly older than the comparison children. This is a further index of disadvantage among the experimental group. While the children in the comparison group were appropriately aged for their grade, the children in the experimental group showed a very wide age range and were, in general, a year or two older than the accepted age for their grade.

Pre- and post-intervention psychometric measures

Both the experimental and the comparison group children showed a mean overall statistically significant improvement in performance from pre- to post-intervention testing on both the Coding (overall score and time taken to complete the task) and Vigilance tests. On the Digit Span test, the experimental group, but not the comparison group, showed a significant improvement from pre- to post-test. The differences between the groups were tested by two-tailed t-tests at a 1% level of significance. The results of the pre- and post-test assessments are summarised in Table 1. (A more detailed presentation of these results is available in Richter *et al.*, 1997).

TABLE 1: SUMMARY OF RESULTS ON THE EVALUATION MEASURES

MEASURES	RESULTS
Psychometric meaures	
• WISC Coding A&B group comparison	Both groups showed statistically significant improvement from pre- to post-testing
• Mean change scores	No difference between the two groups
• WISC Digit Span group comparison	Experimental but not comparison group improved
• Mean change scores	Experimental group children showed significantly greater improvement than comparison children
• Vigilance group comparison	Both groups showed statistically significant improvement
• Mean change scores	Experimental group children showed significantly greater improvement than comparison children
Teacher Ratings	The experimental group showed a significant improvement on hyperactivity
Videotaped observations	
• Off-task behaviour	The experimental group showed a significantly greater decline than the comparison group
• Out-of-seat	The experimental group showed a significantly greater decline than the comparison group
• Activity level	The experimental group showed a significantly greater increase than the comparison group
• Peer interaction	The experimental group showed a significantly greater increase than the comparison group
• Class participation	The experimental group showed a significantly greater increase than the comparison group

One of the reasons why design features are so important for evaluations is that people (especially children) tend to change in a positive direction as a result of participating in an intervention. They become familiar, and therefore more competent, with the test materials, and simply because they grow older they consolidate cognitive gains and developments. So merely showing that the experimental children improved is insufficient. To conclude that the intervention is effective, the experimental group need to improve to a greater degree than the comparison group, and the individual children in the experimental group need to improve on their pre-test scores to a greater extent than the comparison children.

In terms of individual change scores, there were no significant differences between the two groups on the WISC Coding scores, although the experimental group showed significantly greater mean individual improvement on both the Digit Span and the Vigilance tests.

Teacher ratings of classroom behaviour

Class teachers were asked to rate each child's customary classroom behaviour before and after the intervention. There was only one significant change in the groups from pre- to post-intervention assessment, and this occurred among the experimental group of children who showed lower scores on the hyperactivity scale after the intervention ($t = 6.4$; $df = 50$; $p<0.01$). Hyperactivity, as rated on the ACTeRS, refers to negative, disruptive behaviour. The five items included in the scale are: extremely overactive, overreacts, fidgety, impulsive and restless.

Videotaped classroom behaviour

Two sets of scores were calculated for the observed classroom behaviour. The first consisted of observations in each coding category, or occurrence. The second set consisted of the mean number of observations during which a particular behaviour code was rated as present on a continuous basis, or duration. Because of a low level of occurrence of behaviours in some code categories, duration scores were only calculated for on- and off-task, activity level and peer interaction.

In general, the experimental group of children, but not the comparison children, showed significant changes from pre- to post-intervention testing on behaviour occurrence scores, as given in Table 1. They showed a decline in off-task and out-of-seat behaviour, and an increase in activity level, positive peer interaction and class participation. No significant differences were found in the behaviour of comparison children at pre- and post-intervention assessment.

On duration scores, the children in the experimental group again showed significant changes – a decline in the duration of off-task behaviour ($t = 3.4$; $df = 50$; $p<0.01$) and an increase in the duration of active episodes ($t = 4.1$; $df = 50$; $p<0.01$).

Absenteeism and school results

Absenteeism was tracked for each school term, including the fourth school term (late September to early December), during which the intervention took place. In all terms, including the fourth, the experimental group showed higher levels of absenteeism than the comparison group.

School results for the year showed that all the comparison children passed and were promoted into the next grade. In contrast, nearly a quarter of the experimental children failed the year and were retained in their grade to repeat the school year. Children who failed in the experimental school were most likely to be children who did very poorly on the general ability test administered at the start of the study. These were also the children who came from the poorest and most disadvantaged homes. On the whole, children who showed marked improvements on the psychometric and videotaped classroom observations were not statistically more likely to pass than children whose performance improved less dramatically or only marginally. These results indicate that, at least as assessed over a relatively short term, school progression depends more on long-standing historical and situational factors than on vertical interventions, such as a school-breakfast programme. While there is little doubt that the experimental children suffered early morning hunger which was curbed by the school breakfast, and that the school breakfast improved their ability to engage in educational activities and benefit from the school environment, in itself the breakfast was not able to reverse or compensate for enduring social and personal adversity.

Relationships between measures of children's cognitive and behavioural functioning

While there were very high correlations between the three psychometric measures – Coding, Digit Span and Vigilance – there were only scattered statistically significant correlations between the psychometric measures and the videotaped classroom behaviour. For example, Digit Span performance was negatively associated with overactive behaviour in the classroom ($r = -0.49$) and with off-task behaviour ($r = -0.37$). The same inconsistently patterned relationships were found between the psychometric tests and teacher-rated classroom behaviour. For example, a negative correlation was found between Digit Span performance and teacher-rated hyperactivity ($r = -0.34$). No significant correlations were found between teacher-rated classroom behaviour and videotaped classroom behaviour. In general, it seemed as though the psychometric tests, the teacher ratings and the observed classroom behaviour were tapping different, although overlapping, dimensions of children's attentional and task-related behaviour at school.

Summary of results

Consistent with recent data from developing countries showing promising educational effects of school-feeding programmes (Jacoby, Cueto & Pollitt, 1998; Simeon, 1998), this evaluation indicated that, as a group, children with demonstrated undernutrition experienced beneficial psychological and behavioural effects following the introduction of a school-breakfast programme. Psychometric indicators of attention and concentration improved, teacher ratings of disruptive behaviour declined, and videotaped observations of classroom behaviour showed that children became significantly more active, participatory and task-oriented.

By contrast, absenteeism in the experimental school was unaffected by the intervention and close to a quarter of the children in the experimental school still failed to progress to the next grade at the end of the year. There was, in fact, little reason to expect that the school breakfast, introduced during the fourth term in the year, would have any effect on the pass rate and progression of children in the experimental school. School-feeding programmes may have limited impact on broad educational achievement, as opposed to specific cognitive performance.

One argument could be that this result is a function of structural and functional problems in the educational system, and the poor quality of the schools that cater to the most vulnerable children. So, even when children's attention and concentration improve as a result of supplementary feeding, the lack of coherent educational processes in poor schools prevents children from converting their cognitive gains into educational achievements. While this argument probably has much relevance for the limited benefits that can be expected from school feeding in many South African schools, it does not apply to this particular farm school.

As indicated previously, the experimental school had far better than expected material and human resources because of its unique situation. Nevertheless, it is unlikely that much immediate educational benefit from school feeding can accrue to children whose home environments are so wretched. The conditions of farm workers and their families, especially on high-labour enterprises in peri-urban areas, are known to be singularly exploitative. Many of these children have suffered and continue to experience multiple deprivation. Their parents are poorly educated, badly paid and overworked. The children are underfed and receive little prolonged care and attention from adults. In addition, they are also obliged to work in the fields as soon as they return home from school.

In the main, the results support two firm axioms of the benefits of intervention. The first is that the poorest performing groups, or those most in need, show the greatest gains in response to intervention. The second is that vertical interventions have limited impact on multi-disadvantaged children. In short, needy children are responsive to interventions but the expected impact of the intervention is limited by the social and other constraints which operate at the same time.

The results also confirmed the importance of including multiple, triangulating measures of outcomes to assess intervention. Thus, improvements in psychometric test performance were not invariably associated with changes in classroom behaviour. Similarly, changes in observed classroom behaviour were not always reflected in improved psychometric performance (Richter *et al.*, 1997). If the evaluation had been limited to the assessment of children's performance in only one domain, both 'Type I' and 'Type II' errors might have occurred. For example, improvements in psychometric performance might have been taken as sufficient evidence of the effectiveness of the intervention – even though they may not have been associated with benefits in classroom behaviour. Conversely, lack of improvement in psychometric performance might have led to the erroneous conclusion that the intervention had no positive effects on classroom behaviour.

Evaluation frameworks

Evaluation theory and method has evolved rapidly over the last two decades, and currently several models exist within which to frame evaluation research. The suitability of any particular model to an evaluation exercise depends essentially on the purpose and requirements of the evaluation (Herman, Morris & Fitz-Gibbon, 1987).

The models of the 1960s and 1970s were driven by the need for formative and summative information required for programme revision and accountability to sponsors. In the main, these models adopted experimental designs on the assumption that relatively clear cause–effect relationships could be established between interventions and outcomes (Campbell, 1969). This information was then used to provide a rational basis for decision-making and planning.

In the 1980s these evaluation models were criticised for lacking sensitivity to contextual issues (Cook & Shadish, 1986). 'Rather than assuming that social programs were discrete and easily specified in terms of process and outcomes, these models [qualitative models] acknowledged that social and other programs often are complex, amorphous mobilisations of human activities and resources that vary significantly from one locale to another, embedded in and influenced by complex political and social networks' (Herman *et al.*, 1987, p. 9). While process models of evaluation stress the importance of naturalistic, qualitative methods for understanding the operation and effects of interventions, they lack credible ways of generalising information beyond the unique situation, and thus are less useful for high-level decision-making.

As indicated, the approach taken to any particular evaluation needs to be responsive to the goals and requirements provided in the evaluation brief. The evaluations conducted of the PSNP, referred to earlier, took a holistic qualitative approach to describe the effects of the programme from a broad systemic perspective. The evaluation described in this chapter adopted a quasi-experimental design to examine, more specifically, the effect of a school breakfast on children's cognitive and behavioural performance in the classroom.

Drawing on the processes involved in biomedical research, one can consider the development of interventions as occurring in three stages, characterised by attempts to establish, first, efficacy, then effectiveness and, finally, cost-effectiveness. In the first stage, which requires an experimental approach, the principal components of the intervention are tested to find out if they have an effect on the targeted systems. For example, food intake after deprivation might be tested to see if it increases attentional capacity. If efficacy is established in a laboratory-like environment where implementation and exposure can be controlled, effectiveness is then tested under real-world, quasi-experimental conditions. One needs to establish whether the benefits hold up under variable conditions of implementation, and in interaction with various other factors. Thus the study reported in this chapter would be classified as an effectiveness trial. Lastly, the cost of the intervention is calculated and compared to the cost and logistical effort of other interventions which could achieve the same ends as effectively. For example, one would need to examine whether the expenditure on the PSNP in relation to the benefits achieved is justified in relation to other potential programmes designed to achieve educational improvements (Walker, Labadarios, Vorster, Glatthaar & Meulenberg-Buskens, 1993).

Complexity of effectiveness evaluations

As indicated, it is one thing to demonstrate a relationship between an intervention and an effect under the controlled conditions of an efficacy trial, but quite another to design a study to test the effectiveness of an intervention under real-life conditions. First, it is difficult to achieve even quasi-experimental conditions in programmes that confer social benefits. For example, it would have been unethical to randomly assign one group of children to a feeding group and not feed the other group of children. Similarly, it was neither practical nor desirable to use a time-series design within which one group of children were fed a breakfast for a specified time period, followed by the other group being fed a breakfast for the same duration. Although these possibilities were discussed, neither the parents, the teachers nor the sponsors were in favour of a design that prejudiced any group of children, even temporarily. It is also difficult to find control groups in other settings, for example another school, with precisely comparable features to the experimental group. These constraints on design in implementation environments can significantly weaken the demonstrable benefits of the intervention for recipients.

Second, it is difficult to conceptualise and design salient outcome measures. This was particularly problematic in this evaluation, as there was a need to find measures falling between laboratory psychometric-type measures and those measuring school achievement or progression as an ultimate outcome. There are no 'strong' measures of learning capacity, concentration, distractibility and so on, so the measures used were selected from available psychological techniques to complement one another. Under such circumstances, triangulation of measurement is not only practically useful, it also provides an opportunity for construct validation. Thus, relationships between the data collected through different measurements give some indication of the validity of the instruments to reflect the same presumed underlying construct.

Evaluations of effectiveness also need to take account of unintended negative consequences that sometimes accompany programme benefits. For example, school-feeding programmes sometimes result in changes in the access children have to household food, as the family makes adjustments to the additional food being provided outside the home. Although we heard anecdotal accounts from children and teachers that children were receiving less food at home because they were being fed at school, the formal evaluation was deficient in that it did not systematically investigate this particular issue. A second unintended consequence, for which the study did not adequately prepare, was the overall increase in the classroom activity and participation levels of the experimental children following the introduction of the school breakfast. Teachers informally complained that children were becoming unmanageable as they were not accustomed to alert, active, participating children in their classrooms!

Interventions in complex social systems

The complexity of the social systems into which interventions are placed also needs to be borne in mind. The evaluation of an intervention directed at an isolated system in the lives of multi-disadvantaged children poses several problems. Thus, many issues that are addressed by specific interventions, such as poor attendance and high failure rates in the school system, are linked – through poverty – to other levels of system, and ultimately to inequalities of power and opportunity in the society as a whole (Farran, 1990; Garbarino, 1989; Halpern, 1990; Jones-Wilson, 1991). For this reason, discernible effects as a result of specific interventions are likely to be small. Such interventions are classified as 'weak treatments' if they are not accompanied by sustained interventions at several other levels of the social system (Gallagher, 1991).

In conclusion, although statistically significant improvements were found in the experimental group that were not paralleled among the comparison group of children, we cannot deduce without doubt that cognitive and behavioural benefits accrued to the children who received a school breakfast. 'On the other hand', cautions Ernesto Pollitt (1994, p. 26), 'it must be recognised that the lack of evidence may be due to inherent complexities of the evaluation, and not due to a genuine lack of effects.'

School feeding in South Africa

The PSNP was introduced in 1994 as part of the visible drive to address issues of equity and redress in South Africa. Feeding young children who are hungry has moral and political force, as well as clearly being one of a number of interventions necessary to address problems of early school performance among poor children. No one will deny that the PSNP has been difficult to implement, that the necessary infrastructure had not been created to support it, and that its achievements to date are far more limited than were ever anticipated. In the main, the PSNP has not created jobs in rural areas, it has not strengthened school governance structures by involving parents, nor has it improved community levels of nutrition knowledge and application. What is more, adverse secondary effects have almost certainly occurred. Local women food vendors around schools have lost business; many children probably do with less food at home as part of a household strategy to maximise resource use; and some persons in power have used their positions to benefit themselves financially at the expense of the children.

Nonetheless, the PSNP represents a massive commitment to children, to their health, nutrition and education. Much has been learnt during the early years of implementation that can be built on in the future. The national Integrated Nutrition Programme, which was finalised in 1997, will be implemented through appropriate provincial frameworks. The government has declared that the PSNP will be increasingly integrated into community development, and 240 community-based nutrition programmes will be established by 2000 (Government Communication and Information System, 1998). It is hoped that the community benefits of increased access, knowledge and participation will accrue to school feeding in future.

Perhaps the greatest benefit of the PSNP has been, and will be, the fact and extent of its existence. It is very difficult for governments to remove benefits from its citizens. Having made school feeding available to children, and having justified it from a rights perspective and as a commitment to education and social development, present and future governments will find it extremely problematic to withdraw from this commitment. Many advocates, programmers and scholars, including ourselves, believe the state has a responsibility to meet the basic needs of children. Providing food at school is one way of meeting that responsibility. The fact that there are other competing priorities in nutrition, and that we have blundered in our first attempts to implement a national feeding system at primary schools, is cause for concern but not for dismay. Pressures on national economic resources will ensure that the scheme becomes more effective by better targeting, administration, community involvement and evaluation.

This evaluation has provided important feedback on the benefits and limits of school feeding for children's educational achievements. We have emphasised the need for careful attention to the gap between the aims and objectives outlined by efficacy expectations and those that can realistically be achieved in effectiveness trials, when interventions are extended into real-life contexts. Exacting assessment often tempers high hopes but, at the same time, renders increasingly sophisticated understanding of the processes and outcomes for which we strive in social programmes. It is part of the never-ending process of refinement in policy and intervention to create a better society.

REFERENCES

Babu, S. & Hallam, J. (1989). Socio-economic impacts of school feeding programmes: Empirical evidence from a South Indian village. *Food Policy, 14,* 58–66.

Bacon, E. (1992). Review of the ADD-H Comprehensive Teacher's Rating Scale. In J. Kramer & J. Conoley (Eds.), *The Eleventh Mental Measurements Yearbook* (pp 14–16). Nebraska: University of Nebraska Press.

Baker, I., Elwood, P., Hughes, J., Jones, M. & Sweetnam, P. (1978). School milk and growth in primary schoolchildren. *The Lancet, 2,* 575.

Barret, D. & Frank, D. (1987). *The effects of undernutrition on children's behavior.* Montreux: Gordon and Breach.

Beaton, G. & Ghassemi, H. (1982). Supplementary feeding programmes for young children in developing countries. *American Journal of Clinical Nutrition, 35,* 864–916.

Benton, D., Owens, D. & Parker, P. (1994). Blood glucose influences memory and attention in young adults. *Neuropsychologia, 32,* 595–607.

Campbell, D. (1969). Reforms as experiments. *American Journal of Psychology, 24,* 409–428.

Carlson, J. & Jensen, C. (1981). Reliability of the Raven Coloured Progressive Matrices Test; Age and ethnic group comparisons. *Journal of Consulting and Clinical Psychology, 49,* 320–322.

Chao, E. & Vanderkooy, P. (1989). An overview of breakfast nutrition. *Journal of the Canadian Dietetics Association, 50,* 225–228.

Cook, T. & Shadish, W. (1986). Program evaluation: The worldly science. *Annual Review of Psychology, 37,* 193–232.

D'Costa, A.G. (1992). Review of the ADD-H Comprehensive Teacher's Rating Scale. In J. Kramer & J. Conoley (Eds.), *The Eleventh Mental Measurements Yearbook* (pp 16–17). Nebraska: University of Nebraska Press.

Farran, D. (1990). Effects of intervention with disadvantaged and disabled children: A decade review. In S. Meisels & J. Shonkoff (Eds.), *Handbook of early education intervention* (pp. 501–539). Cambridge: Cambridge University Press.

Gallagher, J. (1991). Longitudinal interventions: Virtues and limitations. *American Behavioral Scientist, 34,* 431–439.

Garbarino, J. (1989). Early investment in cognitive development as a strategy of reducing poverty. *Early Education and Development, 1,* 64–76.

Gordon, A. (1986). Black education in South Africa: Psychological and sociological correlates of achievement. In L. Ekstrand (Ed.), *Ethnic minorities and immigrants in a cross-cultural perspective* (pp. 240–255). Lisse: Swets & Zeitlinger.

Government Communication and Information System. (1998). *The building has begun: Government's report to the nation '98.* Pretoria: Government Printer.

Griesel, R. & Richter, L. (1987). Psycho-social studies of malnutrition in Southern Africa. In G. Bourne (Ed.), *World review of nutrition and dietetics, Special Edition, Vol 54: Nutrition in the Gulf countries – Malnutrition and minerals* (pp. 71–104). Basel: Kruger.

Griesel, R., Richter, L. & Belciug, M. (1990). Electroencepalography and performance in a poorly nourished South African population. *South African Medical Journal, 78,* 544–547.

Griesel, R., Richter, L., Windell, P. & Oberholzer, D. (1986). A review of Southern African studies on malnutrition since 1970 – Polemics and possibilities. Fourth National Conference of the Psychological Association of South Africa, Johannesburg.

Haber, R. & Hershenson, M. (1973). *The psychology of visual perception.* New York: Holt, Rinehart & Winston.

Halpern, R. (1990). Poverty and early childhood parenting: Toward a framework for intervention. *American Journal of Orthopsychiatry, 60,* 6–18.

Harrison, D. (1995). Nutrition. In *South African Health Review 1995* (pp. 151–162). Durban: Health Systems Trust and Henry J. Kaiser Family Foundation.

Health Systems Trust. (1997). *Evaluation of the Primary School Nutrition Programme (PSNP).* Durban: Health Systems Trust.

Herman, J., Morris, L. & Fitz-Gibbon, C. (1987). *Evaluator's handbook.* Newbury Park, CA: Sage.

Jacoby, E., Cueto, S. & Pollitt, E. (1998). When science and politics listen to each other: Good prospects from a new school breakfast program in Peru. *American Journal of Clinical Nutrition, 67,* S795–S797.

Jones-Wilson, F. (1991). Alleviating the force of poverty on urban poor children. *Early Child Development and Care, 73,* 103–120.

Jooste, P., Wolmarans, P. & Oelofse, A. (1993). *A needs assessment for school feeding programmes in low socio-economic areas.* Cape Town: Medical Research Council.

Kopp, C. (1987). Regulation of distress and negative emotions: A developmental view. *Developmental Psychology, 25,* 343–354.

Levinger, B. (1984). School feeding programmes: Myth and potential. *Prospects, 14,* 369–376.

Liddell, C. & Kemp, K. (1993). Providing services for young children in South Africa. *International Journal of Educational Development, 7,* 127–131.

Lipsey, M. (1998). Design sensitivity: Statistical power for applied experimental research. In L. Rogman & D. Rog (Eds.), *Handbook of applied social research methods* (pp. 39–67). Thousand Oaks, CA: Sage.

Makorapong, T. (1987). Hungry children: Women in action. *World Health Forum, 8,* 25–27.

McKay, H., Sinisterra, L., McKay, A., Gomez, H. & Lloreda, P. (1978). Improving cognitive ability in chronically deprived children. *Science, 200,* 270–278.

Myeni, A. & McGrath, E. (1990). Swaziland: Perspectives in school health. *Journal of School Health, 60,* 351–356.

National Progressive Primary Health Care Network. (1995). *Rapid appraisal of the Primary School Nutrition Programme: An assessment of the impact of the programme on beneficiaries. Final Report for the RDP in the Office of the State President.* Johannesburg: National Progressive Primary Health Care Network.

Pollitt, E. (1994). Poverty and child development: Relevance of research in developing countries to the United States. *Child Development, 65,* 283–295.

Pollitt, E., Cueto, S. & Jacoby, E. (1998). Fasting and cognition in well-nourished and undernourished schoolchildren: A review of three experimental studies. *American Journal of Clinical Nutrition, 67,* S779–S784.

Pollitt, E., Gorman, K.S., Engle, P.L., Martorell, R. & Riviera, J. (1993). Early supplementary feeding and cognition: Effects over two decades. *Monographs of the Society for Research in Child Development. NO. 235, 58*(7).

Pollitt, E., Golub, M., Gorman, K., Grantham-McGregor, S., Levitsky, D., Schurch, B., Strupp, B. & Wachs, T. (1996). *A reconceptualization of the effects of undernutrition on children's biological, psychosocial and behavioral development.* Social Policy Report: Society for Research in Child Development, X, No 5.

Raven, J., Court, J. & Raven, J. (1990). *Coloured Progressive Matrices – Sets A, A$_b$, B.* London: Oxford Psychologists Press.

Reichardt, C. & Mark, M. (1998). Quasi-experimentation. In L. Bickman & D. Rog (Eds.), *Handbook of applied social research methods* (pp. 193–227). Thousand Oaks, CA: Sage.

Reitsma, G., Vorster, H., Venter, C., Labadarios, D., de Ridder, J. & Louw, M. (1994). A school feeding scheme did not improve nutritional status of a group of black children. *South African Journal of Clinical Nutrition, 7,* 10-18.

Richter, L. & Griesel, L. (1994). Malnutrition, low birthweight and related influences on psychological development. In A. Dawes & D. Donald (Eds.), *Childhood and adversity: Psychological perspectives from South African research* (pp. 66–91). Cape Town: David Philip.

Richter, L., Rose, C. & Griesel, R. (1997). Cognitive and behavioural effects of a school breakfast. *South African Medical Journal, 87,* 93–100.

Rogosa, D., Brandt, D. & Zimowski, M. (1982). A growth curve approach to the masurement of change. *Psychological Bulletin, 92,* 726–748.

Sattler, J. (1986). *Assessment of children* (3rd ed.). San Diego: Jerome M. Sattler.

Simeon, D. (1998). School feeding in Jamaica: A review of its evaluation. *American Journal of Clinical Nutrition, 67,* S790–S794.

Soemantri, A., Pollitt, E. & Kim, I. (1986). Iron deficiency anaemia and educational achievement among school-age children in a rural community in Indonesia. *American Journal of Clinical Nutrition, 42,* 1221–1228.

Strupp, B. & Levitsky, D. (1995). Enduring cognitive effects of early malnutrition – A theoretical reappraisal. *Journal of Nutrition, 125,* S2221–S2232.

Taylor, N. (1989). *Falling at the first hurdle.* Educational Policy Unit Research Report No 1, University of the Witwatersrand.

Ullmann, R., Sleator, E. & Sprague, R. (1988). *ACTeRS.* Illinois: MeiriTecd.

Vorster, H., Barnard, H., Reitsma, G., Venter, C., Silvis, N., Greyvenstein, L., Bosman, M. & Kruger, A. (1994). Nutritional status of eight to ten-year-old white, black, coloured and Indian boys in a multi-cultural school. *South African Journal of Food Science and Nutrition,*

6, 18–23.

Walker, A., Labadarios, D., Vorster, H., Glatthaar, I. & Meulenberg-Buskens, I. (1993). Dietary interventions in South African populations: Where are we going? *South African Journal of Clinical Nutrition*, 6, 3–5.

Wechsler, D. (1949). *The Wechsler Intelligence Scale for Children*. New York: The Psychological Corporation.

Wigton, A., Makan, B. & McCoy, D. (1997). Health and nutrition. In S. Robinson & L. Biersteker (Eds.), *First call: The South African children's budget* (pp 33–64). Cape Town: IDASA.

WORKING WITH AGGRESSIVE PRESCHOOLERS

5

A systemic community-based intervention

HEATHER JONES PETERSEN & RONELLE CAROLISSEN

BACKGROUND AND AIMS

On the outskirts of Cape Town lies Lavender Hill, a coloured working-class community of about 60 000 people. It is subject to high levels of unemployment, gangsterism, and community and domestic violence, and has few social services. This chapter describes a violence prevention intervention implemented at preschool level. The programme was initiated by Community Psychological Empowerment Services (COPES), one of the projects of the Trauma Centre for Survivors of Violence and Torture based in Cape Town, and the New World Foundation (NWF), a community-based NGO.

The NWF has operated a community centre in Lavender Hill for some 15 years, and aims to assist the local community to work against poverty, oppression and personal powerlessness. Among other projects, the NWF runs a preschool in Lavender Hill that serves about 300 children aged 2 to 6, as well as a satellite preschool in Vrygrond, a nearby informal settlement. Both preschools share in many of the problems endemic to under-resourced preschools, where the child–teacher ratio is high and most teachers are not formally trained. The children exhibit a range of emotional and behavioural problems in the classroom with which the teachers feel ill equipped to cope. They include sexually provocative behaviour, aggression, enuresis, developmental delays and excessive fearfulness.

The NWF contacted the first author with the request to address some of the difficulties in the Lavender Hill preschool. The organisation was concerned in particular with the fact that their teachers used corporal punishment as their primary form of discipline, and furthermore seemed unable to manage the considerable range of children's behaviour problems evidenced in the classroom. They requested a full assessment of the problems and recommendations on how to address them.

Initial observation of children in the classroom by the authors confirmed that there was indeed a range of significant behavioural and developmental problems. One child was echolalic, for example, unbeknown to the teachers, who described him as 'naughty' for parroting them. Later diagnostic testing found two children with pervasive developmental disorder and many severely mentally handicapped children, some of whom demonstrated the impact of foetal alcohol syndrome. It was decided to conduct a systematic needs assessment in the preschool. Teachers, parents and pupils were involved in this process.

Initially, two focus group meetings were held with the teaching staff. A few parents from each class were also included, to assess their definition of both the difficulties and successes they experienced with the children. The wider parent body was then informed about the needs assessment in a well-attended Parent–Teachers Association (PTA) meeting. Those who were interested in participating were invited to contact their child's teacher in order to be included in the assessment. As a result, 20 interviews with parents from all classes were arranged. Many parents of children from the 4-, 5- and 6-year-old classes volunteered to be interviewed, but none from the 2- and 3-year-old classes. Teachers made special arrangements with two sets of parents from these younger classes to be interviewed. Developmental evaluations were conducted with the children of those parents interviewed to get a more accurate picture of their behavioural, emotional and cognitive abilities.

The needs assessment of the teachers and parents revealed that both groups experienced significant problems. Teachers reported that their greatest difficulty was the high percentage of aggressive children in the classroom – estimated to be between 25 and 50% of all the children. They complained that these children disrupted their lessons and absorbed much of their attention. Most of the teachers reported suffering from physical and emotional symptoms including headaches, migraines, muscle pain, irritability and fatigue. They attributed these symptoms to the stresses they experienced in the classroom.

Parents reported that the many stressors in their everyday lives negatively affected their ability to be effective caregivers. The most common stressors were domestic violence, unemployment, financial problems, alcoholism, and exhaustion due to long hours at work. Almost half of the parents experienced similar difficulties to the teachers in managing their children's aggressive and non-compliant behaviour. They reported that their children were physically and verbally aggressive towards siblings, peers and, to a lesser extent, adults. They were verbally aggressive towards other children, and shouted insults at adults. Many parents described how difficult it was to get their children to comply with requests to wash, get dressed, go to bed and, most worrying for them, return home at night. A few parents said their 4- and 5- year-old children stayed out until 22h00 or later. The primary form of discipline used by all parents was hitting their children, which brought only temporary compliance.

The assessment of the children included a qualitative evaluation, which took the form of classroom observation and individual play therapy, as well as a quantitative evaluation in the form of diagnostic assessments. Formal testing was done to establish possible developmental delays, since behavioural problems in children of this age could have been the result of a developmental delay. The test battery included an intelligence test (the Junior South African Individual Scale – the GIQ8 Afrikaans version, with the use of vernacular terms), the Beery-Buktenica Developmental Test of Visual–Motor Integration (Beery, 1997) and the Draw-a-Person test. The results revealed pervasively low verbal skills, with only one child managing to score in the low average range. A number of behavioural problems was evident: approximately 25% of the children had poor impulse control and low frustration tolerance. This supported the teachers' experiences.

The recommendations from the needs assessment included a pragmatic behaviour management training course for teachers, a parent training group and therapeutic groups for aggressive children. This package of interventions constituted a major task, and COPES was established as a Trauma Centre project to undertake this work at the NWF and elsewhere. In addition, COPES agreed to help the NWF with other developmental evaluations and appropriate referrals. COPES now focuses its interventions mostly on at-risk preschoolers who have been identified as being aggressive, disruptive and oppositional by their teachers. Its objective is to reduce levels of aggression in the preschoolers, and to increase their social skills and prosocial behaviour. The NWF also responded in other ways to the problems highlighted by the assessment, taking measures to improve the quality of the education at the preschool. These included the employment of a full-time remedial teacher and a part-time early learning specialist. Occupational therapy students were also brought into the community centre to work with children requiring special attention.

THEORETICAL BASIS OF THE INTERVENTION

Life-course research has shown that there are different pathways in the development of aggressive and delinquent behaviour from childhood to adulthood (Loeber & Stouthamer-Loeber, 1998). However, there is evidence that aggression is a behaviour that is frequently stable across time (Farrington, 1991; Huesmann, Eron, Lefkowitz & Walder, 1984; Patterson, DeBaryshe & Ramsey, 1989). Many research examples can be cited. For example, the longitudinal Cambridge Study in Delinquent Development (Farrington, 1991) found evidence of continuity of aggression and violence from ages 8 to 32. Huesmann *et al.* (1984) have also reported stability in the trait across a similar period and across generations. An aggressive preschooler is likely to become a primary school child with a behaviour disorder (oppositional defiant disorder). In addition, non-compliance, irritability, inattentiveness and impulsivity in toddlers have been associated with conduct problems in middle childhood, and to a lesser extent, in adolescence (Offord & Bennett, 1994; Conduct Problems Prevention Research (CPPR) Group, 1992; Loeber & Stouthamer-Loeber, 1998; Moffitt, 1993).

These findings are cause for concern, particularly as conduct disorders are apparently not rare in childhood. In the United States there is some evidence that the incidence of conduct problems in young children is growing (Webster-Stratton & Hammond, 1997). Depending on criteria and type of study, it is estimated that 7–25% of North American children are affected, with higher rates occurring in boys than in girls. South African research, while quite limited in extent, suggests that conduct problems, particularly among young males living in poor communities, are also extensive (Dawes *et al.*, 1997).

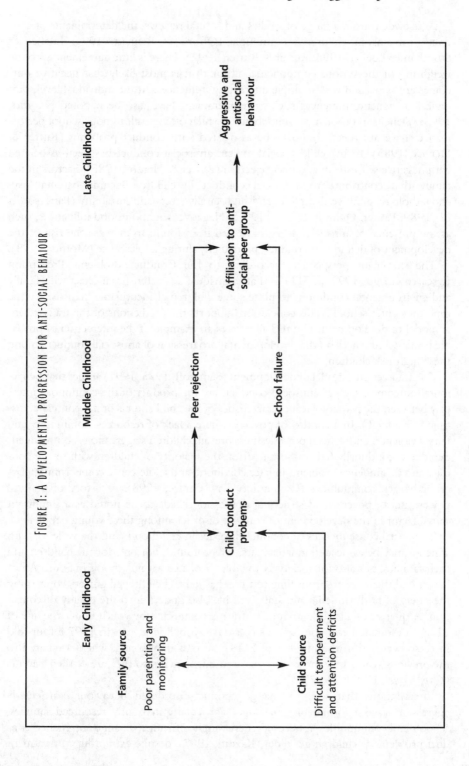

FIGURE 1: A DEVELOPMENTAL PROGRESSION FOR ANTI-SOCIAL BEHAVIOUR

Early Childhood

Middle Childhood

Late Childhood

Family source

Poor parenting and monitoring

Child source

Difficult temperament and attention deficits

Child conduct probems

Peer rejection

School failure

Affiliation to anti-social peer group

Aggressive and antisocial behaviour

As is evident from a range of studies and several reviews, the determinants of conduct problems in children are multiple (Offord & Bennett, 1994; Loeber & Stouthamer-Loeber, 1998; Rutter & Rutter, 1992). There is little agreement as to the weighting of the various components, although it is most likely that negative outcomes are associated with multiple interacting influences. At the individual level, biological or genetic influences such as temperament have also been noted (Moffitt, 1993). Deficits in problem solving-abilities, which often result in poor school performance, have also been found to be associated with conduct problems (Rutter & Herzov, 1985). In the child's social milieu, antisocial conduct has been associated with negative self-esteem and peer rejection (Rutter & Herzov, 1985). Factors in the family that contribute to antisocial conduct in children include parental psychopathology, punitive discipline, and high family stress and instability (Patterson *et al.*, 1989; Rutter, Quinton & Yule, 1977). Negative neighbourhood influences, such as the presence of antisocial peers, have also been found to increase the risk of the development of delinquent conduct, particularly during adolescence (Moffitt, 1993).

The dominant perspective, according to the Conduct Problems Prevention Research Group (1992, p. 511), is that 'individual characteristics interact with family and environmental conditions to place some children at identifiable high risk by the time they enter school'. This conclusion supports the predictions of the transactional model of development. Figure 1 illustrates an example of the interaction of probable primary influences on the developmental progression of antisocial conduct among these high-risk children.

The transactional model of development (Sameroff, 1975; 1991) argues that behavioural outcomes, such as antisocial conduct, are the product of the continuous interplay between the psychological characteristics of the child and his or her context across time (Chapter 1). In a context of poverty, where a lack of resources, community and family violence, and general powerlessness prevail, children's aggression is both engendered and continually fed. In South Africa, the majority of children with severe conduct and delinquency problems in later childhood and adolescence come from impoverished black communities (Community Law Centre, 1998). A history of political powerlessness, poverty and structural oppression needs to be noted as a significant causal factor in the development of conduct disorder among these young people.

The social consequences of conduct disorder in childhood, and the violence with which it may be associated in later years, are profound, not only for the children and their families, but also for society as a whole. Violence within schools in South Africa has caused their closure from time to time, has led to heightened anxiety concerning the safety of both students and staff, and has also undermined the quality of education. A quarter of all crime in South Africa is committed by youth under the age of 21 at an estimated cost to taxpayers of over R15 billion a year. In 1997 a four-fold increase occurred in the number of 7–14-year-olds imprisoned, when compared to the previous year. Many more were released uncharged into the care of their parents (*Cape Times*, 17 July 1997).

Interventions that seek to change conduct-disordered behaviour, particularly aggression, face a formidable challenge. Particularly in poorly resourced families, schools and communities, it becomes increasingly difficult to change entrenched conduct problems as children get older (Kazdin, 1987), despite extraordinary treatment efforts. The implication is that early intervention in the preschool period is necessary if conduct problems are to be prevented from becoming well-established patterns of behaviour (CPPR Group, 1992). There is therefore considerable acceptance among mental health professionals of the value of preventive work with high-risk young children and their families (e.g. Yoshikawa, 1994).

Transactional development models suggest that early interventions may usefully focus on the behavioural exchanges that take place between parents and their children (Sameroff, 1991). Interventions likely to influence the pattern of parent–child exchange include a focus on remedying the deficit in the child, helping the family to redefine the child's problem, and improving parenting skills.

Parental re-education is seen to be of great importance, especially in contexts where there is a high prevalence of adolescent parenting, and where a community suffers significant deprivation. Thus parent training has become one of the major strategies used to reduce conduct problems in children (Webster-Stratton & Herbert, 1993). This form of intervention assumes that as a result of parenting skill deficits, negative interactions within the family develop and sustain aggressive behaviour in children (Offord & Bennett, 1994; Kazdin, 1987; Patterson, Reid, Jones & Conger, 1975). There is well-established evidence of the short-term effectiveness in clinical populations of a treatment strategy called Parent Management Training (PMT), with the majority of the children (and their parents) showing significant improvement (Webster-Stratton, 1985).

In certain cases, however, these interventions have not been particularly effective. Webster-Stratton and Hammond (1997) have argued that the reason for their failure might be risk factors which are not affected by parent training. These would include factors in the child, as well as influences operating in other contexts such as the school and the neighbourhood. Traditionally, child factors have been addressed in programmes that focus on changing the behaviour of the individual child. These have shown some success. However, combined approaches are likely to be most effective. For example, in a study which compared the effectiveness of parent training (PT), child training (CT) and a combined approach (PT–CT), the combined approach produced more significant improvements across a broad range of outcomes. These included improved child behaviour, and better parent–child interactions and child social skills (Webster-Stratton & Hammond, 1997). The FAST track programme (CPPR Group, 1992) has also argued that such multi-modal interventions which include interventions with the children, their parents and their schools are likely to have the greatest chance of success.

In summary, interventions with conduct-disordered and antisocial children have reported improved success when they
• are preventive in nature
• take place with the preschool and early grade school child
• extend beyond parent training
• extend beyond the child to the family by concentrating on the interactional axes of development
• include other normative institutions in the community, such as the church and the school (CPPR Group, 1992).

The first author of this chapter was involved at an earlier point in an intervention programme with conduct-disordered children and their parents in Chicago. She believed that the intervention model developed by Webster-Stratton and Hammond (1997) could be adapted successfully for the COPES project to address the problems identified in the Lavender Hill preschool. The specific objectives of the COPES intervention were the following:

• to reduce the level of aggressive behaviour in the preschool children
• to increase their pro-social behaviour
• to increase the competency of the teachers to reinforce the children's positive behaviour and to set limits non-punitively
• to increase the competency of the parents to reinforce the children's positive behaviour and set limits non-punitively

DESCRIPTION OF PROJECT

The phases of the intervention were as follows:
• a two-week assessment phase
• the intervention itself, which took place over eight weeks
• a follow-up evaluation after another two weeks

Activities were structured around groups of parents, children and teachers who met separately, but in parallel, over the eight weeks. The parent and teacher groups usually met at a central venue in the community while the children's groups met at their schools. The programme began with teachers identifying the aggressive children in their classroom. If the parents were willing, the teacher arranged an interview between the parents and the COPES team. This initial extended interview with the psychologist was considered important to build rapport with the parents and demystify the role of the psychologist (an unfamiliar professional to the target community). The clinician also used the interview to discuss the parents' difficulties with their children, to explore any family problems, to reduce levels of blame felt by parents about their children's problems, and to explain the intervention. Finally, the first interview was also used to complete a battery of measures, later used to evaluate the success of the intervention (the 'pre-tests').

Following completion of the assessments, parents were advised that their children would only be accepted into the programme if they agreed to attend the parent training component of the intervention. At the end of the intervention programme, a graduation ceremony was held for parents, teachers and children. All three sets of participants received certificates if they had attended at least 80% of the sessions. Representatives were invited from the organisations involved in the initiative, and parents were given the opportunity to talk about their experiences. The graduation process was important in achieving closure for trainers, teachers, parents and children.

The parent training group

Activities for the parents were arranged to
• teach parenting skills
• help them to understand their child's behaviour
• increase the empathy felt for the child

• support them in their frustrations with their child, as well as with their personal emotional difficulties

Components of Webster-Stratton's parenting programme, especially video material, were used, together with material developed by the COPES team (Webster-Stratton, 1994). A typical parent group would start with a revision of skills-based parenting homework from the previous week. This gave parents the opportunity to solve child management problems, and to receive support and encouragement if their attempts were not successful. Role-plays were used both to re-enact and solve problems. In addition, members were encouraged to discuss personal difficulties that impacted upon their ability to do the parenting homework. A strong sense of support and cohesion developed rapidly in almost all groups. After the review of the home tasks and role-plays, new material was presented and discussed. Video clips and role-plays were used to demonstrate and reinforce the specific skill. New homework was then given based on the skills learnt.

Here is an example taken from a recording of one of the groups:

'Peter' [the child] presents with aggressive behaviour in that he consistently fights with other children in the classroom. 'Mary' [the mother] was given homework the previous week to spend more positive time with Peter by playing with him for short periods in the evening. This week she reports to the group that she was surprised to see how well Peter responded to her during the periods of play. She confesses that this exercise has been difficult as she has forgotten how to play and feels silly and uncomfortable about doing it. She also says that her own parents never played with her and she thought that children's play involved only other children and not adults. Some parents in the group echo her belief about children's play but say that they will try to play with their children more often because they can see how the positive attention improves the interactions between them and their child. Mary thus feels supported in her insecurities as other parents are experiencing the same feelings. She is also encouraged to persevere because of other parents' positive experience of the exercise.

To provide an alternative forum where parents could express opinions about the intervention process and to encourage continued participation, a community visitor was appointed in consultation with the host community organisation (NWF). The visitor made two home visits to the parents, once during the first two weeks, and again in the last two weeks of the intervention. During this time the psychologist played a supervisory and supportive role. When the cycle of groups was complete, the community worker, together with the staff from the NWF, attempted to integrate the participants into the life of the community centre. The community centre did most of the follow-up work, where required. The community worker met regularly with the psychologist and requested specific 'booster' groups for the parents on a six-weekly basis.

The teachers' group

The activities of the teachers' group were arranged to
• teach teachers behaviour modification principles to reinforce children's positive

behaviour in the classroom and set limits non-punitively
- help teachers to develop proficiency in these skills by setting homework and help-ing them to evaluate successes and failures
- assist teachers to think critically about behavioural problems by discussing the etio-logical factors underlying inappropriate behaviours
- support teachers and teach them how to de-stress

A typical example of what happened in these groups is given below:

'Denise' [the teacher] expressed concern about 'Wayne' [the pupil] during our session on 'special inappropriate behaviours'. He would go into the dolls' cor-ner at school and imitate adult sexual behaviour with one of the large dolls, despite her attempts at distracting him. This would also impact on the other children as they would either laugh or imitate his behaviour at different times. Therefore, while dealing with themes on 'my body' in the classroom and about 'good touching' and 'bad touching', she talked about inappropriate sexual behaviour, directing it at the whole class. She had also previously called in Wayne's mother to discuss this matter. His behaviour abated for a short while, but then reverted to the old pattern. Different teachers had different sugges-tions, such as enlisting the help of a social worker, looking at the possibility of Wayne's own possible sexual abuse, or the possibility of his exposure to adult sexuality.

When focusing on what to do in the classroom, most teachers found it diffi-cult to formulate a coherent plan. We spoke about the need to provide Wayne with close supervision in order to intervene before his behaviour becomes sex-ualised. We recommended the need to integrate Wayne into appropriate play with peers who were nurturing but also displayed some leadership in the class. It was suggested that they draw on a session in the programme called 'tangible rewards' to set up an individual star chart with Wayne. The teachers were told that they should select an appropriate behaviour to substitute for the inappro-priate one and then reward him for displaying the appropriate behaviour. For example, they could reward him with a star for every half an hour during free play at school that he plays with his peers by sharing toys without fighting or bullying. The stars would be totalled on a daily basis and liberal praise given to Wayne for stars earned. Various levels of reward would be offered depending upon the number of stars earned in that day. The rewards should be reinforcing to the child. They could be social, such as running an errand (thus giving him responsibility and status), or tangible (such as sweets). Gradually, the trading of stars for rewards should become weekly (on Fridays) with only social rewards offered. The next step would be to phase them out altogether, replacing the stars with praise and spot rewards for good behaviour displayed in the class-room.

The following week Denise reported that Wayne's inappropriate behaviour had decreased considerably. She felt that previously he had seldom received pos-itive attention because she found his behaviour so offensive. By being able to draw him into positive activities in the classroom, his need to demand attention for negative behaviours was considerably reduced. In addition, Denise also spoke to his mother again and recommended that she speak with a trusted social worker, if only for help and support. Denise agreed to continue to monitor the situation to see how Wayne progressed.

The children's group

It was not too difficult to utilise the American content of the programme (and the videotapes) for the parents' group, but the content of the children's programme had to be revised substantially. Webster-Stratton's children's programme was too advanced developmentally to transfer directly to children in the Lavender Hill community.

The activities arranged for the children's group aimed to
- introduce them to the notion of rules and consequences with rewards for positive behaviour
- teach specific social and behavioural skills, such as taking turns, sharing and paying compliments to each other
- teach anger management and basic problem-solving skills
- teach them how to identify feelings in themselves and others

The groups were active and playful, with a clear structure and group rituals (songs and activities) to mark transitions and facilitate group cohesion. Puppets were used to convey concepts such as those related to anger management. Here is an example of what happened in such a group:

> When the group started, 'Angela' [the child] found it difficult to adhere to the group structure. She did not move from the introductory song to the revision of what had happened during the previous session when the chime sounded. She would play and sometimes fight with some of the other children and the group would have to wait for her to join. The facilitator increased praise to the children who promptly moved to the next activity. In addition she rewarded children who joined the group promptly by giving them stars. After two sessions, Angela's disruptive behaviour in the group abated as she was getting more rewards and attention for positive behaviours.

OUTCOMES AND EVALUATION

Procedure and assessment

Two preschools in Lavender Hill were selected to act as treatment schools, and two more with similar facilities from the same area were selected to act as comparison schools. The latter schools received no intervention. All the interviews and interventions were conducted at the child's preschool or nearby community centre, depending on available space.

To be included in the study required that
- the child be between 4 and 6 years of age
- the child have no debilitating physical impairment, cognitive deficit or history of psychosis
- the primary referral problem be child misconduct

- teachers and parents rate the child as having clinically significant behaviour problems according to the Achenbach Child Behavior Checklist or the Behar Preschool Behavior Checklist

For those in the treatment group, the parents or caregivers were also required to agree to participate in an eight-week parenting course with sequential sessions lasting an hour and a half, as well as in a pre- and post-intervention interview of two or three hours.

Initially, each child underwent a developmental assessment in order to rule out developmental delays. The COPES team was so concerned by the low cognitive scores which children obtained that they decided to assess an entire preschool class to see whether the children with behavioural problems represented a skewed population. Altogether 49 children at the preschool (23 girls and 26 boys) were screened for developmental delays. Their mean age was 5 years and 8 months, and they were all about to enter the first grade of primary school in January of the following year. The children were assessed in their home language (mostly Afrikaans) using vernacular terms with the use of the JSAIS – GIQ8, the Beery Visual–Motor Integration test, and the Draw-a-Person. This assessment indicated that the cognitive abilities of 65% of the children were below average, with 24% in the mentally handicapped range. Meetings were held with school clinics and other agencies that worked in this area to ascertain whether these scores reflected their assessments, and they corroborated the results.

For the study itself we were interested in three main variables:
- the children's aggressive behaviour
- the parents' competence in managing the children's behaviour
- the teachers' competence in managing the children's behaviour

Aggressive behaviour in the children was the major variable of interest, and two scales were used to assess it. These were the Parent Report of the Child Behavior Checklist (Achenbach, 1991) and the Teacher Report of the Preschool Behavior Checklist (Behar & Stringfield, 1974). Aggression is defined by both Achenbach and Behar as including verbal aggression in which the child threatens people, teases excessively, displays temper tantrums, screams, or is argumentative. In addition, aggression is defined in physical terms. Here children destroy their own or other children's possessions, and fight with, bully or physically attack other children. The definition also includes non-compliance (disobedience at home and at school), passive aggressive acts, and stubborn or irascible behaviour.

The Parenting Stress Index (Abidin, 1983) was used to assess the competency of the parents before and after the intervention. Competency is defined in this index as practical child development knowledge, child management skills, and the confidence to use these skills. Teacher competency was assessed using the Teacher Competency Questionnaire (COPES, 1996a), in which teacher competency was defined as the ability to manage classroom behaviour effectively and to feel in control of the situation. A developmental history questionnaire (COPES, 1996b) provided demographic as well as psychosocial background information. In addition, all parents were asked to complete a Violence Questionnaire (COPES, 1996c) in order to provide a deeper understanding of how violence in the community impacts upon their own and their children's lives.

Of the parents, 38% had a primary school education (Grade 7 or below), 25% had completed Grade 8, and 16% had completed Grade 10. Only 8% of the parents had completed their schooling and matriculated. Of the participating parents 33% were unemployed. Of the women, 62% were single parents.

Levels of violence to which children and their parents were exposed in this community was a key issue in the project. Parental reports of such exposure are presented in Table 1. From the table it is evident that both children and parents in this community are exposed to a range of violent events both at home and in the neighbourhood. Noteworthy are the high levels of parental fears of the violence in the neighbourhood as well as the high levels of assault they have experienced. Nearly half the children in the sample have witnessed violence in their own homes.

Table 1: Responses to the exposure to violence questionnaire

Parental reports of family exposure to violence	% respondents experiencing violence
• Parent afraid of gang violence in their community	77%
• Parent has had a violent experience with a gang member (raped; shot at; robbed or physically molested)	19%
• A family member or close friend has had a violent experience with a gang member	50%
• Parent had witnessed a violent gang-related incident	65%
• Their children had witnessed a violent gang-related incident	39%
• Parents are afraid to walk around their neighbourhood at night	65%
• Parents hear gunshots or violent fighting while at home, typically at night	81%
• House had been burgled	8%
• Parents have been raped, sexually or physically assaulted by a relative, friend or partner	48%
• The adults in the child's house have physically violent fights	46%
• The children have witnessed this fighting	42%
• The child in the programme has seen parents being hit	39%
• A family member is in a gang	15%

Altogether 52 children from the treatment schools were identified as aggressive by their teachers, and were rated by them on the Behar Preschool Behavior Questionnaire. Initially a comparison group of 45 children was selected in the same way from the non-intervention schools. However, 8 were excluded, because they were developmentally delayed. The comparison group that received no intervention therefore comprised 37 children. These were also rated by their teachers on the Behar Preschool Behavior Questionnaire.

Not all the parents completed Achenbach's Child Behavior Checklist, because they either did not complete the post-programme assessments or they moved out of the area prior to the completion of the intervention. Therefore, 26 children in the comparison group and 48 from the treatment group were rated by their parents on this checklist. For similar reasons, not all parents completed Abidin's Parenting Stress Index (31 and 48 from the comparison and treatment groups respectively).

The children participating in the evaluation of the intervention were aged between

4 and 6 (mean age = 5.1 years). The mean age of the treatment group was 5.3 years, and of the comparison group 4.9 years.

Results of the intervention

The outcome of the intervention was assessed by comparing the differences between the children who had been the subjects of the intervention with those who had not. Three questions were investigated:

1. Did the intervention reduce the children's aggressive behaviour, as rated by their parents and teachers?
2. Did the parents feel themselves to be more competent after the intervention?
3. Did the teachers' feelings of competency improve?

Two analyses were performed on each of the measures used to answer these questions. A two-way split-plot Analysis of Variance (ANOVA) was used to determine whether there had been any changes due to the intervention. This analysis compared the two groups (comparison and intervention groups) at two points in time (both before and after the intervention), and compared the degree of change in the two groups over time (repeated measures). The findings are summarised in Table 2.

Did the intervention reduce the children's aggressive behaviour, as rated by their parents and teachers?

The teachers' ratings. The Preschool Behavior Questionnaire's hostile-aggressive scale scores were converted into percentiles before analysis. The two-way ANOVA results indicated that only the main effect for time (the difference from before and after the intervention) was significant (pre-test mean = 90.04 and post-test mean = 84.00; with $F(1, 80) = 13.049$ and $p = 0.0005$). Multiple comparisons using Tukey's HSD test, produced one significant finding, namely the difference in scores before and after intervention in the treatment group ($t' = 5.423$; $p<0.01$). Here the post-test mean was 83.24, and the pre-intervention mean was 90.59. These results indicate that there was a decrease in the children's hostile-aggressive scores after the intervention. The reduction in the number of children in the treatment group with scores in the clinically significant range also lends support to the belief that the intervention had some success in reducing aggressiveness.

The Parents' ratings. The parents' raw scores on the aggressive behaviour scale of the Child Behavior Checklist were converted to T scores and analysed using the split-plot two-way ANOVA. The results indicate that there were no significant main effects for group or time, but the interaction effect of group and time was significant ($F(1, 72) = 11.743$; $p = 0.0010$). The simple effect differences were explored by using Tukey's HSD tests which indicated that there was a significant change ($t' = 4.626$; $p<0.01$) in the treatment group following the intervention (pre-intervention T score mean = 67.83; post-intervention T score mean = 62.27). There was no change in the comparison group from pre- to post- testing. The results on this scale support the results from the teachers in suggesting that the intervention had some effect in reducing aggression. Although the two groups of children differed significantly in aggressiveness prior to the intervention, only the treatment group's scores decreased significantly at the second testing. The significant drop in the number of scores in the clinically significant range of the children in the treatment group after the intervention gives added support to the efficacy of the intervention.

TABLE 2: SUMMARISED RESULTS OF THE INTERVENTION		
Question	**Measures**	**Intervention outcomes**
• Did the intervention reduce the children's aggressive behaviour?	• Teacher rating on the Preschool Child Behavior Checklist (Hostile Aggressive Scale) (Behar & Springfield, 1974)	Teacher ratings • A statistically significant decline in the number of hostile aggressive children was reported by the teachers of children in the treatment group (from 72.5% to 47%) (McNemar test Chi²(1) = 9.600; p = 0.0020). • There was no difference in the comparison group scores from pre to post-testing.
	• Parent rating on the Child Behavior Checklist (Achenbach, 1991)	Parent ratings • A statistically significant drop in aggressive behaviour was reported by parents of treatment group children. Children in the clinical range dropped from 43% to 21.6% after the intervention (McNemar test Chi²(1) = 5.263, p = 0.0218). • There was no difference in the comparison group scores from pre- to post-testing.
• Did the parents feel more competent after intervention? • Did the teacher's feelings of competence improve?	• Parenting Stress Index (Abidin, 1983) • Teacher Competency Questionnaire (COPES, 1996a)	• Only the treatment group evidenced statistically improved parenting competence following the intervention. However, the degree of improvement was relatively small • Of 45 teachers, 39 (86%) rated themselves as more competent following their training

Did the parents feel themselves to be more competent after the intervention?

A two-way ANOVA was performed on the percentiles of the Parent Stress Index. The results indicated that neither the interaction effect ($F(1, 74) = 1.067$; $p = 0.3060$), nor the main effect for group was significant ($F(1, 74) = 0.364$; $p = 0.5483$). However, the pre-post difference (combining both groups) was significant ($F(1, 74) = 5.863$; $p = 0.0179$; post-test mean = 75.59 and pre-test mean = 81.62). Tukey's HSD test was performed on the simple effects to explore the results further. Key findings here were that there was no difference between the comparison group (M = 75.82, SD = 17.18) and intervention group (M = 75.46, SD = 19.87) means following the intervention. Also, there was no change in the comparison group between the two times of measurement. However, the treatment group did improve significantly following the intervention (t' = 4.024; p<0.01; pre-intervention mean = 83.19 and post-intervention mean = 75.46). These results indicate that the intervention programme received by the parents of the children in the treatment group had some effect in improving the parental competency scores, but it did not increase their sense of competency to a point where it exceeded the group of parents who did not attend the programme.

Did the teachers' feelings of competency improve?

From their responses on the Teacher Competency Questionnaire, there was a strong indication that the teachers felt better able to manage difficult behaviour in their classrooms after the intervention (86% of the 45 teachers).

Discussion and conclusion

This preliminary evaluation of an intervention with aggressive preschoolers produced promising results. The programme was effective in reducing the expression of aggression by the children, as indicated by both parent and teacher ratings. The parents' sense of competence as caregivers increased, and there was a strong indication that the teachers also experienced an increase in their ability to manage their classrooms effectively.

Clearly the evaluation has a number of limitations. Overall, the number of participants was small, and the children had to meet a number of criteria before they could be selected for the programme. Sampling procedures were such that it was not possible to ensure that the groups started off as equivalent. Indeed, they differed significantly in the way parents reported on their children's aggressive behaviour. Despite this, there are strong suggestions that the intervention effected positive change.

Longitudinal assessment of these children would be the acid test of whether the effects of the intervention could be maintained over the longer term. It would also help to indicate the nodal points at which further intervention might be necessary. While the programme succeeded in reducing aggressive conduct in the short term, it should be noted that poverty has been pinpointed as a major factor that limits the maintenance of treatment effects (Cousins & Weiss, 1993). Given that these children were drawn from a very poor community, it would be unrealistic to imagine that a one-off intervention will prevent the emergence of behaviour disorders in the longer term. The FAST track programme (CPPR Group, 1992) argues that a multi-modal intervention programme needs to take place at school entry and at the transition into middle school (grade 6). Experience suggests violence prevention also needs to work with the individual, the family and the community, and to acknowledge the dynamic influence that the one has on the other. The COPES preschool programme could therefore be seen as the first phase of a more comprehensive prevention programme.

There is a clear link in the current intervention, with the three strategies identified by Sameroff (1991) as important from a transactional perspective. These are remediation of the initial deficit, redefinition of the problem, and re-education of the child's social network. In the first place, the child groups of the COPES preschool programme ameliorated the aggressive-impulsive behaviours of the children by teaching them alternative behaviours (e.g. talking instead of hitting, calming oneself down when angry, and problem solving). Additionally, the focus on positive reinforcement to foster self-esteem in the teacher and parent groups remediated the deficit by encouraging adaptive behaviours in the children. Secondly, in terms of the redefinition of the problem, the COPES programme situated aggression and violence in a structural context of poverty and political powerlessness. Both parents and teachers discussed the consequences of this on individual and family life and the social stressors and problems that it generates. This redefinition enabled parents and teachers to see the problem as the result of a social process and prevented them from feeling solely responsible. Sameroff's third point, that of re-education, is the core of the intervention.

Internationally, parent training has had poor results in impoverished communities (Cousins & Weiss, 1993; Webster-Stratton, 1994). It is noteworthy that in this intervention, conducted in one of the poorest and most violent communities in South Africa, parent training was not only well attended but, together with the total intervention package, has been effective in reducing aggression. It also signals that interventions developed internationally can be adapted locally.

A major limitation of this intervention was that it targeted only the more extremely behaviour-disordered children in the preschool. The reality of poverty and its concomitant social stressors is that children are at high risk for the development of aggressive behaviour. This then poses the question of whether such behaviour is a necessary and, perhaps, vital coping mechanism of survival in the ghettos. If this is true, it would be helpful if interventions are spearheaded and controlled by the main players in the community who are intimate with the local situation. In addition, normative changes require that interventions affect the wider cultural setting of the child's development, such as the school. This would allow a new behavioural culture to emerge among children, teachers and parents.

In its next phase of work the COPES violence prevention programme intends to work in primary schools. As most South African children do not attend preschool, this will enable the programme to reach more children. In addition, the transition to school is a difficult adjustment for many children, resulting in emotional and behavioural difficulties. This second phase of the programme intends to train teachers of first and second grades to implement significant aspects of the intervention. Through teacher development, a violence prevention initiative can reach right through the school, and teachers can influence large numbers of children in the course of their ordinary teaching activities. Teachers are therefore potentially key actors in violence prevention programmes, provided of course they are well trained and can act on their training.

Research has highlighted the importance of focusing on three particular interventions in the school context (Kellam, Mayer, Rebok & Hawkins, 1998; Kellam, Ling, Merisca, Brown & Ialongo, 1998). They include academic remediation, social skills training provided by teachers for the children, and classroom management skills. All of these are intended elements of the next phase of the COPES programme. Academic remediation (specifically reading and mathematics) is regarded as important, as school failure has been linked to aggressive behaviour. Social skills training, specifically the development of conflict-resolution skills, problem-solving abilities and empathic sensitivity, provides the child with the skills needed to interact effectively with others and hence reduce the risk of rejection by peers. Finally, in-service training for teachers on such things as classroom management skills is likely to help them cope with aggressive children. This sort of training can also help create healthier and more productive learning environments (Donald, Lazarus & Lolwana, 1997). The objective of the next phase is to reduce the level of aggression among the children receiving the intervention, and, more powerfully, change the norms of acceptable behaviour. This, it is assumed, will ultimately reduce the culture of violence within the school.

Just as remedial help is necessary for children with special academic needs, so psychological assistance is necessary for children with particular emotional difficulties. The need remains for assistance to parents and individual children. In the second phase of the programme, all parents will be invited to attend parent training groups, while children with particular emotional, social and behavioural problems will be invited to join therapeutic child groups. We believe a promising start has been made in this process during the preschool intervention phase. The implementation of the next phase of the work will hopefully lead to positive benefits in a community where the need is great.

REFERENCES

Abidin, R.R. (1983). *Parenting stress index.* Miami Florida: Psychological Assessment Resources.

Achenbach, T.M. (1991). *Manual for the Child Behavior Checklist/4–18 and 1991 Profile.* Burlington VT: Department of Psychiatry University of Vermont.

Beery, K.E. (1997). *Beery-Buktenica Developmental Test of Visual–Motor Integration.* Parsippany N.J.: Modern Curriculum Press.

Behar, L. & Stringfield, S. (1974). Rating Scale for the preschool child. *Developmental Psychology, 10*(5), 601-610.

Community Law Centre, University of the Western Cape (1998). *Children in prison in South Africa: A situation analysis.* Bellville, South Africa: University of the Western Cape.

Community Psychological Empowerment Services (COPES) (1996a). Unpublished Teacher Competency Questionnaire. Cape Town: COPES & The Trauma Centre for Survivors of Violence and Torture.

Community Psychological Empowerment Services (COPES) (1996b). Unpublished Developmental History Questionnaire. Cape Town: COPES & The Trauma Centre for Survivors of Violence and Torture.

Community Psychological Empowerment Services (COPES) (1996c). Unpublished Violence Questionnaire. Cape Town: COPES & The Trauma Centre for Survivors of Violence and Torture.

Conduct Problems Prevention Research (CPPR) Group (1992). A developmental and clinical model for the prevention of conduct disorder: The FAST track programme. *Development and Psychopathology, 4,* 509–527.

Cousins, L.S. & Weiss, G. (1993). Parent training and social skills training for children with attention-deficit hyperactivity disorder: How can they be combined for greater effectiveness? *Canadian Journal of Psychiatry, 38,* 449–457.

Dawes, A., Robertson, B., Duncan, N., Ensink, K., Jackson, A., Reynolds, P., Pillay, A. & Richter, L. (1997). Child and adolescent mental health policy. In D. Foster, M. Freeman & Y. Pillay (Eds.), *Mental health policy for South Africa* (pp. 193–215). Cape Town: M.A.S.A.

Donald, D., Lazarus, S. & Lolwana, P. (1997). *Educational psychology in social context: Challenges of development, social issues and special need in southern Africa.* Cape Town: Oxford University Press.

Farrington, D.P. (1991). Childhood aggression and adult violence: Early precursors and life outcomes. In D.J. Pepler & K.H. Rubin (Eds.), *The development and treatment of childhood aggression* (pp. 5–30). Hillsdale, N.J.: Lawrence Erlbaum.

Huesmann, L.R., Eron, L.D., Lefkowitz, M.M. & Walder, L.O. (1984). *Stability of aggression over time and generations. Developmental Psychology, 20*(6), 1120–1134.

Kazdin, A.E. (1987). *Conduct disorders in childhood and adolescence.* Newbury Park, CA: Sage.

Kellam, S., Mayer, L., Rebok, G. & Hawkins W. (1998). Effects of improving achievement on aggressive behavior and of improving aggressive behavior on achievement through two preventive interventions: An investigation of causal paths. In B.P. Dohrenwend (Ed.), *Adversity, Stress, and Psychopathology* (pp. 486–505). New York: Oxford University Press.

Kellam, S.G, Ling X., Merisca, R., Brown, C.H. & Ialongo, N. (1998). The effect of the level of aggression in the first grade classroom on the course and malleability of aggressive behavior into middle school. *Development and Psychopathology, 10,* 165–185.

Loeber, R. & Stouthamer-Loeber, M. (1998). Development of juvenile aggression and violence. Some misconceptions and controversies. *American Psychologist, 53,* 242–259.

Moffit, T.E. (1993). Adolescence limited and life-course persistent antisocial behaviour. *Psychological Review, 100*(4), 674–701.

Offord, D.R. & Bennett, K. (1994). Conduct disorder: Long term outcomes and intervention effectiveness. *Journal of the American Academy of Child and Adolescent Psychiatry, 33*(8), 1069–1078.

Patterson, G.R., DeBaryshe, B.D. & Ramsey, E. (1989). A developmental perspective on antisocial behaviour. *American Psychologist, 44,* 329–348.

Patterson, G., Reid, J.B., Jones, R.R. & Conger, R.E. (1975). *A social learning approach to family intervention: Volume 1, Families with aggressive children.* Eugene, O.R.: Castalia.

Rutter, M. & Herzov, L. (1985). *Child and adolescent psychiatry: Modern approaches.* Oxford: Basil Blackwell.

Rutter, M. & Rutter, M. (1992). *Developing minds: Challenge and continuity across the life span.* New York: Basic Books.

Rutter, M., Quinton, D. & Yule, B. (1977). *Family pathology and child psychiatric disorder.* London: John Wiley.

Sameroff, A.J. (1975). Transactional models in early social relations. *Human Development, 18,* 65–79.

Sameroff, A. J. (1991). The social context of development. In M. Woodhead, P. Light & R. Carr (Eds.), *Becoming a person* (pp. 167–189). London: Routledge and The Open University.

Webster-Stratton, C. (1985). Comparisons of behavior transactions between conduct-disordered children and their mothers in the clinic and at home. *Journal of Abnormal Child Psychology, 13*(2), 169–180.

Webster-Stratton, C. (1994). Advancing videotape parent training: A comparison study. *Journal of Consulting and Clinical Psychology, 62*(3), 583-593.

Webster-Stratton, C. & Hammond, M. (1997). Treating children with early-onset conduct problems: A comparison of child and parent training interventions. *Journal of Consulting and Clinical Psychology, 65*(1), 93–109.

Webster-Stratton, C. & Herbert, M. (1993). 'What Really Happens in Parent Training?' *Behavior Modification, 17*(4), 407–456.

Yoshikawa, H. (1994). Prevention as cumulative protection: effects of early family support and education on chronic delinquency and its risks. *Psychological Bulletin, 115*, 28–54.

HEALTH-PROMOTING SCHOOLS 6

Lessons from Avondale Primary School

ALAN J. FLISHER, KEITH CLOETE, BRIDGET JOHNSON, ALYSSA WIGTON, ROSE ADAMS &
PAM JOSHUA

BACKGROUND AND AIMS

Although young people are generally construed as having good health, their vulnerability to the 'new morbidities' (Dryfoos, 1991, p. 630) has been receiving increased international attention. Such new morbidities can result from risk behaviour, defined as behaviour that places adolescents at risk for adverse effects in terms of their physical, social or psychological development (Jessor, 1991).

In the Cape Peninsula, where this project was carried out, high prevalence rates for selected risk behaviours among high school students have been documented (Flisher, Parry, Evans, Lombard & Muller, 1998; Flisher, Ziervogel, Chalton, Leger & Robertson, 1993). In one study, 18% of the 7340 participating students smoked cigarettes daily; 15% had drunk five or more alcoholic drinks on one or more occasion in the previous fortnight; 8% had attempted suicide in the previous year; of those who had driven a motor vehicle on a public road in the previous year, 63% had done so without a licence and 8% while under the influence of alcohol or cannabis; 17% had participated in sexual intercourse, of whom 40% did not use any form of contraception or disease prevention during their last coital episode; and 13% and 10% had been injured by another person at home and school respectively (Flisher et al., 1993). In another Cape Town study conducted among 60 children in a children's home, and a part of Khayelitsha characterised by high levels of community violence, 95% had witnessed violence and 56% had experienced violence themselves (Ensink, Robertson, Zissis & Leger, 1997). Furthermore, there is evidence that the prevalence rates of risk behaviour will continue to rise with the increased urbanisation of young people in South Africa (Flisher & Chalton, 1998).

In addition to these new morbidities, it is important to remember that many South African students remain at risk for poverty-related conditions, such as malnutrition and poor sanitation (see Chapter 2). In the light of these challenges, several provinces have developed programmes and initiatives aimed at the prevention of ill health among young people of school-going age. A recent survey of provincial programme managers in education and maternal, women's and children's health found that approximately half of all provincial Departments of Health and Education have developed policy documents regarding school health; in most provinces there is collaboration between Departments of Health and Departments of Education in developing programmes for school-aged young persons; and in almost all provinces school health programmes are currently being implemented in primary and secondary schools and (in some cases) pre-primary schools (Abrahams, Wigton & De Jong, 1997). Such programmes include counselling and other mental health interventions, feeding programmes, and education regarding the environment, sexuality and life skills.

The current project is an example of a demonstration project being carried out in the Western Cape. The Reference Group for Health-Promoting Schools (HPS) was formed in October 1995 in the Western Cape with the following aims (Department of Health, 1997):

- to facilitate and co-ordinate appropriate training and capacity building around the health-promoting schools concept
- to facilitate networking and liaison between and within different sectors
- to access resources for the implementation and sustaining of projects and programmes
- to monitor and evaluate programmes
- to advocate, lobby and make policy recommendations for the different sectors

The group includes individuals from the provincial Departments of Health, Education and Welfare, non-governmental organisations, and the private and business sectors. While the reference group supports the development of health-promoting schools, it aims not to be prescriptive. Schools are encouraged to embrace the concept and adapt it according to the needs of the school and the particular school community. The group recognises that each school is unique and that the staff members at the school are the most qualified to understand the school and the community in which it is situated. Much of the work of the Reference Group for HPS is carried by area co-ordinating teams.

In the Western Cape, many schools have taken steps to transform into health-promoting institutions. They proceed at their own pace and are at various stages of development. The Reference Group for HPS recognises and commends each attempt, however preliminary or limited. This is in line with the understanding fostered by the World Health Organisation (1996) of a health-promoting school as a place that is constantly strengthening its own capacity as a healthy setting for living, learning and working.

Avondale Primary School is situated in Atlantis, which is a semi-rural town situated about 50 kilometres from Cape Town. It was established during the apartheid era as an industrial town with promises of employment for the community. However, today most of the inhabitants are unemployed, with resultant socio-economic problems such as gangsterism, substance abuse and broken families. Despite these difficulties, there exists a strong determination amongst the inhabitants to protect the children and to ensure a brighter future for them. The development of schools in

Atlantis such as Avondale Primary School into health-promoting institutions is seen as one way of achieving this.

THEORETICAL AND RESEARCH BASE

The 1993 World Bank Development Report identified school-based programmes as one of the most cost-effective approaches to health and development, and included it in a short list of five public health priorities (World Bank, 1993). There are several compelling reasons why school-based programmes enjoy such a high priority.

Although current health policies entitle all people in South Africa to free primary-level health care services, these services are still inequitably distributed and inaccessible to many South Africans. The Central Statistical Service (1994) estimated that 56% of the rural population in South Africa were living more than 5 kilometres from a medical facility. The ratio of doctors ranges from 143.8 per 100 000 in the Western Cape to 15.5 in the Northern Province (Development Bank of Southern Africa, 1994). For psychiatrists, the ratios range from 24.7 per million in the Western Cape to 0.2 in the Northern Province (Flisher, Riccitelli, Jhetam & Robertson, 1997). Similar discrepancies are present for nurses: the ratio of nurses ranges from 683 per 100 000 in the Western Cape to 266 in Mpumalanga (Development Bank of Southern Africa, 1994).

Alongside this inadequate access to health facilities young people aged less than 19 years constitute almost half the population of South Africa, the majority of whom are school-aged (Central Statistical Service, 1996). The Human Sciences Research Council (1996) estimated that there were more than 10 million pupils attending primary and secondary schools in 1996. A survey of 4000 households found that at least 90% of children aged between 6 and 15 years were attending school (Community Agency for Social Enquiry, 1995). This is compatible with data produced by the National Institute for Economic Policy (1996) which found that 75% of children aged 5–9 years, 97% of those aged 10–14 years, and 83% of children aged 15–19 years attend school. Given the difficulties of accessing health services, these statistics suggest that school-based health-promotion could increase accessibility and reduce some of the inequalities in access to health services. Also, the school provides an infrastructure from which health services can be launched both for students attending the school and for the broader community (McCoy *et al.*, 1997).

International recommendations focus on health and nutrition interventions as methods for achieving better educational outcomes (Miller del Rosso & Marek, 1996; United Nations Subcommittee on Nutrition, 1990). The results of one study on school drop-out conducted in a Cape Flats community suggest that programmes which aim to reduce substance use and sexual behaviour may contribute to reducing drop-out rates (Flisher & Chalton, 1995). In addition, improved health status increases the potential of young people to take optimal advantage of their learning environment (McCoy *et al.*, 1997). Conversely, improvements in education have also been shown to impact positively on health outcomes. For example, improvements in the levels of female literacy are associated with declining rates of fertility, infant mortality and sexually transmitted disease (McCoy *et al.*, 1997).

These factors formed the rationale for establishing the Reference Group for HPS and, more specifically, for transforming Avondale Primary School into a health-promoting school. Such a school has been defined as a place where 'all members of the school community work together to provide students with integrated and positive experiences and structures which promote and protect their health. This includes both the formal and informal curricula in health, the creation of a safe and healthy school environment, the provision of appropriate health services and the involvement of the family and wider community in efforts to promote health' (World Health Organisation, 1996, p. 2).

The curriculum should comprise experiences and structures that promote and protect health (World Health Organisation, UNESCO and United Nations Children's Fund, 1992). In particular, it should:

- view health holistically, 'addressing the inter-relatedness of health problems and the factors that influence health, within the context of the human and material environment and other conditions of life' (World Health Organisation *et al.*, 1992, p. 4)
- utilise all opportunities for health-promotion, including drawing on services outside the school
- serve to harmonise the health messages from the various sources that influence students, including the media, the health system, family, peers and the school
- empower children and youth 'to act for healthy living and to promote conditions supportive for health' (World Health Organisation *et al.*, 1992, p. 4)

Because the concept of developing health-promoting schools is relatively recent, there are few studies that have evaluated the efficacy of this specific approach. However, Dryfoos (1990) reviewed 100 diverse school-based programmes in the United States that had the potential to change risk behaviours such as substance abuse, delinquency, teen pregnancy, and school failure and drop-out. She identified themes that characterise these successful programmes. The two themes that stood out above the others were the need for individual attention and the importance of community-wide programmes that involved a range of agencies. Other common components of successful programmes were early intervention; developing basic skills; healthy school climate; parental involvement; peer involvement; connection to the world of work; social and life skills training; and attention to staff training and supervision. Most of these themes are implicit in the notion of a health-promoting school, and indeed were present at Avondale Primary School. This gives grounds for optimism that this intervention had the potential to be successful.

PROJECT DESCRIPTION

The Atlantis Area Co-ordinating Team for HPS is an intersectoral team that co-ordinates the establishment and support of the network of health-promoting schools in Atlantis (see Figure 1). It operates under the auspices of the Reference Group for HPS mentioned above. Although initiated through the provincial Department of Health, the team is constantly being strengthened by the involvement of key role-players from other sectors, such as the provincial nutrition services, school psychological services and social services, the police and non-governmental organisations. It works in close collaboration with all the other area co-ordinating teams falling under the Reference Group for HPS.

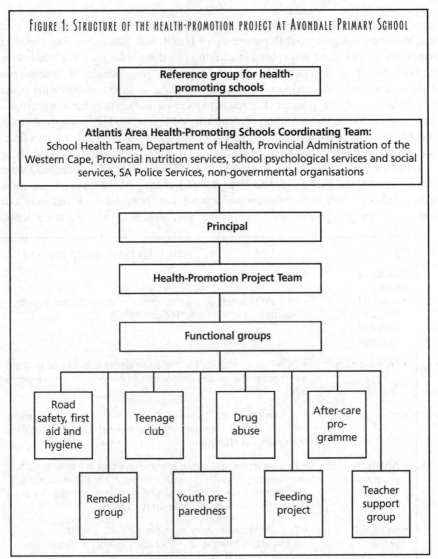

FIGURE 1: STRUCTURE OF THE HEALTH-PROMOTION PROJECT AT AVONDALE PRIMARY SCHOOL

A chief professional nurse and a medical officer first introduced the concept of a health-promoting school to the principal and the staff of Avondale Primary School, taking care not to impose the concept. They encouraged the school to take control and ownership of the process of transforming the school into a health-promoting institution. This is consistent with the health-promotion principle that people should be enabled to increase control over their own health. Indeed, the school embraced the concept and developed it into a working model aimed at the development of the whole school and surrounding community.

Besides initiating the process, other roles of the Atlantis Area HPS Co-ordinating Team included provision of regular inputs in terms of the theory and practice of health-promoting schools; monitoring the process; provision of support to the school, especially when the process was under threat; and liaison with outside agencies, including the provincial Departments of Health and Education. The contribution of the school nurse was crucial in carrying out these roles since she was in contact with the school on a particularly regular basis. The principal played an active role in motivating and encouraging teachers and in finding solutions to difficulties which they encountered. He ensured that teachers received recognition for work done as part of the project. This encouraged others to do the same. He had a strong relationship with the parents and the wider community and was thus able to gain financial and other assistance for the school.

At one of the initial meetings between the Atlantis Area HPS Co-ordinating Team and the school, the staff decided to form themselves into eight functional groups to address priority issues in the physical, social, academic, environmental and emotional domains. These groups built on functions that were already in existence at the school

TABLE 1: FUNCTIONAL GROUPS FOR THE HEALTH	
Functional group	**Goals**
• Road safety, first aid and personal hygiene	• To train teachers to train students, who would train other students • To ensure a better community
• Teenage club	• To prepare students for the adult world • To ensure that students enter the adult world with self-confidence and responsibility
• Drug abuse	• To make students aware of the dangers of drugs • To help students handle peer pressure • To make students aware of their rights as children
• After care programme	• To develop an after-care programme that is interesting, fun, recreational, stimulates cultural interest, contributes to the well-being of the community, and stimulates interest on the part of the students in community events
• Remedial group	• To assist students with learning difficulties in Afrikaans, English and mathematics • To assist students with specific problems related to sections of work
• Youth preparedness	• To create outdoor educational situations such as camps and tours
• Nutrition project	• To be self-sustainable • To improve upon the existing feeding project • To encourage initiative • To facilitate better relations between students • To improve communication between staff, students and parents
• Teacher support group	• To acquire healthy eating habits • To start an exercise programme • To monitor weight and blood pressure • To improve self-image • To deal more appropriately with conflict and depression • To incorporate the above into the curriculum

such as a feeding scheme and remedial interventions. The teams elected their own leaders and reached consensus on the goals of the groups and their projects. These are summarised in Table 1. The functional groups addressed many of the health needs mentioned above in ways that were consistent with the principles of developing a health-promoting school. The Teacher Support Group, for example, included among its goals acquiring healthy eating habits and resolving conflict constructively. In this way they harmonised health messages from various sources – a characteristic of comprehensive health education (World Health Organisation *et al.*, 1992).

The Health-Promotion Project Team, consisting of the team co-ordinator and the leaders of each of the working groups, was the body that co-ordinated all the health-promoting activities in the school. It stood at the core. The quarterly meetings were always attended by the leaders of the various groups, the team co-ordinator and the school nurse (representing the Atlantis Area HPS Co-ordinating Team). Others who

---

PROMOTION PROJECT AT AVONDALE PRIMARY SCHOOL

Projects

• Seminars for teachers on road safety and first aid • Teachers to attend to the personal hygiene of students on a daily basis

• Invited speakers to address topics such as child abuse, teenage pregnancies, personal safety, and various career choices • AIDS and TB drama for students in Grades 6 and 7

• Attendance by teachers at course where they were taught to identify problems, especially drug-related problems • Presentation by the Child Protection Unit, South African Police Services • Videos dealing with peer pressure and drugs

• (This programme did not take place because of an overload of programmes occurring after school, minimal parent and community interest, shortage of accommodation, and lack of funds)

• Provision of assistance by senior students to junior students, all junior primary teachers, and some senior primary teachers

• Speakers from 'The Fairest Cape' • Excursions to Koeberg and Rondevlei Nature Reserves • Camp at Cape Point • Formation of a nature club

• Diet and lifestyle classes for students, teachers and parents • Initiation and maintenance of a vegetable garden, the products of which were used to supplement the primary schools nutrition scheme • Growth monitoring of Grade 1 students • Dietary supplementation for selected subgroups (e.g. athletes)

• 'Walk it off' programme • Aerobics classes • Training in weight and blood pressure measurement • Training in behaviour modification • Workshop on counselling skills

attended on occasions included staff from the school clinic, such as educational psychologists, remedial teachers and speech and hearing therapists; social workers from governmental and non-governmental organisations; community members working in the police and fire services; university academics; and managers from the Department of Education, such as the circuit manager. The Health-Promotion Project Team co-ordinator had several important functions, including the facilitation of the evaluation meeting at the end of each term, consultation with team members, and role modelling.

One of the tasks of the Health-Promotion Project Team was to raise awareness of the need to adapt the curriculum to address the health-promotion needs that had been identified. There were three aspects to the curriculum changes. First, the principle of the spiral curriculum was implemented. This refers to alterations in the content and nature of the material according to the level of the learner (Downie, Tannahill & Tannahill, 1996). In presenting sexuality, for example, the focus in the junior standards was on the basic anatomy of the female and male reproductive systems. In the more senior standards, however, the focus was on the emotional aspects of sexual relationships. Second, lifeskills education was prioritised in the curriculum. This emphasised the development of proficiencies that enable learners to deal with the challenges of everyday life, such as decision making, problem solving, creative thinking, critical thinking, effective communication, interpersonal relating, self-awareness, ability to empathise, coping with emotions and coping with stress (De Jong, Ganie, Lazarus & Prinsloo, 1995). Finally, health-promotion issues were 'infused' throughout the curriculum (Donald, Lazarus & Lolwana, 1997), thus giving expression to principles of comprehensiveness and consistency. This effectively reduced the amount of 'extra' time that the teachers needed to devote to health-promotion since it was incorporated into the normal curriculum. Nutrition, for example, was included in the following subjects: geography, in which preparations necessary for the introduction of a vegetable garden were discussed; English, in which the issue of recycling was addressed; health education, in which healthy eating habits were presented; and mathematics, in which ways of presenting data obtained during weight monitoring were explored.

Another manifestation of comprehensiveness and consistency in the programme was the collaborative relationship developed between the school and parents. This was achieved by fostering a mutually respectful and trusting attitude; informing the parents about what was happening at school; ensuring that the importance of parents in the lives of their children and the school was explicitly recognised; encouraging parents to visit the school and even attend lessons; recognising that parents provide services in the community that could be beneficial to the school; establishing personal connections through social functions; and involving the neighbourhood watch in providing security for parents and students during night functions at the school. Attempting to involve parents in the activities of the functional groups met with little success, however, as employed parents were not generally able to attend meetings during the working day, and unemployed parents were reluctant to assist without remuneration.

Finally, the children themselves were important team members in the effort to transform Avondale into a health-promoting school (Hanbury, 1996; World Health Organisation *et al.*, 1992). They were taught to carry health messages into their homes, thereby strengthening the bond between the school and community. They assisted at school functions such as the inter-house athletic programme. They were encouraged to help one another, including providing emotional support during difficult times. A very specific form of help involved older students providing educational support to more junior students who were experiencing academic difficulties. This formed part of the activities of the remedial group (see Table 1). There were several benefits of this 'child-to-child' approach (Hanbury, 1996): it conveyed important values of co-operation and social responsibility; it enabled a greater amount to be achieved than would otherwise be the case (for example, in the area of remedial education); and it may have resulted in direct benefits for the adults, in that they may have been more responsive to messages conveyed by children than by the media and the health system (Hanbury, 1996).

OUTCOMES AND EVALUATION

Ongoing 'internal' monitoring, which takes the form of quarterly evaluation sessions, has been conducted by the Atlantis Area HPS Co-ordinating Team on a continuing basis. This evaluation aims to identify successes and obstacles, and to develop strategies to strengthen the successes as well as to overcome the obstacles encountered. Progress reports from all the areas are given to the Reference Group for HPS on a quarterly basis.

In addition, during 1996 the project was subject to an 'external' evaluation by a postgraduate student at the University of the Western Cape (Johnson, 1997). There were four sources of data. First, in-depth interviews were conducted with the principal, the school nurse and the leaders of each of the support teams. Second, focus groups were held with a group of students and a group of parents. Third, one of the quarterly evaluation meetings mentioned above was evaluated. Fourth, documents were examined for each of the functional groups containing details of the group's goals, objectives and activities.

The in-depth interviews, focus group discussions and evaluation meetings were tape-recorded and transcribed verbatim for analysis. A thematic analysis was conducted of the project's strengths, weaknesses and future proposals, the results of which are presented in Table 2.

There were many gains in terms of interpersonal relationships among both the teachers and the students. In many cases, the students were functioning as peer counsellors, one commenting: 'If someone had hurt him at home and he was feeling down when he came to school, you can quickly see this – and you are always there to help',[1] and another: 'Through helping others you help yourself, you become stronger.'* They were also encouraged to take home key health-promotion messages. One parent described how her child had influenced her smoking habits: 'One day the little one said to me, "Mammie, how can you smoke in this room with us, we sleep together in one room." Now I must smoke through there. I realise that I'm smoking less.'*

In general, the parents expressed their satisfaction that the school was able to offer so much to their children. The good relationship between parents and teachers was emphasised in comments such as 'The parents and teachers at Avondale get on well together'* and 'They know the children's situations so well that they really care.'*

TABLE 2: EVALUATION OF THE HEALTH-PROMOTION PROJECT AT AVONDALE PRIMARY SCHOOL

Domain	Group	Comments
Strengths		
• Interpersonal relationships	• Teachers	• Worked well together in the functional groups and developed a better understanding of each other • Supported each other regarding both project-related and personal issues, thus building trusting relationships
	• Students	• Relationships between students in general improved • Senior students showed a greater interest in junior students and were keen to help them • Social responsibility of the students towards each other increased in that they helped each other not only in terms of work but also with finances, food, clothing and emotional difficulties
	• Parents	• No complaints regarding the school or individual teachers • Expressed satisfaction with programme
• Skills development	• Teachers	• Developed skills as a result of the project, e.g. in conflict resolution • Dormant skills came to the fore, increasing self-confidence • Knowledge of activities improved, e.g. gardening
	• Students	• Senior students developed leadership skills and hence self-confidence • Report-writing skills improved through reports on assisted students and excursions
• Attitudes	• Teachers	• Attitudes towards education improved • Some teachers who were initially sceptical became more positive once they had started to work in their functional groups • All agreed that there was progress in all the functional groups that were operating (albeit slow in some cases)
	• Students	• Particularly well disposed to the child-to-child projects • Generally were more interested in their school-work

Domain	Group	Comments
Weaknesses		
• Motivation	• Teachers	• A subset of teachers never became interested or motivated • Much dissatisfaction about the fact that the planning tended to take place after school • Some teachers had to spend a considerable amount of time motivating others
	• Parents	• Difficult to get parents involved • Some parents wanted remuneration for their involvement
• Workload	• Teachers	• Amount of work involved was underestimated • Difficult to arrange meetings because of sport and other extramural activities • Teachers involved in too many activities • Too many functional groups • Quality of work suffered
• Broader educational change	• Teachers	• Introduction of new curriculum • Many teachers leaving
Future proposals		
	• Teachers	• Should be evenly spread between the groups • Should be motivated to participate • Should serve on groups in which they are interested • Should reach out more to the community
	• Groups	• Should be combined so there are fewer • Notice of meetings should be given in a timely manner • Group leaders should consult more
	• Parents	• Need for greater involvement • Should also serve on the groups
	• Planning	• Should be done earlier • Fewer projects should be planned • Focus should be on doing fewer things well rather than many things and experiencing failure • Group leaders should do planning in collaboration with subject heads

Teachers developed many skills through the project. While the principal supported the teachers, he refrained from doing things for them since he believed it was important for people to have confidence in their own abilities. This was also a conscious approach taken by the school nurse: 'I don't want to do it for them because it is their project, I will do it with them.' Teachers thus saw themselves developing skills which they had not known about, as in this comment: 'Many teachers were unaware of their talents and this project brought them to the fore, and developed them as well.'* They also felt that the project had contributed substantially to their professional development and growth. Those who were regarded as shy and having little self-confidence managed to get projects going, liaise with relevant people and make arrangements. Thus, 'I've learnt a lot, managing, organising and all that this year'. In addition, students developed skills in leadership, report writing and peer counselling. Parents felt that the child-to-child approach demonstrated that the teachers trusted the children and that this helped the children themselves to become more responsible.

Teachers and students were well disposed to the project. The Health-Promotion Project Team co-ordinator made the following comment in the context of her impending retirement: 'I'll miss teaching, but I'll miss this health-promoting school more ... because I found it so interesting ... as it progressed, I saw what could still be done in future ... and I saw things happening, how we are reaching out.' Equally, the project contributed to positive attitudes towards schooling on the part of the learners, one parent remarking, 'It's really quite strange to see the children so keen to go to school!'*

A key weakness of the project was the additional demands it made on teachers, some of whom resented this, particularly at the beginning. Dissatisfaction centred around the time required after school hours and the number of meetings needed to manage the programme. This resulted in staff friction. The introduction of the new curriculum and the rationalisation crisis necessitated additional meetings, which served to multiply the friction. As one teacher put it: 'It was a heavy year and teachers felt the pinch.'

There were several suggestions for improvements in the project in future. These included improved deployment of the teachers, arrangements for the groups and planning in general (see Table 2). Although parents were involved in the project, staff believed that this could be improved through 'making more of a point to get them here'.* The overall impression was that the project should continue, expressed in emphatic comments such as: 'It definitely must go on next year' and 'The programme must continue.' Teachers felt that the following year would be better as they 'had learned from their mistakes and problems'.*

During the following year, 1997, the school was exposed to several sources of stress. Financial problems affected the number of activities that the functional groups could carry out. The principal, who had been at the school since its inception twenty years previously, had retired and there were delays in appointing a replacement. The staff was reduced as part of a general and stressful rationalisation process in the province. The first half of the year was particularly difficult. Despite the difficulties, the teachers persisted with their health-promotion efforts. The encouragement which they received from the school nurse and medical officer were particularly important sources of motivation through these difficult times.

There were also several positive developments during this time. As a result of the evaluation the preceding year, several changes were introduced. There was, for example, a reduction in the number of functional groups from nine to five. This reduced the work load of the teachers, which in turn made them more relaxed and confident. The extent of involvement by parents was greater than the previous year; for example, many participated actively in a community fun run and the sports day.

The health-promotion programme received recognition from several sources. Teachers from the school introduced the project to several other schools in Cape Town that were interested in transforming to health-promoting schools. They were also involved in the launch of health-promoting schools initiatives in Oudtshoorn and the Boland–Overberg region. A group of visitors from the United States were so impressed that they donated much-needed books and writing material to the school. The project was presented at two Teacher Inservice Project (TIP) colloquia. Finally, the project has been regularly presented as an example of a health-promoting school initiative in courses offered by the Public Health Programme at UWC.

ISSUES AND INSIGHTS

Vergnani, Flisher, Lazarus, Reddy and James (1998) identified a number of critical tasks that need to be pursued in the implementation of health-promoting schools in South Africa. We have selected some of these tasks to serve as a framework in which to situate some concluding remarks about the programme at Avondale Primary School. Specifically, we shall assess the extent to which this programme addressed these tasks, and point to some of the work that still needs to be done.

Intersectoral collaboration

Collaboration between different state services as well as between sectors such as teachers, parents and students is a vital component of any health-promotion initiative. It is necessary for interdisciplinary co-ordination; to rationalise scarce resources in a context of enormous need; to co-ordinate planning, development and evaluation; and to engage all stakeholders so that ownership of policy, services and programmes is promoted (Lazarus & Donald, 1997).

On at least three levels, this project has been a living example of the benefits of intersectoral collaboration. On the level of state departments, there has been extensive collaboration between the health and education sectors. The main responsibility for implementation of the project has been with the education sector (specifically the school itself, in collaboration with Education Support Services, Curriculum Advisory Services and the circuit manager). However, the School Health Team is located in the Department of Health. Also, several additional state services were involved in the activities of the functional groups, such as the police, traffic control and environmental services (see Table 1).

On the level of academic disciplines, the representatives of the departments just mentioned have various academic backgrounds. Indeed, the authors of this chapter represent various disciplines including education, maternal and child health, medicine (including psychiatry), educational and clinical psychology, public health and nursing science.

Finally, there has been collaboration between different 'types' of sector. Non-governmental organisations were involved in several activities of the functional groups. Universities were involved in the evaluation of the programme. Within the school itself, several sectors were intimately involved in the development and implementation of the programme, in particular the staff, students and parents.

Of course, there are several potential problems that can arise in a context of intersectoral collaboration. These include fear of loss of influence by particular disciplines, destructive group dynamics relating to issues of control, inadequate organisational support for intersectoral collaboration, and alienation of health workers in the education sector because their work is not perceived as being central to the academic goals of education (Lazarus & Donald, 1997). In the present project, these problems did not manifest themselves to any significant degree. Possible reasons for this may have included the style of collaboration, with ownership of the programme being vested securely with the school and its community.

Optimal utilisation of resources

Optimal utilisation of resources is particularly necessary in schools that are situated in poor communities. One means to achieve this is through intersectoral collaboration. Two additional strategies were employed at Avondale Primary School. First, the teachers were primarily responsible for many of the activities of the functional groups. They developed skills specifically for this purpose – or reactivated dormant skills (see Table 2). The teachers reported psychological benefits for themselves through skills development, such as increased self-confidence. This enabled them to function more effectively as teachers, thus benefiting the students and the school in general. The project also provides a good example of the synergy that health-promoting schools can engender.

Secondly, senior students, supervised by teachers, assisted junior students who were having learning difficulties in Afrikaans, English and mathematics or with specific sections of the syllabus. If remedial teachers or even subject teachers had been the only ones to provide such services, a very small proportion of students requiring help would have received it. As mentioned above (see Table 2), senior students also started to take a greater interest in the junior students and their sense of social responsibility was enhanced, thus illustrating another synergistic effect. Although information was not collected on this, it would have been interesting to know how effective this process was in helping the junior students.

The development and implementation of appropriate research

The qualitative methodology employed during this project certainly provided rich and detailed data that illuminated different aspects of the project – and had practical and formative effects. It was shown, for example, how the results of the evaluation had a direct influence on the project the year after the research was conducted.

However, some quantitative information could have complemented the qualitative study. Thus, whether the programme as a whole, or components of it, achieved the desired outcomes is not entirely clear. Many specific research questions could have been informed by the collection of appropriate quantitative data, such as the question of how effective the student 'remedial' system was. Many of the specific findings emerging from the qualitative study (see Table 2) could have been subject to quantitative scrutiny to investigate how generally applicable they were. Other questions might have been addressed more specifically and quantitatively, such as whether the relationships between the students and teachers improved through the programme; whether the self-confidence of the teachers improved; whether the AIDS and TB play had an effect on the sexual knowledge, attitudes or practice of the students; whether the videos dealing with peer pressure and drugs improved the capacity of the students to withstand peer pressure, etc. In addition, quantitative evaluation should address the economic or cost-effectiveness aspect of a project such as this.

Such research questions are not of academic interest only. Answers to these questions have the potential to influence not only the immediate programme but also decisions about whether such activities should be introduced at other schools at regional, provincial, national or even wider levels. Of course, further questions would emerge which might, in turn, require a more qualitative focus. If an aspect of the programme is found not to be effective, one would immediately ask why. Answers to this might be better obtained through a qualitative analysis of, say, the pattern of functional group interactions. Qualitative and quantitative methods can thus inform each other in a mutually beneficial loop.

The development of demonstration programmes

The current project differs from most other South African school-based health-promotion demonstration programmes in important respects. Most of these programmes appear to have been initiated by researchers based at a university or the Medical Research Council. By contrast, the main impetus for the current project came from the school itself, as opposed to people from outside the school. Although the School Health Team initiated the project and has remained involved, the responsibility for the development and implementation of the project has rested firmly with the school. This has unquestionably contributed to the sustainability of the project.

In addition, most of the other programmes have focused on specific risk behaviours, such as cigarette smoking or sexual behaviour. The current project was comprehensive. Not only did it address diverse risk behaviours such as unsafe sexual behaviour and drug abuse, but it included attention to issues such as remedial education and sexual and physical abuse. The appropriateness of a comprehensive approach which does not limit its focus to a single aspect has been supported by epidemiological research in Cape Town that has documented the interrelationships between risk behaviours (Flisher, Ziervogel, Chalton, Leger & Robertson, 1996). Whatever the reason for this co-variation (Wallace, Flisher & Fullilove, 1997), intervention programmes that fail to recognise it are unlikely to achieve their maximum potential (Flisher & Reddy, 1995).

Despite the existence of the Avondale Primary School project, there is a need for further demonstration programmes. These would inevitably exist in different communities, have different personnel involved, have different structures, and address dif-

ferent specific issues. However, it is absolutely essential that new demonstration programmes incorporate lessons learned from previous projects (including that at
Avondale Primary School). With time, it may be possible to identify those aspects of
South African programmes that appear to have the most potential for positive outcomes, as Dryfoos (1990) has in the United States.

National commitment to health-promoting schools in South Africa

Advocacy for the development of a national commitment to health-promoting
schools needs to take place at a number of levels, including the national, provincial,
regional, community, school and personal level. The current project was partly a consequence of such lobbying. Both the Reference Group for health-promoting Schools
and the School Health Team in the provincial Department of Health have lobbying
as key aims. The present project has itself served as a vehicle for further lobbying.

In conclusion, the project at Avondale Primary School serves as a model for other
schools wishing to develop into health-promoting schools. It reflects the successful
application of theoretical concepts in a practical and meaningful way. It is a project
that is owned by the school and its community, and it has been able to develop its
own identity, at its own pace, in collaboration with others.

NOTES

[1] Translated from the original Afrikaans. This applies to all subsequent quotes marked
with an asterisk.

REFERENCES

Abrahams, E., Wigton, A. & De Jong, R. (1997). Workshop in an integrated policy for school
health: Discussion document. Cape Town: Child Health Policy Institute, University of Cape
Town.
Central Statistical Service (1994). *October 1994 Household Survey.* Pretoria: Government
Printer.
Central Statistical Service (1996). *Census '96: Preliminary estimates of the size of the population
of South Africa.* Pretoria: Government Printer.
Community Agency for Social Enquiry (1995). *A national household survey of health inequali-
ties in South Africa.* Washington, DC: The Henry J. Kaiser Family Foundation.
De Jong, T., Ganie, L., Lazarus, S. & Prinsloo, E. (1995). Proposed general guidelines for a
lifeskills curriculum framework. In A. Gordon (Ed.), *Curriculum framework for the general
phase of education* (pp. 91–108). Johannesburg: Centre for Education Policy Development,
University of the Witwatersrand.
Department of Health, Republic of South Africa (1997). *Health-promoting schools. Report on
provincial health-promoting schools networks.* Pretoria: Department of Health.
Development Bank of Southern Africa (1994). *South Africa's nine provinces: A human devel-
opment profile.* Halfway House: Development Bank of Southern Africa.
Donald, D., Lazarus, S. & Lolwana, P. (1997). *Educational psychology in social context:
Challenges of development, social issues and special need in southern Africa.* Cape Town:

Oxford University Press.

Downie, R.S., Tannahill, C. & Tannahill, A. (1996). *Health-promotion: Models and values.* Cape Town: Oxford University Press.

Dryfoos, J.G. (1990). *Adolescents at risk. Prevalence and prevention.* New York: Oxford University Press.

Dryfoos, J.G. (1991). Adolescents at Risk: A summation of work in the field – Programs and policies. *Journal of Adolescent Health, 12,* 630–637.

Ensink, K., Robertson, B.A., Zissis, C. & Leger, P. (1997). Post-traumatic stress disorder in children exposed to violence. *South African Medical Journal, 87,* 1526–1530.

Flisher, A.J. & Chalton, D.O. (1995). High-school dropouts in a working-class South African community: selected characteristics and risk-taking behaviour. *Journal of Adolescence, 18,* 105–121.

Flisher, A.J. & Chalton, D.O. (1998). Urbanisation and risk behaviour among high-school students. Paper presented at the 45th Annual Meeting of the American Academy of Child and Adolescent Psychiatry, October/November 1998. Anaheim, California.

Flisher, A.J. & Reddy, P. (1995). Towards health-promoting schools in South Africa. *South African Medical Journal, 85,* 629–630.

Flisher, A.J., Riccitelli, G., Jhetam, N. & Robertson, B.A. (1997). A survey of professional activities of psychiatrists in South Africa. *Psychiatric Services, 48,* 707–709.

Flisher, A.J., Parry, C., Evans, J., Lombard, C. & Muller, M. (1998). The South African Community Epidemiology Network on Drug Use (SACENDU): Methodology and preliminary results (abstract). *South African Medical Journal, 88,* 1191.

Flisher, A.J., Ziervogel, C.F., Chalton, D.O., Leger, P.H. & Robertson, B.A. (1993). Risk-taking behaviour of Cape Peninsula high-school students: Parts II to VIII. *South African Medical Journal, 83,* 474–497.

Flisher, A.J., Ziervogel, C.F., Chalton, D.O., Leger, P.H. & Robertson, B.A. (1996). Risk-taking behaviour of Cape Peninsula high-school students: Parts IX and X. *South African Medical Journal, 86,* 1090–1098.

Hanbury, C. (1996). The Child-to-Child programme. In T. Vergnani, S. Lazarus, S. Swart, K. Bility, P. Reddy, S. James, L. Moore & O. Mbombo (Eds.), *health-promoting schools in South Africa: challenges for the 21st century. Conference Proceedings* (pp. 64–79). Cape Town: University of the Western Cape.

Human Sciences Research Council (1996). *Education database.* Pretoria: HSRC Publishers.

Jessor, R. (1991). Risk behavior in adolescence: a psychosocial framework for understanding and action. *Journal of Adolescent Health, 12,* 597–605.

Johnson, B.A. (1997). Teacher support teams. A school-based strategy for the provision of education support services and health-promotion. Unpublished M.Psych dissertation, University of the Western Cape.

Lazarus, S. & Donald, D. (1997). Education and mental health. In D. Foster, M. Freeman & Y. Pillay (Eds.), *Mental health policy issues for South Africa* (pp. 94–110). Cape Town: Medical Association of South Africa.

McCoy, D., Saitowitz, R., Saasa, M., Sanders, D., Wigton, A., MacLachlan, M., Mokoetle, K., Swart, R., Kvalsig, J., Gordon, A., Hendricks, M., Dhansay, A. & Barron, P. (1997). *An evaluation of South Africa's primary school nutrition programme.* Cape Town: Health Systems Trust.

Miller Del Rosso, J. & Marek, T. (1996). *Class action: Meeting the nutrition and health needs of school age children in the developing world*. Washington, DC: World Bank Human Development Department.

National Institute for Economic Policy (1996). *Children, poverty and disparity reduction: Towards fulfilling the rights of South Africa's children*. Pretoria: Reconstruction and Development Programme, Office of the Deputy President.

United Nations Subcommittee on Nutrition (1990). *Summary report of the 16th session of the Subcommittee on Nutrition of the United Nations*. Paris: UNESCO.

Vergnani, T., Flisher, A., Lazarus, S., Reddy, P. & James, S. (1998). Health-promoting schools in South Africa: Needs and prospects. *Southern African Journal of Child and Adolescent Mental Health, 10*, 44–58.

Wallace, R., Flisher, A.J. & Fullilove, R. (1997). Marginalization, information and infection: The correlation of ghetto risk behaviors and the spread of disease to majority populations. *Environment and Planning A, 29*, 1629–1645.

World Bank (1993). *Investing in health. World development report*. Oxford: Oxford University Press.

World Health Organisation (1996). *Regional guidelines: Development of health-promoting schools. A framework for action*. Geneva: World Health Organisation.

World Health Organisation, United Nations Educational, Scientific and Cultural Organisation and United Nations Children's Fund (1992). *Comprehensive school health education. Suggested guidelines for action*. Geneva: World Health Organisation.

THE THOUSAND SCHOOLS PROJECT 7

Evaluating a whole school development initiative

JOHANN MOUTON

'All who have meditated on the art of governing mankind have been convinced that the fate of empires depends on the education of youth' (Aristotle, 348–322 BC)

BACKGROUND AIMS OF THE PROJECT

The Thousand Schools Project (TSP) was launched in 1993 on the initiative of the Independent Development Trust (IDT), a development facilitation agency established in 1990 by the South African government. The IDT's decision to launch the TSP was borne out of a concern to make a significant impact on improving the quality of schooling in South Africa. Decades of inferior education had debilitated the system for the majority of South African pupils. Education had become highly politicised resulting in a succession of school boycotts, the alienation of schools from their communities, and a general erosion of the culture of teaching and learning in the classrooms.

At least four factors played a major role in the original decision to initiate the TSP:
- the nature of the South African state in the early 1990s
- the special role and place of educational non-governmental organisations (NGOs) in South African society in the late 1980s and early 1990s
- international experiences of school improvement
- the credibility of the IDT

The nature of the South African state in the early 1990s

It is now common knowledge that the abandonment of apartheid by the South African government during the late 1980s led to a crisis for central state authority. It became increasingly impossible for the South African government to govern the country and implement its various policies (even policies of 'reform'). The effects of international sanctions and pressure were being felt in all spheres of society. The general crisis of legitimacy that had developed during this period further eroded the authority of the state. Within such a context, it is not surprising that organs of civil society (churches, NGOs, business, foundations, aid agencies and community organisations) played an increasingly important role in the delivery of much-needed services to communities.

The special role and place of educational NGOs in South African society

NGOs were at the forefront of the struggle to ameliorate the effects of apartheid. Significant amounts of local and international funding were directed to NGOs in the 1980s and early 1990s to support them in their work. This was especially true of educational NGOs working in such fields as adult basic education, in-service education and training, literacy and educare.

The IDT recognised that educational NGOs were playing an important role in educational development, especially as far as the disadvantaged majority was concerned. The IDT, therefore, hoped that it could use the TSP as a vehicle to get NGOs working together more efficiently and thereby improve the delivery of schooling in society. In fact, in their document on the first year of the TSP, Mehl, Gillespie, Foale and Ashley (1995) motivated this decision as being in line with the new government's philosophy:

> The IDT experience in its School Building activities in particular, and its role in greatly strengthening educational NGOs, suggested it has qualifications well suited to the challenge of improving the quality of schooling ... Such a role is recognised in the policy framework for the Reconstruction and Development Programme of the new government. 'Civil society must be encouraged to play an active part in the provision of learning opportunities as a part of the national human resources development strategy' (ANC, 1994, p. 60 in Mehl *et al.*, 1995, p. 5).

All of the above resulted in the IDT actively seeking partnership with the major educational NGOs in the country. Eventually about 81 NGOs would participate in the TSP, making it the biggest collaborative effort in educational development in the history of the country.

International experiences of school improvement

The IDT was also influenced by international developments in its initial conceptualisation of the nature of the TSP. Mehl *et al.* (1995) specifically refer to overseas experiences within the paradigm of 'whole school development' as being particularly pertinent to South Africa. They list the following as important principles adopted from these experiences:

In the first place, the importance of placing the school at the centre of activity was recognised – the so-called 'school-based' approach. Other features of that experience – the importance of leadership and management in the school; the need for resource-based, learner-centred teaching; the inclusion of thinking skills in the curriculum; ongoing evaluation and in-service teacher education to operate in this progressive environment – were all within the capability of available NGOs to provide (Mehl *et al.*, 1995, pp. 6–7).

The philosophy of 'school-based' educational development eventually became the core idea that drove the TSP. These and related ideas (such as the necessity of community involvement) will be discussed in more detail under the following section.

The credibility of the IDT

Although not spelled out in any of the official documents of the IDT, there is no question that the IDT saw the TSP as an initiative to enhance its own legitimacy within educational circles and the broader society. In an article in 1996, Brown and Ashley wrote:

> The IDT was set up in 1990 by the previous South African government with the mandate of aiding the 'poorest of the poor'; those most detrimentally affected by apartheid. In view of the source funding for the Trust the organisation immediately faced an issue of legitimacy in the eyes of the at-the-time disenfranchised majority, who tended to view any Nationalist Government initiative with skepticism (Brown & Ashley, 1996, p. 1).

In a personal interview with the author, Ashley (November 1997) indicated that this perceived lack of credibility also accounted for the IDT's reluctance to intervene too strongly in matters of project administration in the provinces. The decision to devolve a substantial part of the authority of the TSP to provincial Boards of Trustees can, therefore, be seen both as part of the underlying philosophy of decentralisation of the TSP, but also specifically as a consequence of the IDT's own interpretation of its lack of credibility as facilitator.

Nevertheless, the IDT's decision at the time to embark on an ambitious programme of school reform and rehabilitation was an innovative, and even visionary, initiative that was sorely needed. It attempted to address a situation in primary and secondary education in South Africa that had reached crisis proportions. Evidence from various studies has shown how the culture of learning in the schools had all but been eroded. Coupled to a general lack of resources, poorly qualified teachers, a general lack of school discipline and the inability of provincial departments of education to manage the schools in their areas properly, such an intervention – to address conditions of widespread educational adversity – was sorely needed.

Project goals and early implementation

The concept of 'whole school development' became the catchword of the TSP. It embodied the core philosophy of the main actors both at the IDT and within the

NGO community. In their 1995 document, Mehl *et al.* define the notion of whole school development in the following way:

> 'whole school development' implies a change in the whole environment that surrounds and contains the school, including the pupils, the teachers, parents, college lecturers, governing council, inspectors, subject advisors and others. It involves redefining the school as a Community Learning Centre with negotiated relationships between the above-mentioned stakeholders (Mehl *et al.*, 1995, p. 12).

For those involved in the TSP, the concept of 'whole school development' would need to manifest itself in the following practical ways in the school environment:
• co-operation between the teachers and the principal
• child-centred, discovery-based learning across the curriculum
• care for the physical infrastructure, a demonstrated pride in the grounds, and class-rooms in a condition that is conducive to learning
• on-going staff education and development
• the provision of resources for colleagues and others
• outreach to other schools in the area
• the encouragement of parental involvement in the life of the school
• an ongoing and thorough process of evaluation

The emphasis from the outset was on systemic educational change. This implied at least four types of changes: (1) There should be both top-down and bottom-up change, with all components of the system being supportive of the change. (2) Everyone at all levels should be accountable. (3) Capacity building should be prioritised in order to leave the system with better prepared and trained staff. (4) Schools should be 'given back' to their communities.

The IDT's attempt to relate the TSP to international trends, and especially to the notion of 'whole school development', was a positive feature of the project. Unfortunately, no systematic attempt was made to translate this notion into practical, concrete and measurable outcomes. A continued lack of attention to the challenge of operationalising 'whole school development' remained a problem feature of the project.

One could argue that it was more important for the IDT, at this stage, to get the NGOs and other stakeholders on board. Hence, the use of broad value-statements and catchwords such as 'holistic transformation', 'empowerment' and 'contributing to the RDP' would find widespread support, not only because they formed part of the educational paradigm of the time, but also because they resonated with the discourse of democracy, transformation and capacity building of the new government. It is, of course, essential that any initiative, especially a major national one such as the TSP, should attempt to get widespread ideological acceptance. There was, therefore, nothing wrong with the IDT and its partners reaffirming their commitment to the broad goals and values of transformation, reconstruction, development and empowerment. However, from the perspective of programme implementation, it was also essential that such broad goals and aims be translated into concrete objectives and tasks. It should have been imperative to get clarity early on in the process about the appropriate means that would lead to the realisation of these goals.

The first eighteen months of the project (mid-1993 until the end of 1994) were mainly devoted to setting up the required national and provincial structures in order to deliver the necessary services. An Executive Committee was established in early 1994, and was accountable to the National Management Forum, which in turn consisted of the nine' provincial co-ordinators and nine trustee members. Thus each province had two representatives on the National Forum.

Another important early decision concerned the total number of schools to be selected per province. At a meeting held in July 1994, it was decided that the following province-specific considerations would be taken into account in this selection: the proportion of African and coloured students; pupil–teacher ratios; pupil–classroom ratios; a poverty index; and overall literacy rate. After the provincial allocations were made, it would be the responsibility of the provincial structures (at this stage mainly NGO consortiums) to undertake the selection of schools within provinces. At the same meeting, it was decided that the final stage of school selection should meet the following criteria:

- The programme as a whole should be 'do-able'.
- Schools should be selected in consultation with stakeholders.
- There should be broad-based community support for schools chosen.
- The proportion of primary to secondary schools should be justifiable within the composition of the province.
- The balance of metropolitan, rural and peri-urban schools should reflect the composition of the province.
- The neediest magisterial districts and the provincial poverty indicators should be taken into account as a matter of priority.
- There should be a justifiable balance between 'hard-to-do' and 'easier-to-do' schools.

It should be obvious from the criteria listed above that the TSP was aimed at the 'neediest of the needy'. On the whole the thousand schools selected for the TSP were most representative not only of those which had been most disadvantaged under the previous education system, but of those which were additionally disadvantaged because of their location (deep rural), the social environment (high illiteracy) and general economic conditions (high poverty). The identification of schools was finalised late in 1994 with Eastern Cape and KwaZulu-Natal having 200 schools each; Northern Province 170; North West Province 85; Mpumalanga 75; Gauteng, Free State and Western Cape 70 each; and Northern Cape 40.

As mentioned earlier, provincial empowerment and decentralised management were seen as key principles, which in turn were translated into decisions that gave significant powers to provincial structures. Once the national management forum had been established, the focus shifted to provincial structures. Provincial consortiums, initially dominated by the NGOs, were constituted. One of the first tasks of these consortiums was to canvass for support for the TSP amongst key stakeholders in the respective provinces. Thus, representatives of the education departments, teacher organisations, trade unions, civic bodies and others were invited to participate in the TSP. Once the wider commitment had been gained, the consortiums established smaller bodies to actually drive the TSP. In this way, steering committees, working committees and forums came into being in the different provinces. All provinces were required to follow these guidelines about wide consultation, representative management structures and having a legally binding overseeing body. However, it was also recognised that provincial differences (size, politics, etc.) could mean that some differences in administration and organisation might have to be tolerated by the centre (Minutes of meeting held on 1 June 1994).

In overview, the early stages of the TSP exhibited a number of positive features. These included: (1) continuous consultation and discussion between the IDT and the provincial representatives; (2) detailed discussions and reflections on practical matters of project administration and implementation; (3) an authentic attempt to put into practice some of the key values and goals of the IDT–TSP, such as provincial autonomy and the involvement of all stakeholders in the provinces; (4) facilitating new forms of partnership amongst the NGOs; and (5) concentrating the intervention on the truly needy and disadvantaged schools. There was good leadership and guidance from the IDT during this stage. The minutes of the meetings of this period reflect a general sense of purpose and commitment to the process together with evidence of efficient central management and enthusiastic support from the provinces.

On the other hand, negative features included (1) the lack of sufficient attention to operationalising the central notion of 'whole school development'; and (2) insufficient attention to the demands of a proper evaluation study. As to the former, there is no doubt that more effort should have been devoted to refining and articulating the broad goals of the TSP into measurable and observable indicators. It should have been a major priority of TSP management to ensure that clearly defined outcome measures be developed and agreed upon, so as to ensure that every stakeholder knew exactly what to work towards. As to the latter, the evident lack of insight into the nature of implementation evaluation as opposed to outcome or impact evaluation, seriously compromised any potential value that such evaluations might have had.

THE EVALUATION STUDY

Terms of reference

In November 1996 the IDT approached the Centre for Interdisciplinary Studies at the University of Stellenbosch to develop a framework for the national evaluation of the TSP for 1997. In order to ensure some degree of consistency and comparability across provinces, as well as a more co-ordinated national evaluation, the Centre proposed an evaluation plan which would be co-ordinated by a Central Co-ordinating Agency with the following functions:
- To provide central co-ordination and administration for the national evaluation effort in 1997, to ensure effective and efficient execution of every aspect thereof
- To ensure that the evaluation projects were planned and undertaken in such a way that the comparability, validity and integration of the final results were guaranteed
- To plan and manage the research capacity component in such a way that it (1) would support the projects meaningfully and (2) was fully integrated with the actual evaluation process

- To take responsibility for the capture and analysis of the core evaluation study data and the writing of the final integrated report

The Provincial Implementation and Management Study (PIMS)

With a focus on process evaluation, it was proposed that all provinces participate in a study of the provincial implementation and management systems. The aims of this project were defined as follows:

- To document in detail how the TSP in a particular province had been set up and implemented
- To provide a detailed profile of the degree of implementation of the TSP in each province by collecting quantitative data on courses delivered
- To record what the particular problems were in the implementation of the TSP in each province
- To record what successes and achievements had materialised in a particular province

The Core Evaluation Study

It was furthermore proposed that all the provinces participate in the Core Evaluation Study. This study was to be planned and executed as a non-equivalent control group (or comparison group) design. This meant that a certain number of schools would be selected (using criteria discussed below) as experimental schools, and others as control schools, for purposes of comparison. The basic logic of this design was to establish whether the intervention (the TSP) was effective in those schools where proper implementation had taken place (the experimental schools) compared to a situation where no or very little TSP intervention had taken place (control schools).

The TSP was unique in that, outside of government, it was the largest intervention (both in monetary terms and scope) in the history of South African education. It was aimed at 'whole school development' in 1000 schools over all nine provinces. This had two immediate implications for any evaluation initiative: the decentralised and widely distributed nature of the intervention introduced a variety of new and potentially complicating factors. Thus, it raised issues about contextual differences (nine provincial histories and political settings), the question of adequate capacity across nine sites of project management as well as problems of consistency in implementation and monitoring. The relation between the centre and the provinces also created particular complications of management such as relations of power and authority between the centre and the periphery, lines of communication, separation of responsibilities and so on. These complexities can be seen in Figure 1.

PROCESS EVALUATION: THE MAIN FINDINGS OF PIMS

This section is devoted to a discussion of the implementation of the TSP in the nine provinces. Main trends that developed are summarised and there is some discussion about why, apparently, certain processes became derailed. The findings are based on a variety of data sources: secondary analysis of programme documents, field reports

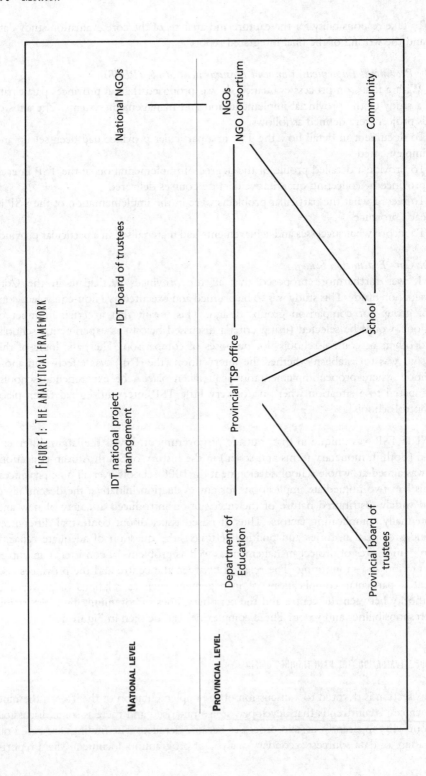

FIGURE 1: THE ANALYTICAL FRAMEWORK

and other provincial reports; observations in classes; and individual interviews with the major role-players in the provinces. Data collection was conducted by the provincial evaluation teams, which submitted three reports during 1997. These reports were discussed at joint workshops held during the year.

The tension between the centre and the provinces

Any decentralised project management contains the seeds of a tension between the centre and the periphery. This tension arises from the challenge of sharing power in such a way that delivery of services is still efficient and in compliance with central guidelines and policies.

It is possible to distinguish three main stages in the IDT's management of the implementation of the TSP in the provinces:
- a 'hands off' stage: inception – mid-1995 (two years)
- a controlled 'hands on' stage: (mid-1995 – end of 1996)
- withdrawal (1997)

From the outset, the IDT deliberately chose to devolve much decision-making power to the provinces. Provincial structures, most notably the Boards of Trustees, were given extensive powers to manage the TSP in their provinces. Further, the National Management Forum, which was set up to oversee the process at the national level, decided in March 1994 to devolve most of its authority to a six-person Executive Committee under the chair of the TSP Project Manager. In his assessment of the early stages of the TSP, Ashley interprets this as further evidence of the IDT's philosophy of managing the project in a removed manner.

When implementation commenced during the first half of 1995, it soon became apparent that many of the systems and procedures that had supposedly been put in place were not working as effectively as anticipated. With increased administrative problems, the National Management Forum, and the IDT, expressed the view that power should revert from the Executive Committee. In his assessment of these developments, Ashley (1995, pp. 2–3) says:

> The Executive Committee concept, however, had run into difficulty for two reasons. Firstly, that with monthly meetings and incomplete agendas at those meetings, decisions were not being made. Secondly, two of the provinces had repudiated the authority of the Executive Committee to make decisions, arguing that as its membership was drawn from the National Management Forum, the people concerned could not be players and referees at the same time. The new Education Portfolio director had come to the conclusion that stronger central management was needed, and therefore welcomed the motion which came from the stakeholder body that the IDT should adopt a stronger central managing role with the appointment of a project co-ordinator.

This change in management philosophy was also evidenced in the decision by the Executive Director of the IDT, Merlyn Mehl, to address the National Management Forum at its meeting of 18 August 1995. From the minutes of the meeting, it is clear that the IDT deemed it essential to intervene through a high-level presence at the Forum. Other developments that signalled tighter central management were the launch of a first internal audit by the IDT in the provinces in March 1996, as well as the decision early in 1996 to establish 'Joint Venture Agreements' between the IDT and the provincial Boards of Trustees.

Although a shift in management philosophy could alone not resolve some of the serious problems that were starting to emerge as early as the first half of 1995, it is clear that the IDT's decision to take stronger and more direct responsibility in the running of the project was justified. In the final assessment, however, the evaluation team argued that the IDT should have taken an even stronger role in getting the project on track when it became clear that essential objectives were not being realised.

This reconstruction of the three stages of management clearly illustrates the problems of managing a large project with a limited time span. The TSP only reached a significant level of implementation during the second half of 1995 (in some provinces only in 1996). By the middle of 1997 (less than two years later), most provinces were scaling down and phasing out. The true implementation of the TSP turned out to be closer to eighteen months than the expected three years!

Differential rate of implementation

There is abundant evidence from the minutes of various national meetings, the provincial evaluation reports as well as the regular assessments by the consultant to the IDT that implementation did not commence simultaneously, nor did it proceed at the same speed and intensity in all nine provinces.

During the first round of provincial reports (April 1995), it was reported that some implementation had commenced in the Northern Province and the North West. The report from the North West, however, revealed that while some implementation had taken place, various serious logistical and organisational problems were occurring, not the least of which was indecision about the co-ordinator and the lack of availability of NGO services in the province. The Western Cape report indicated that the co-ordinator was still setting up structures, consulting with various stakeholders and ensuring that the necessary infrastructures and systems were in place before implementation could start. It was disconcerting – at this early stage in the history of the TSP – to hear from this co-ordinator that 'All TSP staff members are feeling stressed and over-stretched. There are side effects, conflict in the office, more physical illnesses are becoming apparent. If we all collapse from sheer exhaustion and stress, where will that leave the project? We need to be developing ideas around getting the NGOs to take on more responsibility but we are stuck for ideas.' How the centre responded to this very obvious appeal for assistance and support is not recorded.

By the middle of 1995 the provincial reports painted the following picture: There were conflicts of interest on the Boards of Trustees in Mpumalanga and Free State. Two provinces (Free State and Western Cape) expressed concern that the administration budgets had not yet been approved. Implementation had commenced in the Western Cape and Gauteng. It had begun but been temporarily interrupted in the Northern Province, Mpumalanga and the North West (only one NGO operating). There was no implementation as yet in the Northern Cape, Eastern Cape and Free

State. No information was provided on the situation in KwaZulu-Natal.

From the reports tabled at national meetings, as well as an analysis of NGO statements, it is clear that implementation in the nine provinces followed very different time tracks. The main reasons for this were the following:

Provincial politics

The legacy of apartheid education had affected provinces differently. For example, the process of integrating previously different departments under one provincial Department of Education was more complicated in some provinces than in others. These processes not only delayed the TSP in various ways (the appointment of provincial co-ordinators, who were mainly from Departments of Education), but also made consultation between stakeholders more difficult. Some provinces were more politically sensitive, which led to lengthy consultative processes before the practical problems of implementation could be addressed.

Lack of appropriate human resources

Finding an appropriately qualified and experienced project co-ordinator in each province was not a straightforward matter. Neither was it easy to find appropriately qualified members of the Boards of Trustees. Given the key role of the provincial co-ordinator, and the responsibilities and duties of the Board members in the management of the programme at provincial level, it was imperative that the right people be appointed. Unfortunately, as the later history of the TSP showed, too many individuals were appointed in TSP offices and Boards of Trustees who did not have the required skills and experience for the job. This affected the implementation of the project from the outset.

Availability of NGOs

Educational NGOs were key players in the TSP. However, these organisations were very unevenly distributed across the country, with the majority based in Gauteng and the urban centres of Durban in KwaZulu-Natal and Cape Town in the Western Cape. By contrast the Northern Cape had no NGOs, and the North West had only one. To a lesser degree Free State, Mpumalanga and Northern Province faced similar problems. The late start to implementation in the Northern Cape and interruptions in the North West were directly related to the lack of NGO capacity in these provinces.

Overall, two important effects of the very different rates of implementation should be noted. First, differential implementation made management and administration (especially financial administration) from the centre much more difficult. Second, with different starting points and subsequent differences in the levels of implementation, it became nearly impossible for the evaluation team to conduct a systematic process evaluation, or outcome evaluation.

Systems, policies and procedures

It is entirely to be expected that a multi-site, multi-province development project such as the TSP would generate a host of administrative challenges for the IDT. It has already been mentioned that much of the extensive initial planning stage (during

1993 and 1994) was devoted to setting up a project management and an administration system that would provide effective support to the TSP. For such a system to have worked well, three essential conditions should have been met:
1. Systems and procedures appropriate to the demands and needs of the project should have been in place.
2. Policies and procedures should have been clearly spelt out and uniformly administered.
3. Adequate and continuous support from the IDT should have been provided, including training, maintenance of systems, and on-line help.

This was not the case. Indeed, a view of the chronology of events which relate to matters of management and administration shows how soon in the history of the project specific problems began to appear – and then continued to plague it.

The first half of 1995 was devoted to the installation of the computerised system that would support the financial management of the project. However, by April 1995 financial and management training had only been given in four provinces. Other provinces noted interference during the training from the co-ordinator, unavailability of all staff during training, and a lack of established office procedures.

The first documentation of problems with financial matters appears in the minutes of the meeting of 22 May 1995. At this meeting, it was noted that differences in the costing of services across provinces were observed and the provinces were requested to submit their policies on transport, catering and provincial delivery by 1 June to the IDT. At two subsequent meetings in 1995, concerns continued to be raised about the payment system, as well as with the policies regarding transport. These recurring problems led the IDT to document in a more detailed fashion which actual policies and procedures had to be followed. A project handbook was distributed to delegates at the next meeting of the National Management Forum. However, problems with the payment system continued to plague effective implementation. It became so bad that a decision was taken, later heavily criticised by the auditors of the IDT, to switch temporarily from the computerised system to a manual system of payments. At the same meeting (March 1996) mention was first made of outstanding payments to the NGOs. As became apparent from later provincial and NGO reports, late payment became a major bone of contention and led to the withdrawal of some NGOs from the TSP during 1996.

From the evidence in this brief chronological overview, it is clear that the three requirements listed earlier (appropriate systems and procedures, clarity and consistency in policies and procedures, and adequate and continuous support from the IDT) were not sufficiently met. The following could be concluded:

Management and administration systems

This was clearly experienced very differently from the perspective of the IDT on the one hand, and most of the provinces on the other. The IDT saw the computerised system as a major management tool that could meet the challenges that the TSP faced. By contrast, the computerised system of management was seen by most provinces as complex, cumbersome and not easily workable. These very different perceptions suggest – at the very least – that the initial training for the proper use of the system had been inadequate and underestimated.

Policies and procedures

The IDT went to a lot of trouble to develop guidelines and manuals on key aspects of financial administration. At the same time it should be said that the policies regarding some essential matters (most notably on costing of services and transport) remained ambiguous for a long time.

Training and support

The IDT undertook some initial training (especially on the administration of the computerised system). The request to the IDT – quite late in the history of the programme – to hold a training workshop for provincial co-ordinators suggests, however, that the IDT should have anticipated other training needs. There were other areas in the management of the project that required more proactive training. For example, what was lacking was training of members of Boards of Trustees regarding their duties and responsibilities, training of project co-ordinators in project management and administration, support to provincial offices regarding the setting up of a Trust, and conditions of service for staff.

It was the considered opinion of the evaluation team that of the three requirements listed above, the IDT could, in particular, have done much more to train and support personnel in the provinces. It seems as if the IDT relied too much, especially during 1995 and 1996, on feedback at the national meetings to identify emerging problems. The very fragmented and irregular way in which provincial co-ordinators reported to the IDT indicated that no proper monitoring and reporting system had been put in place. If it had, it might have been possible for the IDT to identify problems in capacity building and training at an earlier stage – and have allowed it to intervene in time.

Overall findings

The main findings of the PIMS are presented according to the eight analytical categories that guided both the collection and analysis of data.

Context of implementation

The overall context of the first years of TSP implementation was not conducive to the establishment of such a major initiative. It is commendable that the IDT wanted to make a major positive impact on the quality of schooling in South Africa. One also has to comment positively on the initial responses, commitment and enthusiasm from the provinces. However, ultimately the odds were heavily stacked against a successful start-up of the TSP. Neither the political climate nor the administrative infrastructure of the education departments was supportive or adequate for the establishment of such a major intervention. In fact, the severity of the conditions of adversity under which the project had to be implemented was such that it is doubtful that any intervention could have made a major impact.

Issues of governance

Although most members of Boards of Trustees were highly committed to the TSP and helped to sustain it throughout its implementation, the lack of experience and expertise in certain areas, as well as the continued conflict of interest within some Boards, should have been addressed much sooner by the IDT.

Programme model and programme evaluation

Most provinces tried to clarify the concept of 'whole school development'. However, the nature of implementation eventually made it impossible to put any consolidated, integrated and co-ordinated plan of this concept into practice. The way in which NGOs were funded individually, the lack of intervention from both the IDT and Boards of Trustees in this matter, as well as continuing differences of interpretation between NGOs, all contributed to the situation where the concept of 'whole school development' remained a good idea on paper but an ill-defined one in practice.

All provinces would have benefited from support and intervention from the IDT on programme monitoring and the utilisation of evaluation findings. The general lack of experience and understanding about the crucial role of programme monitoring and continuous self-evaluation within Boards of Trustees was one of the main factors that impacted negatively on implementation within the provinces. There is no question that the IDT should have taken a stronger role in rectifying this situation as soon as it became apparent.

Administrative structure and procedures

The overall picture with regard to office management and administration was not a positive one. Numerous cases were cited of lack of continuity in TSP offices, ineffective and inefficient management, unprofessional behaviour amongst staff members, and a lack of expertise in critical areas. The provincial Boards of Trustees as well as the IDT should have addressed these issues. There is evidence from various national meeting documents and provincial reports that the IDT was aware of most of the issues listed above. Although some of the problems (such as financial mismanagement) only surfaced during audit reports, there were opportunities for the IDT to intervene. If more care had been taken initially in specifying conditions of employment and codes of conduct for staff, and more intensive and continuous training and support had been put in place, some of the problems could have been avoided or minimised.

Stakeholder involvement

During the start-up phase and initial implementation, most provinces managed to secure the involvement and commitment of significant stakeholders in their respective provinces, especially as far as official representation on the Boards of Trustees was concerned. However, as the project continued, some stakeholders lost interest and it became difficult for the Boards of Trustees to keep everyone involved.

It was a major oversight that no province ever did a systematic and rigorous needs assessment survey before embarking on actual implementation. The results of such surveys could have made a significant contribution to collaboration amongst NGOs on the focus of implementation, and between the NGOs and schools on what needed to be delivered.

Service delivery and implementation

Any intervention is only as good as the delivery of its services. There is ample evidence from the PIMS reports that various aspects of the actual implementation went awry. It is clear that there was inadequate monitoring of actual delivery of services by the TSP offices. More care should have been taken to put into place mechanisms that could have alerted the provincial Boards of Trustees when problems arose in the field. Ultimately there was a 'patchwork' of implementation: there was no consistency in the delivery of services across and within provinces; there were insufficient checks to monitor the quality of training sessions; payments were not effected; and materials support and follow-up visits were inadequate.

NGOs

The NGOs played a crucial role in the TSP. There could not have been a TSP without significant NGO involvement. In retrospect it seems as if a more rigorous selection of participating NGOs could have been to the advantage of the TSP. While the IDT aimed to involve all relevant NGOs countrywide, the lack of selection certainly had a negative effect on the quality of service delivery. Also, with the wisdom of hindsight, it is clear that some 'code of conduct' with regard to commitment, materials support, professionalism and follow-up visits to schools by NGOs might have been useful.

Province–IDT relationships

Despite various attempts by the IDT to put guidelines and instructions for the TSP on record, these were not perceived by the provinces to be satisfactory. Lines of communication were clearly not adequate. This could be attributed to at least two factors: turnover of key staff at the IDT as well as under-resourced project management staff.

The overall impression, as far as communications and head office support are concerned, was not positive. All of this reaffirms a point made earlier that the IDT should have assigned more staff (especially more senior staff) to the project, and perhaps have considered appointing one person as a dedicated liaison officer within each province to deal with all queries, trouble-shooting and general support.

THE CORE EVALUATION STUDY

Whereas the PIMs addressed process issues of project implementation and management, the Core Evaluation Study focused on the school and issues of school management, classroom practices and student performance. Before discussing the findings, something needs to be said about the research process and how data were collected for this study. In order to ensure acceptable degrees of comparability across the nine provinces, a series of instruments was developed to be used for primary data collection. These were:

School profile questionnaire

This questionnaire aimed at collecting information about the overall profile of each school. It included information on the pupil and staff profile, as well as the physical resources available in each school. The main purpose was to gain a more systematic idea of how well schools were resourced (in order to construct an index of school resourcing) and of general student and teacher profiles.

Interview schedule for principals

This schedule aimed at gathering information regarding matters of school management. It was focused on management attitudes and practices in the school.

Observation schedules

Two observation schedules were developed: a School Observation Schedule and a Classroom Observation Schedule. The former focused on issues of school discipline and practical administration as well as on physical resources. The latter focused on various aspects of classroom practice including teacher competence and confidence, student participation and learning, assessment techniques in the classroom, physical conditions of the classroom, and education resources.

Student performance grid

In an attempt to document the performance of students in the experimental schools, their examination results in mathematics, science and English for 1995 and 1996 were collected.

School checklist

This was administered during the final phase of data collection and aimed to provide the evaluation team with (1) some corroborative information on questions asked earlier in the year; (2) detailed information on the perceptions and experiences of teachers involved with TSP; and (3) qualitative information about various aspects of 'whole school development'.

Although it was not always possible to discuss the contents of all these instruments in sufficient detail at national workshops, or even to pilot newly developed questionnaires, the results show that most of the instruments were adequate. The administration of the various instruments used in the Core Evaluation Study was done over six visits to each school, conducted between March and October 1997. Three national workshops were held in the same period which afforded evaluators the opportunity to discuss problems encountered in the field.

School management issues

Two different conclusions can be drawn from the empirical results on school management. The results revealed few differences between the TSP and non-TSP schools. Although this might suggest that the TSP training in management had not had any substantial effects, one must be cautious in jumping to this conclusion. The fact that there were a small number of non-TSP schools in the sample, which could easily distort any statistical trends, needs to be kept in mind. Other reasons might also explain the results. For example, principals in non-TSP schools might have been on similar training programmes or they might have been in contact and communicating with principals in TSP schools.

On the positive side there seemed to be a healthy appreciation of the importance of management issues amongst most principals interviewed. Where management support had been provided through the TSP, it was rated as either 'very useful' or 'useful'. Most principals operate with school management teams that meet quite often (the majority meet either weekly or fortnightly) discussing a wide range of issues. Finally, TSP schools fared slightly better when asked to produce certain school policy documents on management issues.

Classroom practices and teaching methodologies

All teachers were rated as performing between moderately well and very well with regard to the following aspects of lesson presentation: spelling out instructions, familiarity with lesson content, the use of assessment techniques, and methods to encourage pupil participation in the classroom. TSP teachers were rated as doing better than their counterparts in the non-TSP schools in one area only, namely the use of assessment techniques.

The most significant result concerned the difference in the use of group exercises between TSP classes (39%) and non-TSP classes (14%). This finding is consistent with the findings on the use of small group discussions and group work as facilitation techniques and the use of 'group assessment' between the two groups. This would suggest that TSP teachers had adopted group-based techniques in facilitating and assessing learning, as well as in their consolidating strategies. Such strategies are in line with the philosophy of child-centred learning.

With one exception, all ratings indicate that teachers in TSP and non-TSP schools succeeded well in keeping students focused on the learning task. The striking exception was in the ability of teachers (in all schools) to get students to ask questions. Only approximately half of all students were observed to ask questions during lessons.

TSP teachers were rated as doing better in task definition than their counterparts (80% compared to 60%). However, the majority of all teachers apparently do not have problems with lack of order or discipline in their classrooms. Also, most teachers use verbal praise and encouragement extensively to reward good performance in the classroom.

Attitudes towards the Thousand Schools Project

An overwhelming majority (90%) of teachers interviewed responded positively to the role and value of TSP courses that they had attended. The most common areas of value cited were improved competencies; increased confidence to deal with issues of classroom management; innovative approaches to teaching; empowerment to participate more spontaneously in matters of school management; and overall professional development benefiting from TSP intervention.

The majority of school principals indicated that the TSP had had a significant to moderate impact on most aspects of their schools' activities. Areas that received the highest ratings were school management, general school culture and atmosphere, and teaching skills. An analysis of principals' qualitative comments on the influence of the TSP revealed that approximately 55% of the comments were positive. When asked whether they had changed their management style over the past three years, the majority of school principals indicated that they had done so. Of the 30–40% who could produce key policy documents on school management, most indicated that these documents had been generated as a result of the TSP.

On the basis of these results, the following general conclusion would seem to be justified. A significant proportion of the school principals in the TSP benefited from the TSP, making them more aware of aspects of school management and the advantages of a participatory management style. In some cases (approximately 30%) it led to concrete actions such as the development of school mission statements and school development plans, as well as more democratic forms of decision-making in the school.

School performance data

This section deals briefly with evidence from student performance. It must be emphasised, however, that in the absence of reliable baseline data, any conclusions should be viewed as extremely provisional.

Three instruments were used to gather data about the students in the TSP:

- As part of the school profile data, information on student 'progression' rates (students who wrote examinations as a proportion of those who attended classes) and pass rates (proportion of students passing the examination as a proportion of those who wrote it) were gathered. These results were available for 1995 and 1996.
- A standardised HSRC test to measure English competency was administered. The thinking behind this was to test whether there would be noticeable differences between TSP and non-TSP schools after three years of the intervention.
- Finally, student performance data were gathered towards the end of the year. The scores of students in English, mathematics and science for December 1995 and December 1996 were gathered on the hypothesis that students in the experimental schools would have shown some improvement over the two years of the TSP.

Progression and pass rates

Using the differences between the 1995 and 1996 progression and pass rates, a 'mean difference progression score' and 'mean difference pass score' for all grades were calculated. These mean scores are tabulated (separately for TSP and non-TSP schools) in Table 1 below.

These results should be interpreted as follows: The score of −1.36 in the top left cell for Grade 1 (TSP school) means that 1.36% fewer students wrote examinations in 1996 compared to 1995, as a proportion of those who were enrolled. Similarly, if we look at the top right, the score for Grade 1 (−0.57) means that 0.57% fewer students passed in 1996 compared to 1995, as a proportion of those who wrote.

We would contend that no consistent pattern can be derived from these results. Although it is true that non-TSP schools received more positive mean scores (8 compared to 4 on progression rates, and 3 compared to 2 on pass rates), most of the differences are negligible. Ultimately, these results do not assist us in making any assessments regarding TSP impact on students.

Human Sciences Research Council tests

Standardised tests were administered to most schools during April–May 1997 to measure English listening, reading and writing skills at Grade 4 and 5 level and English proficiency at Grade 9. With few exceptions, average scores ranged between

TABLE 1: MEAN DIFFERENCE PROGRESSION AND PASS SCORES

GRADE	MEAN DIFFERENCE PROGRESSION SCORE		MEAN DIFFERENCE PASS SCORE	
	TSP Schools	Non-TSP Schools	TSP Schools	Non-TSP Schools
Grade 1	-1.36	3.52	-2.58	-0.57
Grade 2	1.09	-4.83	-3.56	-13.24
Grade 3	-27.61	-0.44	-2.69	3.56
Grade 4	-0.35	9.01	-2.42	1.24
Grade 5	1.01	-5.32	2.46	-3.75
Grade 6	-0.57	3.23	-3.15	-0.69
Grade 7	0.05	2.67	-1.85	1.79
Grade 8	3.85	-0.75	-1.94	-12.55
Grade 9	-0.69	4.08	-1.82	-12.68
Grade 10	-13.01	0.32	-6.52	-13.91
Grade 11	-1.11	1.39	-6.60	-25.65
Grade 12	-7.11	0.48	13.86	-4.21
Total positives	4	8	2	3

10 and 15 (stanine values of 1 or 2), indicating that the results of these classes were comparable to the lowest 11% of the original norm group. The results clearly showed that the tests were too difficult for the target groups.

Not only did feedback from the provincial evaluators confirm that the tests were experienced as too difficult by most students, but various problems were encountered during the administration of the tests. For most students, this was their first exposure to a standardised test and a lot of time had to be devoted to explaining procedures before testing could start. Furthermore, the quality of the audiocassettes which were used to administer the listening test (Grades 4 and 5) was found to be extremely poor. From discussions with the researchers who were involved in the construction of the tests, it became clear that the tests were originally standardised for urban students. The fact that such large proportions of the students in the sampled schools were from rural environments would have a major effect on the outcome of testing. Because of the above problems, these results were of little or no value.

Student performance data

Student examination scores were collected for December 1995 and December 1996 in three subjects: English, mathematics and science. Owing to a lack of comparison group data, a summary of the TSP school data only is provided. Figures 2, 3 and 4 present the data for these three subjects. The solid lines represent the 1995 examination marks, while the broken lines represent the 1996 marks.

The main trends from these three graphs are as follows:

• As far as English scores are concerned, there are no statistically significant differences between the December 1995 and 1996 scores of the pupils. The average scores for Grades 4, 9 and 10 are slightly higher in 1996 compared to 1995, but the converse holds true for other grades.

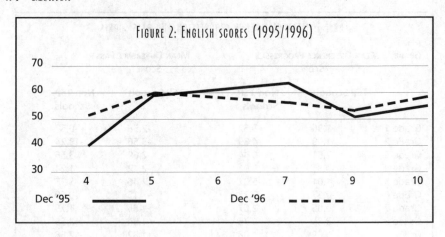

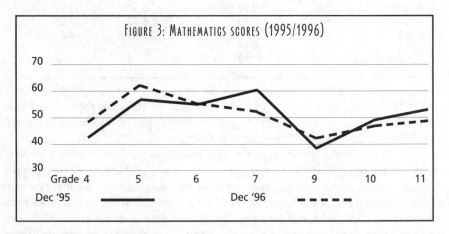

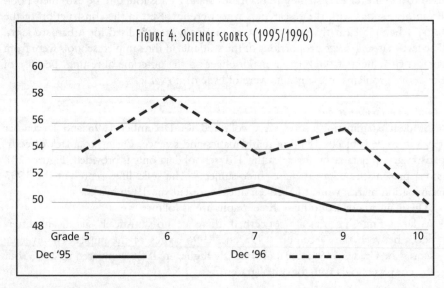

- A similar picture emerges as far as the mathematics scores are concerned: some grades did marginally better in 1996; the remainder did slightly worse.
- The results for science show a clear pattern of improvement across all grades from 1995 to 1996: the average improvement was 5%.

Concluding assessment

Although providing interesting information about the profiles of students in the TSP schools, the three measures used to collect data on student performance unfortunately shed very little light on the effect of TSP itself. This is mainly due to the lack of reliable baseline data, major methodological problems in measurement (e.g. HSRC tests) and the problem of comparability across provinces. For the sake of completeness, therefore, these 'results' have been included, but no attempt will be made to draw any further conclusions from them.

FINAL ASSESSMENT

With regard to the national implementation and management of the TSP, the evaluators' final assessment was that the programme had suffered because of a lack of continuous, high-level, efficient management. The IDT should have committed more human resources to the TSP, so as to ensure adequate, on-line training and support to the provincial offices for the duration of the project. Equally, the TSP was severely constrained by the lack of continuity of a senior-level project manager. Finally, as far as conceptualisation and design are concerned, more effort and time should have been invested in making project goals more concrete and attainable.

The timing of the project turned out to be a major constraining factor. If this initiative had been launched two or three years later, conditions in the provinces would have been more stable and the chances of success would have been higher.

Indeed, the Provincial Implementation and Management Studies paint a rather bleak picture of how the TSP was implemented in the provinces. As emphasised, the general socio-political and educational climate in most provinces was not conducive to the implementation of such a complex educational intervention. The necessary conditions for the successful implementation of a decentralised national project of such scope were not in place. The PIMS reports clearly document how underprepared most of the provinces were in terms of basic human resource capacity, infrastructure and basic project management competencies. The lack of experience and expertise, both at the level of TSP office management and the Board of Trustees, was pervasive and led to inefficient administration of the project, no proper monitoring and assessment, and mismanagement of funds. The PIMS reports also suggest that implementation was more efficient in some provinces than in others. Because of a lack of systematic baseline data, however, it remains impossible to identify province-specific outcomes. The overarching image is one of a 'patchwork' implementation.

With regard to schools, three levels of impact or potential 'benefit' were identified: school management, classroom practices and student performance. Regarding the last, the evidence is inconclusive as to whether students benefited in any way. The results with regard to school management and classroom practices are clearer. The evidence indicates that some benefits accrued to principals and teachers who participated in the TSP. These benefits included a greater awareness of school management principles and the value of participatory decision-making; new teaching methodologies and positive changes in classroom practices in favour of child-centred learning; and reported improvements in competence and self-confidence. It would be difficult to claim that these benefits accrued equally to all schools and teachers who participated in the TSP. However, there is sufficient evidence that these positive outcomes were not merely chance-related and, in the final analysis, they constitute the most positive outcomes of the TSP.

ISSUES AND INSIGHTS

Reflecting on the TSP as a whole, it is clear why a decentralised management policy was attractive to the IDT. In any context, the value of decentralising educational management has been seen as related to the creation of greater equity, improved decision-making at the local level, increased community and parental involvement, empowerment of schools and school management structures, and greater accountability at the grassroots level. It is also clear, however, that for decentralisation to be effective, certain minimum conditions need to be in place. Four categories of conditions are commonly identified in the literature: adequate local political and administrative support; behavioural and attitudinal factors (commitment, motivation, enthusiasm); organisational factors (clarity of structures and procedures); and adequate human and physical resources (capacities, expertise, experience).

The question, therefore, becomes: Were the necessary conditions in place when the TSP was initially implemented? This question translates into four more specific questions:

- Was it clear at the time (1993–4) that the required political and administrative support would be forthcoming from the provinces?
- Were there sufficient motivated and enthusiastic 'champions' of the project, especially at provincial level?
- Were the appropriate organisational systems, policies and procedures in place, or being put in place, to sustain such a decentralised programme?
- Were there sufficient numbers of trained and experienced people in the provinces (education departments, TSP offices, schools, NGOs) to carry the implementation?

In an insightful discussion of the preconditions of successful educational change, Verspoor (1989) lists three factors:

- Experience: lack of prior experience of planners, administrators and teachers with change is regarded as a major constraint in implementing change in developing countries.
- Organisation strength: the way in which the administrative structures and systems at individual schools give effective support for staff implementing change plays an important role.
- Professional capacity: the degree of professionalism of individuals and institutions is an important factor and is closely associated with the capacity for change.

The situation in schools at the inception of the TSP in 1994 provides a view of the many challenges to programme implementation at that time. The start of the project coincided with the enormous socio-political changes taking place in the country. In addition to this, all the education departments of the old regime were being transformed. Their staff were under considerable strain, teachers were under threat of redeployment, and there was often a vacuum at leadership level. All these factors impacted negatively on the effective functioning of schools and teacher motivation in many regions.

Poor discipline existed in many of the schools. Teaching and learning in the majority of cases were not taking place and the school community needed to be reorientated towards the primary aim of schooling. The culture of resistance in schools during the early 1990s, impacted negatively on school improvement projects in general.

The project was officially ended at a time when the culture of teaching and learning was in the process of being restored and a general commitment to education began to emerge in the country. It was felt by the stakeholders that the time towards the end of 1997 was more conducive to school improvement initiatives. It was a major concern amongst all stakeholders that the TSP had to end at this point in time. In essence, the timing of the TSP could not have been worse! With the wisdom of hindsight, it is clear that the IDT embarked on an ambitious and worthwhile initiative, but under the most adverse of conditions.

This is also the main lesson learnt from this particular project. Conditions of adversity affected the intervention at two levels: not only did the TSP face severely adverse conditions within the selected schools and their surrounding environments, but the actual process of implementing the intervention, and the conditions under which it was managed, were themselves adverse and not conducive to successful implementation. Thus, poor project management, lack of sufficient capacity in the provinces, and wholly inadequate infrastructure and systems constituted a second level of adversity. Ultimately, the relative lack of success that characterised the TSP may be seen as due to both these levels of adversity and their inevitable interaction.

AUTHOR'S NOTE

Although I am the only author of this paper and take full responsibility for the views expressed here, I would like to express my appreciation to every member, especially the team leaders, of the provincial evaluation teams who participated in the evaluation of the TSP. Without their contributions no report would have been possible.

REFERENCES

Ashley, M. (1995). *The state of the project in mid-August 1995*. IDT Report.

Brown, M. & Ashley, M. (1996). The Thousand Schools Project and Stephen's quality wheel. Unpublished report.

Mehl, M., Gillespie, G., Foale, S. & Ashley, M. (1995). Project in progress: The first year and a half of the Thousand Schools Project. May 1993 – December 1994. IDT Working Paper 7.

Verspoor, A. (1989). *Pathways to change. Improving the quality of education in developing countries*. Washington: World Bank.

SCHOOL ORGANISATION DEVELOPMENT

8

A success story

TERRY DE JONG

BACKGROUND

Many schools in South Africa are adverse environments. They are often characterised by low staff morale, poor resources and facilities, mismanagement, social problems such as gangsterism and substance abuse, and disillusioned learners. Schools desperately need to be more 'learner friendly'. It is thus not surprising that the greatest challenge that faces the education reform process in South Africa is the restoration of a culture of learning, teaching and services. The new education policies are clearly concerned with this critical challenge. However, structural transformation is not enough to transcend education's deep malaise. As Parker (1997, p. 39) points out: 'Changing South Africa's education system requires both structural and cultural transformation. Not just one or the other but an integration of the two'.

There is an alarming misconception that new policies will automatically bring about better schools. This has to be corrected. In a recent report on 'The Culture of Learning and Teaching (COLT) in Gauteng Schools' (Chisholm & Vally, 1996, p. 1) this issue was emphasised:

> The phenomenon, evocatively referred to as the 'collapse of a culture of learning and teaching', was most pronounced in secondary schools. In many, attendance was sporadic, the principal had given up attending to problems of the school, teachers lost their desire to teach and there were tensions between rival organisations and between all elements of the school community. Vandalism, gangsterism, rape and drug abuse were rampant. The morale of all parties in the school community was low. These realities, in many cases, overwhelmed those members of the school community who courageously, despite the unfavourable conditions, attempted to instil a new vision and ethos. While it is important not to understate the successes many school communities achieved, a cursory examination of the low pass and high dropout and repetition rates highlighted the

generalised failure of many schools. The misplaced and disarming hope that the new political dispensation at the national and provincial levels would automatically translate into better schools, accentuated the pervasive sense of powerlessness and hopelessness.

Despite this somewhat gloomy picture, let us not forget about the successes that have been achieved by many school communities. This, broadly speaking, is the purpose of this chapter. Based on a case study, it briefly tells the story of an historically disadvantaged secondary school which, in spite of extremely adverse conditions very similar to those described above, has manifested demonstrable improvements over the past five years (1993–1998). It describes the nature, role and impact of a particular school organisation development intervention which the school had engaged in over this period of time.

What are the characteristics of a successful school?

The central theme of 'learning from success' in this chapter raises the somewhat problematic question of how to define 'success'. This is more complex than it might appear to be. First, can the characteristics of a 'successful' school be defined independently of the context in which it finds itself? The critical role of context in understanding school improvement has been strongly asserted by key figures in the field (Fullan, 1991; Hargreaves, 1997; Hopkins, Reynolds & Farrell, 1996; Proudford & Baker, 1994). In South Africa, Christie and Potterton (1997) and Davidoff and Lazarus (1997) have asserted the complexity of interdependence that exists between schools and their environments. Although common characteristics of successful schools can undoubtedly be identified, these will always have to be interpreted within particular contexts.

Another difficulty occurs in asking the question 'What are the characteristics of a successful school?'. Ostensibly this requires that the characteristics of 'good' schools be identified and described. But in so doing the question neglects to focus on what makes schools become good (Austin & Reynolds, 1990). The former has largely been the concern of research into 'school effectiveness' and has focused mainly on descriptors of success, while the latter has been the concern of 'school improvement' research and has focused more on processes and strategies that lead to success. However, both are important, and both need to be taken into account in attempting to understand the characteristics of a successful school.

Despite these complexities, a review of the literature, including research studies conducted in developing contexts (for example, Christie & Potterton, 1997; Dalin, Biazen, Dibaba, Jahan, Miles & Rojas, 1994; Levin & Lockheed, 1993; Verspoor, 1989), reveals that there are many characteristics common to successful schools, even in widely different contexts. A synthesis of the most common characteristics identified across this literature review has yielded the following twelve 'generic' characteristics (De Jong, 1999). Taking the particular context of the case study school into account, these characteristics – which are a mix of descriptors and strategies – provided a useful source against which to compare the specific successes described in the case study.

Twelve generic characteristics of a successful school

It is likely that a successful school will:

- Have a shared educational vision or central philosophy which provides the school with a guiding spirit, a sense of direction, and a set of educational goals which have been collaboratively developed by all or most of the school's stakeholders
- Manifest strong and competent leadership which is generally focused on the principal but often will include the management team and other teachers
- Reflect a culture in which, generally, there is a commitment to teaching and learning, a willingness on the part of the staff to be proactive and to take responsibility for their own destiny, a collaborative approach to planning, a collegial atmosphere amongst teachers, and between teachers and students, and a sense of community, identity, pride and belonging
- Have a relatively stable staff with a low teacher turnover
- Include ongoing and regular staff development, with many opportunities for teachers to learn together, and an emphasis on personal as well as professional development
- Have a system of order and discipline which is linked to the school's educational vision, which emphasises the well-being of the students and school at large, and which is understood by teachers and students alike, is generally unobtrusive, and includes praise and encouragement and not punishment alone
- Focus strongly on teaching and learning where:
  - there is a well-organised teaching and learning programme
  - there is an emphasis on effective classroom practice
  - actual learning time is maximised
  - student progress is systematically monitored
  - the curriculum is integrated and adapted according to local needs
  - lessons plans are well organised
  - appropriate teaching and learning materials are produced and used
  - a learner-centred approach is encouraged (according to Christie and Potterton (1997) this was not uniformly present in the successful South African schools they visited)
  - teachers have high expectations and positive views of the capabilities of their students
  - success (academic, sporting, cultural, etc.) is recognised and celebrated
- Have many teachers who provide good role models by showing a commitment to teaching and learning, exhibiting good time management, and displaying concern for the well-being of students inside and outside the school
- Be a safe and secure environment both physically (the school building and grounds are secure and generally well tended) and socially (there is minimal threat of social problems such as drug and alcohol abuse, or danger to the personal safety of the teachers and students)
- Reflect a community involvement where the school addresses community needs in its educational programmes, and the community contributes to the school financially or in kind, and is involved in the life of the school. (Although this was a key characteristic identified in other developing contexts by Levin and Lockheed (1993) and Dalin *et al.* (1994), Christie and Potterton (1997) reported that

parental involvement in the 32 South African successful schools which they studied was limited)

• Have sufficient funding and basic resources – this includes technical and professional support, and a good working relationship with education authorities who provide support but respect the school's autonomy (Christie and Potterton (1997) did not find this to be a key factor in the South African context)

• Show some evidence of individual and organisational self-understanding and self-analysis, inquiry and reflection, problem-solving capacity, and an ability to use these for ongoing development and management of change (most successful schools had engaged in some form of external support or school improvement programme)

SCHOOL ORGANISATION DEVELOPMENT AS A STRATEGY TOWARDS SUCCESS

It is evident from the literature that institutional development is considered to be one of the central strategies in transforming schools. In South Africa this is evident in a number of key policy documents (Chisholm & Vally, 1996; Department of Education, 1995; 1996a; 1996b). Furthermore, there are a number of NGO initiatives at present which advocate variations of a 'whole school development' approach. Although at this stage very little research has been conducted in this area (Human Sciences Research Council, 1995), school organisation development appears to be receiving increasing attention as a potentially useful change strategy in South Africa's educational transformation process (Davidoff & Lazarus, 1997; Davidoff, Kaplan & Lazarus, 1995; De Jong, 1996; Donald, Lazarus & Lolwana, 1997; Druker & De Jong, 1996).

Definitions and theory of school organisation development

There are many definitions of school organisation development. Early definitions reflected a process orientation, emphasising the development of human resources. Later definitions sought to balance human and structural factors in the development process, while others have stressed the importance of self-renewal in the process. Based on an extensive review in the late 1980s, Miles, Fullan and Taylor (cited in Dalin, 1998, p. 185) produced this integrated definition:

> Organizational development in schools is an interrelated, systematically planned, supportive effort for achieving self-analysis and renewal. The various schemes direct their attention in particular to changes in formal and informal procedures, processes, norms and structures by the application of behavior-developing concepts and methods. The goal of organizational development is two-fold: meeting the needs of the individual ('quality of life') *and* improving the way an organization functions and the subsequent results.

More contemporary definitions (for example, French & Bell, 1995; Schmuck, 1995) appear to have a wider application, and emphasise managing the school's culture and improving student performance. In the South African context, Davidoff and Lazarus (1997, pp. 35–36) have defined school organisation development as follows:

Organisation development can be described as a 'normative re-educative' strategy for managing change, which is aimed at facilitating development of people and the organisation as a whole for the purposes of optimising human fulfilment and increasing organisational capacity.

This means that the school needs to be a learning organisation – an organisation which is constantly and systematically reflecting on its own practice, and making appropriate adjustments and changes as a result of new insights gained through that reflection. In this way we are talking about *professional* teacher development (with the emphasis on 'people' change) and *organisation development* (organisational change) in order to equip the school as a whole to become more effective in its purpose and goals. We cannot develop an organisation (school) without developing the people who work in the school; thus professional (human resource) development is seen to be a necessary aspect of organisation development.

TABLE 1: KEY THEORETICAL ASSUMPTIONS, GOALS AND STRATEGIES OF SCHOOL ORGANISATION DEVELOPMENT

Theoretical assumptions	Goals	Strategies
• The school is the unit of change	• Human resources development	• An inclusive and collaborative approach for task accomplishment, including participation in problem-solving and decision making by all levels of the organisation
• The school is the driving force of change	• Development of structures	
• Change is a complex process. There is no blueprint for change	• Changing and managing the culture and processes of the school	
• Views organisations as complex social systems	• Organisational self-renewal	• Focuses on conflict which creates possibilities for change
• Holds a developmental view of change that seeks the betterment of both individuals and the organisation;	• Create an enabling environment which supports the social, emotional, spiritual and cognitive development of all learners	• Emphases continuous learning through self-analytical methods
• Organisation improvement as an ongoing process in the context of a constantly changing environment;	• Minimises barriers to effective learning	• Takes on an action research or experiential learning approach
• A human-systems theory base which embraces democratic values		• Utilises the three fundamental strategies of process consultation, content consultation, and consultative assistance with a dual focus on person-centred and structural change
		• Rational planning, including goal-setting and planning accordingly
		• Sees organisation development practitioners a as facilitators, collaborators, and co-learners

Table 1, which is intended to be read vertically rather than horizontally, summarises the key theoretical assumptions, goals and strategies of school organisation development.

The Teacher Inservice Project's school organisation development approach

The Teacher Inservice Project (TIP), which played a central role in the intervention described below, originated from the Teacher Action Research Project, which was a small project located within the Faculty of Education at the University of the Western Cape. In the face of an impoverished education system in South Africa, the focus of this project was to assist teachers to engage more critically in their own classroom practice. However, it became apparent that a focus on the teacher in the classroom was not sufficient to ensure sustained improvement in the quality of teaching. In short, teacher development in a disabling environment appeared to have limited impact. Thus, in 1993, TIP was established with a focus on working with the school environment as a whole. In order to build the capacity of the school to manage change effectively, TIP made use of school organisation development theory to develop its particular *modus operandi*.

Briefly, TIP sees schools as organisations made up of a number of interdependent elements each of which needs to be functioning healthily for the school as a whole to be functioning healthily (Davidoff & Lazarus, 1997). The school is considered to be in a dynamic relationship with its broader context. In particular, TIP focuses on vision building, developing leadership and management capacity, establishing democratic school governance strategies and structures, and building a culture of good discipline, respect and authority in the school.

THE CASE STUDY

The story of Modderdam High School: Its context and relationship with TIP

Context

Modderdam High School is situated in Bonteheuwel, a predominantly 'coloured' suburb which was established in 1959 as a result of the Group Areas Act. The suburb is approximately 15 km from Cape Town and is characterised by small brick houses complemented in many cases by wood and iron structures in the backyard. The inhabitants of Bonteheuwel are mainly working class. Unemployment, crime, substance abuse and gangsterism are major problems in the suburb.

The school was established in 1965 and has a current roll of about 1100 learners. The present staff complement consists of 36 teachers and 2 custodial members. The curriculum is essentially academic. As a result of the school's admission policy opening up in 1990, English was added to Afrikaans as a medium of instruction to accommodate African students, who now constitute about 40% of the school's enrolment. The lack of facilities and resources in the school is pronounced. In spite of this, the school offers athletics, soccer, netball and rugby. Other extracurricular activities include the Association of Christian Students, the Muslim Youth Movement and the school choir.

Modderdam High School has a long history of being at the forefront of the 'struggle'. 'People's education' was an influential source of development at Modderdam, especially in relation to the critical appraisal of textbooks and the extension of learning beyond the syllabus. This activist energy still appears to be part of the school's culture. Many staff are key figures in teacher unions, particularly the South African Democratic Teachers' Union (SADTU). The school is also characterised by an unusually stable staff, the majority of whom have been at the school for more than eleven years. The current principal was a learner at the school from 1973 and has been an educator at Modderdam since the early 1980s. He was appointed principal in July 1997.

The political changes of the early 1990s launched Modderdam into a different kind of 'struggle'. There was a shift from protest politics to reconstruction politics. Traditionally the 'enemy' had been the state. Now the new state required the support and input of educators to make the transition towards a democratic order. This posed a major challenge to the school.

At the time, Modderdam appeared to be an 'unsuccessful' school. It presented as a severely adverse learning environment characterised by socio-economic problems such as gangsterism, substance abuse, poor discipline amongst learners and staff, and high levels of absenteeism and drop-out.

Relationship with TIP

This was the context in which TIP became involved in development work with Modderdam during 1993. The main interventions in TIP's development programme over the period 1993–8 were:

- The introduction of the Mentor Programme to the school in the latter part of 1993. The aim of this programme was to build enabling environments in which student teachers could be supported in their development while on teaching practice.
- Workshops were presented in November 1993 and in February 1994 which focused on vision building. A baseline was established in terms of the school's positive aspects, shortcomings and areas of vision building. The second workshop looked specifically at the nature of the school as an organisation and where it needed support to grow and develop. Critical issues for development were identified.
- A number of workshops were conducted during 1995 on developing criteria for a new teacher appraisal system. This process included support staff and management and aimed to develop a better standard of teaching.
- Three workshops in May 1996, with educators, learners and parents respectively, facilitated the establishment of an effective governance structure in the school.
- Follow-up workshops were conducted from August to November 1996 on governance at the school.
- An evaluation workshop on the appraisal system was conducted with all the educators in November 1996.
- A strategic planning workshop was held in May 1997. This involved all stakeholders at the school (educators, learners, support staff and parents) in a process of identifying the school's strengths and weaknesses, its developmental needs, and goals and resources for the next five years. This was followed by a review workshop in October 1997 which focused on taking stock of what was working and what needed further strategic attention.

- Two intensive workshops in November 1997 for all the educators took a critical look at planning for the implementation of Curriculum 2005.
- A review workshop was held in April 1998. In the light of decreasing resources, increasing pressures and a change in management, this workshop sought to clarify the role of management and staff in terms of the management of the school.

What this linear sequence does not reveal are the ripple effects and circular influences which characterised the ongoing developments in the school over this period. For example, the Mentor Programme raised a number of issues, one of which was the absence of an effective teacher appraisal system. Thus began the development of an appropriate teacher appraisal system at Modderdam through 1995. Ultimately, through this process, criteria were established for the appraisal of administrative, ground, educator and senior management staff in a collaborative manner. This, in turn, acted as one of a set of positive influences on relationships at all levels in the school.

What difference did TIP's organisation development approach make to Modderdam High School over the five-year period in question? Addressing this question was the basic focus of the following case study.

Aims of the study

There were a number of broad aims, two of which are most relevant to this chapter:
1. To identify what improvements had occurred at Modderdam High School over the period 1993–8, during which the school had engaged with TIP in its school organisation development intervention.
2. To determine what role TIP's school organisation development intervention had played in these improvements.

The research design

The phenomena under study, namely school improvements at Modderdam High School and the role of TIP's school organisation development intervention in these improvements could not be separated from the context in which they occurred. The contextual specificity of this study was one of the fundamental considerations in selecting the single-case study as the research methodology. As Yin (1993, p.3) puts it: 'The case study is the method of choice when the phenomenon under study is not readily distinguishable from its context. Such a phenomenon may be a project or program in an evaluation study.'

Miles and Huberman's (1994) processes of data reduction, data display and conclusion drawing provided the qualitative data analysis base for the study. Sources and methods of data collection included the following:
- 21 documents on workshops, reports, minutes and letters that reflected school development work carried out at the school from September 1993
- 22 individual semi-structured interviews with a range of staff (including 'non-teaching' staff)
- a school development questionnaire which was administered to all the staff at the school

- 9 focus group interviews with 20 Grade 11 and 20 Grade 12 learners at the school
- 40 semi-structured interview questionnaires administered to the parents or guardians of these learners
- a data verification meeting with the staff
- field notes based on on-site observation

The period of data collection and analysis ran from June 1997 to February 1999. A pilot study was conducted initially where key people were interviewed and key documents analysed. The focus of data collection during this phase was on establishing what had changed in the school since 1993. The data pointed strongly to the school having experienced many successes in its development. Subsequent data collection, for example the school development questionnaire and other sources, aimed to triangulate the findings and elaborate on these successes.

FINDINGS OF THE CASE STUDY

Areas of improvement

What were the outcomes of TIP's intervention at Modderdam? Nine major areas of improvement in the life of the school were identified from the data. The data display in Table 2 summarises them.

Security

This area of improvement was apparent across every data source. With the building of a wall around the school grounds and the inclusion of security guards, security at the school had improved considerably. This had resulted in a much lower incidence of gangsterism in the school, staff and learners generally feeling much safer, and the incidence of burglaries and vandalism decreasing. In the recent 'verification' meeting with the staff (February 1999) it was reported that there had been no burglaries at the school over the whole summer holiday – an extraordinary change.

The role of the security staff, especially in relation to their improved work ethic and pride, and the fact that they were armed, had contributed to this improvement. Reference was made to the school as being a safe haven and sanctuary where learners could find protection from the hostile environment in which they lived. Awareness programmes and a more vigilant community also appeared to improve the safety at the school. Nevertheless, some staff felt that the wall tended to constrain learners so that their energy was often channelled negatively (being destructively mischievous, fighting amongst themselves) instead of being channelled constructively into running and playing games on the sports field. Personal observation confirmed this, particularly when learners were confined to the limited space of the building during bad weather in winter and the very hot weather in summer.

The magnitude of the gangsterism problem of the past and its impact on learning were raised by the majority of the learners. Although there was an initial perception amongst learners that the school felt like a prison when the wall was first erected, they were unanimous that the improved security at Modderdam had made a very positive difference to the learning environment. Some learners pointed out that the improved security system also minimised truancy. Reference was also made to the improved

TABLE 2: AREAS OF IMPROVEMENT

NATURE OF IMPROVEMENT	WHOSE PERSPECTIVE	IMPACT ON SCHOOL
Security		
The wall	S, L & P	Lower incidence of gangster-
Security guards	S, L & P	ism
Greater control of attendance	S, L & P	Lower incidence of burglaries and vandalism
		Staff and learners feel safer
		Minimised truancy
		Can learn better
Physical conditions		
Broken windows replaced	S, L & P	Protection from the 'elements'
Improved cleanliness	S & L	School environment more con-
Greener environment	S	ducive to learning
More welcoming staff room	S	
Relationships between staff		
Better communication	S	Improved culture of teaching
Greater tolerance	S	and learning
Common understanding	S	
Team spirit	S	
Relationships between staff and learners		
More mutual respect	L & S	Improved culture of teaching
Relaxed and friendly atmosphere	L & S	and learning
Caring culture	L & S	
Greater commitment to teaching	L & S	
Learners more confident	L & S	
Relationships between learners		
Low incidence of racism	L & P	Improved culture of teaching
Acceptance of different cultures	L	and learning
Integration of cultures	S, L & P	
Broader use of 2nd languages	L & P	
Relationship between school and parents		
Better communication	P	Community support
Parents called in when there is a problem	S & P	Improved discipline of learners
Greater attendance of parents at meetings	S, L & P	

Management and governance		
Decentralisation	S	Improved discipline amongst
Ownership	S	staff and learners
Democratisation	S & L	Better financial management
All stakeholders represented	S, L & P	School better organised
Committee system	S & L	Learners more punctual
Participative and consultative	S	Better attendance
Accountability	S & L	
Modernising of administration	S	

Quality of teachings		
More innovative	S	Learners more serious about
Less reliant on textbooks	S	work
More learner-centred	S & L	Learners more assertive with
Better preparation of exam	S	staff
papers – greater relevance		Greater confidence for exams,
Staff more committed	S , P & L	especially matric
Positive role-models	L	Better motivated
Extended curriculum	S & L	Lower drop-out rate
Inclusion of computers	S & L	
Inclusion of technical drawing	S	

Sense of identity and community		
Increased pride	S, L & P	Increase in number of learners
The school as a 'family'	S, L & P	wanting to register at school
More school uniforms worn	S & P	Best school in Bonteheuwel

Key: S=Staff; L=Learners; P=Parents.

management of attendance at the school where learners had to receive written permission to leave the school grounds. Most parents commented extensively on the improved security at Modderdam. They emphasised the importance of their children being safe. Many made connections between the better security and improved discipline, also with particular reference to truancy.

Physical conditions

The majority of staff, learners and parents made several references to the improved physical conditions of the school. The replacement of broken windows was consistently raised by all three groups. Many of the staff commented that there were considerably fewer windows broken or missing than in the past. Perspex instead of glass windows had clearly played a part in this. Most of the learners made reference to how this positive development had contributed towards a better learning environment by keeping the rain, wind and cold out of the classrooms. The involvement of the custodial staff in the decentralised management system of the school appeared to have contributed to this improvement.

Reference was made by approximately half the staff and learners alike to the improved cleanliness of the building. Although there was a fairly high consensus amongst staff that the school was 'greener' than in the past, concern was expressed by a few that vandalism involving theft of trees and plants had restricted the greening of the school. There was also a consistently high agreement amongst staff that the staff room environment was more welcoming (e.g. curtains, tablecloths and personal touches such as photographs on the walls).

Relationships between staff

There was generally a strong consensus amongst staff that relationships between themselves had improved, especially in terms of better communication. This was manifested in greater collegial assertiveness: people seemed to have the courage and willingness to speak out in a 'public' forum (e.g. staff meetings). Tolerance of different views amongst staff and a common understanding of issues were further characteristics of the improved relationships.

There was some evidence that staff relationships had been negatively affected during the first year with the new principal (June 1997–June 1998). Team spirit was considered by some to be not as strong as in the past. References were made to the recent change in management structure and style as having had a negative influence on staff relationships, especially in relation to ownership issues and less participatory decision-making. Relationships amongst staff were also unusually strained over this time as a result of pending rationalisation.

Relationships between staff and learners

At least two-thirds of the staff said that there was a better relationship between themselves and the learners especially since the new principal took over in 1997. Some suggested that this shift could have been a result of his firm management, which contributed towards better discipline amongst the learners and staff. There was a strong indication that there was more respect between staff and learners and that they were more open and direct with each other. This characteristic was raised consistently by the majority of learners and parents too, with references often being made to a more caring culture in the school and a greater commitment to teaching by the staff.

Staff generally felt that learners were more confident about speaking to them, expressing their opinions and being more assertive, especially in the classroom. One explanation for this was that the school had made an effort to implement the new South African Schools Act which, amongst other things, advocates learners' rights, learner representation on the Governing Body, and greater accountability of staff to their learners. Documentation had indicated that a number of workshops facilitated by TIP on the Act had been attended by many staff and learner representatives. Trust and accountability seemed to be a feature of this improvement. Many learners also made reference to their improved confidence in communicating with the staff. The theme of caring and commitment often pervaded their perspectives.

In spite of the above improvement there were some striking comments on the role of the education crisis and its impact on relationships between staff and learners. Reference was often made to the tremendous pressure that they were experiencing as a result of rationalisation and the abolition of corporal punishment.

Relationships between learners

Almost every learner (and, to a lesser extent, the staff and parents) said that the relationships between themselves had improved. Most referred to the lower incidence of racism at the school. This was a view expressed by both coloured and African learners. Some made comparisons between Modderdam and other schools, pointing out that there was a much higher and healthier level of integration between the two groups at Modderdam than at other schools. Many referred to the positive role that the staff were playing in developing this integration and the 'zero' tolerance rules at the school concerning racist behaviour. Some of the African learners commented specifically on feeling accepted in the historically 'coloured' community at the school. Many parents also commented on the school being successfully integrated and non-racist.

Relationship between school and parents

There was some evidence, albeit limited, which suggested that there was a better relationship between the school and parents. A few parents commented on improved communication, which they felt was facilitated by regular circulars and newsletters. Some parents and staff referred to the school's policy of calling parents in when there was a problem with the learner. A few parents referred to the caring culture of Modderdam.

An indicator which supported the improved relationship between the school and parents was the greater attendance of parents at school meetings. However, parental involvement was still considered to be limited. Most of the learners pointed out that their parents took an interest in their school work but found it difficult to attend meetings.

Management and governance

This area of improvement was strongly evident across all the sources of data. One of the most celebrated changes in the management and governance of the school was its democratisation through the involvement of all stakeholders. Many staff associated this with TIP's organisation development work. The decentralisation of management, whereby committees had been established to run the school, was considered by most staff to be a highly successful strategy. However, concern was raised by many staff that, since the new principal had taken over, this structure had been replaced with a more centralised system. This issue was acknowledged by the management team, some of whom suggested that the rationalisation process had increased the workload of the staff, leaving them with less time to be involved in managing the school.

There was a high consensus amongst staff that the school's finances were being managed more efficiently and transparently. One indicator of this was that school fees had been paid more readily (80% of the 1998 school fees had been collected by June). This was seen by some staff to be a reflection of improved parent support. The modernising of the school's administration through the use of computers was also considered to be an improvement in the management of Modderdam.

There was also some indication from staff that there had been an improvement in the discipline of both staff and learners in terms of more arriving at school on time and being in their classrooms. This development was associated by some staff with better accountability of staff towards learners and the firmer management of the learners by the new principal. However, there were mixed feelings amongst the staff as to whether discipline had in fact improved, with a few commenting on how the rationalisation process had affected the morale and commitment of some staff and how the strain on resources and larger classes had contributed towards learners being at times undisciplined.

Expressed through a range of comments, at least half of the learners believed that the school had improved in its management and governance over the past few years. These comments referred to the school being better organised, and there being a more consultative approach to governance through the establishment of structures such as the school's governing body and the SRC. The establishment of governance structures was also seen as helping to facilitate collective problem-solving. Most significant were views expressed on the improved discipline amongst staff and learners alike. Many learners associated this with the improved security at the school and the increased commitment to quality teaching by the staff. The new principal was considered by a large number of learners to have contributed to the improved discipline through his firm and fair management of the learners and staff.

Better management of the school was also raised by almost all the parents. Many commented about the more stringent control the school had over the learners, especially in terms of permission having to be obtained should a learner wish to leave the school premises. Mention was often made of the positive effect that the wall and added security had had in keeping the learners in the grounds. This was linked to the gates being kept closed, improved punctuality and a lower incidence of truancy. A few parents commented on the neater appearance of the learners, who were required to wear the correct school uniform. Some parents referred to the strict but caring management style of the current principal as being responsible for many of the improvements at the school. Reference was made to the better communication between parents and the school, especially in relation to disciplinary matters.

Quality of teaching

There was a high level of consensus amongst the staff that the quality of teaching at Modderdam High had improved substantially. Staff saw this in more innovative approaches to lesson preparation (e.g. worksheets were more creatively prepared), less reliance on textbooks (e.g. materials used from a range of resources such as newspapers and outings), using a more learner-centred approach (e.g. learners worked more often in groups on a co-operative basis, and were expected to research information more independently of the teacher), and a more creative preparation of examination papers with greater relevance to current affairs and issues. Apart from the opinions of staff, this was also apparent through independent observations of the quality of worksheets and examination papers.

Some staff suggested that with the cutback in resources these improvements had developed out of necessity rather than pedagogical wisdom! Other issues raised concerned staff being overloaded, needing more support in developing their teaching methods, and concern that learners should take more responsibility for their learning.

The majority of learners referred to the greater levels of commitment to teaching compared to a few years previously. They said that many of the staff 'went the extra mile' in offering extra lessons, encouraged and motivated the learners to apply themselves seriously to their work, manifested a more caring and mentoring disposition towards them, and facilitated a more interactive process of teaching and learning in the classroom (e.g. encouraging more questioning). A few learners pointed out that as a result of these positive changes learners were generally more serious about their work, and more assertive and challenging of staff in class. Some learners said that with the improved teaching at the school many Grade 12 learners felt more confident about their matriculation exams. Although unacceptable social behaviour of some of the staff (e.g. smoking in the corridors, smelling of alcohol) was mentioned, there was a strong sentiment amongst learners that staff were taking their teaching more seriously than in the past, and some felt that staff at Modderdam presented positive role models.

Learners commented on the improved extended curriculum, referring to the inclusion of career education, environmental awareness and sexuality education. Many said that the recent inclusion of computer work at the school was a great improvement given the importance of computer literacy in the workplace. It was suggested that the number of computers should be increased so as to give more learners access. Recent information (February 1999) confirmed that there were now 26 computers available and that all classes had a computer period in a 7-day cycle.

A few staff raised the recent addition of technical drawing to the curriculum as being an improvement, especially as it allowed learners to enter into a technical senior certificate at a technical training school after Grade 9. The inclusion of Xhosa and extension of Afrikaans to second and third languages were also considered by some staff to be an improvement to the school's curriculum.

The most prominent theme that emerged from almost all the parent interviews was the improved commitment of the staff. This was often referred to in terms of their offering extra support to the learners (e.g. afternoon classes), their caring and encouraging approach to teaching, and the better communication between staff and learners.

Sense of identity and community

There was a very high consensus amongst the staff that there was an increased pride in being a member of Modderdam High School within the school community. Increased enrolment at the school was taken as a positive indicator, and was linked to the good security and firm discipline. Some staff and parents talked about the school as being a family. Learners used the 'family' metaphor too, referring to the principal as a strict but encouraging guardian or parent of the learners at the school. There were numerous comments made by the learners about the improved sense of identity and pride in being a member of the Modderdam community. Another indicator of this, which many parents mentioned, was the better dress code at the school: many more learners than in the past wore the correct school uniform. The Grade 12s made particular reference to their smart tracksuit tops which identified them as the 1998 matriculants of Modderdam High School.

In strong support of these improvements was the exceptionally high level of consensus between staff, learners and parents that Modderdam High was the best school in Bonteheuwel.

TIP's role in the development of Modderdam High School

How did these improvements develop at Modderdam? There was a considerable amount of evidence that TIP's school organisation development intervention played a major role. However, the extent of TIP's influence varied according to the source of data examined. It was apparent from the documents, observation of workshops, and the staff's perspective that TIP had played a direct and important role in the development of the school. However, TIP was not mentioned at all by the learners and parents as being a source of influence. This was not surprising as the development of staff was a critical feature of TIP's work. Although learners and parents were included in the school development process, their involvement was limited in comparison to the staff. Nevertheless, the main sources to which the learners and parents had attributed the school's improvement were, in fact, the development of the staff and governance structures – elements on which TIP had focused most directly.

From the data seven major themes were identified as representing the key strategies that contributed to the success of TIP's organisation development work at the school.

People development

People development was a consistently strong theme that kept on emerging in the data. There were three main dimensions to this. Firstly, and perhaps most profoundly, was TIP's focus on self-reflection. Some staff used the term 'self-investigation', highlighting the fact that they seemed to discover a lot within themselves of which they were previously unaware. Others emphasised the problem-solving nature of this process whereby answers to problems had to be created by staff themselves.

Secondly, the development of self-confidence and empowerment appeared to be themes intrinsic to TIP's people development focus. The building of the wall was a good example of staff problem-solving and their having the confidence to raise the funds through the Reconstruction and Development Programme. Many comments suggested that introspection and change within people are fundamental to organisational change.

Thirdly, there was the ongoing formative evaluation of the development process. This strategy was manifested most significantly in TIP's emphasis on co-operative reviewing and planning, often based on extensive auditing of the views and needs of all participants. In sum, it would appear that TIP placed considerable emphasis on the personal development of staff in its work. It took a critical humanistic approach which focused most particularly on the development of people-in-context.

Relationships

Implicit in the above was the facilitation of more open, honest and respectful relationships amongst staff. A range of strategies was used in support of this process; for example, involving all the stakeholders in vision building. This included teaching staff, 'non-teaching' staff, learners and parents. Central to vision building was the development of a common understanding of issues and challenges amongst staff. In the data, many references were made to team building and the role that workshops played in facilitating better communication.

Critical entry points

A core element of TIP's consultative and co-operative planning was the strategic use of critical entry points. In conjunction with key people in the school, this involved identifying important areas in need of development and then facilitating a project to address those needs which would be most likely to benefit the whole school context. TIP's history with Modderdam reflected how a range of projects, initiated from particular needs, became vehicles for wider organisation development. In the earlier years (1993–5) this included the Mentor Programme and Teacher Appraisal Programme. More recently, the Strategic Planning Programme has focused on the implementation of the new Schools Act, especially the establishment of governance structures. Curriculum 2005 also became a focal point in TIP's work with the school.

Workshops

When TIP conducted its first workshop on the school's strengths and weaknesses in September 1993 there was much scepticism amongst the staff about this method. Its novelty and uniqueness took on a somewhat humorous tone when the educator primarily responsible for initiating and driving the development process was labelled 'Mr Workshop'. However, the facilitative role that the workshops played in improving communication and relationships amongst the staff was later consistently appreciated. As a facilitative strategy, workshopping had come a long way since 1993. Thus, in February 1999 three educators at the school themselves conducted a workshop for the staff on strategic planning.

Strategic planning

Workshops were used among other things to facilitate strategic planning. The significance of this strategy was raised in relation to the intensive work TIP had done with staff, learners and parents in preparing them in advance for the establishment of a School Governing Body. It was apparent, mainly from the documents, that strategic planning included specific input on the content of certain policies such as the criteria for electing a Governing Body. While most of TIP's development strategies appeared to be process-oriented, there was a parallel focus on establishing structures and procedures in strategic planning. The creation of committees to manage the school, such as the Disciplinary and Finance Committees, was a good example of structures which had to ensure that the process of democratising the management of the school stood a good chance of being successful.

Quality of facilitation

The quality of TIP's process of facilitation also seems to have been important. Reference was often made to the respectful manner in which TIP guided the process of the school's development, and many staff appeared to benefit personally from observing the facilitation skills of the TIP people when they were conducting workshops.

Understanding how a school functions as an organisation

Although a concern was expressed by a few staff that the developmental process of building a healthy organisation at Modderdam was poorly understood, there was considerable evidence to suggest that, ultimately, most of the staff had a sound understanding of school organisation development as a process. Perhaps TIP's visual presentation of its organisation development 'map' had contributed to this. One staff member explicitly credited the 'map' with helping him understand how a school functions as an organisation. It is also possible that the emphasis on self-reflection contributed to the level of insight shown by staff.

ISSUES AND INSIGHTS

How do Modderdam High School's successes compare with the twelve 'generic' characteristics of a successful school identified from the literature? What can we learn from the success story of this school? What are the implications of these insights for the development of healthy learning environments in South African schools? The discussion that follows attempts to address these questions.

There are striking similarities between this case study's profile of success and the 'generic' profile of a successful school: for example, the presence of good management and leadership, developing a common educational philosophy, a focus on teaching and learning, and having a stable staff. How does this relate to the contextual specificity of the case study? Even though safety and security is one of the 'generic' elements of a successful school, in this social context it needs to be given special priority because of the profoundly negative impact problems such as gangsterism and vandalism have on the lives of staff and learners. Thus the wall at Modderdam reflects more than physical safety. It symbolises a hierarchy of needs reminiscent of Maslow's 'pyramid'. Without people's basic needs being met, little meaningful learning can take place. The bitter irony of the wall is that it has been created to protect the school community from the very community which it is serving – this at a time when the educational rhetoric is crying out for schools and the community to work closely together. Perhaps it is not so surprising after all that Christie and Potterton (1997) discovered that community relationships and parental involvement played a minimal role in contributing towards the success of the 32 primary and secondary schools which they examined from a range of adverse rural and urban contexts in South Africa. The shocking poignancy of this parent's comment sums up the critical importance of ensuring safety and security of learners in many of our embattled schools: 'Hulle kan maar sê dat Modderdam is nou 'n tronk maar ek sê dis liewers 'n tronk waar dit veilig is as wat dit 'n oorlogsveld is.' (They can say that Modderdam is now a jail but I say better a jail where it is safe than it being a war-zone.)

Schools are microcosms of society. One of the most pressing issues in South Africa at present is the unacceptably high level of crime that besets all. Although in other contexts a wall may not be the appropriate answer, it is likely that all schools, not only those in historically disadvantaged communities, will have to take practical steps to protect their learners. Certainly, the pervasive culture of violence in South Africa will have to be tackled on a macro level as well, in order to make a real difference to the well-being of all citizens.

Another sobering lesson from Modderdam's story is the basic importance of establishing a physical environment in a school which enhances learning. This includes the condition of the school building and facilities. Chisholm and Vally (1996, p. 13) point out from their study that 'in contexts where schooling has collapsed, the condition of school buildings and facilities makes an incalculable difference to the climate of learning and teaching in a school. The morale of school-goers and teachers alike is deeply influenced by the physical environment.'

Good relationships across all the natural boundaries in a school's social fabric are fundamental to a healthy learning environment. Modderdam's story of success reinforces the importance of establishing and maintaining open, honest and respectful relations between all the stakeholders in the school community. Vision building in an inclusive and collaborative way was a powerful strategy used to achieve this and was implemented as a key strategy by TIP from the beginning. As reflected in the generic features of successful schools, a collaborative and evolutionary approach to planning, and developing a common understanding of issues, should be a core activity in team building.

People development was a major element in the success of TIP's intervention. This humanistic perspective regards the individual's contribution in organisations, and the interaction between people within the organisation, as central to the life of that organisation (Dalin, 1998). The empowerment of staff through the development of self-reflection and problem-solving skills was a central strategy adopted by TIP. Being able to be proactive and to manage change effectively are key processes in sustained school development, and are themselves firmly rooted in effective empowerment. In an education system which has historically fostered subservience, the development of independent, critical and creative thinking amongst school staff poses a mammoth task. As Christie and Potterton (1997) observe, a successful school will feature a willingness and ability on the part of the staff to take initiatives and move from passivity and feeling victimised to active agency. In an educational culture which has been marked by authoritarianism this will require much effort.

External support from a change agent and the education authorities is essential to sustained development work. This includes sufficient school funding and resources, without which there is a serious threat to the morale and commitment of staff. Recent observations of staff morale at Modderdam reflect a disturbing disillusionment with the lack of support and guidance from the education authorities. Clearly external changes and forces such as rationalisation have a profound effect on schools, especially those which are having to 'downsize' in historically adverse contexts. Even with intensive human resources development in a school, there is a fine line between being able to manage change effectively – and giving up under the sheer pressure of adversity. Schools cannot go it alone!

Schools are notorious for their unequal power relationships. A key factor in Modderdam's success was the 'flattening' of the management structure whereby real power was given to the staff through a decentralised committee system. The participatory-democratic leadership style of the previous principal established the foundation for this. It was evident too that the learners were more aware of their rights, and looked to the staff as role models of democratic practice. If South Africa's fledgeling democracy is to grow in strength, then schools really do need to model democratic values and behaviour in this way.

Arising from the above is the fundamental issue of 'readiness' for development. This is particularly relevant in an educational climate which requires schools to do more and more with less and less. Is it feasible for schools to embrace participatory decision-making and a decentralised management system, both of which require much energy, under such strained circumstances? Recent observations have pointed to strong signals at Modderam that many staff were finding it difficult, under increasingly heavy teaching loads and the stresses of large classes, to participate in any meaningful way in the management of the school.

Development is an ongoing, organic process which requires consistent nurturing. It takes time, and seldom responds in any sustained way to 'quick-fix' solutions. The case study of Modderdam spanned a five-year period which can only be considered a 'snap-shot' in the life of the school. In spite of the many improvements experienced by the school, sustainability of the development process remains very much an issue. The ideal is that a school becomes a learning organisation which has a self-renewing capacity to manage change in a proactive manner. It would seem from recent developments at Modderdam that the external pressures and stretched internal resources have placed a serious threat on the sustainability of the development process.

Evaluation of school development programmes is often driven by the need to measure impact with a predominantly summative objective in mind. Notions of linear causality tend to underpin this approach, which is further compounded by political and economic pressures to induce change at the quickest and cheapest rate with instant tangible results. Little cognisance is taken of the complexities of change, which is an intricately interconnected and often unpredictable process. In concluding this chapter it is appropriate to caution against oversimplifying the evaluation of school development programmes into distinct areas of outcomes and process. In evaluating any social development intervention we need to recognise that change outcomes and change processes are inextricably bound to one another. The building of the wall at Modderdam was a distinct outcome of TIP's intervention. It became the powerful source of a complex change process in itself. The security at the school improved, which in turn contributed to numerous other positive change outcomes and processes. Thus, change outcomes and processes affect, and are affected by, each other. This recursive feature of social and educational change poses a formidable challenge to any evaluation process.

ACKNOWLEDGEMENTS

The author would like to acknowledge the University of Cape Town for providing funding for the research described in this chapter.

REFERENCES

Austin, G. & Reynolds, D. (1990). Managing for improved school effectiveness: an international survey. *School Organisation, 10*, 178–197.

Chisholm, L. & Vally, S. (1996). Report of the committee on the culture of learning and teaching in Gauteng schools. University of the Witwatersrand, Johannesburg.

Christie, P. & Potterton, M. (1997). School development in South Africa: A research project to investigate strategic interventions for quality improvement in South African schools. Final report for Education Department, University of the Witwatersrand, Johannesburg.

Dalin, P. (1998). *School development. Theories and strategies.* London: Cassell.

Dalin, P., Biazen, A., Dibaba, B., Jahan, M., Miles, M. & Rojas, C. (1994). *How schools improve. An international report.* London: Cassell.

Davidoff, S. & Lazarus, S. (1997). *The learning school. An organisation development approach.* Cape Town: Juta.

Davidoff, S., Kaplan, A. & Lazarus, S. (1995). Organisation development: An argument for South African schools. In G. Kruss & H. Jacklin (Eds.), *Realising change* (pp. 170–182). Cape Town: Juta.

De Jong, T. (1996). The educational psychologist and school organisation development in the reconstruction of education in South Africa: Issues and challenges. *South African Journal of Psychology, 26*, 114–119.

De Jong, T. (1999). School organisation development (OD): Learning from a success story in South Africa. PhD thesis: University of the Western Cape.

Department of Education, Republic of South Africa (1995). *White Paper on Education and Training.* Pretoria: Department of Education.

Department of Education, Republic of South Africa (1996a). *White Paper on the Organisation, Governance and Funding of Schools.* Pretoria: Department of Education.

Department of Education, Republic of South Africa (1996b). *Changing management to manage change in education. Task team report on education management development.* Pretoria: Department of Education.

Donald, D., Lazarus, S. & Lolwana, P. (1997). *Educational psychology in social context.* Cape Town: Oxford University Press.

Druker, B. & De Jong, T. (1996). The educational psychologist as organisation development consultant in South African schools: A framework for conceptualising substantive issues. *School Psychology International, 17*, 17–32.

French, W.L. & Bell, C.H. Jr. (1995). *Organization development. Behavioral science interventions for organization improvement.* New Jersey: Prentice Hall.

Fullan, M. (1991). *The new meaning of educational change.* London: Cassell.

Hargreaves, A. (1997). Rethinking educational change: Going deeper and wider in the quest for success. Paper for the International Centre for Educational Change, Ontario. Institute for Studies in Education of the University of Toronto, Ontario, Canada.

Hopkins, D., Reynolds, D. & Farrell, S. (1996). Moving on and moving up: Confronting the complexities of improvement. Paper presented to the Symposium on School Effectiveness and School Improvement. Annual Conference of the British Educational Research Association. University of Lancaster, September 1996.

Human Sciences Research Council (HSRC) (1995). Printout of South African research abstracts in the field of school organisation development and school improvement. Pretoria: HSRC.

Levin, H.M. & Lockheed, M.E. (1993). *Effective schools in developing countries.* London and Washington: The Falmer Press.

Miles, M.B. & Huberman, M.A. (1994). *Qualitative data analysis.* Thousand Oaks: Sage.

Parker, B. (1997). Valuing education construction. In a report on the COLTS campaign consultative conference held from 22 to 24 August 1997 at the Eskom Conference Centre. Pretoria: Department of Education.

Proudford, C. & Baker, R. (1994). Looking at school improvement from a contextual perspective. *School Organisation, 14,* 21–35.

Schmuck, R.A. (1995). Process consultation and organization development today. *Journal of Educational and Psychological Consultation, 6,* 207–215.

Verspoor, A. (1989). *Pathways to change. Improving the quality of education in developing countries.* Washington DC: The World Bank.

Yin, R.K. (1993). *Applications of case study research.* Newbury Park, CA: Sage.

HEALING WOUNDS OF WAR IN ANGOLA 9

A community-based approach

MICHAEL WESSELLS & CARLINDA MONTEIRO

BACKGROUND AND AIMS

Childhood adversity is often particularly severe in situations of war. War destroys children's rights, damages children's physical and psychological well-being, and shatters the communities that constitute children's life-support systems. The adversity is also long-term. War destroys infrastructure, heightens political and economic turmoil, disrupts education, and amplifies poverty, one of the primary sources of armed conflict. Even after the fighting has ended officially, violence remains widespread and normalised, placing children at risk. This chapter focuses on an attempt to address the adversities created through decades of war in Angola (see Figure 1).

The Angolan war

Initiated in 1961 as a liberation struggle from Portugal, the Angolan war has roots in the wider, regional political struggles in southern Africa (Minter, 1994). Angola achieved its independence in 1975. Soon afterwards, the Angolan war became a mixture of internal war and external proxy war, as the former Soviet Union and Cuba backed the socialist government party (MPLA) while the US and South Africa backed the opposition forces of Jonas Savimbi and UNITA. Following a brief interlude in 1991, Angola conducted its first democratic elections in 1992. But UNITA rejected the results, plunging the country into the most vicious phase of fighting, from October 1992 to May 1994. By mid-1993, nearly 1000 people were dying daily in the war from starvation and disease if not from direct attack. In the 21-month siege of the city of Kuito, an estimated 20 000–30 000 people died, mostly women and children (Human Rights Watch, 1994). By 1993, the number of internally displaced people had reached 1.2 million, and an estimated 3.3 million people were in need of emergency assistance (UNICEF, 1995). Overall, approximately 900 000

FIGURE 1: ANGOLA AND ITS PROVINCES

Underlinings designate the provinces where the project work reported on
in this chapter were conducted

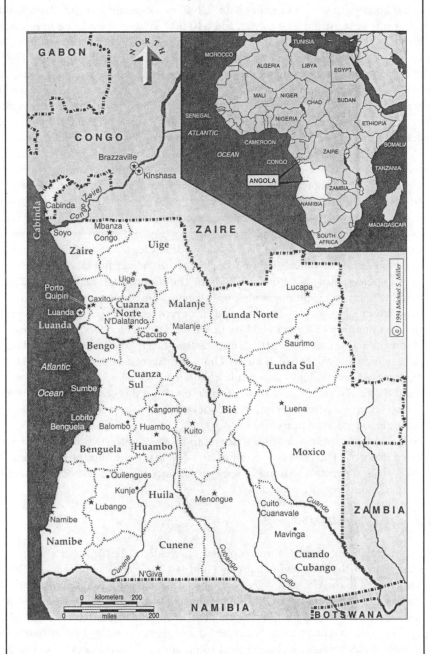

people have died in the war. Since the war extended over several decades, two generations of Angolans grew up in conditions in which war was a daily part of social reality.

Children, who comprise half the population in Angola, shouldered some of the heaviest burdens of war and its aftermath. UNICEF estimated in 1993 that 500 000 child deaths were attributable to war, and 840 000 children were living in especially difficult circumstances. In Luanda, there were large numbers of unaccompanied children, who are particularly vulnerable physically and psychologically (Boothby, 1988). The war devastated the health infrastructure, aggravated already extreme poverty, and ushered in outbreaks of diseases such as measles, malaria and tetanus. The mortality rate for children under 5 years of age soared to over 300 per 1000. Malnutrition rates for children under 5 was approximately 15% by 1995. Nearly 60% of children had no regular schooling, and literacy rates for women were under 10% (Tvedten, 1997).

Although the war ended officially in 1994 with the signing of the Lusaka Protocol, peace has not been achieved in Angola, as large-scale fighting re-erupted in late 1998. This chapter focuses on the time period from late 1994 to September 1998, before the most recent round of war. Following the signing of the Lusaka Protocol, the problems facing children and communities continued. War stresses strongly affected families already stressed by poverty and other issues, leading to increased rates of family violence. The war left a deadly legacy of 6 million landmines, which have disrupted agriculture, impeded the return home, and created large numbers of amputees, many of whom are children. The aftermath of war produced a wave of criminal violence, including widespread banditry involving youth who had little formal education, no job training and few prospects of gainful employment. Significant numbers of former child soldiers have been demobilised, but the process of reintegrating former soldiers back into civilian society has gone slowly. Although an integrated Government of National Unity and Reconciliation was established in 1996, tensions remain high. As a result, children are socialised into a system of violence at the family, community and societal levels. Since this system is self-perpetuating, intervention is needed to interrupt cycles of violence and to transform the situation in the direction of peace.

This chapter examines a large-scale, multi-province intervention to assist war-affected children. The project evolved from a Luanda-based pilot project (Wessells, 1996), which warrants discussion in some detail since it guided the development of the larger, multi-province project.

The initial, Luanda-based project

Recognising the emotional burdens placed on children, the Angolan government invited in 1994 the Christian Children's Fund (CCF), a non-denominational NGO headquartered in the US, to provide psychosocial assistance to children in Luanda. In a site visit and situation analysis, CCF representatives confirmed that virtually no psychosocial services existed for assisting children, as Angola had few trained psychologists. The initial situation analysis entailed dialogue, networking and integration of data from diverse groups, including local communities. This dialogue was viewed as a process of building partnership and a step towards possible collaboration.

The situation analysis led to five key strategic decisions:

- First, psychosocial work should begin in Luanda, which had absorbed massive waves of displaced people yet was relatively stable in comparison to rural areas, where fighting continued. Safety and access were major constraints that guided this decision.

- Second, the emphasis would be on building local capacities through the training of local trainers, who in turn would train adults who work with children in sectors such as health, education and social services. This decision recognised the multi-faceted needs of local peoples and the importance of integrating psychosocial assistance into wider systems of service.

- Third, the project would be community-based and oriented towards partnership with local people. Since nearly everyone was war-affected, it made little sense to single out any particular group or to focus on individually oriented interventions. These would, in any case, be ill suited to a collectivist society.

- Fourth, the project would assist children by working through adults, whose emotional support has a strong influence on children's well-being. Since adults were also war-affected, it was necessary to assist adults in coming to terms with their own war experiences to enable them to support children.

- Fifth, Angolans should lead the project, thereby enhancing capacity building, cultural relevance and the use of local resources. The second author of this chapter, having extensive local professional experience, was employed by CCF to lead the implementation of the project in Angola. In general, local people were viewed not as victims but as survivors and actors who, though in need of assistance, were capable of constructing a positive future. These emphases on local participation and the construction of culturally grounded, sustainable approaches are congruent with participatory approaches developed in Latin America (e.g. Lykes, 1994; Métraux & Aviles, 1993) and other parts of the world (Boothby, 1996).

The goals of the initial project were to increase the capacity of adults who work with children to recognise psychological trauma in children (under 18 years of age) and to assist war-affected children in expressing their feelings and coming to terms with their experiences. The need for this kind of approach was highlighted by the results of an early study by CCF/Angola of some of the most severely war-affected children (UNICEF, 1996). In a sample of 200 children living in Luanda as displaced people, it was reported that 27% had lost their parents; 94% had been exposed to attacks; 66% had witnessed mine explosions and 5% had been victims thereof; 36% had lived with troops; 33% had suffered injuries by shooting or shelling; 65% had narrowly escaped death; and 7% had fired guns. In the same sample, children reported fright and insecurity (67%), disturbed sleep (61%), intrusive images (59%), frequent thoughts about war (89%), and sensory-motor disturbance (24%). Not all these effects can be attributed directly to war since children may also have been affected by the violence that is so prevalent in the aftermath of war.

Preparation of trainers

To address these needs, CCF/Angola assembled a core team of four Angolan trainers having extensive experience of working with children. To train this team, the second author combined her own knowledge of the Angolan culture and context with that of a trauma specialist from the Taylor Institute in Chicago. The training curriculum included children's psychosocial development, impacts of war-related violence on children, rituals surrounding loss and bereavement, and methods of assisting violence-affected children.

Following training, the members of the core team initiated extensive networking and dialogue in Luanda with both service-provider groups and local communities. In entering local communities, the typical process entailed meeting with the *soba* or local chief, his council of elders and influential women. These meetings served as occasions for relationship building and mutual sensitisation and learning. The team member learned about the needs of children in that particular community, about the community power structure and resources, and about which adults within the community were best positioned to assist them, enabling selection for training. The community members learned about the planned work of CCF/Angola and how war experiences affect different children. For example, some community leaders commented that, before this dialogue had begun, they had not recognised that a child's chronic isolation might be attributable to the effects of exposure to violence. The respect shown for local practices in these dialogues was instrumental in building relationships with traditional healers and enabling learning about centuries-old practices that constituted key community resources.

Using participatory methodology, the trainers conducted week-long training seminars for adults who had been selected by their communities as being highly motivated and in a position to assist war-affected children. The basic content of the curriculum was as outlined above. It also evolved through discussion with trainees. For example, trainees from different communities (including *deslocados* who had come from different geographic regions and ethnic groups) described variations in local beliefs and rituals. These were regarded as sources of new learning, and the ideas presented often became integrated into the training curriculum. In addition, dialogue with trainees indicated that harsh corporal punishment was used in many families and that war stresses were being played out in the home. Since it made little sense to focus only on healing without also working to prevent trauma, material on non-violent conflict resolution was incorporated into the curriculum.

Assistance to children

Following training, the trainees engaged in a variety of activities on behalf of children in their communities and work settings. To encourage emotional expression and reintegration, they encouraged children to draw freely in a secure, supportive setting. In a group context, they used dance, song and story-telling to enable emotional expression, social support and co-operative behaviour. To complement these expression-oriented methods, they developed collaborative relations with local healers, asking them to intervene when it seemed appropriate to do so. In one case, unaccompanied children in an 'orphanage' reported an inability to sleep since a spirit haunted the premises. To address the children's sleeplessness and fear, a trainer sought the assistance of a local healer. By conducting a traditional ritual for correcting spiritual contamination or discord, the healer restored the children's sense of well-being. This experience and others like it strengthened the respect and valorisation of traditional healing that became a hallmark of the project.

With regard to project effects, children demonstrated reduced nightmares, bed-wetting and concentration problems, and they exhibited improved social relations with adults and other children. Community leaders said that by valorising local methods of healing, the project had helped to re-establish traditions that had been weakened by decades of war but were important sources of continuity and strength in difficult circumstances. Community leaders reported improvements in children's behaviour and said that they saw children differently as a result of the training and activities, which had led them to provide more structured activities for children. One community of displaced people which had previously allowed children to spend large amounts of time in unsupervised activity initiated informal educational discussions in the shade of nearby trees. The *soba* reported that the community had become more active and hopeful as a result. This outcome, replicated in other communities, suggested that the intervention had valuable effects in mobilising communities around the needs of children (Green & Wessells, 1995; Wessells, 1996).

The project successes, together with advances in the peace process, opened opportunities to expand the project to different geographic areas. This wider project, however, is best viewed against its theoretical and research background and in terms of the evolving discourses that informed it.

THEORETICAL AND RESEARCH BASE

The conceptual underpinnings of the project derive partly from psychological research on stress, trauma and healing, and from the view that victimisation by violence places people at risk of continuing cycles of violence (Volkan, 1997; Widom, 1989). Although highly valuable, much of this research has been conducted in Western societies, embodies universalistic views of child development, and may not apply directly to the Angolan context. Accordingly, it is discussed below in the context of a cultural critique that attempts to integrate the most helpful elements of Western and local approaches to healing.

Stress, trauma and healing

Research on children in situations of political violence has had to steer between simplistic images that portray children either as badly damaged or as highly resilient (Cairns & Dawes, 1996). Although most research indicates that a small minority (typically, under 10%) show signs of severe psychological problems (Cairns, 1996), the reality of war zones is that most people are war-affected in some respects (Dawes, 1994).

In war zones, affected children may exhibit both acute and chronic reactions, both of which are normal responses to highly stressful events. Prominent among the acute psychological disturbances are problems of flashbacks, nightmares and sleep disturbances, concentration problems, heightened alertness or hypervigilance, and avoidance of people and situations that evoke memories of the traumatic events. In Western cultures, this often falls under the clinical diagnosis of Post-Traumatic Stress Disorder (PTSD) (Friedman & Marsella, 1996; van der Kolk, McFarlane & Weisaeth, 1996). Straker (1987), as well as Dawes, Tredoux and Feinstein (1989), however, have noted that children in war situations often face chronic, ongoing stressors, not least of which is poverty, and that categories such as PTSD cease to have meaning under these conditions. The chronic stressors associated with armed conflict may lead to problems of aggression (Baker, 1990; Chimienti, Nasr & Khalifeh, 1989), depression (Macksoud & Aber, 1996), truncated moral development (Ferguson & Cairns, 1996), changed attitudes and beliefs, personality changes (Terr, 1991), and diminished hope for the future (Cairns, 1996).

Children's responses vary according to situational and personal factors. Situational factors include the intensity, quality, duration, number and frequency of the stressors. Children exposed to multiple stressors show greater psychological impact (Garbarino & Kostelny, 1996), though effects of violence vary according to the nature of the stressors and the role played by children (Macksoud & Aber, 1996). Children's resilience in situations of violence depends on protective factors (Rutter, 1985) such as the presence of a well-functioning caregiver who can provide effective emotional support. Unaccompanied children, particularly under the age of 7 years, are at much greater risk of psychological damage (Boothby, 1988; Felsman, Leong, Johnson & Felsman, 1990). Furthermore, children react strongly to the cues provided by their caregivers, typically their mothers, who themselves suffer the effects of armed conflict and who may not be in a position to provide the needed quantity or quality of emotional support to their children (Dawes *et al.*, 1989; Punamäki, 1987).

Children's reactions to stress also vary according to personal factors such as age, gender, level of development and temperament. Stress, however, is personally and socially constructed, and children's reactions to stressors depend on the meanings they attribute to them. Strong ideological commitment, as evidenced in war glorification and defiant attitudes towards a feared or hated enemy, enables youth to find meaning in political violence and is associated with reduced anxiety and depression (Punamäki, 1996; Straker, Moosa, Becker & Nkwale, 1992).

Stress and healing in the Angolan context

Western ideas about stress and healing are grounded in a cultural system saturated with individualistic, materialistic and mechanistic values and worldviews. Typically, trauma is viewed as an individual phenomenon, and discourses and practices of healing are steeped in a medical model. Applied to war children, this approach tends to medicalise problems that are inherently political, social and economic (Punamäki, 1989). The impact of trauma on children cannot be separated from the devastation of families and communities (Reichenberg & Friedman, 1996). Conceptualised in Western terms, a focus on individual trauma underestimates the importance of culturally constructed meanings and interpretations of war-related events. In Angola, as in other contexts, children are not passive but are active interpreters, who assign meanings shaped powerfully by Angolan cosmology. This cosmology is the soil in which methods of traditional healing are rooted.

Although Angolan culture is diverse and dynamic, one may nevertheless describe general features that apply across ethnic groups and regions. Particularly in rural areas in Angola, as in much of sub-Saharan Africa, spirituality and community are at the centre of life. The visible world of the living is regarded as an extension of the invisible world of the ancestors. These two worlds are fused into a continuous community of the spirits and those alive today (Altuna, 1985). When a person dies, he or she continues life in the spirit world, which protects the living community. The visible and spirit worlds interact continuously, as if the world were a spider's web and any touch of a single thread reverberates throughout the entire structure (Tempels, 1965). It is the invisible world, however, that is most fundamental, and all major events are attributed to it. If the ancestors are not honoured through the teaching of traditions and the practice of appropriate rituals, their spirits cause problems manifesting in poor health, misfortune, social disruption and even war.

Consider the implications of this belief system for a boy whose parents had been killed in an attack, who had to flee for his life, and who exhibited symptoms of PTSD such as sleep disturbance and hypervigilance. Concerned about the magnitude of the boy's loss and trauma, a Western psychologist might encourage expression of grief and working through in a safe, supportive context. Although valuable, this approach fails to address the communal, spiritual dimensions of the boy's experience. Case studies conducted by the Angolan team indicate that the biggest stressor for a boy in these circumstances might be his perception of spiritual discord stemming from his inability to have conducted an appropriate burial ritual for his parents. In Angola, rites surrounding death honour the solidarity between the living and the ancestors, and the performance of rites enables the successful spiritual passage of a person from the visible world to the next world. Failure to conduct the rites, thus causing a breach with the ancestors, is believed to create spiritual discord in which the dead person's spirits are unavenged and cause personal and communal problems.

In this context, analyses of individual trauma are severely limited since the perceived stressors and their origins are inherently communal. Further, a term such as 'PTSD' can mislead since it does not focus attention on the pivotal elements of spiritual distress. Because the wounds are communal and spiritual, the healing interventions must also be communal and spiritual. To assist the boy, a traditional healer would recommend the conduct of a communal burial ritual believed to enable spiritual transition, honour the ancestors, and restore spiritual harmony. This is not to imply that emotional expression and 'working through' are unhelpful or inappropriate, though they may be under some circumstances (Honwana, 1997).

To succeed in the sub-Saharan context, work on healing must step beyond Western boundaries and include culturally defined practices situated in a larger process of social reconstruction. Western psychologists often think of healing occurring in therapeutic spaces constructed in individual and small group-counselling sessions. In contrast, healing in rural Angola is probably better conceptualised as a process of social integration involving the re-establishment of normal patterns of living and the recovery of traditions weakened by war. Participation in traditional patterns of agriculture, the formation of attachment to land and animals, and the resumption of normal patterns of living are themselves important avenues for psychosocial healing and reconstruction (Gibbs, 1997). Economic and political reconstruction cannot be separated sharply from psychosocial reconstruction, which entails systemic transformation. A potentially important role for psychologists is to document and learn about these culturally grounded, socially reconstructive processes and their impacts. This role is best fulfilled through action research, an integral part of the Angolan project.

Action research

Issues of cultural bias such as those discussed above are symptomatic of deeper problems of power and the privileging of particular knowledge systems. When an external NGO undertakes a particular intervention, it enters a local community as an outsider, yet it often wields enormous influence. Typically, the NGO has access to wealth and resources far beyond the reach of local governments or communities. Living in desperate circumstances and wanting access to jobs and resources, local leaders may 'play along' with an NGO even if they doubt the value of its proposed work. In most psychosocial projects, an NGO provides trained psychologists, 'experts' who tacitly carry the authority of Western science and who observe the community situation, define the problems and design interventions.

In this situation, local knowledge and practice is easily marginalised. Wanting to bring forward the best tools of contemporary science, Western experts may impose their own systems of knowledge, training and practice. Internal silencing, however, may also occur. Out of a desire to appear scientific and to avoid embarrassment, local people may downplay their own traditions of knowledge and practice. Either way, the end results are cultural imperialism (Dawes, 1997), the continuation of colonial patterns of injustice (Wessells, 1992), and the removal of local resources that might be useful in addressing local needs. Often there is an erosion of respect for indigenous cultural practices, which themselves may provide psychosocial support and a sense of continuity and meaning in difficult, changing circumstances. Wanting to correct this imbalance, NGOs may also react by romanticising indigenous traditions in ways that obscure important questions about efficacy and ethics. Another problematic reaction is to place all the power in the hands of local actors. This approach, however, risks privileging some actors over others and strengthening ongoing patterns of inequity.

Action research constitutes one appropriate, though imperfect (Chataway, 1997), means of negotiating this power asymmetry and creating new forms of knowledge and practice. Although action research takes many different forms, the common elements are critical consciousness, partnership, local participation and leadership, and the construction of knowledge and practice in ways that address injustice and social problems, and ongoing testing of ideas and practices with an eye towards increasing the socially transformative power of such knowledge and practice (Brydon-Miller & Tolman, 1997; Fals-Borda & Rahman, 1991). Methodologically, the emphasis is on dialogue and conscientisation (Freire, 1970), facilitation and consultation, joint problem-solving, elicitive rather than directive approaches (Lederach, 1995), and systematic collection and use of collectively owned data. With an external change agent, such as a Western NGO, operating in an existing community of practice, an action research approach would entail working jointly to define tasks and emergent goals, constructing new tools and practices, and stimulating joint interpretation of the data. The emphasis is on creating a joint community of practice (Gilbert, 1997) that integrates the values, perspectives, understandings and tools of both the NGO and the local actors.

This integrationist approach lies at the heart of the work of the CCF/Angola team. From its inception, it has worked to construct knowledge and practice in ways that address the damage and injustice inflicted by war and that empower communities to transform themselves. Although Western consultants contribute to the work, their knowledge and practice is not viewed as superior to local knowledge and practice. Through dialogue and partnership, ways of interweaving Western and local practices are constructed and then tested jointly. As the work proceeds, new, emergent goals take shape and become the focus of common discourse. The result is an emerging psychosocial technology that incorporates elements of very different social worlds.

THE PROVINCE-BASED PROJECT

The enthusiasm of the government and local communities for the participatory, culturally grounded approach developed by CCF, together with widespread needs, led to plans to extend the initial project on a national scale. The Luanda-based team of trainers from the initial project became the national team that planned and guided the implementation of this extended and wider, province-based project.

Scaling up brought with it issues of focus, leadership and cultural tailoring. Because of limited resources, Angola's size, and issues of workload, transportation and language, it was not seen as possible for the national team to conduct the project in all provinces simultaneously. People were needed who knew the local languages and situation and who lived on site. Since existing data indicated that the war had affected some areas more strongly than others, a decision was made to focus efforts on the most severely war-affected provinces. These included Benguela, Bié, Huambo, Huila, Malanje, Moxico, and Uige (see Figure 1). To ensure quality control and effective local leadership, the national team decided to structure the project through a mixture of national and province-based leadership. For each province, there was a team of three paid trainers who would function locally. Each province-based team worked closely with one member of the national team. The formation, training and co-ordination of a national team and seven province-based teams required a strategy of building psychosocial capacity at multiple levels, and of combining the benefits of central organisation and locally distributed practice.

The goal of the province-based project was to integrate traumatised children into families and communities through the training of paid local trainers, who in turn trained adults to work with war-affected children. The project aimed to train over 4000 adults, who in turn would interact with and assist approximately 320 000 children. The project collaborated with many government ministries and NGOs, and it partnered with UNICEF in Huila and Moxico provinces. The stated focus on 'trauma' was congruent with the original focus of the initial project, but for reasons outlined above, the discourse evolved well beyond considerations of trauma. By 1996, the CCF/Angola team seldom spoke of 'trauma', preferring to speak instead of war-affected children. The multiple discourses within the project reflected the need to speak effectively to different constituencies. They also reflected different worldviews and understandings of stress and healing. Extensive time and sharing are required to build new communities of practice having unified discourse.

Preparation of province-based teams

Figure 2 shows the project in outline form. As Panel B indicates, the national team conducted a situation analysis using existing data to focus scarce project resources on

Figure 2: The province-based project in outline form

Panel A: The cycle of work at each level

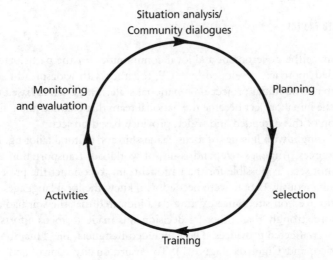

Situation analysis/
Community dialogues

Monitoring
and evaluation

Planning

Activities

Selection

Training

Panel B: The sequencing of activities from national to local level

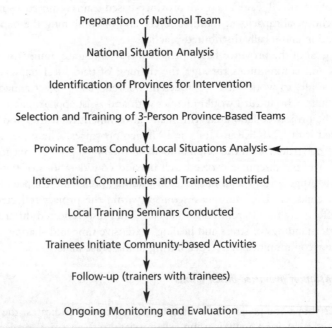

Preparation of National Team

National Situation Analysis

Identification of Provinces for Intervention

Selection and Training of 3-Person Province-Based Teams

Province Teams Conduct Local Situations Analysis

Intervention Communities and Trainees Identified

Local Training Seminars Conducted

Trainees Initiate Community-based Activities

Follow-up (trainers with trainees)

Ongoing Monitoring and Evaluation

those provinces that had been affected most severely by war and had the fewest services available for assisting children. Next, the national team selected the three-person province-based teams. The members of the provincial teams were selected through dialogue with local leaders, government ministries, NGOs, and UN agencies. The criteria used included motivation, commitment to children, effective working relations with different communities, understanding of local language and culture, articulateness and dynamism. To prepare these trainers, the national team provided three-week seminars that included the curriculum as outlined earlier. Issues of programme supervision, province office management, monitoring and evaluation were also covered. The seminars were highly participatory and enabled the national team to learn more about local customs and healing methods in regions populated by different ethnic groups. This joint learning was valuable for members of the national team, most of whom had lived many years in Luanda, where Portuguese influences were very strong. Participants reported that these dialogues were important in rebuilding a unified Angola, which the war had fragmented.

Once trained, the province-based teams initiated the cycle of work illustrated in Panel A. They conducted situation analyses aimed at identifying the most severely war-affected, underserved communities, as there was a need to focus resources, even within provinces. Further, security and access were important issues at the province level, as rural areas remained dangerous. Entrance into UNITA-controlled areas was often impossible. Early on, the national and province-based teams decided not to work in areas that posed security risks to project personnel. By collecting data from various government ministries and NGOs and by conducting focus group discussions with local *sobas* and communities, the province-based teams constructed a picture of the local needs, the situation of children and the security situation. This process served both to sensitise communities to children's emotional needs and to educate the trainers about resources already available in the community for assisting children. When the dialogues disclosed physical needs such as food or water, the provincial team worked through its networks with other NGOs and agencies to help meet these needs. This work helped to build the trust and relationship needed for the next stage, the selection and training of adults from the communities.

Selection and training in local communities

Within the most severely affected, accessible communities, the selection of people for training was guided by dialogue with local chiefs, community influentials and parents. The strategy was one of drawing on existing networks and resources, thereby strengthening partnership and sustainability. Since the project aimed to integrate psychosocial awareness and work into various areas, prospective trainees were selected from venues such as schools, churches, health facilities, government ministries and NGOs working to meet material needs. In the selection process, special emphasis was placed on people working in schools which had been damaged badly by war. Reconstruction of the educational system is an important element of psychosocial rebuilding. Furthermore, in the rural areas schools provide access to the largest numbers of children. In selecting trainees, care was taken not to train too large a number of people within a particular community. The aim was to plant seeds in various communities while at the same time creating conditions where a group of trainees could support each other in their work on behalf of children.

The training seminars for adults from local communities followed the lines that had been established in the initial project. Working in pairs, the members of the provincial teams conducted week-long seminars for groups of 20 to 25 trainees, half of whom were women. The curriculum included topics such as children's psychosocial needs and development, the impact of war and violence on children, rites associated with death and bereavement, Western and traditional methods of assisting war-affected children, and non-violent conflict resolution. Since a key lesson from the initial project was that the trainees learned best through the use of highly participatory methodology, the pedagogy of the province-based project became increasingly centred around participatory, elicitive methods. Rather than lecture on children's psychosocial needs, for example, the trainers evoked discussion by asking questions such as 'What do children need for healthy development?'. Through dialogue, trainers and participants co-constructed a basic ecological model (see Figure 3).

Pedagogically, a key challenge arose from the low levels of formal education of most trainees (typically about four years). To illustrate key points, concrete images and demonstrations were developed. For example, to illustrate the profound effects of war, and the difficulties of rebuilding, participants were given a sheet of paper and asked to spend two full minutes destroying it and ripping it up into small pieces. This they all did playfully. Then the trainers asked the trainees to spend 20 minutes trying to put the paper back together. This demonstration evoked considerable frustration – and laughter – and also provoked discussion about why it is so difficult to put the pieces back together following protracted war. To encourage trainees to talk about their own war experiences and to begin the process of coming to terms with them, the trainers asked, 'What was the worst thing that happened to you?' Trainees often commented that the opportunity to step back and reflect on their own experiences was one of the most valuable parts of the seminar. The seminars also stimulated extensive discussion of Angolan culture, rituals associated with death and mourning, and healing methods. Although the seminars provided no training in the use of traditional methods of healing, they valorised the importance of traditional beliefs and practices, encouraging participants to work with traditional healers when it seemed appropriate to do so.

To prepare the participants to work effectively with children in their daily settings, the seminars discussed the identification and interpretation of problems such as sleep disturbances, concentration lapses, aggression, severe isolation and withdrawal, and hopelessness. There was also discussion of the damage that could be done by singling out or stigmatising severely war-affected children. The seminars included training in how to use basic methods such as free drawing or storytelling to encourage emotional expression in children. Through discussion, participants analysed how best to assist children using a mixture of Western, expressive methods and traditional, ritual-oriented methods, all of which were subject to critical discussion. In this manner, trainers and local people constructed a discourse oriented towards the use of locally available resources and integration with tools derived from Western practice.

The seminars were designed as the beginning of an ongoing process of training accomplished through on-site follow-up visits. In the first three months, the trainers

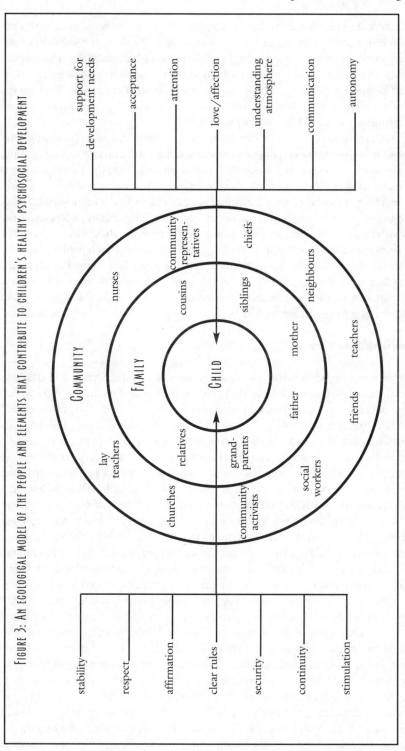

FIGURE 3: AN ECOLOGICAL MODEL OF THE PEOPLE AND ELEMENTS THAT CONTRIBUTE TO CHILDREN'S HEALTHY PSYCHOSOCIAL DEVELOPMENT

Note: Through dialogue, seminar participants and trainers constructed this model, which places the child at the centre surrounded by the social ecologies of the family and the community. At each level, key influences are indicated such as mothers, fathers, teachers and friends and basic psychosocial needs such as love, security and acceptance. (Original in Portuguese.)

made a follow-up visit to each trainee at the site where he or she worked with children, with bi-monthly visits thereafter. The follow-up visits allowed discussion of difficult cases; analysis of what had worked or failed and of how to make adjustments; monitoring of whether concepts and tools were being used appropriately; and reinforcement of previous learning. These visits provided an important field check on the impact of training and enabled trainers to observe how the project activities were actually being implemented in local communities.

Projects of this size often fail by becoming too regimented, and not allowing local innovation. In Malanje, many trainees were teachers who were unable to devote a full, continuous week to the training seminar. To accommodate this, the training sessions were conducted over a period of five months in monthly meetings of one day each. At each meeting, trainees received a practical assignment such as a request to conduct a drawing session or to organise a game for children. The trainees completed the assignment at their work sites, and the subsequent meeting enabled discussion of the activity, its impact and adjustments that were needed. This approach, which also integrated the seminar and follow-up elements of training more fully, served as a pilot for possible extension to other areas. This enablement of local adaptation and mutual learning between trainers and trainees was a microcosm of what the national team hoped to develop in the larger project.

Community-based activities

Trainees arranged group activities such as singing, story-telling, drama and dancing, all of which enabled emotional expression. Themes of war and its impact were woven into these activities and sometimes emerged even when they had not been included intentionally. But themes of war and loss were not exclusive focuses. The activities were also intended as venues for the encouragement of play, expression of positive feelings, and social integration. They served too as vehicles for the construction of social meaning, as children learned the songs, myths and symbols of their ethnic group and community. Activities were also used to teach survival skills. Thus, following a model developed by UNICEF, trainees used drama as a means of teaching children about the hazards of landmines and how to avoid them. Particularly for young or withdrawn children, trainees often encouraged free drawing, giving children a sheet of paper and crayons and asking them to draw whatever they wanted. Typically, children drew pictures of their war experiences, enabling discussion and emotional reintegration in a safe environment. In all these activities, the trainees worked in an inclusive, non-stigmatising manner, trying to engage previously isolated children but without labelling them or giving them excessive attention. Trainees also networked with and valorised the work of traditional healers, referring particular problems to them. This networking enabled the integration at the community level of Western and traditional healing, and it also facilitated the documentation of indigenous methods.

More broadly, the trainees acted as change agents who worked to transform communities by heightening their sensitivity to children's needs and by activating communities around meeting children's needs. Within the community, they conducted public dialogues on the situation of children, working to get children's issues on the agenda and to boost vigilance regarding children's well-being. Village meetings served as occasions for educating leaders and parents, bringing insights from the training seminars to the community. For example, trainees pointed out that children had too much free time and might benefit from additional structured activities and supervision. In addition, they noted that problems such as heightened aggressiveness stemmed not from disobedience but from exposure to violence. They also created a space in which adults in the community at large could begin to talk about their own war experiences and hopes for the future. Trainees regularly encouraged their communities to be hopeful and to take active steps to build a positive future for children. They assisted in organising structured activities such as youth soccer or community drama productions.

Increasingly, trainees became facilitators of community rebuilding projects. Throughout the project, discussions with community leaders indicated the centrality of structural and economic rebuilding in the healing process. Parents, teachers and children all pointed out, for example, the need for schools. Community influentials noted the need for a community hut or *jango* that could serve as a focus for community meetings, child-care and informal educational activities. Numerous communities, energised by discussions of their future, sought seed money for small income-generating projects. Viewing these emergent directions as positive opportunities, the national team instituted a system of small grants using funding from the World Bank and the Dutch government. In this programme, communities conceptualised a project and then proposed it along with an implementation framework to the national team, which worked with the province-based teams and the proposing community to refine the approach. Projects judged to be valuable and well-conceptualised received funding. This was usually used to purchase construction materials, while the local community then supplied the labour to build the structures.

Project staff and trainees also worked in the public arena on behalf of children. To institutionalise the project's methodology and insights on how to recognise and assist war-affected children, teams are working to have the training built into teacher preparation curricula. In addition, both the national and province-based teams engage in public policy analysis and advocacy on issues pertaining to children's well-being. For example, in several provinces unaccompanied children were placed in 'orphanages' that were poorly staffed and constituted adverse environments for development. Recognising the under-use of extended families as local resources, the province teams advocated increased emphasis on the reunification of children with extended families. These and related policy activities were regarded as steps towards prevention and making a positive difference on behalf of large numbers of children. The national team has also worked consistently to get children's issues onto the agenda, using radio interviews and other means to boost awareness. Just as trainees have become change agents at the community level, so trainers have become change agents at the provincial and national levels.

OUTCOMES AND EVALUATION

In the tradition of action research, the project includes a participatory, open-systems approach to ongoing monitoring and evaluation. Since the project receives major financial support from a donor that must justify its expenditures to the US Congress, the goals and methodology are driven partly by donor accountability. However, evaluation is oriented primarily towards improving the project, addressing children's psychosocial needs, and enabling communities to do a better job of constructing a positive future for children. Like the wider project, the evaluation process aims to enable communities to see with new eyes, to ask new questions about children's needs and how to meet them, to collect systematic information in addressing those questions, and to reflect on their own traditions. This is part of a larger project of strengthening planned, forward-looking community processes that are empowering and transformative while also being respectful of local traditions.

The evaluation system itself is a product of extensive dialogue between the first author and the national team. Methodologically, the system entails a mixture of quantitative and qualitative tools, with an emphasis on the latter since Angolan culture has strong oral traditions. To assess children's war experiences and their psychosocial impact, the team used Exposure and Impact Scales, modified to fit the Angolan context. Among the evaluation methods were the following:

- Pre- and post-tests to assess efficacy of training seminars
- Regular follow-up meetings with trainees at their work site to consolidate learning, provide support and assist in handling difficult situations
- Assessment of children's war experiences, through an Exposure Scale that measured the kind and frequency of events such as shelling, seeing dead people, loss of parents, hunger, etc.
- Repeated measures of an Impact Scale designed to assess the occurrence of psychosocial difficulties such as sleep disturbances, reliving bad experiences, concentration problems and rapid heart beat
- Direct observation of children by adults
- Focus group discussions with *sobas*, elders, parents and teachers
- Collections of children's free drawings
- Narrative descriptions of traditional beliefs and healing methods
- Process descriptions of community entry and steps in relationship building with communities
- Pictorial and narrative descriptions of community projects
- Records of sensitisation meetings and media interviews

Since many of these measures track processes rather than document outcomes, the possibility exists that improvements in children's behaviour that appear to be attributable to the project intervention may instead be due to economic or political changes not associated with the project. To identify changes associated with the project, the system uses a quasi-experimental design that establishes a temporally relevant baseline by comparing matched communities that receive project interventions (training, activities and follow-up) at different times.

Operationally, the evaluation system began with the national situation analysis. Following the conceptualisation of the project and its evaluation system, the national team included in the training seminars for province-based trainers material on how to collect and use evaluation data. The province-based teams began their work on evaluation by conducting a local situation analysis designed to identify the principal needs of children and the main strategic points of intervention (schools, age groups, etc.). Teams collected information on a continuous basis as they entered communities, conducted trainings, made site visits, and so on. They used this information to identify strengths and weaknesses in their work and to make adjustments as needed. The province-based teams sent their information to the national CCF/Angola office, which monitored the project consistency and quality across provinces, kept global measures such as the total number of people trained, and constructed a picture of where the project stood in relation to its goals. To help guide this work, the national office hired a half-time monitoring and evaluation person, who constructed a national database on computer. In implementing this evaluation system, careful attention was paid to ethical issues. Through frequent dialogue between the province-based and national teams, CCF/Angola monitored the security situation and took steps to ensure that data collection efforts protected children's confidentiality and well-being and endangered neither the project personnel nor local people.

The evaluation system is supplemented by both external and informal review processes. The mid-term evaluation, conducted in April 1997, was structured to include external evaluations by an anthropologist and a psychologist. The results, discussed below, were used systematically to make project improvements. Informally, the project has developed a norm of discussion about what works and does not work. When a national team member visits a province, this typically becomes an occasion to visit community people and to talk about the situation of children, about the intervention accomplishments and difficulties, and about improvements that might be made. Similarly, when province-based teams visit the national office, they convey informally their own sense of the accomplishments and problems. This norm has been fostered by the teams' strong commitment to children, the non-punitive use of the evaluation system, and the spirit of participation and joint ownership that has informed evaluation discussions at all levels.

Training

By its endpoint of 30 August 1998, the project had conducted 172 training seminars. Table 1, which shows the number of adults trained in each province, indicates that five of seven provinces surpassed their initial goals. Further, the project surpassed its training goals by several hundred people. The inability to achieve the training goals in Malanje and Moxico stemmed mainly from security problems. Overall, the project

TABLE 1: THE NUMBER OF TRAINEES BY PROVINCE AND GENDER					
Province	Male	Female	Total	Target	% Target reached
Luanda	177	130	307	200	153.5
Benguela	319	300	619	572	108.2
Bié	374	469	843	572	147.4
Huambo	284	401	685	572	120.0
Malanje	228	264	492	572	86.0
Uige	372	335	707	572	123.6
Moxico	421	188	609	572	106.5
Huila	363	269	632	572	110.5
Total	2 538	2 356	4 894	4 204	119.5

achieved relative gender balance, as 48% of the trainees were women and 52% were men.

The mid-term evaluation included focus group discussions with both trainers and groups of trainees (Green & Wessells, 1997). These discussions revealed high levels of satisfaction with the training seminars, which had become so popular in some areas that the demand exceeded the supply by a substantial margin. Across provinces, trainees particularly valued the seminars for their participatory style, discussions of war impacts and traditional healing, and the content pertaining to child development and how to assist children. Many trainees commented spontaneously that the seminars had provided the first occasion on which they could step back and take stock of how they had been affected by the war. They also said that the seminars had started a process of their own healing, which continued after the seminars ended and increased their ability to assist children. Furthermore, trainees indicated that they saw children differently as a result of the training, recognising isolation behaviour and aggression as possible impacts of violence. Having been trained, they were less likely to use harsh punishment and more likely to listen to children, both at home and in their work with children outside the family. Trainees reported that on a regular basis they engaged significant numbers of children in activities such as singing, dancing, drawing, drama and sporting events. These reports were corroborated by observations made by trainers during follow-up visits, of which 1393 have been documented. On a more critical note, trainees suggested that the seminars should provide greater emphasis on specific, concrete activities and methods for working with children. This feedback was built into the training conducted in the second half of the project

Children

Nearly half the children worked with were in preschool or school. The rest were in the community at large. The project estimated that by its endpoint, over 298 000 children had been reached. Focus group discussions conducted as part of the mid-term evaluation indicated that trainees, community leaders, teachers and parents observed positive changes in children following the implementation of activities by trainees. These changes included improved child–child and child–adult relationships; improved behaviour in the classroom; less evidence of war-related games and toys; diminished isolation behaviour; reduced violence and aggressive behaviour; fewer concentration problems; decreased hypervigilance; increased hope; and improved school attendance (Green & Wessells, 1997). Although data from matched, delayed intervention communities is still being analysed, no such rapid, positive changes have been reported in communities where training and intervention work have not been conducted.

Children's free drawings also provide evidence of emotional improvement. When the project was first implemented in a community, the content of free drawings focused on war experiences such as bombings, shootings and burning villages. For example, Figure 4 shows the drawing of a 13-year-old boy from Kuito, a city that was the site of heavy fighting. Following several months of activity associated with the project, children's drawings often became more hopeful, including content related to school, athletic events and home. Similarly, in discussion groups children showed a more positive, hopeful attitude towards the future, and many expressed a desire to enter teaching, mechanics or other professions. It remains to be seen, however, whether these hopeful, short-term improvements are pathways to positive long-term outcomes for children. The evaluation system makes provisions for tracking children over the next several years.

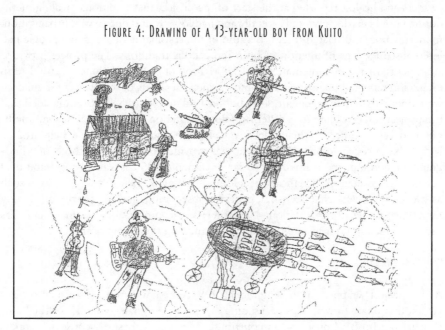

FIGURE 4: DRAWING OF A 13-YEAR-OLD BOY FROM KUITO

Communities

The project stimulated many activities that built community awareness of how children had been affected by war and of how to assist them. By August 1998 trainers had facilitated 88 public, consciousness-raising meetings in communities across the seven provinces and Luanda. In addition, they had conducted 67 interviews for the media, mostly radio. Awareness was also raised by conducting activities on behalf of children in public spaces, thereby inviting dialogue and participation within the community. During the mid-term evaluation, community leaders reported that the project had increased their understanding of children's emotional needs and behaviour. For example, they perceived unruly children not as troublemakers who required corporal punishment but as war-affected individuals who needed assistance. Leaders also reported that as a result of their new learning, community people in addition to trainees had instituted more structured activities, providing supervision and support for children.

Overall, the project stimulated 119 community development projects such as *jango* construction and school rehabilitation; the formation of dance groups, drama groups and soccer teams; and literacy development. Community leaders report that these projects have mobilised communities around children and strengthened processes of planning and community activity. As a result, they report feeling more hopeful about the future. An evaluation conducted in September 1998 (Wessells & Kostelny, 1998) reported that new structures built became symbols of community healing and hope, and the building process itself was part of community transformation. It is too early, however, to discern the long-term economic impacts of these activities.

The project has also enabled communities to recover their traditional practices. Leaders and healers reported at the start of the project that traditional healing methods had not been documented carefully and had lost ground due to war, urbanisation, modernisation and related forces. Because of the colonial heritage, many people had internalised feelings of inferiority about indigenous traditions. The project provided an impetus for the documentation and valorisation of those traditions. The mid-term evaluation reported that some of the most beneficial effects of the project for children were due to the encouragement of traditional healing methods. It recommended that the project undertake a more systematic documentation of traditional healing methods and case studies of their effects on children. With consultative help from a Mozambican social anthropologist, who has provided training in methods of ethnographic recording, the teams have so far documented 35 cases involving traditional healing. Assessment of the efficacy of tradition healing is made difficult by issues such as selection, demand characteristics, intrusive observation, and the paucity of training for ethnographic documentation. Nevertheless, the process of documentation has itself increased interest in traditions and in examining them empirically.

ISSUES AND INSIGHTS

As the project wrapped up in September 1998, Angola was moving steadily towards yet another phase of war. This backsliding serves as a poignant reminder of the limits to what psychosocial projects can contribute to peace. At best, psychosocial work is only one element in a much wider project of social reconstruction, and powerful political and economic forces limit what psychologists can accomplish. Still, this project indicates that community-based psychosocial work has much to contribute to human well-being in a war zone, and it points the way towards the kinds of comprehensive reconstruction efforts that are needed. It is appropriate, then, to examine the issues and insights associated with the project.

Issues

Throughout the project, security issues were recurrent and powerful. Security threats necessitated curtailment of project activities in particular areas, compromises in data collection, and high levels of vigilance and concern on the part of everyone involved. These risks, inherent in work in a war zone, were managed by careful monitoring and by attaching a high priority to the safety of project personnel and the people they serve. Towards the end of the project, rising tensions and the threat of war also necessitated changes in the content of the training seminars. Peace education had been a prominent theme initially, but communities became, understandably, reluctant to talk about peace on the eve of war. Accordingly, the training sessions focused less on societal peace than on non-violent conflict resolution at the family and community levels.

Poverty has also been a continuing issue. The team has struggled with the questions about why and how to conduct psychosocial work in situations where people are hungry, jobless and facing economic desperation. At the community level, trainers noted that it was difficult to maintain the enthusiasm produced by initial training and project activities in the face of profound, unmet physical needs. People needed to see tangible, physical improvements. To address these issues, the team developed the strategy of conducting psychosocial work not as a stand-alone measure but as an integrated, comprehensive approach to social reconstruction. In many respects, the project learned through experience that psychosocial and economic reconstruction go hand in hand. People who suffer war stresses are not in a good position to learn new skills, to benefit from education, or to work and plan effectively. At the same time, economic reconstruction is a source of psychosocial well-being. Economic issues motivated projects aimed at structural rebuilding, and physical rebuilding became part of the healing process.

Staff motivation and development have also presented challenges. People who work with children face enormous stresses as they see, learn about and carry the horrors that children and families experience in war zones. The prospects of burnout are immense, and are amplified by the heavy workload. In many ways, the evaluation process itself contributed to the workload and the stresses experienced by the team. Moreover, rapid inflation and the difficulties of keeping the salaries of project staff at reasonable levels have reduced motivation and led to more time being spent on other jobs. These concerns were not swept under the rug but were regarded as problems to be addressed through dialogue, problem-solving, and the evaluation processes. Thus, the mid-term evaluation called for salary increases, leading to appropriate adjustments. To address issues of stress, the project arranged several workshops on burnout for the national team and agreed that the team should make workload management a high priority. Further, the national team decided to make ongoing training for itself a priority in order to enable more effective analysis, planning and implementation. Team discussions about workload indicated that the expectations for evaluation had been too high, leading to selective cutbacks in the monitoring and evaluation system. These efforts highlight the importance of helping the helpers and of consciously managing one's expectations and workload.

Another key issue was the paucity of training to enable effective evaluation. Without training, it was not possible for the province-based trainers to perform systematic content analyses of community dialogues (conducted in local languages) which they had facilitated. As a result, the data from focus group discussions tend toward the impressionistic. Hopefully, this problem can be corrected as sequel projects get under way. This training issue was particularly conspicuous in connection with the documentation of traditional healing. Initially, the province-based trainers had little background in ethnographic methods, and they were ill prepared to record accurately local views of life and death, health and illness, and healing rituals. Having been educated in a colonially constructed school system, they had little prior knowledge and considerable doubt about traditional beliefs and practices. To address this situation, it proved necessary to provide repeated, ongoing training designed to increase both openness and skills of documentation in regard to traditions.

Insights and lessons learned

One of the main insights of the project was that children often benefit most through the integration of indigenous and Western approaches. As one *soba* put it, 'We teach you; we learn from you.' Since many of children's war-related stresses were spiritual and were grounded in a local belief system, Western approaches by themselves would have been incomplete and ill suited to the local context. Through valorising and learning about local healing, the project helped to bring forward local psychosocial resources that are far outside the scope of Western psychology. At the same time, the project benefited from Western approaches. Without sensitisation and training, local people typically do not connect their children's problematic behaviours – social isolation, heightened aggression, sleep and concentration problems, etc. – with the children's experiences of war and violence. Nor is there typically a comprehensive understanding of children's psychosocial needs. The Western elements of the training seminars enabled people to see their children with new eyes, to understand their children's needs more completely, and to learn a variety of methods for helping children to come to terms with their war experiences and to achieve healthy social integration. No cultural system for understanding and assisting children is complete in itself. The dialogue across cultural boundaries featured in this project helped to create a richer approach to assisting children.

A key insight concerns sustainability. The successes of the project owe much to the use of culturally grounded methods, reliance on local resources, and the integration of project work into existing community social processes. By fitting the project with local beliefs and practices, the likelihood is increased that community activation on behalf of children will continue after funding has ceased. The damage that can be done through imposing outsider approaches, and the marginalisation of local voices, is also minimised.

The project also demonstrates the importance of community mobilisation in assisting children. In view of the importance of social ecologies of the family and community in shaping children's psychosocial development, this is not surprising. Still, Western interventions tend to focus on individuals and families, when communities are the life support systems for both. Further, community interventions are needed to heal community wounds. Little real healing can occur without the restoration of community practices, routines of daily living and economic development. Through mobilisation, communities address the passivity, loss of control and hopelessness that constitute some of the most damaging and paralysing effects of armed conflict. Community empowerment may be achieved by focusing on the needs of children, whom parents and community leaders care about deeply. As communities become active and oriented positively towards the future, they become better places to protect children's rights and enable children to thrive.

A key insight concerns the interplay between economic reconstruction and psychosocial well-being. The training seminars helped communities to come to terms with their past, to build hope, and to help adults move into a position in which they could engage in effective self-transformation. To sustain the hope, however, it was vital to have concrete, tangible markers of progress. As communities planned and built structures such as schools, the buildings became tangible symbols of hope and reconstruction. Although outside support was valuable, the hope and reconstruction arose not through things done by outsiders but through the planning and action initiated by the community itself. Taking control over their own rebuilding was a key step towards community healing. The final evaluation also suggested that the community healing process, in turn, enabled community planning and development on a wider scale. This suggests the limitations of traditional approaches where outside agencies build schools or other structures. Physical development and rebuilding may be enhanced by the addition of psychosocial programming that encourages community healing, mobilisation and planning.

Although much remains to be learned about its long-term impact, the project suggests that it is possible to implement on a large scale relatively effective programmes that build local capacities to assist war-affected children. Psychosocial work on behalf of children is most likely to succeed when it is community-based, respectful of local culture, and oriented towards the integration of Western and indigenous concepts and tools. Despite the many challenges encountered, the project accomplishments give testimony to the power of the Angolan spirit.

ACKNOWLEDGEMENTS

Funding for these projects from the Swedish International Development Agency, the Bernard Van Leer Foundation and the US Agency for International Development is gratefully acknowledged.

REFERENCES

Altuna, P.A. (1985). *Cultural tradicional banto*. Luanda.

Baker, A. (1990). The psychological impact of the Intifada on Palestinian children in Occupied West Bank and Gaza. *American Journal of Orthopsychiatry, 60*, 496–505.

Boothby, N. (1988). Unaccompanied children from a psychological perspective. In W. Ressler, N. Boothby & D. Steinbock (Eds.), *Unaccompanied children: Care and protection in wars, natural disasters, and refugee movements* (pp. 133–180). Oxford: Oxford University Press.

Boothby, N. (1996). Mobilising communities to meet the psychosocial needs of children in war and refugee crises. In R.J. Apfel & B. Simon (Eds.), *Minefields in their hearts: The mental health of children in war and communal violence* (pp. 149–164). New Haven, CT: Yale University Press.

Brydon-Miller, M. & Tolman, D.L. (Eds). (1997). Transforming psychology: Interpretive and participatory research methods. *Journal of Social Issues, 53*(4), 597–827.

Cairns, E. (1996). *Children and political violence*. Oxford: Blackwell.

Cairns, E. & Dawes, A. (1996). Children: Ethnic and political violence – a commentary. *Child Development, 67*, 129–139.

Chataway, C.J. (1997). An examination of the constrains on mutual inquiry in a participatory action research project. *Journal of Social Issues, 53*, 747–765.

Chimienti, G., Nasr, J.A. & Khalifeh, I. (1989). Children's reactions to war-related stress: Affective symptoms and behaviour problems. *Social Psychiatry and Psychiatric Epidemiology, 24*, 282–287.

Dawes, A. (1994). The emotional impact of political violence. In A. Dawes & D. Donald

(Eds.), *Childhood and adversity: Psychological perspectives from South African research* (pp. 177–199). Cape Town: David Philip.

Dawes, A. (1997, July). Cultural imperialism in the treatment of children following political violence and war: A Southern African perspective. Paper presented at the Fifth International Symposium on the Contributions of Psychology to Peace, Melbourne.

Dawes, A., Tredoux, C.G. & Feinstein, A. (1989). Political violence in South Africa: Some effects on children of the violent destruction of their community. *International Journal of Mental Health, 18*(2), 16–43.

Fals-Borda, O. & Rahman, M.A. (1991). *Action and knowledge: Breaking the monopoly with participatory action research.* New York: Apex.

Felsman, J.K., Leong, F., Johnson, M. & Felsman, I. (1990). Estimates of psychological distress among Vietnamese refugees: Adolescents, unaccompanied minors, and young adults. *Social Science and Medicine, 31*, 1251–1256.

Ferguson, N. & Cairns, E. (1996). Political violence and moral maturity in Northern Ireland. *Political Psychology, 17*, 713–725.

Freire, P. (1970). *Pedagogy of the oppressed.* New York: Seabury.

Friedman, M.J. & Marsella, A.J. (1996). Posttraumatic stress disorder: An overview of the concept. In A.J. Marsella, M.J. Friedman, E.T. Gerrity & R.M. Scurfield (Eds.), *Ethnocultural aspects of posttraumatic stress disorder: Issues, research, and clinical applications* (pp. 11–32). Washington, DC: American Psychological Association.

Garbarino, J. & Kostelny, K. (1996). The effects of political violence on Palestinian children's behavioral problems: A risk accumulation model. *Child Development, 67*, 33–45.

Gibbs, S. (1997). Postwar social reconstruction in Mozambique: Reframing children's experiences of trauma and healing. In K. Kumar (Ed.), *Rebuilding war-torn societies: Critical Areas for International Assistance* (pp. 227–238). Boulder: Lynne Rienner.

Gilbert, A. (1997). Small voices against the wind: Local knowledge and social transformation. *Peace and conflict: Journal of Peace Psychology, 3*, 275–292.

Green, E. & Wessells, M. (1995). *Evaluation of the Mobile War Trauma Team Program of Meeting the Psychosocial Needs of Children in Angola.* Richmond, VA: Christian Children's Fund.

Green, E. & Wessells, M. (1997). *Mid-term evaluation of the province-based war trauma team project: Meeting the psychosocial needs of children in Angola.* Richmond, VA: Christian Children's Fund.

Honwana, A. (1997). Healing for peace: Traditional healers and post-war reconstruction in Southern Mozambique. *Peace and conflict: Journal of Peace Psychology, 3*, 293–305.

Human Rights Watch (1994). *Angola. Arms trade and violations of the laws of war since the 1992 elections.* New York: Human Rights Watch.

Lederach, J.P. (1995). *Preparing for peace.* Washington, DC: US Institute of Peace.

Lykes, M.B. (1994). Terror, silencing, and children: International multidisciplinary collaboration with Guatemalan Maya communities. *Social Science and Medicine, 38*, 543–552.

Macksoud, M.S. & Aber, J.L. (1996). The war experiences and psychosocial development of children in Lebanon. *Child Development, 67*, 70 – 88.

Métraux, J.C. & Aviles, A. (1993). Training techniques of non-professionals: A Nicaraguan preventive and primary care programme in mental health. In M. McCallin (Ed.), *The psychological well-being of refugee children: Research, practice and policy issues* (pp. 226–243). Geneva: International Catholic Child Bureau.

Minter, W. (1994). *Apartheid's contras: An inquiry into the roots of war in Angola and*

Mozambique. London: Zed Books.

Punamäki, R. (1987). Psychological stress response of Palestinian mothers and their children in conditions of military occupation and political violence. *The Quarterly Newsletter of the Laboratory of Comparative Human Cognition, 9*, 76–79.

Punamäki, R. (1989). Political violence and mental health. *International Journal of Mental Health, 17*, 3–15.

Punamäki, R. (1996). Can ideological commitment protect children's psychosocial well-being in situations of political violence? *Child Development, 67*, 55–69.

Reichenberg, D. & Friedman, S. (1996). Traumatized children. Healing the invisible wounds of war: A rights approach. In Y. Daniele, N.S. Rodley & L. Weisaeth (Eds.), *International responses to traumatic stress* (pp. 307–326). Amityville, NY: Baywood.

Rutter, M. (1985). Resilience in the face of adversity: Protective factors and resistance to psychological disorder. *British Journal of Psychiatry, 147*, 598–611.

Straker, G. (1987). The continuous traumatic stress syndrome: The single therapeutic interview. *Psychology in Society, 8*, 48–78.

Straker, G., Moosa, F., Becker, R. & Nkwale, M. (1992). *Faces in the revolution*. Cape Town: David Philip.

Tempels, P. (1965). *La philosophie bantoue*. Paris: Presence Africaine.

Terr, L. (1991). Childhood traumas: An outline and overview. *American Journal of Psychiatry, 148*, 10–20.

Tvedten, I. (1997). *Angola: Struggle for peace and reconstruction*. Boulder, CO: Westview.

UNICEF. (1995). *The state of Angola's children report*. Luanda: United Nations Children's Fund.

UNICEF. (1996). *The state of the world's children 1996*. New York: UNICEF.

Van der Kolk, V.A., McFarlane, A.C. & Weisaeth, L. (Eds) (1996). *Traumatic stress: The effects of overwhelming experience on mind, body, and society*. New York: Guilford.

Volkan, V. (1997). *Bloodlines: From ethnic pride to ethnic terrorism*. New York: Farrar, Straus and Giroux.

Wessells, M.G. (1992). Building peace psychology on a global scale: Challenges and opportunities. *The Peace Psychology Bulletin, 1*, 32–44.

Wessells, M. (1996). Assisting Angolan children impacted by war: Blending Western and traditional approaches to healing. *Coordinators' Notebook: An International Resource for Early Childhood Development, 19*, 33–37.

Wessells, M. & Kostelny, K. (1998). *The province-based war trauma team project: Community mobilization and psychosocial assistance for Angolan children*. Richmond, VA: Christian Children's Fund.

Widom, C.S. (1989). Does violence beget violence? A critical examination of the literature. *Psychological Bulletin, 106*, 3–28.

CARING FOR CHILDREN IN FRAGMENTED COMMUNITIES 10

CRAIG HIGSON-SMITH & BEVERLEY KILLIAN

BACKGROUND AND AIMS

KwaZulu-Natal: A challenge for child support

Although KwaZulu-Natal is not the poorest or the least educated of South Africa's provinces, it does contain the greatest number of people facing the challenges of severely impoverished rural life. This is due to a high population density in the rural areas. Despite the province only constituting about 7% of South Africa's land area, 21% of the population resides in it (Central Statistical Services, 1997), and nearly two-thirds of these live in rural areas. In addition, 23% of the people living in KwaZulu-Natal are between 0 and 5 years of age (Central Statistical Services, 1997). Taken together with the degree of rural poverty, it is clear that KwaZulu-Natal is faced with great challenges in the appropriate and effective care of children.

However, over recent decades KwaZulu-Natal has been most characterised as the province with the greatest incidence of civil and political violence, much of this directly affecting homes and schools. Children have been witnesses to much of the ongoing civil strife – seeing homes being burnt down, schools being ransacked and people fleeing for their lives or being murdered. The effects of this experience of ongoing violence are deep-seated and cumulative. Individuals, families and communities have been exposed to continuous threat and trauma, with little if any opportunity to recover. In relation to this repeated or continuous nature of the trauma, Straker and Moosa (1994) introduced the concept of 'continuous traumatic stress disorder' as a contrast to the concept of 'post-traumatic stress disorder', which is usually associated with a single traumatic event. Herman (1992) speaks of 'complex traumatic stress disorder', a term which encapsulates some of the complex realities of the experience of political violence in South Africa where individuals are exposed to repeated, multiple or prolonged trauma.

In South Africa, as in so many other countries, the effects of violence are superimposed on other sources of adversity. The majority of the children in KwaZulu-Natal not only live in an atmosphere of threat from ongoing civil violence, but are also affected by severe poverty, and many by abandonment and abuse.

Communities are forced to deal not only with a history of poverty and brutal state violence, but also with a more recent history of savage civil conflict. In most rural South African communities, it is usual for breadwinners to live away from their families for extended periods. Child-care and support become the burden of a single parent who is usually involved with both food production and income generation. Children often travel long distances to school and regularly spend nights in the homes of other families closer to school. Youth leave home in their mid-teens in order to find work and assist with the support of the family and younger children. In communities where such family arrangements are the norm, one can expect significantly raised levels of alcoholism and substance abuse, domestic violence, unplanned pregnancy, rates of HIV infection and a host of related concerns.

Where poverty and oppression erode community life, civil violence rips the social fabric apart. Summerfield (1995) maintains that modern warfare targets the destruction of the social fabric in that violence is played out where people live and work, with very little distinction between combatants and others. Children have often become, voluntarily or through coercion, the active combatants and are not necessarily passive bystanders. In relation to this, Staub (1989) suggests that people in such situations can variously take on the roles of perpetrator, victim or bystander, and that most people take on each of these roles at different times. Each of these contrasting roles brings with it specific social and emotional issues.

Children grow to adulthood in an atmosphere of threat, surviving many traumatic events and enduring multiple losses and grief. Individuals, families and communities often adapt to such ongoing conditions and experiences by developing a general suspiciousness and unwillingness to trust. Where children are growing up in constant danger, and have had their trust betrayed repeatedly, suspicion may indeed be a realistic strategy (McKay, 1997). For the most part, such strategies and adaptations allow people to cope on a day-to-day survival basis with the reality of their world. Unfortunately, these adaptive changes are not without their disadvantages. As lasting peace and development become viable options, past adaptations may actually deprive individuals, and the community at large, of valuable healing and growth possibilities.

The KwaZulu-Natal Programme for Survivors of Violence (KZN-PSV)

The KwaZulu-Natal Programme for Survivors of Violence was formed by a group of psychologists in 1991. The programme arose out of a long period of social and political activism by mental health workers who protested against the brutality meted out by the apartheid regime. Simultaneously there were growing divisions between various political parties which frequently erupted into civil violence in the communities surrounding Pietermaritzburg and Durban. This resulted in thousands losing their lives and hundreds of thousands being forced to flee their homes. The conflict affected virtually every community in the province – and continues today in ongoing violence between the various political parties. Under these circumstances, any programme addressing issues around the violence in the region had to be seen as neutral and committed to an ideology of peace and tolerance. In this way, KZN-PSV was born.

Since the civil violence was so pervasive the Programme had to target particular communities (defined geographically). Figure 1 contains a map of KwaZulu-Natal and shows the two centres of operation as well as targeted communities over the past few years. These include both urban and rural communities, as well as informal settlements. Virtually every one of these communities has experienced at least one resurgence of violent civil conflict during the past five years. They have very few health, social welfare and educational services, and are characterised by a lack of infrastructure, high unemployment and high crime levels. The recent political history of KwaZulu-Natal is extremely complex and each of these communities has its own history and dynamics. For detailed accounts of events in particular communities the reader is referred to Jeffrey (1997).

FIGURE 1: MAP OF KWAZULU-NATAL

The ideological and philosophical underpinnings of the programme therefore have clear historical roots. The programme is concerned with the psychosocial impact of political violence at all levels of society. Its fundamental aim is to develop appropriate models of service delivery for survivors of civil violence in KwaZulu-Natal. Beyond this very broad aim it is impossible to lay out a clear set of objectives. Projects have emerged in response to the particular needs and resources of targeted communities. Thus the complete package of work done in any specific community arose out of extensive negotiation between the staff of KZN-PSV, members of the community and other role-players. The primary advantage of this approach to community work is that it ensures that the enterprise remains appropriate to the needs and resources of the target community at all times.

THEORETICAL AND RESEARCH BASE

The need for a theoretical model to guide intervention

When KZN-PSV embarked upon this work in 1991, there was no clear model to guide community-based intervention following civil violence. The social developmental literature is concerned largely with poverty relief at the community level. When one considers the incidence of civil conflict among the world's poorest communities it is somewhat surprising to find this topic receiving so little coverage. The literature of war trauma and post-traumatic stress disorder does deal with the effects of violence, but mainly as it applies to individuals and, in a few cases, families.

It became clear that the organisation needed to develop its own working model. However, this takes time, and immediate intervention was required in several communities as the incidence of civil violence in the province rose alarmingly. It therefore became expedient to proceed, but with adherence to basic principles relating to social development and a community orientation.

Principles of social development and community orientation

In each target community the staff of the programme began by establishing a co-operative and interactive base in order to try to understand the community's particular history, needs and resources. By working hand in hand with local structures, and by continually learning from local people, KZN-PSV has tried to address the problem at community level without confining itself to individual, family or small group work alone.

Attempting to deal with issues at community level has helped to ensure that the work remains culturally relevant – that it has real meaning to all members of the target community. Furthermore, by striving to maintain a facilitative role and to comprehend the subjective meaning of the political struggle and civil violence within different social contexts, the organisation attempts to support existing traditional and cultural structures. In addition, regular critical evaluation is built into all projects as an essential feedback mechanism through which understanding of the challenges that face target communities is refined.

Although the organisation aims at social development, particularly in matters affecting children, it is necessary to accept that it is unlikely to have any direct impact upon certain socio-economic realities. For example, poverty is a highly complex phenomenon seriously jeopardising the quality of life and mental health of many communities and the children in them. But KZN-PSV lacks the capacity to train individuals in marketable skills or to impact directly on their economic status. The organisation deals with these realities by networking with other organisations better equipped to meet specific needs, and by engaging in the process of policy development at wider levels. Nevertheless, these limitations have always been, and continue to be, the source of greatest tension within the organisation.

Conceptualising the effects of civil violence

The principles outlined above served as an appropriate starting point for the work that KZN-PSV aimed to conduct. However, practitioners still lacked a framework that could describe the effects of civil violence on communities, and that might guide effective intervention. The model outlined below is the result of several years of open-minded listening to people from communities that have experienced the worst of KwaZulu-Natal's civil violence, together with an ongoing process of critical reflection. It is important to remember that a model is, by definition, a simplified representation of reality. This or any other model has not been used, and should not be used, to replace the important process of exploring the needs, resources and histories of particular communities.

Crucial to this model is an ecological understanding of the structure of society (Bronfenbrenner, 1979). The Zulu people of South Africa have an important saying: '*umuntu umuntu ngabantu*', which, literally translated, means 'a person is only a person with other people'. The more figurative meaning of this is that it is only within a community that a person can be said to truly become a person. Through a person's contributing to the community, the community in turn adds human qualities to that person. Put another way, society is more than the sum of individual lives. It can be thought of as made up of different levels of system 'nested' within each other. Most basically these can be seen as the individual nested within different forms of small groupings (including the family, the immediate social circle, school, etc.) which, in turn, are nested within communities (defined geographically or by some common affiliation) and these, in their turn, are nested within society in general (see Figure 2).

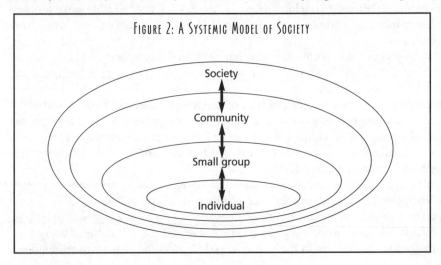

FIGURE 2: A SYSTEMIC MODEL OF SOCIETY

Society

Community

Small group

Individual

Events at each level impact upon all other levels in the system. For example, applying this view to the context of political violence, it sometimes happens that a young person who has been involved in a para-military group is accused of 'selling out' to the enemy. Since many youths have been murdered for this 'crime', such accusations are extremely frightening and traumatic (individual effects). However, such victimisation is seldom restricted to the individual. Very often, family and friends are similarly threatened. In some cases families are forced to protect themselves by turning against their own members or fleeing the community (small group effects). Such suspicion and threat within communities make people reluctant to be seen with others, including agencies, from beyond that community. This isolates the community from important developmental opportunities (community effects). Where this situation exists in numerous communities, social services – including health, welfare, education and security – become compromised (societal effects).

Thus the effects of violence need to be conceptualised as impacting at these different levels of society, both simultaneously and in interaction with one another. Equally, interventions aimed at ameliorating and healing these effects need to be designed to act at all levels simultaneously. Such an ecological framework also allows one to explore the ways in which different types and levels of intervention impact upon each other. For example, it has been observed that young men and women who are part of a support group within their communities (one level of intervention) tend to make much better use of employment training opportunities (another level of intervention) than young people who receive those opportunities but have no support group.

There are many ways in which civil violence impacts upon individuals, families and communities. This picture can be so complex and confusing that it becomes difficult to understand it or intervene effectively in relation to it. One way of simplifying this complexity is to see it in terms of two broad and pervasive ways through which civil violence consistently cripples individuals, families and communities. It disempowers and it fragments.

Disempowerment refers to the way in which civil violence prevents individuals, families and other small groups, as well as community structures, from fulfilling their original purposes. For example, not having a safe place to play is disempowering for children in their development (individual level). When parents are caught up in basic survival strategies, they are disempowered in fulfilling their role as parents (small group effects). Similarly, when local political parties take over the role of ensuring the safety of the community, the local police structures are disempowered (community level).

Fragmentation refers to the breakdown in communication which happens between individuals, within small groups and within and between community structures as a result of violence. When children are sent away from their homes to stay with relatives in safer communities, the family is fragmented (small group level). When community structures become so distrustful of outside service agencies that those agencies are prevented from working in the area, the entire community is fragmented (community level).

Thus, violence disempowers and fragments at each level of society and at different times during the process of conflict and recovery. Bearing this in mind helps to determine what needs to be achieved at each level and at various times. Different types of intervention are required depending upon how long ago the actual violence occurred. Traditional wisdom accepts that emergency relief work is the appropriate intervention directly following an eruption of civil violence. Capacity building, training and other developmental work are not seen as appropriate until relative peace has been attained and the community's basic needs have been met. However, the work of KZN-PSV has demonstrated that this pattern is not always the most beneficial, a finding which is supported by recent work in other similar contexts. Roche (1996) suggests that relief and development agencies essentially participate in four categories of activity ranging from emergency relief to long-term economic, social and political reconstruction. He argues that all of these different activities are necessary at all times following a crisis but that the relative importance of different activities changes over time. The experiences of KZN-PSV support this argument but suggest an even more integrated conceptualisation. It is possible to ensure that a community in crisis receives the necessary shelter and food in such a way that the process empowers community structures and strengthens links both within the community and to organisations outside it. Directly after a crisis the most important linkages might well be with providers of shelter and food, but existing community structures can be empowered to negotiate access to and distribute these resources. This contrasts with a 'rescuing' approach where the delivery of food and tents would be organised without the involvement of the afflicted community.

Understanding violence in terms of disempowerment and fragmentation helps to make sense of these complex dynamics. Similarly, by planning interventions around the contrasting concepts of empowerment and linking, the work is given direction and a clear developmental focus. This is illustrated graphically in Figure 3. There are several reasons why the concepts of 'linking' and 'empowering' are especially useful. First, they translate immediately into practical intervention strategies. Second, they provide a way of integrating both the understanding of, and the responses to, the various effects of civil violence. Third, they steer practitioners away from the pitfalls of interventions which, due to insensitivity or haste, may be detrimental to communities or individuals.

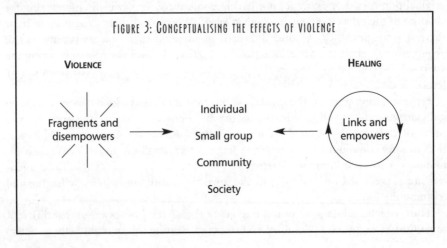

FIGURE 3: CONCEPTUALISING THE EFFECTS OF VIOLENCE

VIOLENCE

HEALING

Fragments and disempowers

Individual

Small group

Community

Society

Links and empowers

PROJECT DESCRIPTION

In the practice of KZN-PSV, the model for understanding the impact of violence has been translated into strategic interventions, tailored to meet the specific needs of particular communities. A very wide range of interventions is therefore possible – and, in fact, occurs (see Figure 4). The following practical principles, developed from long experience of community work, nevertheless run as a common guiding thread through these different interventions.

Guiding principles for effective intervention

Establishing credibility

A range of different individuals and institutions offers assistance to impoverished communities. However, not all are adequately skilled or informed and some projects have been perceived by community members to be a waste of time and energy. On the basis of such experiences, many communities in KwaZulu-Natal are suspicious of the worth of intervention projects. Furthermore, where communities have experienced a great deal of violence, community members and leaders become distrustful of all strangers, including those offering services. It is therefore essential that practitioners establish their credibility through demonstrating competence in the necessary skills, detailed knowledge of the community, and sensitivity in relation to the community's history and objectives.

Maintaining impartiality

A sympathetic understanding of a community's position brings its own problems, especially where an organisation is working with various communities in conflict with one another. To maintain, simultaneously, an empathetic understanding of two communities who are at war with each other requires an understanding of the broader societal issues that have resulted in these two communities being in conflict. It is sometimes difficult to remember that the true sources of conflict lie outside the violence in local situations. It is therefore important for field workers to be given opportunities to discuss and resolve these complex issues properly. For these reasons KZN-PSV attaches great importance to regular and intensive support and supervision of field staff.

Furthermore, in such situations impartiality has to be actively demonstrated. This can only be achieved through the organisation declaring a clear public intention of working on both sides of the conflict, and then being seen to do so. Only by monitoring the number of visits, the number of projects, and the amount of resources being devoted to opposing communities can absolute impartiality be maintained.

Strict adherence to non-pathologising

One of the basic tenets of individual trauma counselling is to view the person's response to trauma as being a normal response to an abnormal event. Extrapolating to the community and societal level, one needs to adhere to a similar view and to avoid falling into the trap of pathologising the responses that occur to the violence. For example, the degree of suspicion that can develop at community level should be seen in this way, and not as a 'sickness' in the community.

Core conditions for effective therapeutic intervention

These conditions have been well documented over the years (Egan, 1994). Since they describe ways of relating to, and working with, others therapeutically they are equally useful when applied to such interventions at community level:

Respect usually grows if the story of an individual, family, or community is really listened to and 'heard'. Respect can be demonstrated in many ways including simple things such as the way one greets members of the community, and attentive and open-minded listening in any context.

Genuine regard for the well-being of the people and their concerns is essential. This is particularly important amongst people who have learnt mistrust and suspicion as survival strategies. Attempts to really understand the complex and interrelated concerns of people in severely disrupted communities demonstrate genuine regard, particularly when accompanied by attempts to find realistic strategies for addressing some of those concerns.

Accurate empathy. From the outside, few can fully comprehend the experience of ongoing political violence, coupled with poverty and discrimination. Accurate empathy can only be approximated through the ongoing experience of active listening and learning on the part of those who attempt to intervene.

Opportunities for emotional expression. In the face of overwhelming community problems there is a temptation to impose solutions – and often too rapidly. When field staff begin to 'manage' communities in this way, opportunities for emotional expression are lost. Space and opportunities for this have to be created. Most often emotional expression comes out in small groups or in individual dialogue with field staff. Good listening skills are vital here. Emotional expression is also powerfully facilitated through writing and drama (especially with adolescents and young adults), singing and prayer (especially with older adults) and through play and art (especially children and adolescents).

A *collaborative relationship* between community members and field workers is essential. Communities that have been severely disrupted by civil violence may initially be resistant to service providers who do not offer them anything tangible. However, to succeed, any developmental community work must begin with the understanding that the role of field workers is to work with people within the community to resolve their own concerns – not to provide resources or solutions from the outside.

Trust is essential for any effective intervention. However, people in violence-torn areas have typically been betrayed and abandoned by more than one authority figure. As a result, it is necessary for field workers to demonstrate absolute trustworthiness. Seemingly small things are very important such as attending every meeting and always being on time. Due to the nature of community work in violence-torn areas, especially in the under-resourced NGO sector, this is sometimes very difficult to achieve. However, the repercussions of not continuously proving trustworthy can be very costly to the work. Field workers need to demonstrate reliability by attending on a regular and completely predictable basis, even if, for example, adverse weather conditions make it highly unlikely that participants will be present. This sends a clear therapeutic message that the framework for intervention is stable and sincere. In evaluations of the KZN-PSV's interventions, community members have indicated that the constancy of the organisation's presence in an unstable community (particularly during upsurges of violence) is both normalising and reassuring. Trustworthiness also requires strict adherence to the ethical codes of confidentiality, beneficence and non-exploitation.

Small group work provides a powerful arena for therapeutic change. When properly facilitated, small groups contain and express many of the diverse dynamics which exist between the participants. KZN-PSV works with groups of children, parents, community leaders, women and youth as is appropriate in particular communities. Membership of groups is open, with some people attending more regularly than others. Groups typically consist of between 15 and 25 individuals. It is essential that the group must have been formed and developed in such a way that participants feel safe to discuss their feelings. In communities which have experienced a long history of violence this is a slow process that requires patience on the part of the facilitator. The

TABLE 1: FRAGMENTATION AND DISEMPOWERMENT – THE EFFECTS OF VIOLENCE AND DISASTER

	Fragmentation	Disempowerment
Individual	Loss of memory of traumatic events Efforts to avoid stimuli (including thoughts) Dissociation of affect Inability to contain feelings of hopelessness, frustration and anger	Loss of control of life Inability to fulfil social roles (parent, teacher, priest, breadwinner, child) Loss of education, training, personal development opportunities High stress, inability to concentrate, sleep disturbances, poor eating habits, substance abuse impairs ability to function Loss of interest in significant activities Sense of foreshortened future resulting in no long-term planning or vision
Small groups	Generalised distrust and suspicion of others Lack of intimacy and emotional support Reduced caring behaviour (parents and older siblings of small children, teachers of pupils, etc.) Envy of friends and family Undermining of attempts to heal by family and friends Breakdown in community communication structures leading to individual isolation (people no longer meet at church, etc.)	Small groups unable to fulfil their role in community (prayer groups, youth clubs, etc.) Loss of meaningful supportive, healing and development resources within community (sports and recreation facilities, skills training opportunities, etc.)

	Fragmentation	Disempowerment
Community	Destruction of valuable and scarce infrastructure and resources Division within community prevents resources from being optimised Generalised distrust of 'outsiders' Results in inability to access resources outside of community or repair/replace damaged infrastructure Nonfunctional community structures prevent community being represented in local government structures (breakdown in democracy) This results in frustration and anger and further conflict	Local structures lose their ability to represent and govern (teachers cannot enforce discipline in schools, breakaway political structures form, conflict between civic and political structures emerges) Local services cannot function (clinics, public transport, churches, etc.)
Society	Isolation of communities hinders peacemaking and facilitates conflict Increase in number of weapons in society Proliferation of paramilitary training	Intolerable strain on virtually all services resulting in inability to function (policing, emergency services, health services, welfare services, etc.) Development programmes constantly undermined, leading to generalised disillusionment with process of social change

usual confidentiality ethic of groups is frequently challenged by family members, particularly by the men in relation to female groups. Men, in this cultural context, believe that they have a right to know what has been discussed, by virtue of their status and their need to protect. The confidentiality code within a group can therefore create suspicious reactions from outsiders to the group process. Group content can be extremely threatening and may contain the risk of rejection and alienation for participants.

Facilitators must have the capacity to contain emotions generated in the group in order for members to feel safe in sharing their traumatic memories and the resultant emotions. Most people in communities that have experienced the trauma of ongoing violence are vulnerable to feeling overwhelmed by the strength of their own emotions or the emotions of others. Trust in the containing strength of the facilitator can only be achieved through a gradual process of testing.

The content of what is dealt with in groups is determined by group members themselves. Thus, for example, youth groups often choose to work on issues of personal development (especially gaining employment and other skills), coping with unemployment, issues of sexuality (including HIV and AIDS) and so forth. Community leaders spend more time discussing local community problems and ways

	Linking	Empowerment
TABLE 2: LINKING AND EMPOWERING – THE GOALS OF INTERVENTION		
Individual	Individual and group trauma counselling aimed at: • processing traumatic events • learning adaptive coping techniques • learning to contain and express emotion in controlled and adaptive manner	Individual and group counselling aimed at: • understanding individuals' personal narratives • developing decision-making skills • planning for the future Relearning of social skills necessary to continue life in a peaceful society Opportunities for personal development Opportunities to develop self-esteem
Small groups	Group work aimed at building relationships: • recognising and naming 'distrust' • exploring barriers to trust • learning how to negotiate trusting relaitonships Opportunities to develop intimacy and social support Developing caring behaviour: • exploring barriers to caring • learning caring behaviour Rebuilding fragmented social groups	Rebuilding small groups and assisting them in carrying out their original purpose (facilitating prayer groups, youth clubs, etc.)
Community	Rebuilding infrastructure and other resources Peacemaking and negotiation so resources become available to whole community Facilitate links with resources outside of communities Empower community structures to work responsibly with outside agencies Facilitate development of proper democratic local government and other community structures	Build the capactiy of local leaders and service providers to deliver effective and accountable services to the community

Society	Foster links between communities, and between different levels of government Active lobbying against proliferation of weapons Active lobbying against para-military training	Support the functioning of different social services (extra training and resources for police and others) Support broader development and public works programmes which offer economic relief to survivors of violence

of accessing resources for the community. Women's groups tend to look at income-generating projects as well as issues of relationships, parenting, substance abuse and domestic violence. Where group content goes beyond the specific expertise of KZN-PSV personnel, other agencies are invited to run the groups as a means of connecting isolated communities with greater expertise and the resources to which they would normally have access.

Transference and counter-transference. As in any therapeutic context, staff need to be able to recognise the ways in which transference and counter-transference operate when one does work in trauma-related communities. The nature of these processes often reflects a contagion of negative emotions; of feeling hopeless, powerless, depressed, angry and victimised – all associated with generalised distrust and anxiety. The natural response in the face of these emotions can take a number of routes. Emotions can be internalised and cause the staff member to become overwhelmed with a sense of futility. On the other hand the staff member may be stirred into the non-productive zones of taking on power, installing facilities, and running projects and events – that is, working in a way that actually perpetuates the disempowerment and fragmentation of the community. The third possible response is burn-out. Supervision, support and fun events for staff are essential elements of any programme in order to sustain the staff's motivation, enthusiasm and drive under such difficult and stressful conditions.

Honesty and transparency. In a community which is at war with itself, it is often very difficult to differentiate truth from lies. Some ways of ensuring honesty and transparency include the keeping of detailed written notes of all meetings and distributing them to all stakeholders to ensure shared understanding. Structures should also be established which allow community members to observe and influence the decision-making of the service provider. For example, representatives of target communities sit on the management committee of KZN-PSV and everyone involved in the organisation's work is invited to an annual general meeting at which the organisation's finances are publicly discussed.

Furthermore, facilitators should be very clear about what it is that their organisation can and cannot offer the target community. Where this is not clear, it is likely that the target community will develop expectations greater than what can realistically be delivered. In time, the participants are likely to feel deceived and dissatisfied. In addition, facilitators must be clear about the constraints on their own resources (often laid down by their funders, parent organisations and other structures) and about the limits of their skills and experience. For example, acknowledging that staff do not have skills for assisting with income-generating projects, or for paying volunteers, prevents false expectations being raised.

Building on existing strengths and coping strategies. Community spirit needs to be supported, respected and developed. Cultural traditions need to be explored as possible mechanisms for adaptive coping. African societies have survived many trials in the past and have a variety of traditions and rituals which facilitate coping. Where possible, such traditions need to be incorporated in intervention strategies.

Unfortunately it is also true that many traditions have been corrupted through Westernisation and industrialisation and no longer effectively fulfil their original function. The speed with which change is coming to urban and peri-urban communities in South Africa also creates an enormous gulf between parents and children. Rebuilding relationships between people of different generations is a slow, painful but very important process.

The spread of Christianity has also impacted on traditional life. Although largely responsible for some communities abandoning their traditional belief systems, Christianity has provided a strong spiritual anchor for many people. In addition, the human rights work of some church organisations has increased their credibility. Nevertheless, Christian teaching is at times accompanied by a fatalistic approach to life in which people are expected to 'bear the cross' of suffering. This is not always productive in terms of the need for empowerment. An uncritical acceptance of either traditional or religious healing mechanisms is not adequate nor does it take into account the complexities which people face in their search for healing. Practitioners need to help people to discriminate more effectively between what does and what does not assist them as individuals and as communities.

Working with culture. Part of respect for individuals and community structures entails respecting the cultural norms prevalent within that community. It is not true that communities are culturally homogeneous. In fact, a range of different cultures exists within target communities, as they do within society at large. For example, the values, beliefs and practices of youth who left school to join the civil conflict are different from those of their parents and grandparents. Also, very few individuals can be characterised as belonging to a single culture. Most people exist between cultures, drawing from them what seems appropriate for the reality of their lives. It is particularly important as a practitioner in such a context to identify one's own values, assumptions and beliefs, especially about such things as distress, health and healing.

Strategic intervention: Application of the empowerment and linking model

Tables 1 and 2 bring together some of the effects of violence and the activities of intervention in terms of the model outlined above. At each level in the model the various effects of violence and the goals of intervention are explored. It is clearly not possible to mention every possible effect or intervention. Nor is it feasible to explain all possible interactions between either the effects of violence or the effects of intervention. Instead the tables contain the most common effects of violence and the most common aspects of intervention. Each community and each situation is different and it is part of the practitioners' skill to assess the main areas of threat and opportunity and to plan accordingly.

An overview of KZN-PSV's work with children

Given the extent of adversity affecting children in South Africa (Dawes & Donald, 1994) and the limited resources available for state child-support programmes (Robinson & Biersteker, 1997), it is essential that priority is given to community-based programmes. Many existing services which are individually oriented are predictably overstretched and unable to cope with the extent of the need for mental health services (Robinson & Biersteker, 1997). Community-based mental health programmes for children, on the other hand, are less well documented and so involve venturing into less clearly understood areas of work.

KZN-PSV uses a range of criteria to select target communities. On the whole, the organisation targets the most needy communities which have experienced the greatest amounts of political violence. Obviously, access is important to avoid staff spending much of their working day travelling to and from the community. Concern for the staff has required regular checks that the area is safe enough for staff to enter. This

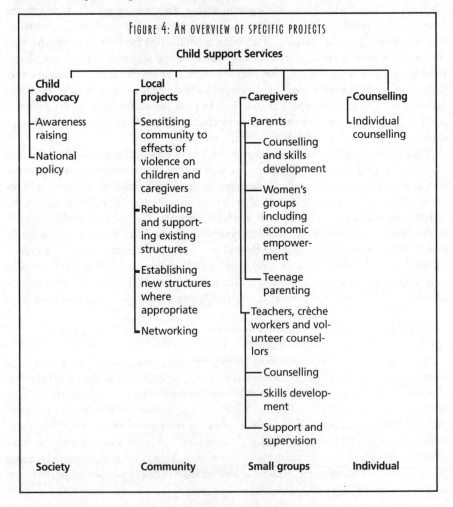

FIGURE 4: AN OVERVIEW OF SPECIFIC PROJECTS

Child Support Services

Child advocacy	Local projects	Caregivers	Counselling
Awareness raising	Sensitising community to effects of violence on children and caregivers	Parents	Individual counselling
National policy	Rebuilding and supporting existing structures	Counselling and skills development	
	Establishing new structures where appropriate	Women's groups including economic empowerment	
	Networking	Teenage parenting	
		Teachers, crèche workers and volunteer counsellors	
		Counselling	
		Skills development	
		Support and supervision	

| Society | Community | Small groups | Individual |

is determined through a network of contacts including helpful people within target communities, community leadership, police, other service providers, the media (particularly radio) and violence monitors. Nevertheless, it is very difficult to predict outbreaks of violence and on several occasions staff have found themselves in extremely dangerous situations. This adds a level of stress to the work which is not adequately recognised.

In keeping with the model, services to children have been conducted at multiple levels. It is important to keep in mind the inter linked nature of all levels and types of intervention. Of particular importance is the intersection of the work with children, adolescents (many of whom are parents and caregiving older siblings), women (many of whom are single, working parents and grandparents), teachers, lay counsellors, health workers, police, and local leadership. Child support programmes cannot be understood or implemented in isolation. Figure 4 outlines the range of activities undertaken with children.

Societal level

KZN-PSV set two broad child-advocacy goals at the societal level. First, it aims to raise awareness of the distress experienced by children who have been affected by violence and other adversities. Second, children's needs, rights and responsibilities have not enjoyed high priority at a societal level. A mere 6% of the social services budget directed towards services for children goes on life-skills training for children, whilst none of the social assistance budget goes to the running of groups for youth (Motala, 1997). Mental health workers need to engage with policy-making on such matters. There are also opportunities for people at grassroots level to give input and make their needs known. Thus KZN-PSV, together with members of the target communities, have organised submissions, meetings and campaigns at local, regional and national level in order to influence decisions which impact upon the well-being of children in our society.

Facilitating the involvement of community in policy development has itself been an important goal. Participation in this level of activity has served to organise communities and create a sense of effectiveness and power within community structures and in the individuals of whom they are composed.

Community level

Although so much damage is done by political violence to particular communities, almost no restorative work has previously been done at this level. Each community is different in terms of its geographical position, its economic strength, the major cultures of its members, the political history of the area, and a range of other factors. Accessing the story of the community is an important aspect of post-trauma work. The story places the experiences of the individuals and small groups within a particular context. It helps to break through the disintegration and alienation experienced at each of these levels. Telling the story provides members of the community with a voice which can be heard and understood, thereby presenting the first elements of linking within the community. Fragmentation of the community leads to extensive isolation of existing structures, many becoming so alienated and disempowered that they are unable to support each other, or network in any meaningful way. Those structures which do survive tend to see themselves as helpless and unable to change as they wait passively for assistance from government or other sources.

One outcome of the process of disempowerment is for people to feel that they have lost control over their own lives – that control is located externally to them. One aim of intervention is to re-establish an internal locus of control, and to sensitise community leaders to these potentially disempowering effects of violence on themselves and their children. Support to rebuild or establish new structures is frequently needed. Regular visits help to reinforce and recognise the work that has been done. All communities need functioning crèches, schools, clinics, recreational facilities and other resources for children. Linking and networking between organisations can result in the formation of powerful lobbies which identify and work towards meeting the needs of children within a community.

Work at the community level entails meeting and working with all the various structures that exist within a community. These may include such groups as development committees, party political structures, traditional leadership, traditional courts, church groups, paramilitary organisations and school structures such as parent–teacher–learner associations. With each of these groups it is useful to evaluate to what extent they are achieving their objectives. Where goals are not being met, it is necessary to determine why and to assist them to find ways of overcoming the obstacles. It is also necessary to determine the extent to which structures are supporting each other within the community and interacting with agencies outside it. Where structures have become isolated, it is important to link them with other agencies which can assist them to achieve their goals.

In the experience of KZN-PSV structures had often broken down due to the civil violence. Examples included schools which were no longer functional, others with no links between parents and teachers, and day-care facilities for young children that had ceased to function. In such cases it was necessary to facilitate the re-establishment of these essential structures through finding local people with the interest and energy to participate, providing skills training to assist people to maintain the structure, and so on. Although painstaking work, the existence of properly functioning community structures is vital to the long-term health of the community.

Small group level

At the small group level the aim has been to create a more supportive environment for children. Important small groups for children are the family, the classroom, the crèche and the peer group. Thus an important aspect of work at this level is developing the emotional capacity and skills of caregivers in relation to the children in their care. In most cases caregivers are women, although not necessarily the mothers of the children. Young children are frequently cared for by grandmothers, aunts, older siblings or neighbours. It is important that service providers recognise that mothers are not always the primary caregivers in young children's lives – a fact rooted deeply in African culture, as well as in the economic and social position of many families.

Targeting caregivers requires a deep understanding of the position of this group within the community. It is imperative to begin by finding out in detail about their lives, fears and aspirations. Caregivers are by definition responsible for both their own and others' well-being. As such they have additional commitments and stresses, and these carry direct consequences for the children in their care. It has been well documented in the literature that children are likely to cope as well as their caregivers, and that adult figures play an important role in modelling adaptive coping (Rutter, 1985). Unfortunately, when the population of caregivers is itself dealing with traumatic experiences, this is not likely to happen.

In part, the high incidence of domestic violence and child abuse can be attributed to parents not having the emotional resources to negotiate their relationships more effectively. Various forms of substance abuse and sexual abuse can be seen as having a similar aetiology. By addressing these problems with caregivers (including teenage parents), the situation of many children in the community can be improved.

Where communities are isolated, it is useful to build basic counselling and debriefing resources into the community. Thus, KZN-PSV has spent time equipping volunteer parents, school teachers, crèche teachers and other trusted adults with the skills to identify various forms of psychological distress, to assist children where appropriate, and to refer where not. Increasing awareness about the effects on children of exposure to violence has been an important part of this work.

Individual level

Much has been written about working with children who suffer from post-traumatic stress disorder, major depression or generalised anxiety disorder (Eagle & Michelson, 1997; Spencer & Pynoos, 1985; Udwin, 1993). A number of children do indeed require individual intervention. However, particularly since this is an aspect of service delivery with which most clinicians are familiar, it is tempting to do only this. The organisation has to be continually conscious of its mental health objectives at other levels and, because of resource limitations, to limit the extent of individual work that can be undertaken.

OUTCOMES AND EVALUATION

A necessary, albeit frequently neglected, part of every intervention must be critical evaluation. This is particularly true when new intervention strategies are being developed and tested. An individual counsellor using a tried and tested debriefing technique has the security of knowing that the method has worked for many others and is thus likely to be effective with her client. There are, however, very few tried and tested models of community intervention. In fact, a central aim of KZN-PSV has always been to develop effective and appropriate methods of intervention with the hope that these might then be implemented by state-supported institutions more widely than has been possible from an NGO. Critical evaluation has therefore been seen as an important process in the organisation's work. A number of difficulties have, however, emerged in the process.

Communities that are recovering from civil violence are exceptionally fragile. There are innumerable cases where incidents in the life of the community have set both peace-making and mental health interventions back months. Under such circumstances, specific outcome indicators may not reflect the complex, staggered and inconsistent movement towards peace and psychosocial health within a community.

Other information is also required in order to create a full understanding of the progress of a particular community.

The fragility of the evaluation context as well as the multiple activities aligned with the complex objectives described above has made it necessary to use alternative methods of monitoring and evaluation. The framework adopted by KZN-PSV has been based on the principles of action-research (Winter, 1987). Stated simply, intervention is planned, implemented, monitored and evaluated through the collaboration of the participants (both beneficiaries and practitioners) in a cyclical, recursive model of development. Action-research relies heavily upon the ability of participants to reflect critically upon the intervention. Because they are both intimately involved with the intervention, this 'closeness' can make practitioners and beneficiaries particularly perceptive in their evaluative judgements – or it can do the reverse. In most cases something of each is probably involved. In the end, a combination of internal evaluation (such as is outlined above) and external or independent evaluation (where an outside evaluator is brought in) probably provides the most convincing assessment of the efficacy of such interventions.

Internal evaluation

Using action-research as a framework for evaluation makes some important demands upon an organisation. First, it demands that there is a sharing of power between practitioners and beneficiaries. This is particularly valuable when one of the aims of intervention is empowerment. It also ensures that the intervention remains responsive to the changing needs of the community. KZN-PSV has met this challenge in several ways. Most importantly, the management committee (the highest decision-making body in the organisation) comprises both practitioners and community representatives. This structure allows representatives of the beneficiary community to have a direct influence on intervention strategies and other aspects of the organisation's functioning. The organisation has also established leadership (including youth leadership) forums at which representatives of various target communities meet with staff to discuss progress in their communities.

A second demand made by action-research is that monitoring and evaluation should be ongoing processes, and that the results should impact immediately and continuously upon intervention strategies. KZN-PSV has responded to this challenge by instituting a continuous collection of outcome and process information, weekly process supervision for all field workers, quarterly reporting on all communities, and six-monthly strategic planning sessions. All this ensures that personnel as well as beneficiaries are constantly reflecting critically upon the programme's work.

Through the various mechanisms and processes detailed above, a range of different information is collected. In addition three other mechanisms for monitoring progress are used:

- *Individual self-report.* All clients coming into the programme – whether for individual counselling, as members of one of the various groups, as volunteers or as trainees – answer a set of questions relating to their current state of health, their concerns and their reasons for getting involved with the programme. At the end of that person's time with the organisation a similar set of questions is asked. The difference in answers allows practitioners to monitor the impact of intervention upon their clients' lives. In addition this process provides a therapeutic way of bringing the intervention to a meaningful close.

- *Objective statistics.* The organisation monitors a wide range of statistics which, on the whole, demonstrate the quantity of work rather than its quality or impact. These include the number of individual clients; referrals; groups; sessions per group; people attending group sessions; trainees; trainees attending follow-up; media presentations; youth on skills training; and youth finding work.

  A range of statistics compiled by other bodies is also monitored. Foremost among these is the number of politically motivated killings per month both in the province and in particular communities. Although these statistics capture something of the impact of the programme (at least on a local level) they are not in themselves sufficient.

- *Process notes.* Case notes are kept by field workers of all interactions within particular communities. Thus a detailed narrative of the intervention process is developed over time and it becomes possible to track trends and patterns. Again this serves a dual function. On the one hand the narrative forms the basis for the supervision of field staff and allows co-ordinators and field staff to develop detailed intervention strategies. On the other hand the process notes provide an account of the complex networks of cause and effect within the process. This allows the impact of intervention to be monitored against the complex and changing context of community life.

Independent evaluation

At various times in the organisation's history particular aspects of the work have been subjected to independent evaluations. These are useful in that they provide an outsider's critique of both the intervention strategies and the organisation's internal dynamics. The reports of such evaluations are then usually workshopped by staff in order that the contents are integrated into the strategic planning of the organisation. These cannot be adequately summarised here, but as an example, the following is taken from the executive summary of one such evaluation conducted under the auspices of the University of Natal (Meintjes, Killian, Govender, 1995, p. 36):

  On the basis of this evaluation, it was felt that the following goals were achieved:

  - Psychological healing: to a certain extent individuals seem to have begun to understand and deal with some of their past experiences.
  - Participants show evidence of, and report increases in, self-confidence and a sense of individual empowerment.
  - Leadership skills training and organisation skills training appear to have been successful.
  - Intergroup and gender prejudices seem to have been challenged by the interaction of different groups.
  - Movement towards more general intergroup reconciliation has been mobilised.
  - Projects in community development have been started.

  The evaluation processes described above have for several years provided a rich source of both summative data, which demonstrate impact, and formative data, which guide the development of intervention strategies. These data have served to sustain the funding base of the organisation and ensure that intervention strategies have developed and remained appropriate to the needs of the beneficiary communities.

ISSUES AND INSIGHTS

Five years ago, when KZN-PSV formally began work, the individuals involved had little idea about how things would develop. Gradually, the development of philosophical and psychological roots to the work of the organisation has provided a firmer position from which to explore and evaluate ways of working with communities that have survived civil conflict. Trauma work by its very nature is overwhelming, demanding and stressful. It is essential that practitioners have a theoretical framework from which to operate and to make decisions. This chapter has outlined a theoretical framework from which KZN-PSV has found it useful to work. It is by no means perfect. The concepts of 'empowerment' and 'linking' need to be more rigorously explored and perhaps extended. Similarly the framework does not yet provide an adequate understanding of the process of recovery following civil conflict, and how this process is facilitated by strategic intervention. Thus, appropriately, the development of theory is an ongoing process.

The authors' experience with KZN-PSV has led to some important insights. First, in such interventions it is not enough to work at the level of the individual and the family. Isolated interventions at this level do not change what happens at community level or affect the social structures which have been the cause of children not being adequately protected and nurtured. Similarly the enormous challenges faced by caregivers, community leaders and other service delivery agencies, including schools, crèches and clinics, are not addressed. It has been the experience of KZN-PSV that it is possible to intervene effectively at the level of whole communities and that, in combination with other levels of intervention, it is essential in dealing with the effects of civil violence.

Second, the authors have come to a fuller appreciation of how exhausting and stressful community-level intervention can be. Such intervention requires field workers to become equally competent in a children's playgroup, in negotiating domestic violence situations, in reporting and following up child-abuse cases with the police and legal system, in training youth and parents, and in negotiations with community leadership. Each of these groups makes its own demands upon the personal and other resources of the field worker and the organisation. As a result the selection, training and support of field staff are of crucial importance. This work requires people with highly developed personal skills, good psychological skills, as well as great vision and tenacity. Most important is constant monitoring and support of personnel. Field personnel are at extremely high risk of secondary traumatic stress, and as, such require compassionate and intensive supervision. One of the ongoing frustrations of staff is their need to recognise their time and personal restrictions. The mental health needs of rural communities in KwaZulu-Natal, especially those that have been subjected to ongoing violence, are overwhelming and will remain so until the resources are made available to provide adequate services to these communities. No single agency can solve all these problems, a fact which many field workers find difficult to accept.

Models of intervention which do not take account of this are likely to fail, at great cost to their field workers and their clients.

As has been the case in KZN-PSV, this problem may be exacerbated by rapid growth in an organisation. Such growth necessitates greater energy and time being placed on administrative, supervisory and other managerial functions. This has the effect of diverting the attention of some of the more senior and experienced staff away from direct service delivery – the work that challenges and has meaning for them personally. Furthermore, the ready access to emotional support that is possible within a small organisation is significantly diluted and greater conscious attention has to be given to 'caring for the carers'.

Third, the authors have come to understand that many fundamental principles of individual or group psychological intervention apply equally to community intervention. These, together with an appreciation of the uniqueness of particular communities and a good understanding of traumatic stress, provide a strong foundation for effective community work. Adopting a collaborative and 'learning' position, it has been possible to conceptualise the effects of violence on a community in the simple yet direct way which informs the ethos of the wide variety of interventions of this programme.

REFERENCES

Bronfenbrenner, U. (1979). *The ecology of human development: Experiments by nature and design*. Cambridge: Harvard University Press.

Central Statistical Services (1997). *October household survey 1995*. Pretoria: Government Printer.

Dawes A. & Donald, D. (Eds) (1994). *Childhood and adversity: Psychological perspectives from South African Research*. Cape Town: David Philip.

Eagle, G. & Michelson, C.L. (1997). Post-traumatic stress in children: presentation and intervention guidelines. In B. Rock (Ed.), *Spirals of suffering: Public violence and children* (pp. 227–254). Pretoria: HSRC Publishers.

Egan, G. (1994). *The skilled helper* (5th ed.). Pacific Grove: Brooks-Cole.

Herman, J. (1992). Complex PTSD: A syndrome in survivors of prolonged and repeated trauma. *Journal of Traumatic Stress*, 5, 377–420.

Jeffrey, A.J. (1997). *The Natal story: 16 years of conflict*. Cape Town: South African Institute of Race Relations.

Kruger, J. & Motala, S. (1997). Welfare. In S. Robinson, & L. Biersteker (Eds.), *First call: The South African children's budget* (pp. 65–114). Cape Town: IDASA.

Malange, N., McKay, A. & Nhlengetwa, Z. (1996). *On common ground*. Durban: KwaZulu Natal Programme for Survivors of Violence.

McKay, A. (1997). The survivors of apartheid and political violence in KwaZulu-Natal. In B. Rock (Ed.), *Spirals of suffering: Public violence and children*. Pretoria: HSRC Publishers.

Meïntjes, B., Killian, B. & Govender, K. (1995). KwaZulu-Natal programme for survivors of violence youth leadership camps: Evaluation report. Unpublished research report.

Motala, S. (1997). Education. In S. Robinson & L. Biersteker (Eds.), *First Call: The South African children's budget* (pp. 115–152). Cape Town: IDASA.

Robinson, S. & Biersteker, L. (1997). *First Call: The South African Children's Budget*. Cape

Town: IDASA

Roche, C. (1996). Operationality in turbulence: The need for change. In D. Eade (Ed.), *Development in states of war* (pp. 160–172). Oxford: Oxfam UK and Ireland.

Rutter, M. (1985). Resilience in the face of adversity. Protective factors and resistance to psychological disorder. *British Journal of Psychiatry, 147*, 598–611.

Spencer, E. & Pynoos, R. S. (1985). *Post-traumatic stress disorder in children.* Washington D.C.: American Psychiatric Association.

Straker, J. & Moosa, F. (1994). Interacting with trauma survivors in contexts of continuing trauma. *Journal of Traumatic Stress, 7*, 1–9.

Staub, E. (1989). *The roots of evil: The origins of genocide and other group violence.* New York: Cambridge University Press.

Summerfield, D. (1995). Assisting survivors of war and atrocity. *Development in Practice, 5*(4), 159–173.

Summerfield, D. (1996). Assisting survivors of war and atrocity: Notes on 'psycho-social' issues for NGO Workers. In D. Eade (Ed.), *Development in states of war* (pp. 352–356). Oxford: Oxfam UK and Ireland .

Udwin, O. (1993). Annotation: Children's reactions to traumatic events. *Journal of Child Psychology and Psychiatry, 34*(2), 115–127.

Winter, R. (1987). *Action-research and the nature of social enquiry: Professional innovation and educational work.* Aldershot: Avebury.

THE EMOTIONAL EXPERIENCE OF WORKING WITH TROUBLED CHILDREN 11

A psychodynamic approach to organisational consultation

KERRY GIBSON

KERRY GIBSON

BACKGROUND

This chapter outlines a model of consultation which can be used by clinical psychologists to provide support and training to organisations which work directly with children in various community settings. The model was developed at the University of Cape Town's Child Guidance Clinic in order to give students an experience of community-oriented work during their clinical psychology training. It has been refined over the past ten years in work with a variety of community organisations involved with the care of children. The aim of the Clinic's various consultation partnerships has been to develop the capacity of key organisations to deal with the emotional needs of children under their care. In particular the programme has targeted organisations which work with groups of children considered at risk for the development of emotional difficulties. The ultimate objective is to improve the standard of care these children receive and, through this, to maximise their opportunities for healthy development.

This chapter describes the way in which the consultation process is conceptualised and implemented. Within the model, consultation includes a range of activities such as training, emotional support or supervision as possible responses to an organisation's needs. In all these interventions the emphasis is on making sense of the powerful emotional and political processes which impact on an organisation's ability to make effective use of a consultation partnership.

It is generally recognised that professional resources in clinical psychology and related fields within the state sector are inadequate to meet the needs of the large numbers of South Africans who may benefit from them (Freeman & Pillay, 1997). Children constitute a particularly under-resourced group, given the relatively small number of psychologists and psychiatrists who are trained to work in this field (Dawes et al., 1997). Ironically the gap between resources and needs has grown even larger as mental health workers have recognised the value of preventive as well as curative services.

In response to scarce resources, many local projects have adopted the well-established community psychological dictum of 'giving psychology away' (Miller, 1969 in Orford, 1992). The aim of this is to use mental health professionals to assist the development of community resources rather than in direct work with clients. In the area of children's mental health this may involve sharing psychological skills amongst people who work with children in a variety of organisational contexts such as schools, clinics or children's homes (Dawes *et al.*, 1997). These so-called 'front-line workers' may have little or no formal training in psychology but are seen to be in a unique position to help the children in their care. They have the advantage, in most cases, of knowing the children well, and the potential for building on already established relationships with them. In addition, this approach is suitable to local contexts where professional knowledge often needs to be adapted to specific cultural norms and practices (Swartz, 1998). In principle, the approach also fits well with the many attempts to empower communities in sectors other than mental health.

THE DEVELOPMENT OF A MODEL OF CONSULTATION

In the mid-1980s, the Child Guidance Clinic, increasingly frustrated with the limitations of the individual and family-based models of psychological intervention, began to experiment with alternative models of community-oriented practice (Swartz, Dowdall & Swartz, 1986). The psychologists, and trainees based there, extended their work to include training and support to organisations, drawing broadly from the principles outlined above (Lazarus, 1991). In response to specific requests, the Clinic began to offer consultations aimed at building the capacity of staff in preschools, clinics and NGOs working with children. Initially this involved training, mostly in counselling skills. With more attention to the specific needs of organisations, however, it became clear that it was not always helpful simply to duplicate the practices of psychologists amongst front-line workers.

Instead, the Clinic adopted the more contextually sensitive aim of increasing the capacity of organisations to deal with the emotional needs of their charges within the context of their own defined area of work; in other words, to create greater capacity amongst nurses, child-care workers, community health workers, teachers and so on to integrate psychological ideas in appropriate ways into their established, everyday activities. Although it was recognised that greater knowledge and skill often did allow workers to identify those children who were particularly in need of psychological assistance and to refer them appropriately, the scarcity of referral resources stopped this from being the primary aim. The intention was rather to provide children with good, ongoing care and, through this, to increase their general resilience.

The widely recognised 'at risk' groups on which the work has focused over the years include children who live in extreme poverty, children living out of the care of their families, those who have been subjected to violence or abuse, and those who are physically or mentally handicapped. The differences between these groups have provided an opportunity to ascertain the model's effectiveness with different kinds of problems, as well as within the very different sorts of organisations working with them.

The broad principles of this consultation approach conformed well to ideas about the appropriate and effective use of resources in mental health (Desjarlais, Eisenberg, Good & Kleinman, 1995). However, the actual process of training and supporting front-line workers in consultation partnerships was found to be far more complicated than the easy idea of 'giving psychology away' had suggested. In practice, consultants were struck by the way in which emotional and social processes within and between organisations often disturbed and, in some cases, completely disrupted the effectiveness of the interventions. Even the most sensitively contracted and mutually developed training processes seemed sometimes to flounder in the face of unexplained resistance or hostility. In some cases, an intervention proclaimed to be a great success by all would mysteriously lead to little change in either thinking or practice. In other instances, when front-line workers did use the ideas developed in consultation, this seemed to be for only frustratingly short periods until they quickly reverted to old patterns and the original problems associated with these.

As the work continued it became important to identify the sorts of factors that affected the success or failure of any consultation. It gradually became clear that the motivation of front-line workers to work with the emotional needs of children was strongly influenced by the stress they experienced in their work. Their ability to develop new skills and knowledge depended on their being able to continue to learn, under the sway of very difficult emotions often generated by the demands of the work itself. Their ability to manage these feelings seemed to depend not only on their individual resources but, more importantly, on the support provided within their organisation. This realisation shifted the focus of attention from the individual worker, and his or her capacity to develop or use psychological knowledge, to the stresses that organisations face as a whole.

Borrowing from psychodynamic ideas about organisational functioning (e.g. Obholzer & Roberts, 1994) we began to recognise that organisations under stress seem to be subject to irrational emotional processes similar to those found in distressed individuals. These, in some cases, seemed to overturn the organisation's own conscious goals and interests as well as their ability to develop through a consultation process. With ongoing reflection and feedback, a model of consultation has gradually been developed which acknowledges the centrality of such feelings in the functioning of organisations. It is only by addressing these dynamics that one can build the motivation, knowledge and capacity of front-line workers to engage with the emotional needs of the children in their charge.

CONSULTATION IN THEORY

Literature in the field of community-oriented psychology recognises consultation as a valuable way of spreading psychological skills to groups who can best use them in their work with people (Orford, 1992). This, in turn, is regarded as an essential component of mental health promotion and prevention (Tudor, 1996). But while there seems to be general agreement on these broad aims of consultation, there are very different ways in which it can be understood and practised. The initial writings in this area tended to emphasise the idea of a temporary relationship between two professionals in which one draws from the expertise of the other (Caplan, 1970). This view was taken largely from the experiences within well-resourced countries where, for example, a psychologist might be bought in to offer expert advice to a paediatric ward on the state of a particular child's mental health.

In our own context this view of consultation has been challenged on a number of different levels. First, given the shortage of resources, consultants working in our context may need to take up a more generally supportive role, including emotional as well as practical support in a range of different areas. They may also need to maintain this support over a significantly longer period of time (Maw, 1996). Second, drawing from authors like Orford (1992), the idea of the consultant as an 'expert' has been questioned. Instead, the value of the consultee's own contribution to the development of shared knowledge has been increasingly recognised. This is particularly important in South Africa where front-line workers can serve as vital interpreters of cultural meaning to professionals who may be out of touch with local concerns and ideas (Swartz, 1998). In this way the consultation relationship needs to be understood as a partnership rather than as one between teacher and pupil. Third, local research has suggested that there needs to be far greater awareness of the political environment and its effects on the consultation process (Holdsworth, 1994; Maw, 1996; Mogoduso & Butchart, 1992; Seedat & Nell, 1992). Finally, the practices of development work suggest that it is more appropriate to adopt a holistic approach to capacity building, focusing on the needs of whole organisations rather than on the interests of particular individuals within them (Orford, 1992). Although all of these theoretical elements have been important in the development of the model of consultation, this chapter will highlight the often neglected emotional processes that form part of consultation work. Particular emphasis will be placed on the way in which organisational stress, with its roots in both personal and political pain, influences the consultation process.

The personal roots of organisational stress

In an attempt to understand some of the roots of organisational stress we have drawn from the combined psychodynamic and systemic models of organisational consultancy. These were developed initially through the work of Menzies (1970) and described more recently in Obholzer and Roberts (1997) as the Tavistock model of consulting to institutions. The essence of this theoretical position is that organisations, like individuals, have an unconscious life which influences and colours their conscious activity. Organisations are understood to struggle with powerful emotional currents which reflect not only the particular concerns of individuals, but also the shared experience of all within the organisation. Intense feelings may originate from various sources, but one of the primary sources for social service organisations is the distress felt by their clients (Halton, 1994). This is directly experienced by front-line workers as they are forced to contend with the difficulties their clients bring to them. Unconsciously they begin to carry the burden of these feelings which, ultimately, infects the organisation as a whole.

For example, the staff of an organisation which deals with abandoned children may find themselves struggling to manage the children's painful feelings of loss and their often excessive emotional neediness. Staff in this situation are forced to find some way of coping with their inability to fulfil the enormous needs of these children. Individual staff might each have their own way of coping with these feelings. For example, they may chose to emphasise the practical care of the children above their emotional care. Over time, however, staff may gradually introduce their own styles of coping into the structures and practices of the organisation itself. So, for example, the children's home may develop a system of shift work which results in staff taking turns in looking after different groups of children. While on the surface this may appear to be a reasonable way of organising the work, it also protects staff members from having to form close personal bonds with any of the children with whom they work. This in turn shields them from the full impact of the children's emotional needs. It also, however, results in the children being deprived of a valuable source of emotional stability. Although it is perhaps helpful to the staff in the short term, in the long term it may deprive them of an important source of meaning in their work and the potential emotional rewards that can come from looking after children. Importantly, these protective strategies seldom develop as a conscious choice, but rather come out of feelings which cannot be consciously acknowledged. Once they are entrenched as practices within the organisation they are seldom questioned, and newcomers to the organisation are quickly initiated into its shared habits and ethos.

The political roots of organisational stress

While the focus of this model is on making sense of the emotional life of organisations, it is important to acknowledge other contextual realities (Obholzer & Roberts, 1994). Although the Tavistock model of consultancy recognises the structures that govern organisational functioning, it does not pay enough attention to the broader political context of organisational activity. Other writers, however, have helped to show how some emotional processes may have their roots in political issues (Holland, 1988). The political divisions that have existed in South Africa have made these links more obvious perhaps than elsewhere. Individuals working within organisations bring with them their own political histories, often from very different sides of the apartheid fence. In addition to strong political or social commitment which may sustain them in their work, they also bring their particular areas of vulnerability and pain associated with their race, gender and class identities. In addition, the clients serviced by the organisations often carry a multitude of experiences related to discrimination and abuse attached both to their identity and to their handicap or difficult circumstances. It is well known that discrimination spirals downwards and it is often children, the weak and the damaged who bear the worst brunt of a prejudiced society.

Organisations reflect their political context even more directly in their relative access to resources, which in turn have for many years been determined according to the inequalities of apartheid. Furthermore, their internal structures often carry the legacy of authoritarian management practices, or manifest inconsistent practices which arise out of a mistrust of authority. Thus the children's home described in the previous example might carry not only the pain of the children's emotional needs but also the added burden of an overworked and underpaid staff who feel they have little power in relation to their own management structures. These kinds of political pressures seem to create, within some organisations, a mirror of the broader political terrain. Feelings of deprivation, envy, conflict and difficulties in establishing effective authority are an understandable response to some of these experiences. These are then added to the pool of difficult feelings within organisations.

Consulting to organisations under stress

Of particular relevance for the Clinic's model is the influence of all of these powerful processes on an organisation's capacity to use the knowledge that should be developed through consultation. Learning and teaching are particularly susceptible to the disruption caused through painful feelings. Effective learning, according to Salzberger-Wittenberg, Henry and Osborne (1990), only occurs in the context of a safe learning environment. Furthermore, the emotional meaning of what is learnt may influence the extent to which it can be taken in, or meaningfully integrated into practice. A psychodynamic approach to understanding an organisation's capacity for learning allows for a more appropriately complex picture of the challenges involved in attempting to develop psychological knowledge through consultation.

Most organisations involved in the caring or social service field find it difficult to present their own needs as legitimate in the face of the overwhelming needs of their clients. An important part of the consultant's job is to facilitate the organisation's recognition of its own underlying emotional needs and experiences, and to provide a temporary container for anxieties that cannot be dealt with by the stressed organisation itself. As these feelings are spoken about, by both the consultant and the organisation, they are experienced as less frightening and are more easily tolerated. This lessens the need to develop ways of coping within the organisation that may be unhelpful to both the clients and the staff. In the context of this shared understanding, the participants can then help to design an intervention which addresses the organisation's development in a holistic way.

This difficult process of making sense of the organisation's deeper needs requires a firm and trusting relationship as a base. This trust is also necessary to cope with often powerful emotions experienced between the consultant and the organisation. Consultation may be fraught in so far as the relationship between university-based professionals and community-based workers often carries many of the political inequalities mentioned earlier. In spite of a stated commitment to cultural dialogue, there may be the added problem of differences in the way that the consultant and the organisation understand or experience problems and their solutions. In addition, the relationship often holds some of the less realistic emotional responses that each group tends to experience in the face of difficulties (Salzberger-Wittenberg *et al.*, 1990). These underlying emotional expectations may include, for example, the hope of members of the organisation that they may be magically rescued from some difficult situation by the consultant – and resentment when this does not occur. On the part of the consultants, it may involve the unrealistic wish to be all-powerful or the fear of having nothing good to offer. It is only when these feelings are acknowledged that they make possible the development of insight in the context of a secure relationship environment.

In summary, this approach to consultancy rests on a holistic and contextualised view of any organisation and its needs. The consultant's role is to work with the organisation in understanding the difficult feelings that may arise out of the nature of their work, the organisational ethos and structure, as well as the broader social and political context. With proper attention to the emotional needs of the organisation, staff can be freed to attend more completely to the needs of their charges, and, with ongoing support, their own capacity to learn and develop can be increased.

CONSULTATION IN PRACTICE

Principles guiding the practice of consultation

A number of key principles have emerged out of the application of these ideas across a range of different consultation relationships. These principles reflect a set of common requirements which appear to apply across different contexts.

Establishing a firm contract

A clear frame which safeguards the relationship between the consultant and the organisation is essential. This translates into paying careful attention in the beginning phase of the consultation to setting up a contract which binds both parties. Both the consultants and organisation need to say clearly what they can and cannot do. As the process of making sense of the organisation's needs is an unfolding one, these have to be repeatedly negotiated. For instance, a consultant to a children's home may have negotiated an initial contract which involved providing training on child development. As the work continues, however, an open group in which staff can talk about their own difficulties may emerge as a more helpful option. While these kinds of contracts are a necessary starting point for a mutually respectful relationship, the emotional processes which affect the work invariably create misunderstandings and disappointments, however well the contract has been negotiated. In practice, establishing a foundation of trust within this relationship can take considerable time. In the Clinic's experience, many of the most significant issues of organisations have emerged only after several years of sustained work with them.

Determining sustainability

The difficult process of dealing with painful feelings and altering established patterns requires a commitment not only on the part of the consultant but also on the part of the organisation. Responding to requests for assistance rather than initiating consultative interventions generally increases the likelihood that organisations will become involved, at least consciously, in participating in a process which may not always be immediately rewarding for them. The Clinic conducts careful assessments of how far an organisation may benefit from a consultation relationship, and whether both parties have the necessary resources to engage with the demands presented. Bearing in mind general cautions about who may or may not benefit from psychological interventions (Malan, 1981), some organisations may not have the necessary infrastructure to deal with the difficulty of learning new ideas or taking on tasks that exceed their already stretched emotional resources. This is particularly so when organisations are undergoing major change involving, for example, mass retrenchments. In this kind of situation it is neither possible nor appropriate for organisations to take on new demands. Maw's (1996) research with individuals in consultation suggests that this kind of assessment may be as valuable in community-oriented work as it is in psychotherapy with individuals.

Establishing boundaries

The work itself often appears to challenge the conventional roles and boundaries which clinical psychologists use in their work with individuals and families. Consultants are inevitably working outside of their familiar surroundings. They may have to fit in with space or other demands over which they have little or no control. There are also often anxieties about how to manage the social demands of the consultancy role. In individual work, roles are clearly defined as client and professional, and the work is strictly focused on therapeutic interaction. The consultant, however, frequently ends up joining the consultees for tea and engaging in normal social chit-chat. These experiences require that consultants are able to respond flexibly and to manage without the clear limits governing more conventional practice.

In spite of this need for flexibility, some clear boundaries are helpful for both the consultant and the organisation. Rules governing the interaction may be as minimal as the consultant arriving at a regular time, or consistently staying after the consultation for a cup of tea. Regardless of what these rules are, provided they are consistently held, they seem to offer a degree of security in the relationship which protects both parties from the sort of unpredictability which can undermine trust. The maintenance of some boundaries also models, for workers, the legitimacy of establishing their own boundaries with their clients (Swartz, 1996). This has been very important for the many organisations who have been driven to the brink of burnout through their inability to protect themselves from the pressing needs of their clients. Paying particular attention to punctuality, consistency and reliability in attendance has proved to be an important professional requirement in the Clinic's work with organisations.

Working with the whole organisation

Focusing on the organisation as a whole is a central principle in the model. This includes a focus not only on management and workers, but on the clients as well. The consultant also becomes a part of the organisational system through his or her involvement with it. In this holistic view, the individual role-players are considered mainly in terms of their position and voice within the organisation, with less concern for their unique histories and issues. This is helpful in directing the consultant away from the temptation to blame an individual or particular group within an organisation for its problems. It redirects the process towards the welfare of the organisation as a whole. It is common, for example, for staff to want to place all responsibility for their difficulties on a director whom they believe to be unfair or autocratic. Such perceptions can be used as a way of protecting staff from having to look more carefully at their own involvement in their work difficulties. In such situations, the consultant is likely to be most helpful through encouraging both staff and management to take joint responsibility for the emotional and practical burdens of the organisation. This view does not exclude the need for staff, and the consultant in the role of advocate, to challenge the reality of unfair labour practices where these exist.

Understanding the context

Organisations are also recognised as closely linked to the communities and structures which make up their working context. They are affected both directly and indirectly by conditions and developments in their surrounding environment. For example, the problems at the children's home already referred to cannot be understood without also looking at the impact of the welfare budget on the home's resources, the effects of gangsterism in the surrounding area on staff morale, or the poverty which is a factor in the initial abandonment of many of the children in the home. The wide range of systems and sub-systems that can be involved in any particular problem may create an unwieldy number of possibilities for intervention. While recognising the deeper or more complex roots of any particular issue, strategic choices in intervention may nevertheless have to be made. Thus, it may be necessary to focus on issues where it is possible to effect some kind of real change. It is still important, however, to understand the influence of a wide variety of factors on the problems of any organisation if solutions are not to be overly simplistic.

Reflecting and changing

Consultation is recognised to be a complex, unfolding and often unpredictable process. This requires constant reflection, reformulation and responsiveness on the part of the consultant in relation to any new or previously hidden needs. It is very easy for consultants and consultees to get stuck in a particular intervention activity which has become institutionalised through repetition. This is especially so when the intervention itself may be serving a defensive function for either organisation or consultant (Bolton & Roberts, 1994). For example, a staff group in which participants regularly moan about the same unresolved conflicts may actually be helping to distract them from their real difficulties around working with the children. In order to prevent this from happening, consultants need to remain open-minded. Where possible, ongoing contact with an external supervisor can help with this. With or without such supervision, however, consultants are encouraged to reflect on their own emotional responses, to challenge their motivations and to acknowledge their own irrational responses to the work. It is only through this that they can remain open to the kinds of things that organisations may be trying to tell them about their changing needs.

Listening deeply

Importantly the consultant has to be able not only to listen to what the organisation is saying at any time but also to listen deeply (Stein, 1994). Halton (1994) describes the consultant as listening on the boundary of conscious and unconscious meanings. In practice this involves being open to the emotional responses of the organisation, to hearing some of the unspoken needs, and tracking the symbolic meaning of what is verbalised. For example, continual references to the helplessness of their charges may also be signalling the staff's own experience of impotence in response to the difficulties of their work. The consultant also needs to track his or her own emotional responses, as these sometimes offer important clues about the emotional experiences of the organisation. Fortunately, organisations, like individuals in therapy (Casement, 1985), are often quite tenacious about letting the consultant know what they need, even when these needs are unconscious. Often the same need will be indirectly expressed in a variety of different ways before it is finally heard by the consultant. Once this need is understood by the consultant its validity can be checked out with the organisation and it can be dealt with in the consultation process.

Keeping the children in mind

Whatever form the intervention takes, the ultimate aim is for it to increase the capacity of the organisation to respond appropriately to the needs of the children in its care. While strengthening an organisation may increase the likelihood that its workers will be able to engage with these needs, this alone is not sufficient. Workers still need to learn about the psychological needs of children and to develop the skills which enable them to respond appropriately to them. Although the ultimate aim of dealing more effectively with the children should be clear, in practice it is easy to get pulled into dealing only with the emotional needs of staff in the organisation, particularly when there are few other supports available. Bion's notion of the 'primary task' is helpful here in maintaining a focus on only those areas of organisational functioning or personal difficulty which directly affect the task of caring for children (Stokes, 1994). This ultimate concern with the needs of children has to be held as a clear, ongoing focus through all the stages of the consultation.

Steps in the process of consultation

Although the model that has been outlined is designed to be flexible, its implementation, as developed by the Child Guidance Clinic, is guided by a series of steps. They provide a framework for making sense of the underlying needs of an organisation, and for determining the kinds of intervention that may be appropriate. These will be described below as they may prove useful to other consultants.

Problem clarification and organisational assessment

Following an initial referral, a series of interviews is conducted with representatives of various sub-systems within the organisation. All groups are asked about their understanding of the problem or request. This information is contextualised by gathering further detail on the aims, structure and functioning of the organisation, its available resources, the community context within which it operates and so on. This information gathering is guided by an 'organisational history-taking format' devised for this purpose (Gibson, 1995). This process has much in common with the standard practice of needs assessment. It differs in so far as it demands more subtle observations about the emotional significance of spoken and observed sources of information. For this process it draws on therapeutic assessment procedures with individuals and families.

Thus, using the example of the children's home again, reasons behind a request for 'training on child development' would be fully explored. It may emerge that the home is actually looking for specific help with age-appropriate discipline techniques for managing the problem behaviour of some of the children. The history taking would also include basic information such as the number and ages of children in the home, the number of staff, and careful descriptions of the tasks they are expected to perform. In addition, however, it may include observations such as the child-care workers' seeming reluctance to discuss their work in front of the director, or the distress expressed by the director when she spoke of the possibility of staff retrenchments.

Making sense of the problem

The background information provided by the organisational representatives is used to reflect back on the significance of the referral problem or request. In practice this involves sifting through the information on the organisation and its functioning to make sense of why the particular referral request was made at this particular time and what other needs it may be expressing. In effect, a causal chain is established between various significant factors in the organisation's history and its current consciously held need.

So, for example, an increase in gang violence in the community in which a children's home is located, coupled with a recent threat of retrenchments amongst staff, may have resulted in an increase in the anxiety experienced by child-care workers, who not only work at the home but also live in the surrounding neighbourhood. Their fears for their own safety and the security of their jobs may add to already existing feelings of powerlessness in relation to meeting the overwhelming needs of the children in their care. In the face of these kinds of feelings, they may find themselves understandably less able to manage a long-standing problem of unruly and aggressive behaviour amongst some of the children. Added to this, the children may respond, unconsciously, with increasingly difficult behaviour to the child-care workers' inability to contain them. The referral request for help to establish effective discipline is a valid need in itself. Symbolically, however, it may also reflect the underlying need for help in dealing with the dual threats of gangsterism and retrenchment as well as the difficulties in working with such a needy group of children. While an intervention focusing simply on the discipline problems in the home may be helpful, it would not address the underlying reasons for the workers' current anxieties. This formulation of the referral request provides a starting point for making sense of the organisation's needs. It will nevertheless require constant development and re-working through the process of consultation.

Negotiating the new understanding

The consultant's ideas about the meaning of the request or problem are discussed with different groups within the organisation. In most cases the process of gathering information has already started participants thinking and talking about their organisation. The questions asked by the consultant often prompt a realisation amongst the staff of the areas that they find difficult. If the earlier information gathering has been conducted sensitively, the staff should already have a better idea of the roots of some of their difficulties. These ideas are then consolidated in discussion with them. This is used not only as an opportunity to develop insight about organisational issues but to allow for the consultant's ideas to be challenged and transformed by alternative interpretations. Although the focus of this process is on the achievement of some kind of shared understanding, it also allows for the development of a recognition that the task is to think together about the needs of the organisation.

Developing an appropriate response

On the basis of the negotiated understanding, an appropriate intervention is planned and agreed to. The intervention can take a variety of forms and in most cases will shift as different needs emerge during the course of the consultation. The kinds of intervention strategies most often pursued include one, or a combination, of the following: staff support groups, formal training workshops, individual supervision or consultation with particular members of the organisation. Help with networking or suggestions for structural change may, on occasion, also occur. These more practical tasks should help to implement ideas gained through insight and reflection. However, they can also represent a flight from more difficult emotional tasks. The development of elaborate 'grievance procedures' for an organisation may harness the energy of consultants and staff alike yet still not deal with the underlying conflict which was the initial problem.

In most cases interventions operate simultaneously on more than one level of need. They often take account of practical needs as well as more hidden emotional needs. Frequently, a single focus can accommodate both, provided attention is paid to the different levels of meaning involved. For example, in the children's home, a series of workshops on discipline techniques may meet the overtly acknowledged practical need. It may also provide staff with a relatively unthreatening forum in which they can begin to talk about their more general feelings of impotence. This in turn may lead to attempts to develop within the home a stronger management structure which would be more capable of providing appropriate protection for the staff and children who live there.

EVALUATING THE MODEL

In the initial phases of the model's development little attention was paid to formal evaluation processes. Like many projects operating in the 1980s, this one developed organically and in response to what appeared to be pressing community needs. Recently, the Clinic has become more aware of the importance of evaluating the model's effectiveness, both in the interests of ongoing work and in response to increasingly stringent demands from funding organisations. Recent attempts to develop an approach to evaluation which is consistent with, and integrated into, the consultation work are a long way from complete. Nevertheless, some early indications of the strengths and weaknesses of the model are apparent.

Principles of evaluation

An important starting point for the process of evaluation is a careful statement of aims. Most basically, the intention of this model is for front-line workers to increase their ability to manage the emotional demands of their work situation, to think psychologically about the needs of the children in their care, and to integrate this thinking into their work with children. Thus the thrust of consultation is to improve the health of an organisation in order to benefit the children who are a part of it. In this sense the intervention aims at improving the environment of children rather than acting directly on them. The intervention is also not time-limited but is aimed at producing and maintaining increased organisational capacity. Evaluation therefore needs to assess the impact of the process of consultation on organisational capacity as it is developed and maintained over a period of time.

In determining whether the consultation is improving an organisation's capacity there are a number of complexities to consider. First, it is difficult to identify a precise moment at which a desired end-point is achieved in the ongoing consultation process. A period of increased distress within an organisation may actually indicate movement to a more healthy state, as staff feel more able to show previously hidden feelings. There can also be considerable fluctuation in the capacity of an organisation, depending on external stressors and internal demands at any time. This suggests a need for repeated evaluations at different stages in the ongoing process of consultation. Second, a multipronged approach to evaluation may be better able to capture the variety of areas influenced by a consultation process. Factors such as increased emotional responsiveness amongst caregivers may best be captured through soft data such as workers' accounts of their own experience. This could be supplemented with more objective indicators of stress or health within the organisation such as rates of absenteeism or work performance (Beehr, 1995). Third, the process of evaluation would need to be sensitively negotiated with organisations as partners in the consultative relationship. In this sensitively balanced relationship there are important issues about whether consultants have the right to evaluate aspects of the functioning of organisations. Evaluation may be focused on the effectiveness of the consultant's intervention, but in doing so it is likely to have to look at the effectiveness of the organisation's staff in performing their work. Finally, it seems that evaluation can only be really helpful if it is part of an ongoing process of reflecting, monitoring and adapting to new understanding or information.

There is an additional aim to this model. This is the development of the field of community psychology in South Africa. In particular, the model is aimed at increasing the number of clinical psychology trainees who are able to do such work and perhaps contributing to broader concerns in the transformation of clinical psychology in this country.

Preliminary sources of data

Although formal evaluation of the impact of the Clinic's consultation work has only just begun, there are several sources of data from which suggestions about its effectiveness can be drawn. Amongst the most valuable of these is the clinical documentation which has carefully recorded the process in each consultation. These records include the formal needs assessment processes conducted with each organisation as well as less formal descriptions of the organisations' experience of the intervention. Basic information such as the frequency and form of the intervention contacts in each case has also been recorded. In addition, there are a number of research reports which, while not specifically aimed at evaluation, have helped to identify strengths and weaknesses in the approach (Swartz & Gibson, in press).

To supplement these existing sources of data, a series of small pilot projects, aimed at developing a more systematic model of evaluation, has recently been undertaken (Abbas, 1998; Hanley, 1998; Marumoloa, 1998). This pilot research has aimed to access the perceptions of organisations through interviews with those participating in various aspects of the consultation. Importantly, these interviews have been conducted by student researchers who have not been engaged directly in consultation with these organisations. In addition, a broadly focused external evaluation of the project has recently been completed (Budlender & Prinsloo, 1998). This offers some perspective on how the strengths and weaknesses of the model may be perceived within the broader needs of the mental health sector.

Strengths and weaknesses of the model

There are currently twelve organisations linked to the Child Guidance Clinic through ongoing consultation relationships based on this model. At various times, the number of organisations involved with the Clinic has been closer to twenty. While quantity does not equal quality, it is significant that a substantial number of organisations have chosen to use the Clinic in a consultative relationship. More importantly, there are an increasing number who are remaining engaged in the partnership. This suggests some degree of satisfaction with the process. One organisational partnership has been sustained over a period of eight years, and the majority of others have run for at least two years. Evidence of commitment on the part of organisations to the process is noted by Budlender and Prinsloo (1998).

During the period in which the project has been running, there have only been two organisations with whom a mutually agreed premature termination has occurred. Useful lessons have been learned from both instances. In the first, although the organisation was experiencing a major funding crisis which limited its capacity to engage in development processes, the consultants had also responded to a crisis by overstepping the boundaries of their responsibility. This lesson reinforced the importance of role definition, and helped to avoid future impulses to act out the panic-stricken experience of organisations. In the second instance, the organisation's expectations of what might be achieved could not be matched. This created considerable frustration for both parties and it was felt to be in the interests of all to end the relationship. This experience reinforced the need for constant monitoring and explicit discussion of expectations and limitations throughout the consultation process.

Ironically, consultation relationships which appear set to continue indefinitely have created more of a problem. Initially the Clinic considered its role to be relatively circumscribed: consultation would occur for a limited period of time, leaving the organisation with increased capacity to deal with children's psychological needs. In reality, most organisations operate in a context where there are few alternative resources from which they can draw. This has led to the realisation that, just as few psychologists would continue their work without some form of continuous supervision, so it is not realistic to expect front-line workers to manage their emotional and occupational burden without some ongoing training and support. Rather than terminating altogether, therefore, consultation relationships have been maintained but with gradually decreasing input as organisational capacity has increased.

However, this ongoing connection to organisations creates another set of difficulties. First, one has to watch extremely carefully the potential for creating dependency within organisations, which would then limit their own potential. Second, it becomes increasingly difficult for consultants to maintain a sense of perspective. As they are progressively drawn in, consultants run the risk of taking on the organisation's issues as their own and losing their valuable capacity to see beyond the prevailing ethos. This also has to be closely monitored.

From the various sources of data available, it seems that the majority of organisations have, generally, experienced the consultative relationship as extremely helpful. There are, however, some differences in the way this has been perceived at various points in the consultation process. Provisional analysis suggests that these perceptions are at least partially determined by the duration of the relationship, the developmental issues the organisations themselves are dealing with, and the variety of external crises that might concurrently be impinging on them. These crises are alarmingly common as the funding terrain shifts and many organisations are faced with enormous pressures to transform themselves, retrench staff or even disband. With regard to the duration of the relationship, the preliminary research suggests that there is a considerable shift in the perception of helpfulness between the early and later stages of involvement. Hanley (1998) notes one organisation's account of their initial ambivalence and uncertainty about what could be offered. This impression changed quite quickly as trust, and a better understanding of what the consultative relationship could yield, were built up. This specific account corresponds closely to the processes described more informally in file notes and case reports of many other consultations. The early ambivalence is often duplicated in a more lasting way in organisations in which there is high staff turnover, absenteeism, or large numbers of new members for other reasons (Abbas, 1998). In all these cases the central ingredient appears to be time of involvement. Organisations take time to understand and trust the consultative relationship and its benefits.

There are also differences in what organisations perceive to be the primary benefits of consultation. In the pilot research, one organisation emphasised emotional support (Hanley, 1998), while another saw the development of skills through training as particularly helpful (Marumoloa, 1998). The author's own preliminary research suggests that the benefits of consultation may be viewed as diversely as 'a kind of therapy', a sense of 'contact with the outside world', or 'conferring authority on staff members'. These differences may reflect the flexibility of the model, which allows it to link with the particular needs of different organisations at different times. At least in one case, an organisation recognised that it would have been unable to deal with the content of a planned workshop on counselling had its more pressing emotional needs not been addressed first (Hanley, 1998). The same research study also notes that the organisation valued the participatory approach of the intervention, while another appreciated the way in which the knowledge of its members was respected and integrated into the learning process (Marumoloa, 1998).

These preliminary research studies also reveal some potential problem areas. First, it appears that a central issue, which has not been sufficiently addressed, is the contribution of the training component of the consultation process to the career development of front-line workers. The workers in one organisation expressed the wish for greater recognition of the training they had undergone and more opportunities to develop their work ambitions (Hanley, 1998). This matches informal feedback from other organisations. The Clinic has, in fact, started to issue certificates recognising the relevant training. However, until this recognition achieves the status of a formal qualification, it is likely that organisations will experience some frustration that their very important learning has not been formally acknowledged. There are also some suggestions from the data available thus far that, while the benefits to organisations as a whole are valued, the personal needs of particular individuals within them are not perceived as being met (Abbas, 1998; Hanley, 1998; as well as clinical notes). This is probably a reflection of the absence of other support resources available to workers in these organisations. But, on the basis of preliminary interview material, it also seems as though the consultants' identity as psychologists may foster unrealistic expectations about their ability to meet all kinds of personal, therapeutic needs.

In terms of the aim of increasing the number of psychologists who are able and motivated to engage in community work, there is an indication of reasonable success. In the period during which the model has been used as a training tool for students, there has been a substantial increase in the number of graduates who are known to be involved in local community-oriented work. Amongst those who began their training in the four years from 1986 to 1989, prior to the development of this model, only a fifth are involved in some kind of community work. This contrasts with the four years between 1993 and 1996 during which the model has been developed and implemented. In this time the number of those involved in community work, post-training, has increased to over a half of all graduates. The use of theoretical ideas and techniques consistent in some way with individual psychological work (Gibson & Sandenbergh, 1998) seems also to have allowed more trainees to engage in work which includes aspects of both areas. This can be particularly helpful given the high levels of burnout which seem to affect those who work only in demanding community settings. A further positive spin-off in training is the usefulness of the model in containing students' anxieties and their reportedly more positive experience of community work as a consequence. This contrasts with many students' experience of this aspect of the work as demanding, frightening, chaotic and ultimately unattractive (Gibson & Sandenbergh, 1998).

The recently released external evaluation report (Budlender & Prinsloo, 1998) provides only limited insight into the Clinic's particular contribution to the mental health sector as a whole, given that it focuses on the work of two other linked organisations simultaneously. However, it does suggest that the Clinic, and the other related organisations, do play an important role in the development of appropriate mental health models for accessing larger groups of children. The report argues that it is important for models of this nature to be developed and emphasises that their effectiveness can only be clearly established if they are sustained for a long period of time. It does suggest the need to pilot the model in an even broader variety of contexts, including the rural areas where it has not yet been tried. While this is clearly an important area of work, there are daunting resource implications for an academic department in taking on this kind of initiative.

ISSUES AND INSIGHTS

The Child Guidance Clinic's model of consultation has developed as an attempt to contribute to the widely acknowledged need for transformation in conventional clinical psychology practice. It is part of the growing trend of exploring various ways of sharing psychological knowledge with broader communities, in an attempt both to address the inadequacies in psychological resources and to facilitate the development of organisations working with disadvantaged children. The model was established in response to the realisation that there could be no quick fixes in the area of community psychology intervention. Establishing effective consultation relationships in which organisations could increase their capacity was discovered to be both time-consuming and extremely complex. In particular, the strong feelings that front-line workers have about working with troubled children and about participating in a consultation relationship needed to be respected and acknowledged as an important part of the process.

A theoretical framework drawing largely from psychodynamic theory has been found to be very useful in making sense of the often unconscious emotional processes that can assist, or get in the way of, the ability of front-line workers to respond sensitively to the needs of children in their care. This strong theoretical framework has also helped consultants tolerate some of the frustrations and anxieties that can be experienced in doing this kind of work. Feelings of powerlessness when confronted by the degree of deprivation in some communities are commonly felt by both front-line workers and the consultants who work with them. These seem to be better tolerated when there is a theoretical framework that can help to explain and normalise these responses. A theoretical approach which emphasises a holistic and contextualised view of the consultancy relationship is also better able to accommodate the wide range of issues which impact on it. These include important issues, often about power and powerlessness or race and cultural difference, which can be addressed and worked through within this model.

While the theory offers a way of making sense of processes that may occur during a consultation, it does not offer a blueprint for intervention. Instead the model is designed to allow both consultant and organisation to work together on developing a response designed to suit the particular needs of any organisation. It is also intended to allow for a flexible unfolding process which can accommodate changing needs over time. The emphasis in this is on a co-operative relationship between the consultant and the organisation in which both contribute to generating knowledge and understanding. A trusting relationship is essential for this kind of mutually beneficial co-operation to occur. The most important factors in facilitating this relationship seem to be time and consistency. The consultant, in this model, is not expected to provide instant solutions. Rather, the consultant needs to offer a safe, reliable connection to the organisation which is capable of withstanding the emotional and practical difficulties that affect both parties during the course of the relationship.

REFERENCES

Abbas, F. (1998). Volunteer child-care workers' perceptions of a training programme provided by the UCT Child Guidance Clinic. Unpublished Honours research project. University of Cape Town.

Beehr, T. (1995). *Psychological stress in the workplace*. London: Routledge.

Bolton, W. & Roberts, V. Z. (1994). Asking for help: Staff support and sensitivity groups reviewed. In A. Obholzer & V. Z. Roberts (Eds), *The unconscious at work: Individual and organizational stress in the human services* (pp.11–18). London: Routledge.

Budlender, D. & Prinsloo, R. (1998). Evaluation of mental health projects for children supported by Radda Barnen 1989–1997. Unpublished Report.

Caplan, G. (1970). *The theory and practice of mental health consultation.* London: Tavistock.

Casement, P. (1985). *On learning from the patient.* London/New York: Tavistock

Dawes, A., Robertson, B., Duncan, N., Ensink, K., Jackson, A., Reynolds, P., Pillay, A. & Richter, L. (1997). Child and adolescent mental health policy. In D. Foster, M. Freeman & Y. Pillay (Eds), *Mental health policy issues for South Africa* (pp. 32–54). Cape Town: MASA Multimedia Publications.

Desjarlais, R., Eisenberg, L., Good, B. & Kleinman, A. (1995). *World mental health: Problems and priorities in low-income countries.* New York: Oxford University Press.

Freeman, M. & Pillay, Y. (1997). Mental health policy – plans and funding. In D. Foster, M. Freeman & Y. Pillay (Eds), *Mental health policy issues for South Africa* (pp. 32–54). Cape Town: MASA Multimedia Publications.

Gibson, K. (1995). History taking format for use with organisations. Unpublished document. University of Cape Town.

Gibson, K. & Sandenbergh, R. (1998, September). We don't want to take sides: Achieving a balance between community and clinical practices in psychologists' training. Paper presented at the *PsySSA* National Conference, September, Cape Town.

Halton, W. (1994). Some unconscious aspects of organizational life: Contributions from psychoanalysis. In A. Obholzer & V. Z. Roberts (Eds), *The unconscious at work: Individual and organizational stress in the human services* (pp. 11–18). London: Routledge.

Hanley, K. (1998). An exploration of community health workers' perceptions of their psychological needs and their response to the Child Guidance Clinic's consultation and training programme. Unpublished Honours research project. University of Cape Town.

Holdsworth, M. (1994). Consulation and training challenges in the Mamre community health project. Unpublished M.A. dissertation, University of Cape Town.

Holland, S. (1988). Defining and experimenting with prevention. In S. Ramon (Ed.), *Psychology in transition: The British and Italian experiences* (pp. 125–137). London: Pluto Press.

Lazarus, J. R. (1991, October). Clinical psychology training into the future. Paper presented at the National Congress of *The Psychological Association of South Africa*, 7–9 October, Pretoria.

Malan. D. (1981). *Individual psychotherapy and the science of psychodynamics.* London: Butterworths.

Marumoloa, M. (1998). Community health workers' perceptions of the training workshops offered by UCT Child Guidance Clinic. Unpublished Honours research project. University of Cape Town.

Maw, A. (1996). The consultation relationship as a complex partnership. Unpublished M.A. dissertation. University of Cape Town.

Menzies, I. (1970). *The functioning of social systems as a defence against anxiety.* London: Tavistock.

Mogoduso, T. & Butchart, A. (1992). Authoritarianism and autonomy. 2. Power, politics and alienated nursing care in a South African primary health care system. *South African Journal of Psychology, 22*(4), 185–193.

Obholzer, A. & Roberts, V. Z. (Eds.) (1994). *The unconscious at work: Individual and orga-*

nizational stress in the human services. London: Routledge.

Orford, J. (1992). *Community psychology: Theory and practice.* Chichester: John Wiley & Sons.

Salzberger-Wittenberg, I., Henry, G. & Osborne, E. (1990). *The emotional experience of learning and teaching.* London: Routledge.

Seedat, M. & Nell, V. (1992). Authoritarianism and autonomy 1. Conflicting value systems in the introduction of psychological services in a South African primary health care system. *South African Journal of Psychology, 22*(4), 185–193.

Stein, H. (1994). *Listening deeply: An approach to understanding and consulting in organizational culture.* Boulder: Westview Press.

Stokes, J. (1994). The unconscious at work in groups and teams: Contributions from the work of Wilfred Bion. In A. Obholzer & V. Z. Roberts (Eds.), *The unconscious at work: Individual and organizational stress in the human services* (pp.11–18). London: Routledge.

Swartz, L. (1996). Crossing or creating boundaries: Challenges in clinical psychology in the community. Inaugural Lecture, University of Cape Town.

Swartz, L. (1998). *Culture and mental health: A southern African view.* Cape Town: Oxford University Press.

Swartz, L. & Gibson K. (in press). The old versus the new in SA community psychology: The quest for appropriate change. In M. Seedat (Ed.), *Community Psychology in the South: Theory, methods and application.*

Swartz, S., Dowdall, T. & Swartz, L. (1986). Clinical psychology and the 1985 crisis in Cape Town. *Psychology in Society, 5,* 131–138.

Tudor, K. (1996). *Mental health promotion: Paradigms and practice.* London: Routledge.

INTERVENING IN ADVERSITY

12

Towards a theory of practice

JOHANN LOUW, DAVID DONALD & ANDREW DAWES

The primary purpose of this chapter is to begin to formulate some of the essential elements of a theory of practice in the area of child-oriented, psychosocial interventions in developing contexts like South Africa. These elements emerge as central threads from the richly varied work that has been presented in this volume.

As mentioned in the Preface, there is a great deal of variation amongst the projects described in this book. Some of these differences have influenced decisions regarding which themes would be appropriate to highlight in this final chapter. On the whole, concern with the particular adversities which the various projects have addressed has not been a central consideration. Conclusions which can be drawn across programmes are of more relevance than those that might relate to particular areas of adversity. On the other hand, the variation in scope across programmes is a central factor. Thus it is apparent that certain sorts of problems and solutions in relation to issues of project implementation, evaluation, sustainability, etc. may be common to large-scale, multi-site projects – like the Thousand Schools Project (Chapter 7) or the programmes addressing the effects of war and violence on children (Chapters 9 and 10) – but not necessarily to smaller, single-site projects – for example, the school-feeding project (Chapter 4) or the organisation development project at Modderdam High School (Chapter 8).

We have organised this final chapter around three major themes which are common to all programmes, large or small, and which must certainly be central to any theory of practice in this area. They are:

* *Linking developmental knowledge and practice*. In Chapter 1 we argued that practical interventions will be strengthened if they build on existing knowledge of children's development. This includes knowledge that is universally applicable, as well as theory and research that has particular relevance in developing contexts like southern Africa. Here, in the concluding chapter, we identify a number of strengths from the programmes reported in the volume, as well as from other relevant mate-

rial. We also describe a number of areas which could be developed further and contribute to an emergent theory of practice.

- *Opportunities and constraints on implementation in developing contexts.* Under this theme, a number of commonalities across programmes are apparent, many of which appear to be particular to conditions in developing countries. This theme is especially important in addressing what is feasible and what is not, and under what circumstances.

- *Evaluation and practice.* Programme evaluation as it relates to a theory of practice was introduced in Chapter 3. A number of important sub-themes of that discussion have re-emerged in the discussions of specific programmes. These call for specific comment, clarification and elaboration.

It is highly likely that readers may discern different themes from those we discuss here. We certainly do not intend our analysis to be exhaustive. What is important is that readers join with us in a systematic process of reflection on what has been presented by the various authors.

LINKING DEVELOPMENTAL KNOWLEDGE AND PRACTICE

Chapter 1 emphasised the central place that an appreciation of 'context' in its various forms must have in the design and implementation of programmes. The potential contribution of an ecological–transactional perspective was stressed. This perspective helps in understanding how various sources of influence in the social context of individuals impact on children and adolescents in different ways at different stages of their development. We also emphasised how an appreciation of cultural practices, whether in major cultural or sub-cultural contexts, is essential in developing interventions which are sensitive to local needs and perceptions, and which can achieve a co-operative working relationship with their target communities. We listed five principles that research and theory would suggest are particularly important for the design of community-based interventions in the southern African context. These will be used as a framework for discussion .

Interventions should be informed by a knowledge of developmental pathways and epochs

In Chapter 1 it was pointed out that as children develop, 'different risk reduction strategies become appropriate, and different areas of risk emerge'. The key point is that children are exposed to different sources of influence at particular points in the life cycle, and that interventions must take this into account.

For many of the projects described in this book, links between different sources of influence and developmental outcomes at various ages, although not always explicitly articulated, were implicit in the design of projects. For example, in Chapter 6 it is clear that the activities in which children at Avondale Primary School engaged were designed to have maximum health-promoting effects at that stage of their development. Equally, interventions involving teachers, parents and peers were designed to be maximally effective with primary schoolers in the particular social context of Atlantis, the working-class community where they lived. This was promoted through teacher, parent and peer involvement in the process of designing and implementing the activities. Similar observations could be made about activities, directed specifically at preschoolers or adolescents, undertaken by the KwaZulu-Natal Programme for Survivors of Violence (Chapter 10), or the link between more democratic teaching styles and the engagement of adolescents in the learning process at Modderdam High School (Chapter 8).

In our view, it is most important that the links between the design of the intervention, in its particular context, and the developmental period to be targeted are made explicit. If this is not done, the specificity of the relationship may be missed. If we are to learn, and be able to generalise, from particular interventions it is important that we try to specify, as exactly as possible, the relationship between intervention and outcome. For example: On what theoretical or research basis do we expect a relationship to exist? Can we show that such a relationship actually exists? Under what circumstances does it operate effectively, when does it not, and for which age group? Only in this way are we likely to advance our understanding of the dynamics of what is happening, and why it might or might not be effective in another context or at another time. Of course this degree of specificity is not always possible, or even desirable, within the aims of the particular project. However, this level of questioning and probing is a dimension of psychosocial interventions in the southern African context that is urgently needed if a systematic approach to intervention is to evolve.

Two projects in this collection do spell out, quite specifically, the developmental pathways that they are attempting to address. Thus, in Chapter 4 (p. 77), Richter and her colleagues specify 'Three pathways, not necessarily independent of one another, [that] have commonly been suggested to explain the link between nutritional deficiencies and cognitive functioning'. This understanding of the nature of the relationship, drawn from the research literature, then frames the intervention and how it is evaluated. Equally, in Chapter 5 the relationship between aggression in children and modes of interaction between teacher and child, and parent and child, at the preschool level is postulated as a critical pathway of influence in development, which in turn shapes the intervention and its evaluation.

Both these interventions demonstrated short-term effects. The question may well arise whether there are any longer-term or more lasting effects, under the complex conditions of extreme poverty that operate in both situations. We might also ask, as Jones Petersen and Carolissen do in the case of their own project (Chapter 5), whether events later in the child's life will undermine the gains made in programmes that target early periods of development. However, it is precisely because attempts have been made to specify and evaluate a particular relationship that the latter questions arise. Where questions like this are raised, they may stimulate research designed to answer them. Often questions about impacts in the longer term encourage programmes to revisit their theoretical underpinning, or to refine or extend their theoretical base. This iterative process can be seen as an important element in extending knowledge and refining practice.

Where possible, interventions should be undertaken at multiple levels

The principle of multi-level intervention, based on an understanding of the various – and often interrelated – ways in which children's contexts influence their development, is well represented in the programmes reported here. Chapter 10, the description of the KwaZulu-Natal Programme for Survivors of Violence, is most explicit in its articulation of an ecological, multi-level model of intervention. This leads the programme to understand that both the effects of violence, and corresponding levels of intervention, are located at the individual, group, community and societal levels. Such a view is also apparent in the Angolan programme addressing the effects of war on children (Chapter 9). In both programmes, the understanding of how different levels of children's contexts influence their development leads directly to interventions which are aimed, simultaneously, at these different levels.

Both Chapter 5, the violence prevention preschool programme, and Chapter 6, the health-promoting schools project, draw explicitly on a systemic understanding of the interaction of families, schools and peers within specific community contexts. In an ecological framework, these positions would relate most closely to Bronfenbrenner's (1986) mesosystem. (Chapter 6 also incorporates the 'exosystems' of services and structures that relate more distally to health promotion in the relevant community.) Again, the theoretical underpinning of these projects ensures that the intervention is distributed across those systems that may be seen to have a simultaneous bearing on the developmental issues at stake.

Two chapters emphasise multi-level interdependencies, but more within the context of organisational functioning: Chapter 8, the organisation development case study at Modderdam High School, and Chapter 11, the project addressing issues of organisational consultation. Both accentuate the systemic principle that an organisation is more than the sum of the individuals who make it up, and that interventions at an organisational level need to take the organisation as a whole, as well as different levels of interaction within it, into account. Both illustrate the complexity, and yet the clear relevance, of trying to work within this theoretical model. Equally, because the multiple interactions and interdependencies that are being taken into account are so complex in such a model, it is not surprising that the specificity of evaluation comes into contention. What both these projects illustrate, however, is a search for ways of evaluating a theoretically complex situation. This, in itself, needs to be an important and ongoing endeavour.

The Thousand Schools Project (Chapter 7) had 'whole school development' – which also has its more formal origins in organisation development theory – as its theoretical base. As Mouton points out, however (p. 134): 'no systematic attempt was made to translate this notion into practical, concrete and measurable outcomes. A continued lack of attention to the challenge of operationalising "whole school development" remained a problem feature of the project.' This emphasises that it is not sufficient to 'claim' a theoretical base to a project. That theoretical base has to be explicitly 'unpacked', and both intervention and evaluation strategies have to be specifically operationalised in terms of the theory.

Finally, there are a number of programmes where the focus of intervention falls more on those working with children than on the children themselves. Thus, although there may be interventions at different levels or with different groups (often including children), the main focus is on educating, supporting or empowering teachers, parents or other caregivers in their close involvement with the development of children. In various ways, this applies to almost all the projects described in this book.

The strength of the multi-level or multi-group aspect of this pattern of intervention has already been emphasised. A different theoretical strength is implicit in the focus on teachers, parents and other caregivers as the 'mediators' in children's development. Since they are operating in proximal contexts, emphasised by theorists such as Vygotsky and Bronfenbrenner as critical to developmental outcomes (see Chapter 1), change in these contexts is likely to have significant impact. This is supported by research which tends to show that interventions in the family and the school are most frequently effective (McLoyd, 1998).

Since it is such a common pattern of intervention, an important reservation should, however, be expressed. Most such programmes aim, ultimately and quite explicitly, to benefit children in their development. But, in many cases, exactly *how* the children are supposed to improve or gain from the intervention is not made clear. The pathway from intervention activity *to* expected mediator change *to* expected child change is not mapped out. As a result of not clarifying this theoretical linkage, specific child-related outcomes are frequently not evaluated. Although the intervention may have other demonstrated benefits, the ultimate benefit to children cannot be assumed without showing that it has indeed happened. In fact, as was argued in Chapter 3, the longer the set of linkages between the actual intervention and the child as ultimate beneficiary, the less likely the effect of the intervention will carry through.

Interventions should combine cultural and developmental sensitivity

The importance of understanding the close relationship between cultural values and practices and child development has been emphasised in a number of places. In practice it requires programmes to spend time and effort in developing a knowledge of, and sensitivity to, local cultural or sub-cultural norms, values and practices in relation to children and their upbringing. These are the 'taken-for-granted ways of seeing and doing things' in relation to children. They may apply in broad cultural contexts, such as a local community, or in more specific settings, such as a school that has its particular 'culture' or way of doing things. Sensitivity to, as well as taking account of, such cultural specifics in the design and implementation of interventions is likely to increase the acceptability, efficacy and sustainability of the programme and its purposes (Chapter 1).

The projects included in this book all demonstrate cultural sensitivity in general terms – after all, it was a criterion of selection. However, some examples of both broader and more specific cultural sensitivity are worth drawing out for illustrative purposes. Both chapters dealing with the effects of violence and war on children (Chapters 9 and 10) reveal a number of effective approaches in dealing with broader cultural issues. Both emphasise the time that was spent in listening to local people. As was stressed in Chapter 1, it is important, where appropriate and possible, to engage with local knowledge and practice in order to develop an approach to intervention that makes local sense, and that is worked out in collaboration with the target beneficiaries. Apart from according respect to the target population, such an approach reinforces the probability that there will be an equalisation of the power relationship between recipient communities and programme personnel. This is likely to render the programme more acceptable to the target community.

Such an approach is demonstrated very clearly in the Angolan project described by Wessells and Monteiro (Chapter 9). They state (p. 180): 'In entering local communities, the typical process entailed meeting with the *soba* or local chief, his council of elders, and influential women.' Time was also devoted to engaging local people in the construction of an 'ecological model' of the factors people saw as leading to healthy child development (Figure 3, p. 189). In the KwaZulu-Natal programme time was devoted to understanding a community's particular history, needs and resources, and structures were created to ensure the representation and input of community members on local project management committees. In management terms, the Angolan project ensured further that it was actually controlled and run by local people. In both cases, intervention practices which drew on local knowledge were incorporated where appropriate – the Angolan project 'valorising' the role of traditional healers in particular. Finally, as part of the sensitivity we speak of, we encourage practitioners to consider culture as something dynamic and changing, as expressed by the authors of Chapter 10 (p. 215): 'the values, beliefs and practices of youth who left school to join the civil conflict are different from those of their parents and grandparents. Also, very few individuals can be characterised as belonging to a single culture. Most people exist between cultures drawing from them what seems appropriate for the reality of their lives.'

Within more specific, sub-cultural contexts Chapter 8, the organisation development project at Modderdam High School, provides an interesting example. The high wall built around the school grounds might, in many other contexts, have been seen negatively – as a symbolic barrier between the school and the community. Indeed, given the policy emphasis on school–community collaboration in South Africa at the moment, this is a value which is being actively promoted at the wider societal level. However, given the particularly violent and gang-troubled area in which the school is situated, the predominant and uncontested value placed on the wall by this school community – parents, learners and staff alike – was one of 'safety and protection'. If it did create a symbolic barrier, this was not seen as important in relation to the far more urgent need for protecting the learners in the culture of *this* school. That the organisation development initiative recognised this is an indication of its sensitivity to the dynamics of the culture of the school.

Another project that demonstrates particular sensitivity to sub-cultural norms, values and concerns is the one described in Chapter 11. This model of organisational consultation, with its holistic, psychodynamic theoretical underpinning, inevitably demands a high degree of sensitivity and perceptiveness on the part of the consultants. In particular they need to be sensitive to the forces and feelings that shape the unique 'culture' or characteristic 'way of seeing things' in different client organisations. Again the chapter brings out the critical importance of creating the space and time to really *listen*.

Finally, it is necessary for projects to pay close attention to unintended consequences that might flow from an intervention. If these are not closely monitored, they can have negative or damaging effects within the social structure of organisations or communities. An example of such an effect was identified in the school-feeding project (Chapter 4). In the very impoverished community in which the experimental school was situated, anecdotal evidence suggested that some children who had been given breakfast at school were seen as needing less of the limited food available at home. The project was unable to check this systematically, but it illustrates the sort of dynamic which can create unintended consequences.

Interventions should promote community participation

Participation in, and ownership of, the programme by those most closely involved – whether they be staff, students and parents in a school or, more widely, members of a local community – have many benefits. Factors that have been mentioned include improving local relevance; promoting identification with and therefore support of the programme; incorporating or questioning relevant cultural practices from an 'owned' position; and promoting sustainability through involvement and building local resources and capacity. Significantly, such participation has also been identified by the Inter-Ministerial Committee on Young People at Risk (IMC) as an important element in facilitating large intersectoral initiatives (Chapter 2).

In one way or another, all projects described illustrate this principle. This is not surprising given that one of the criteria of selection was that 'The project should demonstrate sensitivity to local context and the community in which it is situated'. For this very reason, the principle, and the way different projects have attempted to meet it, should not be taken for granted. It constitutes a very important element within the growing theory of practice.

There are many examples of good practice available in the project descriptions which need not be repeated here. We do need, however, to make one critical comment in relation to the rhetoric around such terms as 'community participation', 'empowerment' and 'democratic transformation'. These terms are common in South Africa at the moment, and often occur in statements of policy and programme goals. Unfortunately, in practice, they are not always applied in realistic or effective ways. One of the major goals of the Thousand Schools Project, for example, was that 'Schools should be "given back" to their communities' (Chapter 7, p. 134). A policy of decentralisation was adopted with the conscious goal of devolving responsibility for implementation to the provinces and the relevant committees and structures within them. Rather than managing the project from the centre, this position was ostensibly in line with calls for 'local capacity-building', 'community participation', 'empowerment', and so on. From the evaluation described in Chapter 7, however, it became apparent that, in practice, expecting people to undertake a large-scale and complex implementation without sufficient financial management and administrative training, infrastructure, and appropriate back-up from the centre was, if anything, 'disempowering'. Again, we learn from this that notions of 'community participation', 'empowerment' and so on have to be examined carefully and critically and, above all, operationalised in ways that are appropriate to the particular contexts of their application.

Interventions should build on, and promote, protective factors

Chapter 1 referred to findings which indicate that it is an effective strategy to build on, and generally promote, factors which protect children against developmental risks of various sorts – particularly in contexts of poverty. One reason for this is that it frequently draws on knowledge of what has worked for resilient children in the same context; i.e. those children who, despite the conditions, 'have come through OK'. Another reason is that protective factors may operate at a number of levels – from capacities built up in the individual, to ways in which families or schools function, to elements in the whole neighbourhood or community. Usually, and significantly, these are structures or ways of coping that have been found to work in that particular context. They have the advantage of not being 'imported' and, therefore, of having established local relevance and acceptability.

Most of the projects implicitly applied this principle of intervention, even if they did not always articulate it. Thus, the school-feeding project (Chapter 4) aimed to increase 'participatory and task-oriented behaviour in class' through the nutritional intervention. This could be seen as promoting a capacity which, through positively affecting the potential to learn, becomes a longer-term protective factor. This is an example of promoting a protective factor at the individual level. Chapter 5 gives an example of promoting one at the family level – assisting parents to reinforce 'their children's positive behaviour and setting non-punitive limits'. Similarly, interventions at an institutional level, having clear protective functions for the organisation as a whole, are apparent in Chapter 8 (developing better staff–learner relationships in the school) and Chapter 11 (child-care workers confronting unresolved feelings of powerlessness in relation to the difficulties of the work in their organisation). The health-promoting schools project (Chapter 6) illustrates the development of elements of health awareness which are clearly protective of the whole neighbourhood or community, as do both projects dealing with the effects of violence (Chapters 9 and 10). These two chapters also talk about involving and building up 'structures', such as crèches or local committees or councils, that would increase resilience and have protective functions at the community level.

Interventions often try to remove the risks that prejudice development. However, it is commonly the case that in very poor communities, or in those affected by ongoing violence such as civil war, this is simply not possible. Stress is likely to remain a fairly permanent feature of the child's life. An alternative approach under such circumstances is to develop strategies that promote resilience through enhancing the coping mechanisms of adults, children and adolescents. If the adults cope better, they will be able to support the young. Also, if the children achieve a sense of mastery despite the difficulties they face, this can serve to boost their confidence and resilience. In this way, individuals become sources of their own resilience.

In Chapters 6 and 8, for example, both Avondale Primary School and Modderdam High School are situated in high-risk developmental environments. Both interventions demonstrate that it is possible to strengthen the school as an organisation, thereby providing teachers and students with capacities that enable them to cope more effectively with the ongoing demands of their situations. Flisher and his colleagues (Chapter 6) also specifically assist students to resist involvement in such risk-taking activities as drug use. This strategy aims to give at-risk youth more control over their own lives. In Chapter 11, Gibson describes a model in which child-care workers are assisted to identify and cope with the stresses associated with their work. Through this approach the project aims to enhance the care that these adults are able to provide to the children. In all these examples, the interventions serve to assist either adults or children, or both, to 'live better with risk'.

OPPORTUNITIES AND CONSTRAINTS ON IMPLEMENTATION IN DEVELOPING CONTEXTS

Virtually all the interventions described here testify to the difficulties faced by service deliverers in South Africa and the region as a whole. For one, there is a serious lack of professional capacity in many areas. In Chapter 7, Mouton provides clear evidence that one of the major difficulties faced by the Thousand Schools Project was that sufficient numbers of trained and experienced people were simply not available in the provinces to carry out the implementation. There are many lessons about such 'reality' issues to be learned from the projects in this book. Some outstanding ones are highlighted here.

Strategic decisions

One consequence of having to face the reality of contextual constraints is that it directs attention to the importance of strategic decisions. Programmes and their staff cannot do everything, and they have to concentrate on some things, based on an informed understanding of what would be the most effective. These strategic decisions are taken at all stages of the programme process. Any programme hopes to address aspects of the problem in which it has most chance of success. To do this, however, programme planners must be able to identify factors as targets for the intervention that are most malleable. This implies at least some explicit understanding of the nature of the problem – referred to in Chapter 3 as 'problem theory'.

Strategic decisions must be, and are, taken all the time. In the Angolan project (Chapter 9), concerns of safety and access meant that services could only be delivered in certain areas. Project staff did not necessarily deal with the problem where it was most acute, but rather with what was practical and strategic. In the Thousand Schools Project (Chapter 7), strategic decisions were evident in the criteria of how the schools were selected. It was impossible to include all the schools, and a decision had to be made to include only some, based on a few acceptable criteria. In KwaZulu-Natal, the programme had to target particular geographically defined communities, given the pervasiveness of violence in the province (Chapter 10). Indeed, it often turns out better to decide to do less rather than more. The health-promoting school project (Chapter 6) showed how strategic reductions in the reach of the project following the initial evaluation had positive effects on the project and its participants.

Implementation and planning

Most projects also showed how difficult it is to install effective practices. When programmes are compromised on this, it often results in incomplete or inadequate implementation. It would be a mistake to discard any programme on this basis, because it has not been given a chance under optimal conditions of implementation to show its worth. This is a powerful argument for monitoring implementation.

Despite the difficulties faced in achieving adequate implementation, it is clear that it is most likely to be consistent and strong if a 'blueprint for action' exists. This could include staffing requirements; the training that staff would require; a detailed account of how the various activities are to be carried out; standards for implementing these activities; descriptions of obstacles most likely to be faced; the characteristics of the communities in which the programme is to take place; and perhaps how much of the planned intervention could be modified, and still be acceptable.

In the Angolan project (Chapter 9), Wessells and Monteiro illustrate the importance of an explicit delivery plan (see Figure 2, p. 186). This sets up a sequence of events which is essential to both implementation and evaluation. By contrast, one of the difficulties with the Thousand Schools Project (Chapter 7) was that the implementation of the programme was not made concrete and operationalised clearly enough.

Programmes improve their chances of being successful if they provide co-ordinated, planned activities. From the work described in Chapter 6 (the health-promoting schools project), the important role of a co-ordinating team emerged. This team was specifically responsible for gathering regular inputs, for monitoring the process of implementation, for providing support, and for liaising with external agencies. Programme activities also need to be co-ordinated to ensure comprehensiveness and consistency in the programme as a whole. All the elements or activities of a programme must work together towards the attainment of its objectives. In short, they must be clearly and explicitly planned and co-ordinated.

Pilot projects

In the light of capacity constraints and implementation difficulties, almost all the projects described in this book were characterised as pilot or demonstration projects. Given the gap between policy and implementation in South Africa at the moment (Chapter 2), this is probably appropriate. Demonstrations of effectiveness in this context are necessary if larger-scale state or other programmes are to be justified. For example, the health-promoting project discussed in Chapter 6 was designed specifically as a demonstration project, to try to concretise the notion of a health-promoting school, and to see how it might work in practice. The insights gained from the project (the importance of intersectoral collaboration, for example), and the way the theoretical concepts found their application in practical and meaningful ways at different levels in this school and community, will serve as important guidelines for other, similar projects. Further examples of projects applying and evaluating specific interventions within limited contexts, but with possible wider applications in mind, include the school-feeding project (Chapter 4), the school organisation development project (Chapter 8) and the preschool violence prevention programme (Chapter 5). Indeed, Chapter 9, the project in Angola, illustrates the evolution from a pilot stage to a large-scale multi-site programme, where lessons learned in the early stages were clearly incorporated in the wider programme.

In developing contexts, given the difficulties of effective implementation, the importance of pilot projects in testing out and clarifying both the opportunities and the constraints of intervention cannot be overemphasised. An explicitly planned and executed pilot project, which attempted to unpack the practical and applied meaning of 'whole school development' in extremely disadvantaged contexts, might have contributed much to the Thousand Schools Project (Chapter 7), for instance.

Sustainability
There is a strong need, expressed in different chapters in this book, to strengthen the

institutions of our society. Many chapters refer to an intention to link up with governmental structures, and to build capacity in institutions, whether governmental, NGO-based or community-based. In Chapter 6, for example, links were enacted between different provincial departments – especially Health and Education – which were seen as essential to the very notion of health promotion in schools. The programme in KwaZulu-Natal (Chapter 10) emphasised the reconstitution of community institutions and structures following the fragmentation which results from civil violence. For Gibson (Chapter 11), the strengthening of institutions was expressed in terms of improving the internal health of organisations which cared for children, and in training future practitioners to have the appropriate orientation and capacity to address such issues in our society.

Funding and sustainability often go together. This is expressed in the common concerns of projects to address the requirements of donors. In the Angolan study (Chapter 9), for example, since the project received funds from a donor which had to justify its expenditures to the US Congress, perceived donor demands played a role in the evaluation. Indeed, this is not an unfamiliar situation in contexts such as our own where community-based, psychosocial interventions for the benefit of children are largely dependent on external funding.

External events

There are many threats to programmes and their evaluation, some of which may be entirely fortuitous. In Chapter 7, the timing of the project was such that virtually none of the essential preconditions for its success were present. Simply by launching it two or three years later, Mouton argues, the chances of success would have been greatly enhanced. The lesson here is that one cannot say that 'whole school development', as an intervention, was a failure. Such a conclusion has not been established because the evaluation showed that contextual factors (time of introduction) were such that the programme really had little chance of succeeding. This is one reason why evaluation is important. It is not just to say that the intervention had no effect, but also to try to understand why it failed.

The environment in which programmes operate is volatile. Schools may be closed, unanticipated budget cuts may decimate programme activities, or violence in the community may disrupt the whole process. There is, however, one context which has to be mentioned separately. Programmes operate in political environments. Policies, and often the programmes to enact them, are created by political decisions, and as such will remain susceptible to political pressures throughout their lifetime. They may receive support from one interest group, who are persuaded that the issues addressed are of social importance and that the programmes offer feasible solutions. At the same time, however, they may be opposed by other interest groups, who may act in ways that jeopardise their long-term future. As a result, programmes may very well find that resources and priorities shift dramatically as a result of changes in the political environment. The most dramatic illustration of this is the effect on the Angolan project (Chapter 9) of, first, the threat of a return to war and, then, the tragic reality of a new conflict that undermined what the programme was attempting to achieve. This constraint requires both resilience and flexibility in programmes themselves.

The majority of the projects described here used evaluation in order to strengthen their interventions. This should be an encouragement to readers who are themselves delivering services to poor communities, to emphasise the evaluation component of their work. Even when faced with great difficulties in evaluating their work under very trying conditions, Higson-Smith and Killian (Chapter 10) used internal evaluation procedures to impact immediately and continuously upon intervention strategies. The data provided by the evaluation processes they describe were clearly valuable in developing and reinforcing the activities of the programme.

In Chapter 3 a step-wise model to conceptualise programmes and their evaluation was suggested as a way to assist practitioners in strengthening their work. Figure 1 shows this model again. Most of the projects included here could be seen as following the model, at least implicitly. Nevertheless, we believe that making this implicit reliance more explicit would encourage a more systematic consideration of programme planning, implementation and evaluation. We return briefly to the main steps of the model and related themes that have emerged from the preceding chapters.

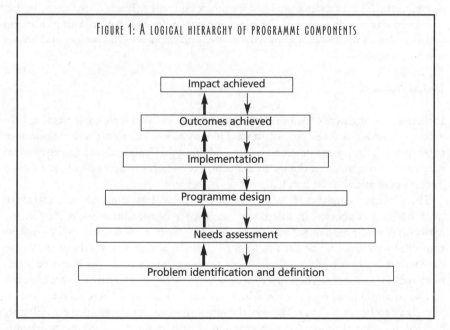

FIGURE 1: A LOGICAL HIERARCHY OF PROGRAMME COMPONENTS

Impact achieved

Outcomes achieved

Implementation

Programme design

Needs assessment

Problem identification and definition

Problem formulation and needs assessment

All the projects which had to do with service delivery relied on some form of needs assessment. This reflects a recognition of how important it is to come to terms with the nature of the social problem the programme is supposed to address, both theoretically and practically. To assist them in their practice, all authors grappled with a theoretical understanding of the problems they faced. Services must relate to the problem, and the better the problem is known and understood, the better are the chances that the services will be appropriately targeted. Gibson, in Chapter 11 for example, describes the development, over some years, of a model to guide the project's consultancy work in relation to child-care organisations. A critical element in this model is the care that is taken in 'uncovering', and developing a shared understanding of, the underlying need of the organisation. In Chapter 10, the programme found that field workers needed a model to help them understand the relationship between the effects of violence and possible solutions in violence-torn communities. The model that was developed creates an explicit link between a way of understanding the needs that are created in such situations and possible solutions to those needs.

In addition, one ought not to forget that the needs assessment often provides an excellent opportunity for the community to 'buy into' the programme and its services. Again, this is illustrated in a number of projects. The project at Modderdam High School (Chapter 8) gives a particularly clear example of needs analysis workshops held at the school in the early stages of the project which helped to cement commitment to the subsequent process of organisation development. In fact, Patton (1990) has drawn attention to the use of evaluation itself to enhance shared understandings between programme staff, boards of governance, evaluators and funders. Applying the logic of evaluation changes the design and delivery of the programme, before data have been collected. People come out of the negotiation with a clear and mutually shared understanding of what is going to happen in the project and how it will be evaluated.

Process evaluation

Earlier, we highlighted a few of the difficulties authors faced with implementing programme activities in developing contexts. Here we would like to stress the importance of monitoring the programme's activities, and using that information in an assessment of what the programme is doing. In evaluation terms, this is typically referred to as a 'process evaluation' or an 'implementation assessment'.

There is much emphasis on 'accountability' at present in South Africa. In terms of what has been discussed in this book, one aspect of accountability relates to the responsibility of programme staff to provide information to funders, policy-makers and other stakeholders that the programme activities are being carried out as intended. Process evaluation is the way to assess that implementation, and is indeed a primary tool for using evaluation in a formative way; that is, in a way which would develop and strengthen the programme. Most programmes described here used evaluation in such a developmental way. The way the health-promoting schools project (Chapter 6) used an internal monitoring system, and regular evaluation sessions, to identify successes and obstacles, and to develop strategies to overcome obstacles, is a particularly good illustration of process evaluation and its uses.

As indicated, many projects saw themselves as 'pilot projects'. Three chapters demonstrated how complex it is to step up from demonstration projects to multi-site, multi-treatment programmes. Mouton (Chapter 7), Wessells and Monteiro (Chapter 9) and Higson-Smith and Killian (Chapter 10) all make it clear that major challenges are involved in the implementation and evaluation of such programmes. Locally this will continue to be a daunting prospect for programme planners and evaluators.

The importance of a delivery plan, of operationalising implementation and of a co-ordinated delivery of services has a consequence in the implementation of the assessment process. Simply put, these things need to be written down and documented. Frequently a process evaluation encourages programme planners and staff to document the intervention in such terms as staffing, theoretical rationale, population planned for, and all that could be relevant to utilising the programme elsewhere. If we want to develop theories of practice, we will need much more descriptive information about programmes – indeed, programmes ought to be encouraged to develop manuals to guide others in their use.

In particular we need good implementation descriptions, to give us an idea of how intensively or superficially a programme has, in reality, been implemented. There is a big difference between a programme where recipients only had brief contact with the programme (e.g. received two hours of group counselling) and a programme where recipients had more intensive contact with the programme (say two hours of personal counselling per week for four weeks). Without this information, it is difficult to assess the outcomes achieved (or not achieved) by the programme. If no impact is achieved, it would be useful to know whether it was the programme itself, or rather the limited exposure of the recipients to key programme elements, that produced the lack of impact.

Outcome evaluation

Posavac and Carey (1997) give some useful guidelines for occasions when evaluations of outcome are particularly recommended. This is when large numbers of people may be affected by the programme, when the costs of the programme are high, or when we know that something must be done about current conditions but don't quite know what.

The authors who contributed to this volume showed that this is not always as difficult as it might appear. Quite simple experimental designs can be effective. In the preschool violence prevention project (Chapter 5), a comparison group was set up to provide data against which possible improvements in the behaviour of the treatment group could be compared. By adding a pre-treatment measure to their evaluation, the authors created a quasi-experimental design which allowed them to make quite confident statements about the changes the intervention brought about in children's aggressive behaviour, as rated by their parents and teachers.

In Chapters 4 and 7 a similar design was used (non-equivalent comparison group, with pre- and post-tests). The outcome evaluation of a school-feeding scheme (Chapter 4) thus enabled the authors to state that very disadvantaged children 'experienced beneficial psychological and behavioural effects following the introduction of a school breakfast programme' (p. 85). Much of Chapter 7 (the Thousand Schools Project) is a process evaluation, asking the question 'How, and to what extent, was the programme implemented in the different provinces?'. This is the only chapter in which impact questions are addressed. This is because the evaluation also asks questions about the longer-term effects of the programme on school management, classroom practices and student performance.

Chapter 8 is unusual in that qualitative methods are used in an innovative way to try to address outcome questions. De Jong did this by examining the Teacher Inservice Project's role in the positive developments at the school via a number of data sources. He produced a 'causal network display' to argue that it was the project that brought about the changes in the school. In other words, he is constructing an argument, just as Mouton, Richter *et al.*, and Jones Petersen and Carolissen did in a quantitative way, that the intervention is the most likely reason for the changes.

Readers can also learn from how projects have defined outcomes, and have often used innovative measures for assessing these outcomes. Outcomes include the number of community projects launched, school security, school management and governance, children's violent behaviour, and much more. Where measurement is concerned, Wessells and Monteiro, in Chapter 9, describe measures ranging from scales to measure sleep disturbances, to direct observation of children's behaviour in classrooms, focus group discussions, children's drawings, evidence of war-related games and toys, and school attendance records. This sort of range and innovation in finding measures which are likely to reflect representative outcomes is an important dimension of programme design.

There is another lesson here which is not immediately obvious. It relates to when outcomes are measured. Most often this is understood as something that only happens after the programme has been delivered, within a 'before-and-after' model. However, it is also possible to monitor outcomes throughout the life of the programme, in a way that is similar to monitoring the implementation (Affholter, 1994). Provided the expected outcomes have been clearly defined, fairly simple measures of these (see the discussion of 'indicators' in Chapter 3) could be built into the monitoring system of the project. In school-based projects, for example, records of attendance, performance, disciplinary actions, and drop-out rate are readily available. Such measures can provide a running record, over time, of how the programme is doing on some of its outcomes.

Utilising evaluation findings

The projects reported generally made good use of evaluation findings. Flisher and his colleagues (Chapter 6), for example, describe how the external evaluation was used to modify the programme so that, amongst other things, the staff at Avondale Primary School felt less under pressure, and parents became more involved. However, such integration of evaluation findings does not always happen.

In the early days of programme evaluation, evaluators believed that it would be sufficient to produce a report on their findings to which interested parties might refer. Since then we have learned that a report is not sufficient, and that evaluation findings need to be actively followed up. Because programmes and their evaluations operate in political contexts, the form of action often needs to be 'political'. Thus, if the findings of the evaluation are perceived to be threatening to particular persons or groups, steps may need to taken to overcome that perception. The best is to do what most projects reported here have done: to prevent the perception of threat or suspicion in the first place. This is typically done by painstaking negotiations with all stakeholders in a programme. It also ensures that the information to be provided by the evaluation will actually be useful, and will be delivered in a timely manner. Posavac and Carey

(1997, pp. 256-260) give a few thumbnail directions to encourage use of findings:
- Work closely with staff and managers to plan and carry out the evaluation.
- Adopt developmental interpretations of findings, especially of failings.
- Frame evaluation findings in terms of improvements; e.g. in the delivery of service.
- Treat findings as working hypotheses to encourage learning on the part of the organisation.
- Recognise the special needs of those who deliver services.

The place of both qualitative and quantitative methods

The projects in this volume have made extensive use of qualitative research methods. Wessells and Monteiro (Chapter 9) describe the value of an action research model in their work with war-affected children and communities in Angola. Higson-Smith and Killian (Chapter 10) make similar observations about their evaluation processes in KwaZulu-Natal. In Chapter 7, Mouton relied essentially on qualitative methods to track the implementation of the Thousand Schools Project across different sites. In organisational contexts, Flisher *et al.* (Chapter 6), Gibson (Chapter 11) and De Jong (Chapter 8) all made use of qualitative techniques. For example, De Jong used a whole set of qualitative data, including interviews, focus groups, field observations and inspection of documents, to build up a case study of what happened at Modderdam High School. He correctly points out that a strength of the case study approach is that it includes context as an important part of what has to be studied. His discussion is thus enlightening in terms of understanding the context in which the project was delivered, and how the context changed as a result. He goes further, elucidating the processes that might have brought about the changes, and attempting a synthesis of what has been learned so that this can be transferred to other schools in similar situations. These are all characteristic strengths of qualitative methods. On the other hand, as De Jong himself points out, it is very difficult for qualitative studies to describe causal relations and to generalise from them. As is evident, qualitative studies are also very labour-intensive.

In Chapter 6, Flisher *et al.* used in-depth interviews, focus groups, observation and recordings of meetings, and documents to provide rich and detailed information about the progress made by the project. However, the authors also argue for a more quantitative study to complement their qualitative approach. This might have yielded answers to such questions as whether the AIDS and TB drama actually had an effect on the sexual knowledge, attitudes or practices of students, or whether the 'child-to-child' remedial intervention actually benefited the junior students or not.

One project which provides a good example of how quantitative and qualitative methods can be used together is the school-feeding project in Chapter 4. Richter *et al.* demonstrate how variables such 'attention' can be measured both quantitatively (psychometric measures) and qualitatively (teacher observations of classroom behaviour).

Programme cost

It is perhaps not surprising that there are no cost-effectiveness or cost-benefit studies included here. For many of these projects this is a question that, possibly, it is too early to address. But if projects aim to be applied as more than mere pilot studies, it is an issue that will have to be faced. For funders and policy-makers, this will always be a major consideration. Certainly, for many of the projects discussed here there is the hope that they may be extended and possibly taken over by government institutions. But given the budgetary constraints and demands (Chapter 2), it is unlikely that this will happen unless it can be demonstrated that these interventions are also cost-efficient. In the end, what programmes cost, and what they are able to deliver for that cost, must be established.

CONCLUSION

Ultimately, all South Africans face the question 'How will we as a society deal with the problems associated with children growing up in adversity?'. On the one hand, the projects in this book affirm that there is much that we can do. On the other hand, they also tell us that we still have far to go in developing an effective theory of practice.

At the very least we need to record and share our observations and experiences. This volume, and this chapters within it, will have served a useful purpose if we have helped to create a culture of sharing, of disseminating knowledge, and of learning from accumulated experience within the world of psychosocial projects that are attempting to address childhood adversity in this region. It is an attempt to build up, critically and constructively, a body of knowledge about what constitutes effective practice, under what circumstances, and why. This can only happen if people are prepared to record their projects and programmes, and to reflect on and share their difficulties as well as their successes. We are grateful to those who have done so in this volume. We trust that their shared experience, which has made it possible to begin to construct the elements of a theory of practice, will stimulate a continuing engagement with this task amongst all involved: practitioners, academics and students alike.

REFERENCES

Affholter, D.P. (1994). Outcome monitoring. In J.S. Wholey, H.P. Hatry & K.E. Newcomer (Eds.), *Handbook of practical program evaluation*. (pp. 96–118). San Francisco: Jossey-Bass.

Bronfenbrenner, U. (1986). Ecology of the family as a context for human development: Research perspectives. *Developmental Psychology, 22*, 723–742.

McLaughlin, J.A., Weber, L.J., Covert, R.W. & Ingle, R.B. (Eds.). (1988). Evaluation utilization, *New Directions for Program Evaluation*, No. 39. San Francisco: Jossey-Bass.

McLoyd, V. (1998). Socio-economic disadvantage and child development. *American Psychologist, 53*, 185–204.

Posavac, E.J. & Carey, R.G. (1997). *Program evaluation. Methods and case studies*. Upper Saddle River, NJ: Prentice Hall.

Patton, M.Q. (1990). *Qualitative evaluation and research methods*. Thousand Oaks, CA: Sage Publications.

Contributors

David Donald is Professor of Educational Psychology in the School of Education, University of Cape Town.

Andrew Dawes is Associate Professor of Psychology in the Department of Psychology, University of Cape Town.

Johann Louw is Professor of Psychology in the Department of Psychology, University of Cape Town.

Linda Biersteker is Research and Information Services Co-ordinator for the Early Learning Resource Unit, Cape Town.

Shirley Robinson is project manager of Budget Information Services for the Institute for Democracy in South Africa.

Linda Richter is Professor and Head of the School of Psychology at the University of Natal in Pietermaritzburg.

Dev Griesel is a Professor Emeritus from the University of South Africa, a Research Professor at the University of Natal in Pietermaritzburg, and Director of the Unit for the Study of Child Development in South Africa: Council for Scientific Development.

Cynthia Rose, who is currently a human resources consultant with DeLoitte and Touche, worked as a research assistant to Professor Richter.

Heather Jones Petersen and Ronelle Carolissen are both clinical psychologists contracted to the Trauma Centre for Survivors of Violence and the New World Foundation in Lavender Hill, Cape Town.

Alan Flisher is Associate Professor in the Department of Psychiatry, University of Cape Town, and Senior Specialist in the Child and Family Unit, Red Cross War Memorial Children's Hospital.

Keith Cloete is Principal Medical Officer in the Sub-Directorate of Public Health Services, Department of Health, Provincial Administration of the Western Cape.

Rose Adams is Chief Professional Nurse in the District School Health Programme, Atlantis: Community Health Services Organisation, Department of Health, Provincial Administration of the Western Cape.

Bridget Johnson is Clinical Psychologist in the Institute of Child and Family Development, University of the Western Cape.

Alyssa Wigton is Senior Research Fellow in the Child Health Unit, Department of Paediatrics and Child Health, University of Cape Town.

Pam Joshua is a teacher at Avondale Primary School, Atlantis: Department of Education, Provincial Administration of the Western Cape.

Johann Mouton is Professor and Director of the Centre for Interdisciplinary Studies, a research centre in the Department of Sociology, University of Stellenbosch.

Terry de Jong is Senior Lecturer in Educational Psychology in the School of Education, University of Cape Town.

Michael Wessells is Professor of Psychology at Randolph-Macon College in Ashland, Virginia (USA) and is a psychosocial consultant for the Christian Children's Fund.

Carlinda Monteiro is Program Director for the Christian Children's Fund/Angola and serves as CCF Regional Advisor.

Craig Higson-Smith previously served as Director of the KwaZulu-Natal Programme for Survivors of Violence.

Beverley Killian is Senior Lecturer in the School of Psychology, University of Natal, Pietermaritzburg, and is chairperson of the KwaZulu-Natal Programme for Survivors of Violence.

Kerry Gibson is Lecturer in the Child Guidance Clinic, Department of Psychology, University of Cape Town.

INDEX

abuse 12, 44, 48; abused children 45, 48–52, 127, 203, 219, 226.

Acts: Basic Conditions of Employment Act of 1997 50; Child Care Act of 1983 48; Child Care Amendment Act of 1996 50; Criminal Procedures Act 51; Prevention of Family Violence Act of 1993 49; South African Schools Act of 1996 38–40, 42, 165, 170.

aggression 96, 98–9, 104, 109–10, 182, 191, 194.

Angolan project 176, 178, 181, 187, 259; evaluation of 191–7, 249, 252–4; insights 198–9; Luanda-based 178–80, 185; province-based 185–8, 190–1; stress and healing 182–3, 185, 187–8, 190, 194, 196–9.

apartheid 26, 31, 37, 74, 131–3, 141, 203, 229.

Avondale Primary School 114–24, 128, 245, 249–51; evaluation of 120–7, 258.

child-care 5, 8, 45–6, 49, 202–3, 225–6, 234–5, 256; caregivers 5–6, 8, 11–12, 14–15, 17, 34, 42, 48, 62, 81, 182, 216, 218–19, 222, 247–8, 251.

child development 2–4, 9–10, 34, 37, 225, 248–9; in poverty environments 2–3, 8–11, 17–18, 98–9; role of cultural practices 2–3, 5, 14–16, 53, 248; role of environment 4, 6, 9–12, 18, 20, 98; role of historical features 5–6, 8, 11; self-regulation 8–9.

child labour 49–51, 78, 86.

Child Support Benefit (CSB) 46–7.

children: abandoned 228–9; disabled 39–40, 43, 45; street 45, 50–1, 53; troubled 44, 241; war-affected 176, 178–81, 185, 188, 190–1, 195, 198, 247–8, 259.

Convention on the Rights of the Child (CRC) (1989) 2, 16, 30–1, 52–3.

cultural practices 15–17, 52, 184, 215, 218, 249.

Department of: Art and Culture 53; Correctional Services 51; Education 114, 117–8, 120, 141, 254; Health 54–5, 114, 116–18, 125, 254; Sport and Recreation 53; Water Affairs and Forestry (DWAF) 36;

Welfare and Population Development 43, 51, 54–5, 114.

development psychology 2–3, 6, 15.

development theory 1–2, 18–19; and cultural practices 15–17; ecological-transactional orientation of 3–7, 14, 18, 20; role of developmental epochs 7–10.

early childhood development (ECD) programmes 39, 42, 45–7, 54–5, 246.

education 37–42, 44, 131; Curriculum 2005 41, 53, 161, 170; intervention through TSP 133, 137; reform of 154, 157; see also early childhood development (ECD) programmes; schools and schooling.

evaluation 55, 60–72, 75–6, 247, 253–9; and intervention 60–1, 89; frameworks 87, 220–1; process 256–7.

fragmented communities 21, 27–8, 211–12, 214, 217, 254, 256.

gangsterism 9–10, 20, 51, 105, 114, 154, 159–60, 162–3, 171.

HIV/AIDS 31–2, 35, 44–5, 66, 127, 203, 212, 259.

health 31–4, 64, 75, 113, 125; and educational outcomes 114–15; and water and sanitation 36–7, 113–14; primary health care services 31–2, 35–7, 54, 115.

Health-Promoting Schools (HPS) 114–17, 119, 125–8, 247, 251–4, 256.

Independent Development Trust (IDT) 131–4, 136, 139–45, 152–3.

infant mortality rates (IMRs) 29, 32, 69.

Integrated Nutrition Programme (INP) 31, 33–4, 36, 89.

Inter-Ministerial Committee on Young People at Risk (IMC) 43–5, 49, 51–2, 55, 250.

intersectoral collaboration 45–6, 48, 52, 54–6, 125–6, 250, 253.

intervention 6, 10, 14, 17–21, 55–6, 60–72, 84, 86–7, 90, 116, 127, 207–10, 213, 216–18, 223, 225, 245, 247; and evaluation 60–1, 89, 173, 215, 219, 245–7, 253–5; community-based 21–2, 37, 205, 216–18, 222–3, 226, 245–6, 250; cost of